Chapter One: Royal Knight Recita Part One

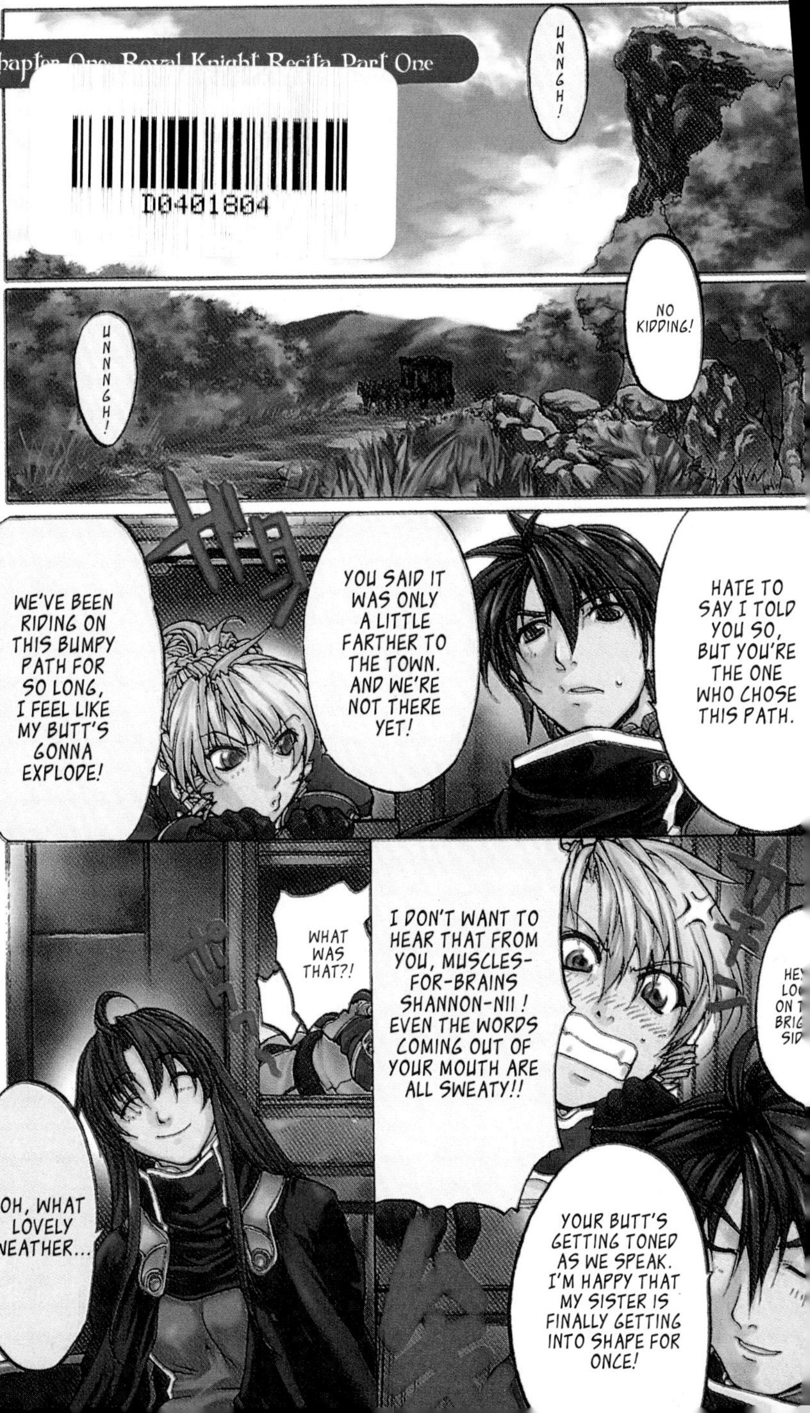
UNNGH!
NO KIDDING!
UNNNGH!
HATE TO SAY I TOLD YOU SO, BUT YOU'RE THE ONE WHO CHOSE THIS PATH.
YOU SAID IT WAS ONLY A LITTLE FARTHER TO THE TOWN. AND WE'RE NOT THERE YET!
WE'VE BEEN RIDING ON THIS BUMPY PATH FOR SO LONG, I FEEL LIKE MY BUTT'S GONNA EXPLODE!
YOUR BUTT'S GETTING TONED AS WE SPEAK. I'M HAPPY THAT MY SISTER IS FINALLY GETTING INTO SHAPE FOR ONCE!
I DON'T WANT TO HEAR THAT FROM YOU, MUSCLES-FOR-BRAINS SHANNON-NII! EVEN THE WORDS COMING OUT OF YOUR MOUTH ARE ALL SWEATY!!
WHAT WAS THAT?!
OH, WHAT LOVELY WEATHER...

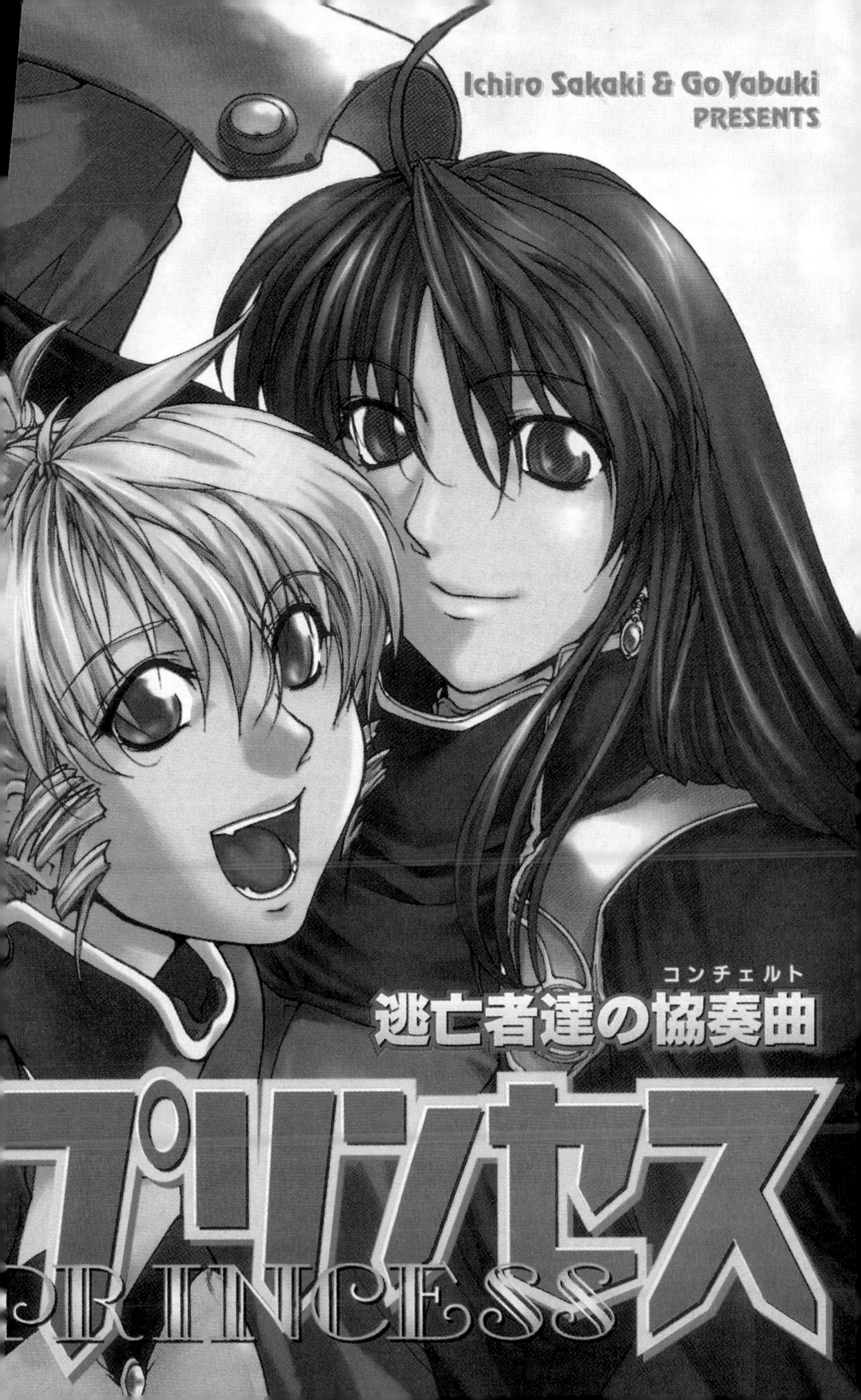
Ichiro Sakaki & Go Yabuki
PRESENTS
コンチェルト
逃亡者達の協奏曲
プリンセス
RINCESS

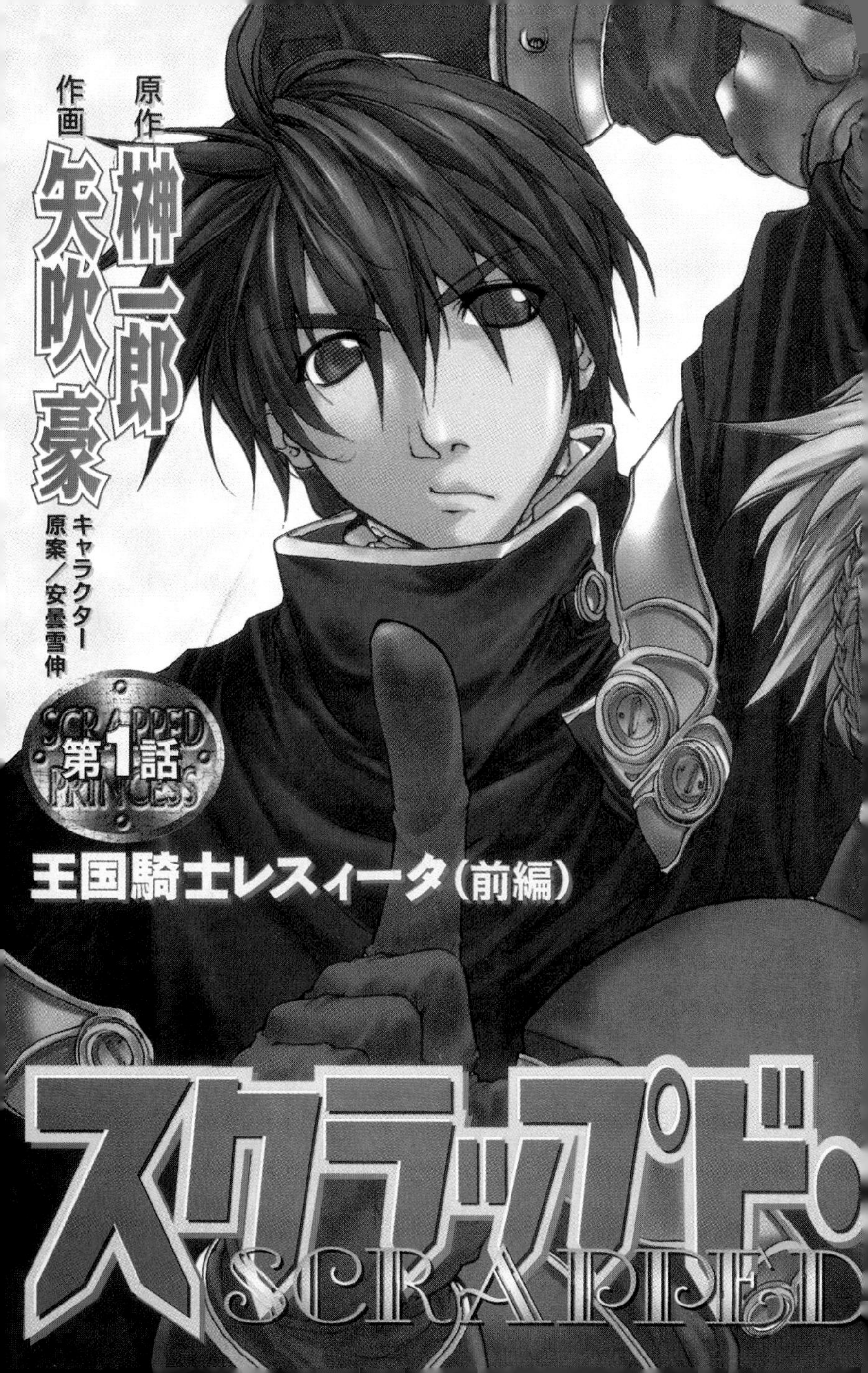
原作 榊一郎
作画 矢吹豪
キャラクター原案／安曇雪伸
SCRAPPED PRINCESS
第1話
王国騎士レスィータ（前編）
スクラップド・
SCRAPPED

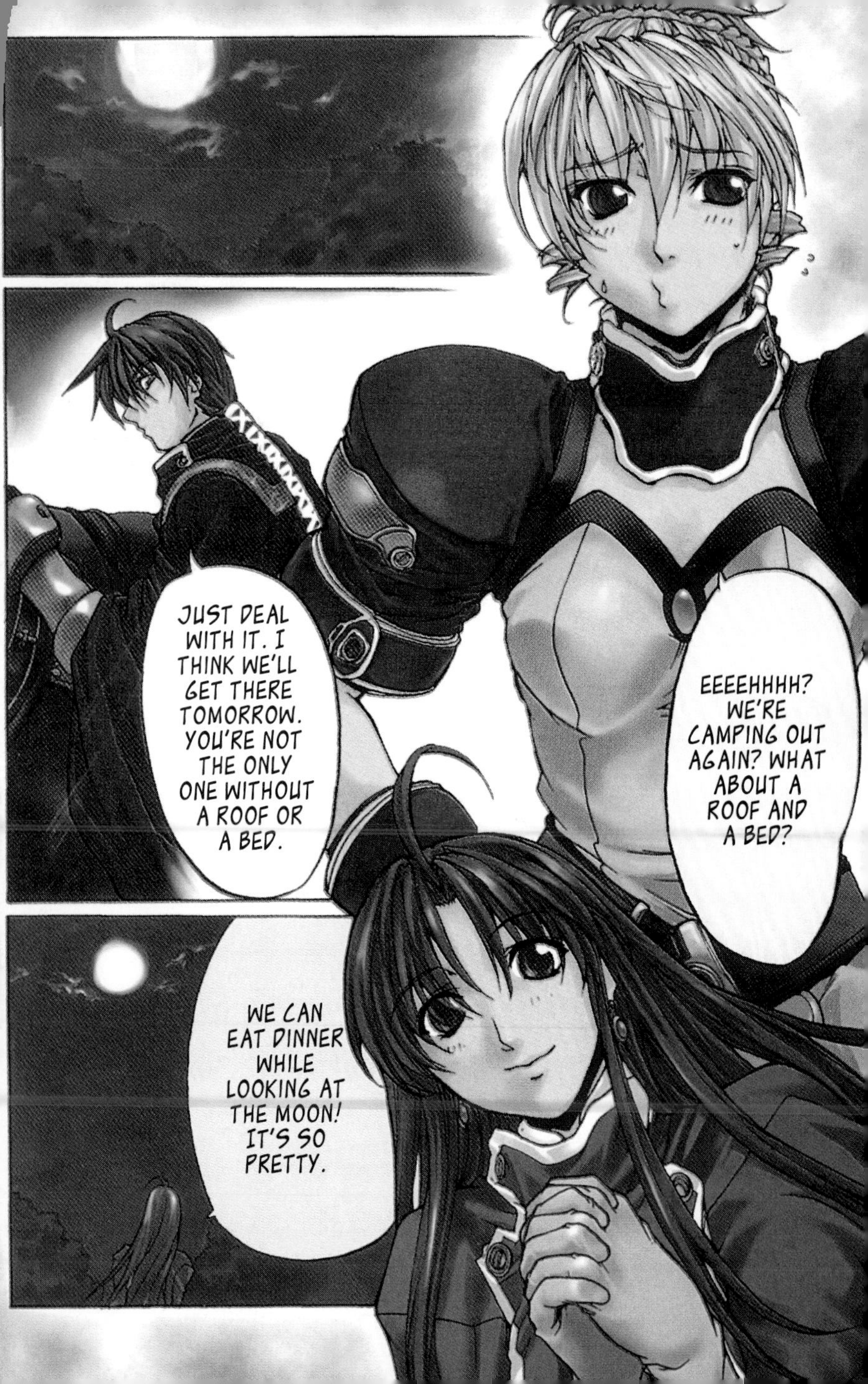
EEEEHHHH? WE'RE CAMPING OUT AGAIN? WHAT ABOUT A ROOF AND A BED?
JUST DEAL WITH IT. I THINK WE'LL GET THERE TOMORROW. YOU'RE NOT THE ONLY ONE WITHOUT A ROOF OR A BED.
WE CAN EAT DINNER WHILE LOOKING AT THE MOON! IT'S SO PRETTY.

SCRAPPED PRINCESS™

Original work: Ichiro Sakaki

Original Character Design: Yukinobu Azumi

Illustrations: Go Yabuki

TOKYOPOP®

HAMBURG // LONDON // LOS ANGELES // TOKYO

Scrapped Princess Vol. 1
Story: Ichiro Sakaki
Art: Go Yabuki
Character plan: Yukinobu Azumi

Translation - Alethea Nibley
English Adaptation - Liesl M. Bradner
Retouch and Lettering - Chris Anderson
Production Artist - James Dashiell
Cover Design - Al-Insan Lashley

Editor - Julie Taylor
Digital Imaging Manager - Chris Buford
Production Managers - Jennifer Miller and Mutsumi Miyazaki
Managing Editor - Jill Freshney
VP of Production - Ron Klamert
Publisher and E.I.C. - Mike Kiley
President and C.O.O. - John Parker
C.E.O. - Stuart Levy

A  Manga

TOKYOPOP Inc.
5900 Wilshire Blvd. Suite 2000
Los Angeles, CA 90036

E-mail: info@TOKYOPOP.com
Come visit us online at www.TOKYOPOP.com

ISBN: 1-59532-981-1

First TOKYOPOP printing: August 2005
10 9 8 7 6 5 4 3 2 1
Printed in Canada

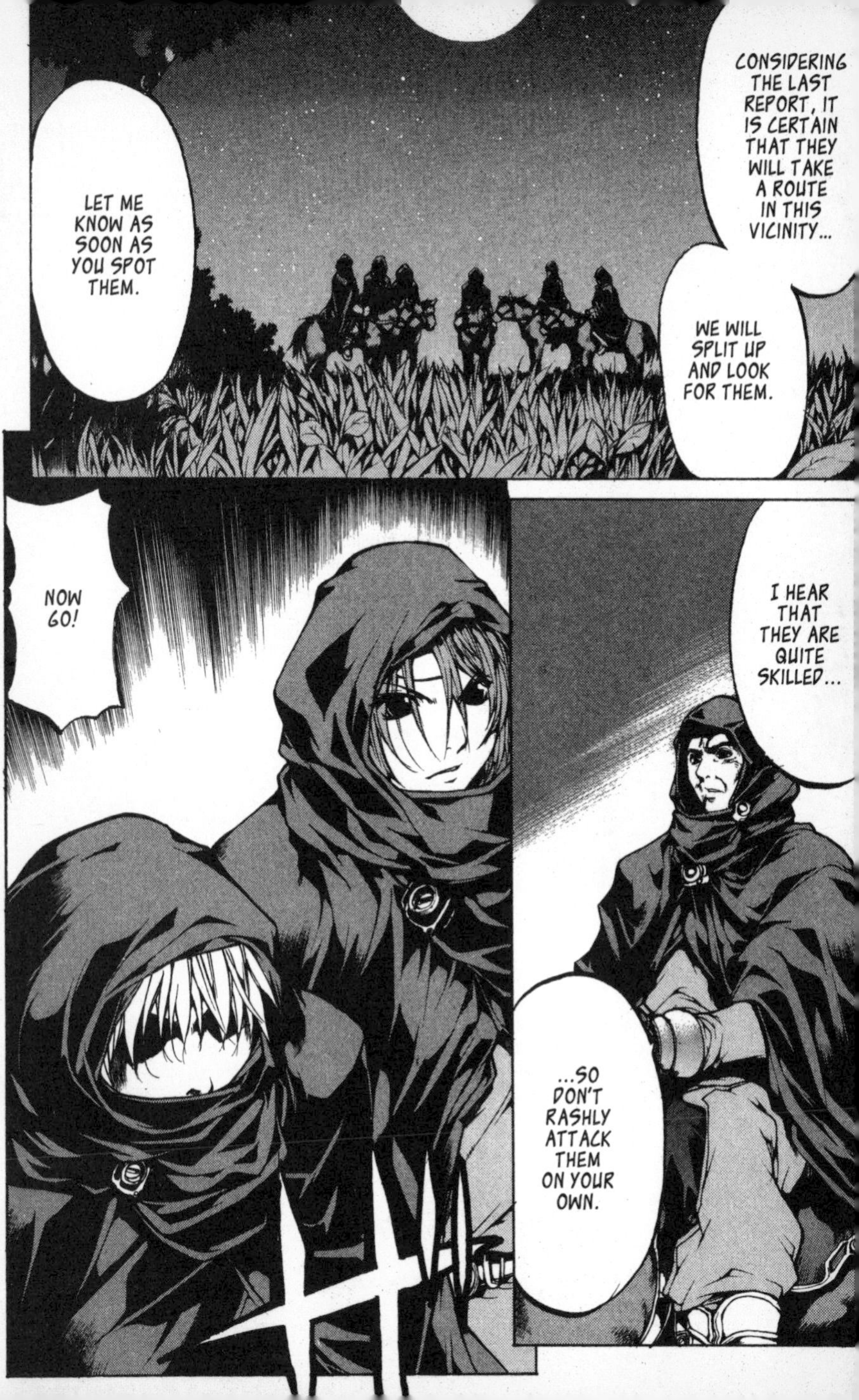
CONSIDERING THE LAST REPORT, IT IS CERTAIN THAT THEY WILL TAKE A ROUTE IN THIS VICINITY...
WE WILL SPLIT UP AND LOOK FOR THEM.
LET ME KNOW AS SOON AS YOU SPOT THEM.
I HEAR THAT THEY ARE QUITE SKILLED...
...SO DON'T RASHLY ATTACK THEM ON YOUR OWN.
NOW GO!

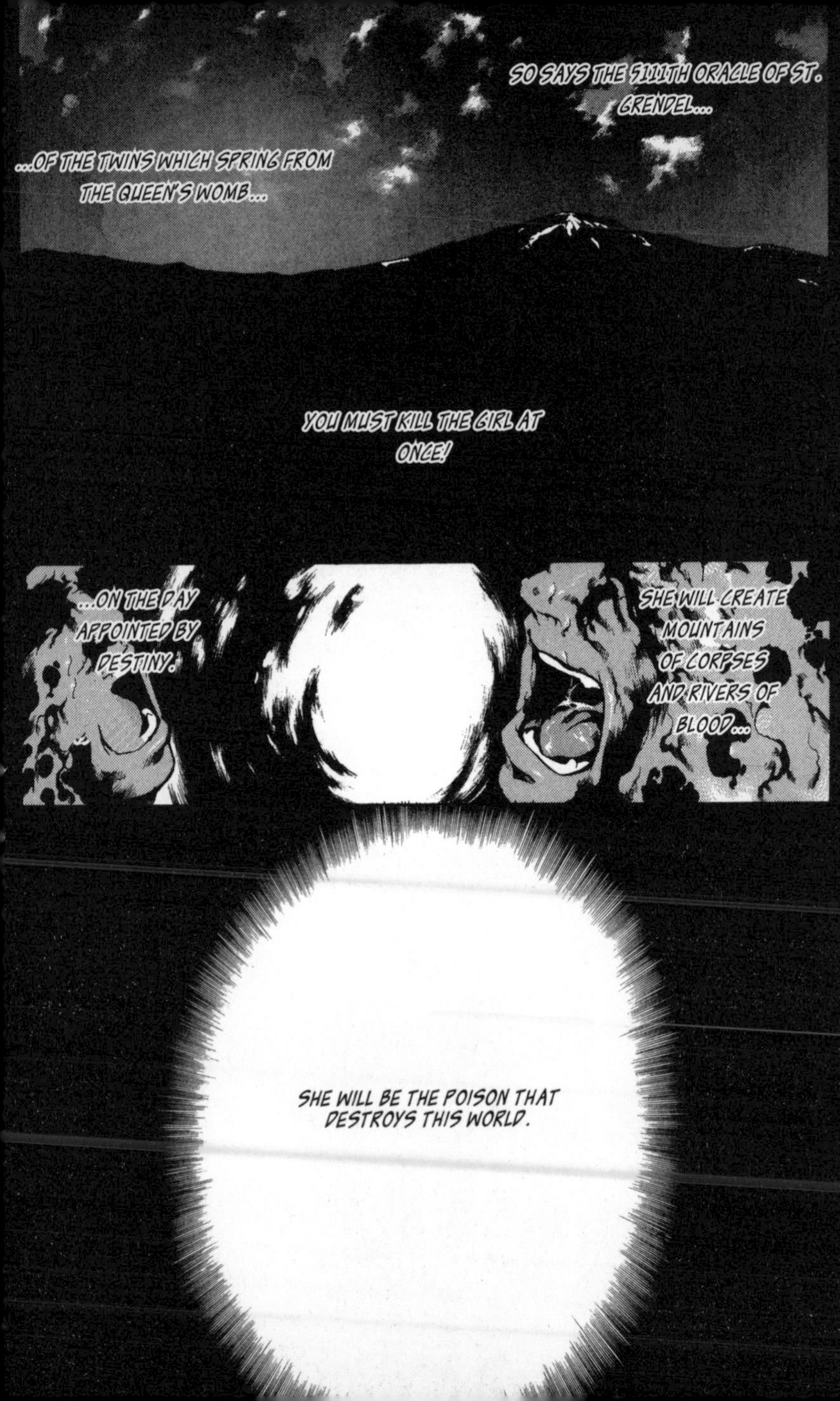
SO SAYS THE 5111TH ORACLE OF ST. GRENDEL...
...OF THE TWINS WHICH SPRING FROM THE QUEEN'S WOMB...
YOU MUST KILL THE GIRL AT ONCE!
SHE WILL CREATE MOUNTAINS OF CORPSES AND RIVERS OF BLOOD...
...ON THE DAY APPOINTED BY DESTINY.
SHE WILL BE THE POISON THAT DESTROYS THIS WORLD.

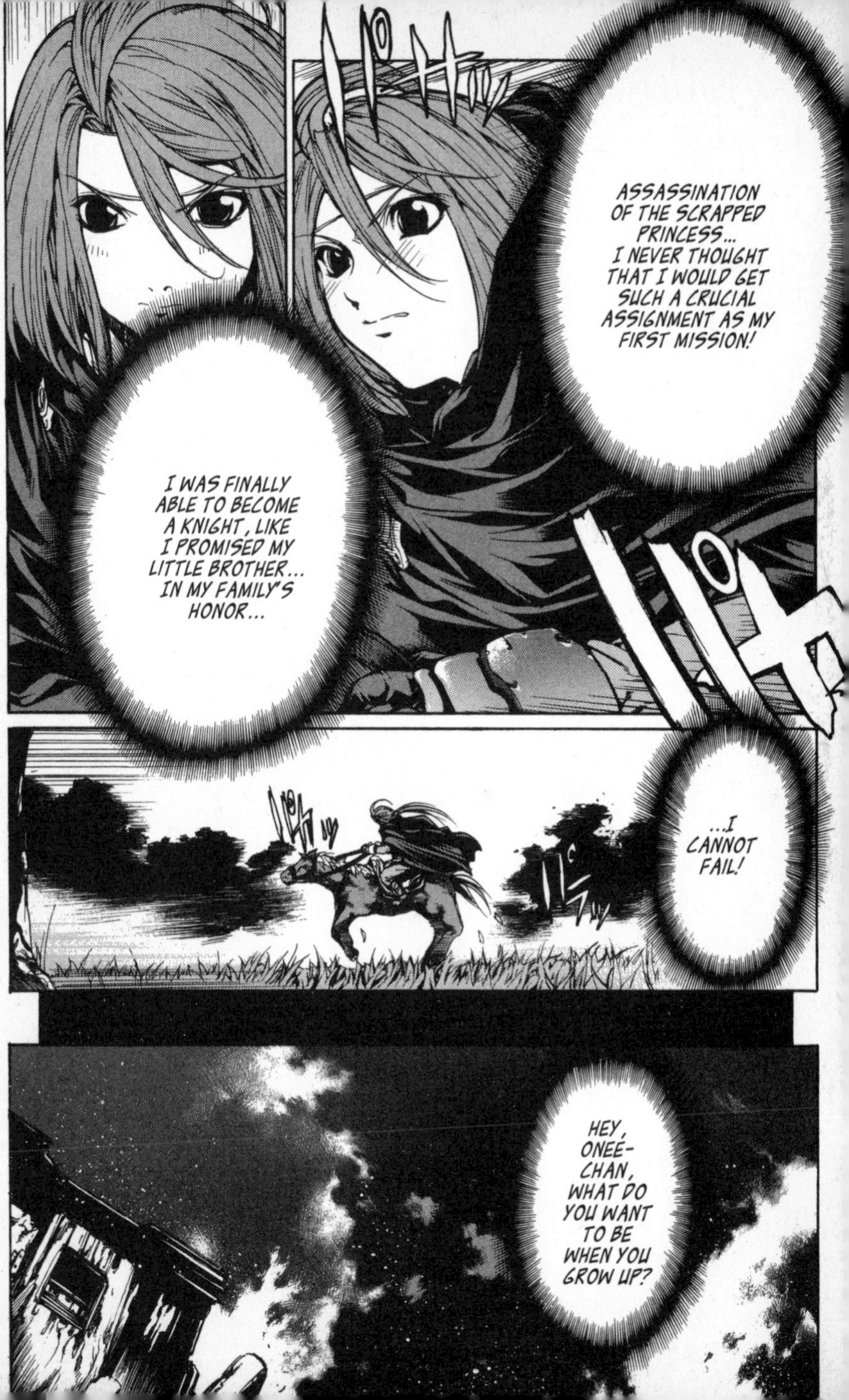
ASSASSINATION OF THE SCRAPPED PRINCESS... I NEVER THOUGHT THAT I WOULD GET SUCH A CRUCIAL ASSIGNMENT AS MY FIRST MISSION!
I WAS FINALLY ABLE TO BECOME A KNIGHT , LIKE I PROMISED MY LITTLE BROTHER... IN MY FAMILY'S HONOR...
...I CANNOT FAIL!
HEY, ONEE-CHAN, WHAT DO YOU WANT TO BE WHEN YOU GROW UP?

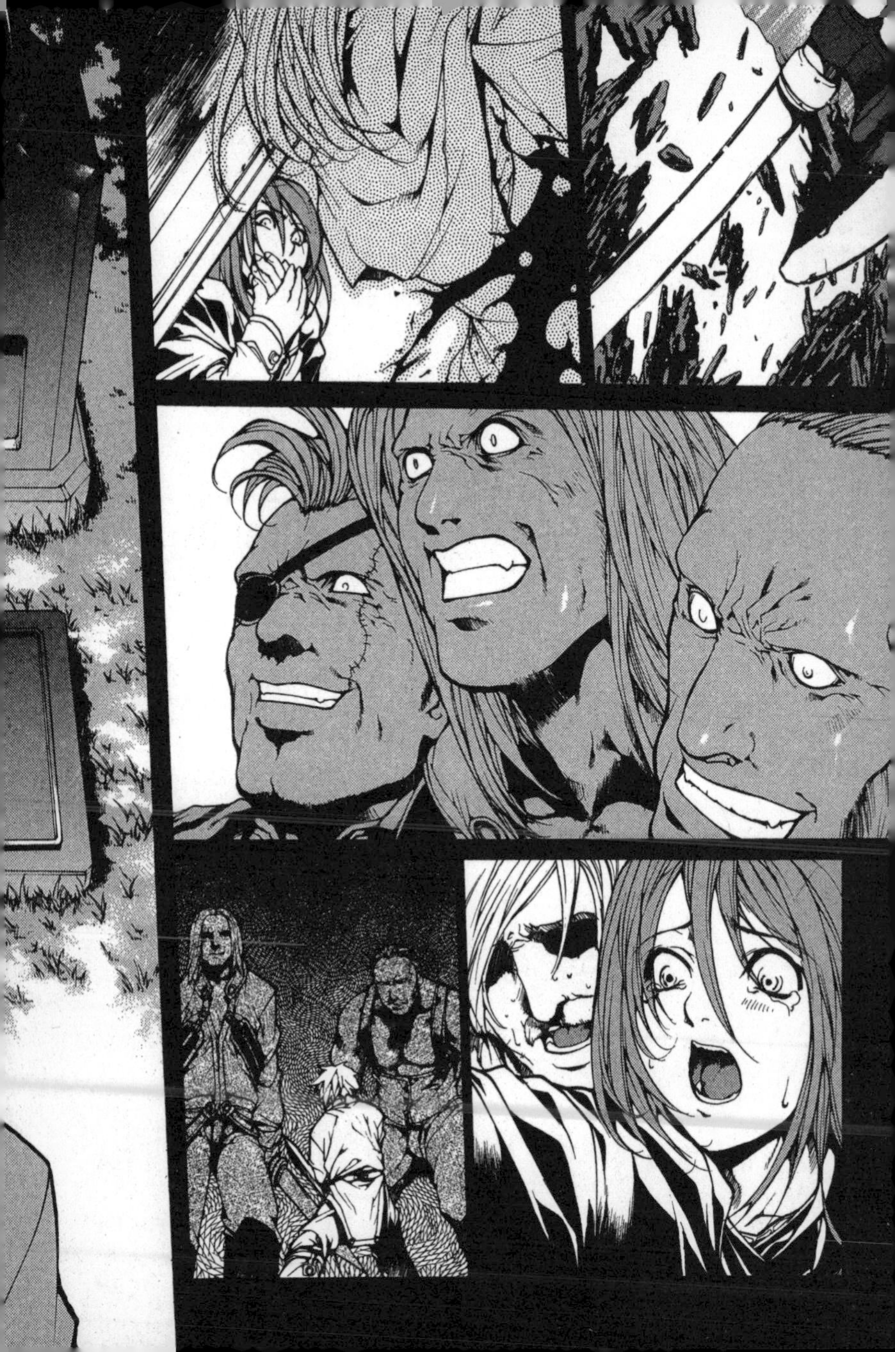

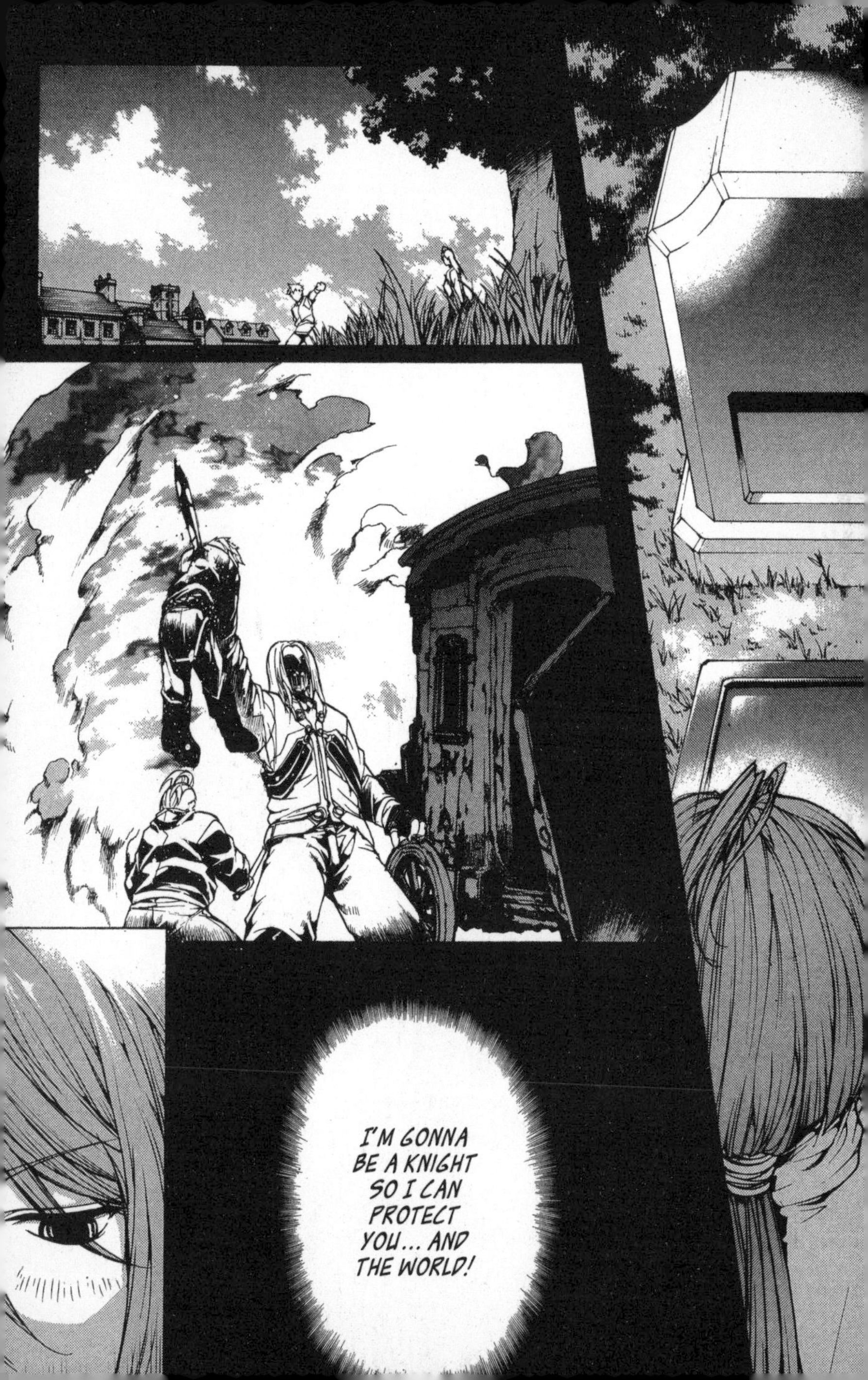
I'M GONNA BE A KNIGHT SO I CAN PROTECT YOU... AND THE WORLD!

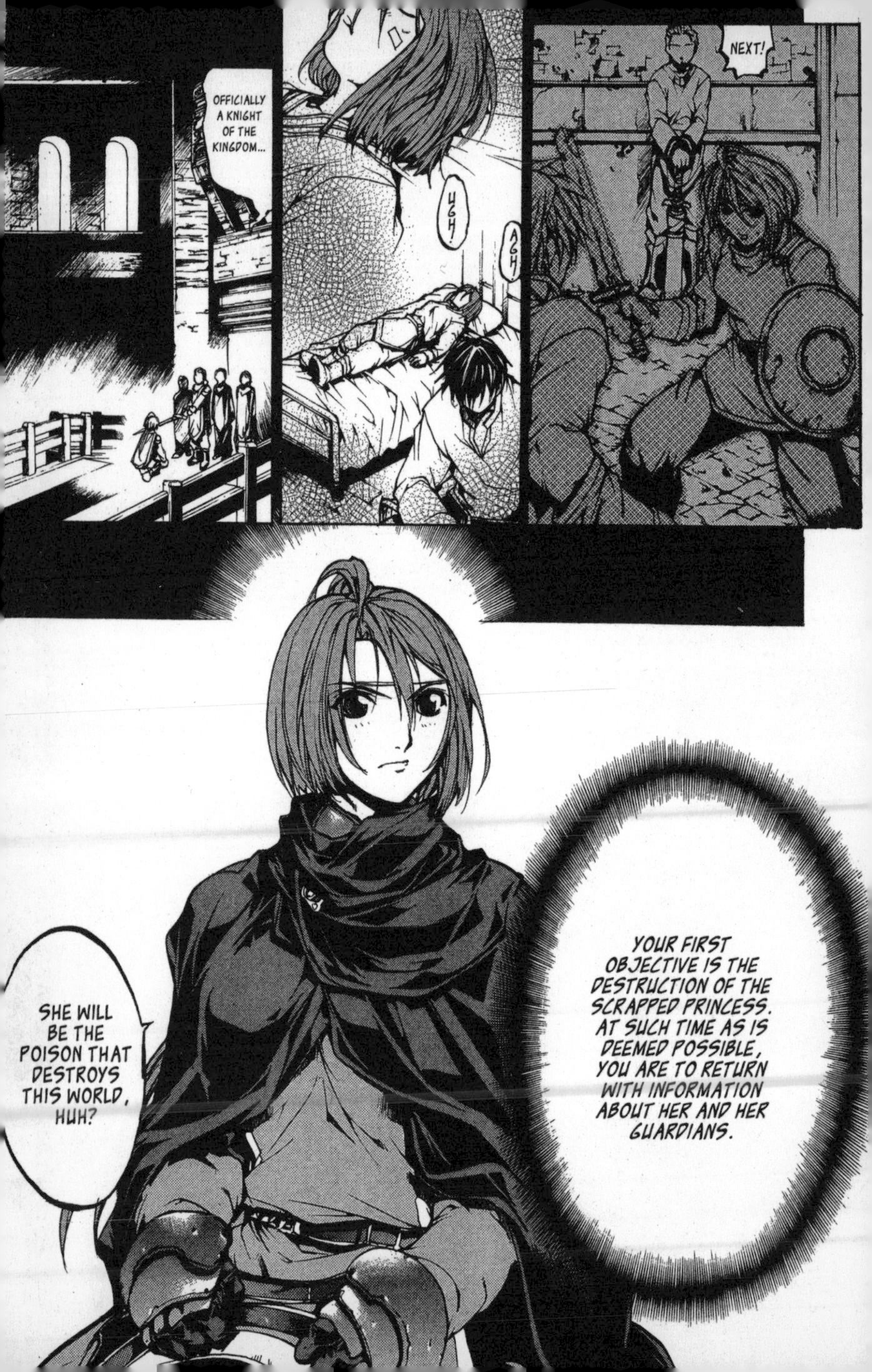
NEXT!
UGH!
AGH!
OFFICIALLY A KNIGHT OF THE KINGDOM...
YOUR FIRST OBJECTIVE IS THE DESTRUCTION OF THE SCRAPPED PRINCESS. AT SUCH TIME AS IS DEEMED POSSIBLE, YOU ARE TO RETURN WITH INFORMATION ABOUT HER AND HER GUARDIANS.
SHE WILL BE THE POISON THAT DESTROYS THIS WORLD, HUH?

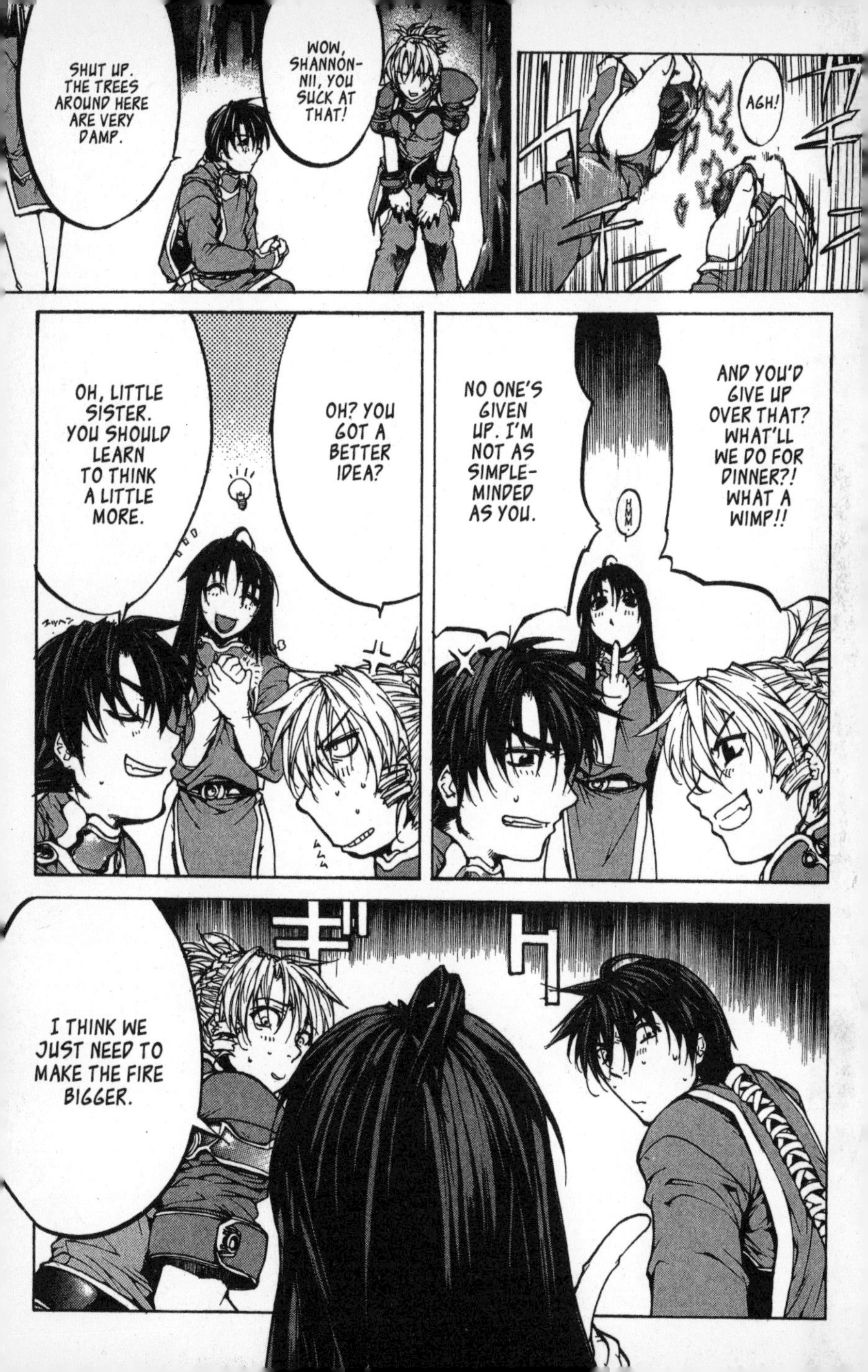
AGH!
WOW, SHANNON-NII, YOU SUCK AT THAT!
SHUT UP. THE TREES AROUND HERE ARE VERY DAMP.
AND YOU'D GIVE UP OVER THAT? WHAT'LL WE DO FOR DINNER?! WHAT A WIMP!!
HMM.
NO ONE'S GIVEN UP. I'M NOT AS SIMPLE-MINDED AS YOU.
OH? YOU GOT A BETTER IDEA?
OH, LITTLE SISTER. YOU SHOULD LEARN TO THINK A LITTLE MORE.
I THINK WE JUST NEED TO MAKE THE FIRE BIGGER.

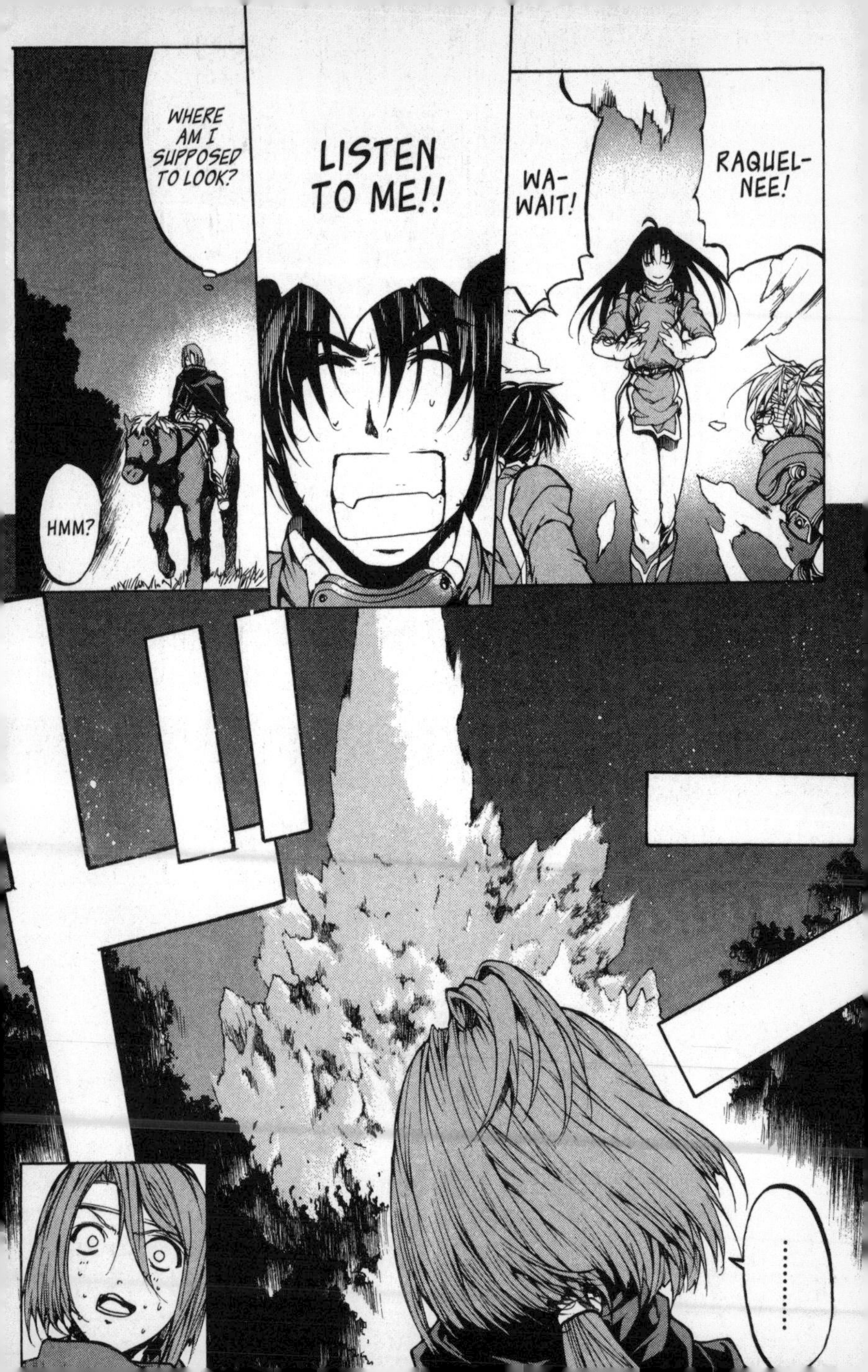
RAQUEL-NEE!
WA-WAIT!
LISTEN TO ME!!
WHERE AM I SUPPOSED TO LOOK?
HMM?
......

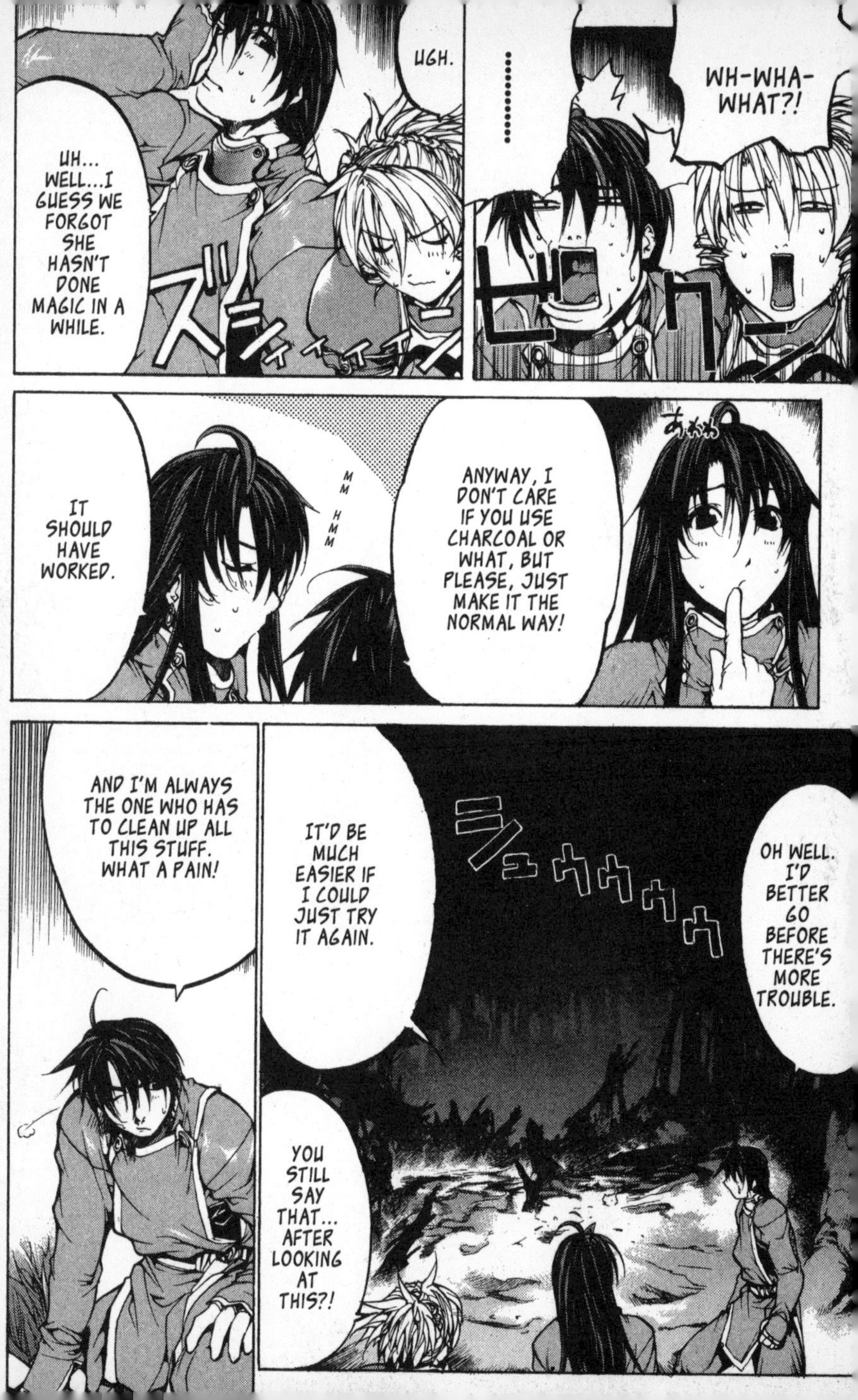
WH-WHA-WHAT?!
....
UGH.
UH... WELL...I GUESS WE FORGOT SHE HASN'T DONE MAGIC IN A WHILE.
ANYWAY, I DON'T CARE IF YOU USE CHARCOAL OR WHAT, BUT PLEASE, JUST MAKE IT THE NORMAL WAY!
MM HMM
IT SHOULD HAVE WORKED.
OH WELL. I'D BETTER GO BEFORE THERE'S MORE TROUBLE.
シュウウウウウ
IT'D BE MUCH EASIER IF I COULD JUST TRY IT AGAIN.
YOU STILL SAY THAT... AFTER LOOKING AT THIS?!
AND I'M ALWAYS THE ONE WHO HAS TO CLEAN UP ALL THIS STUFF. WHAT A PAIN!

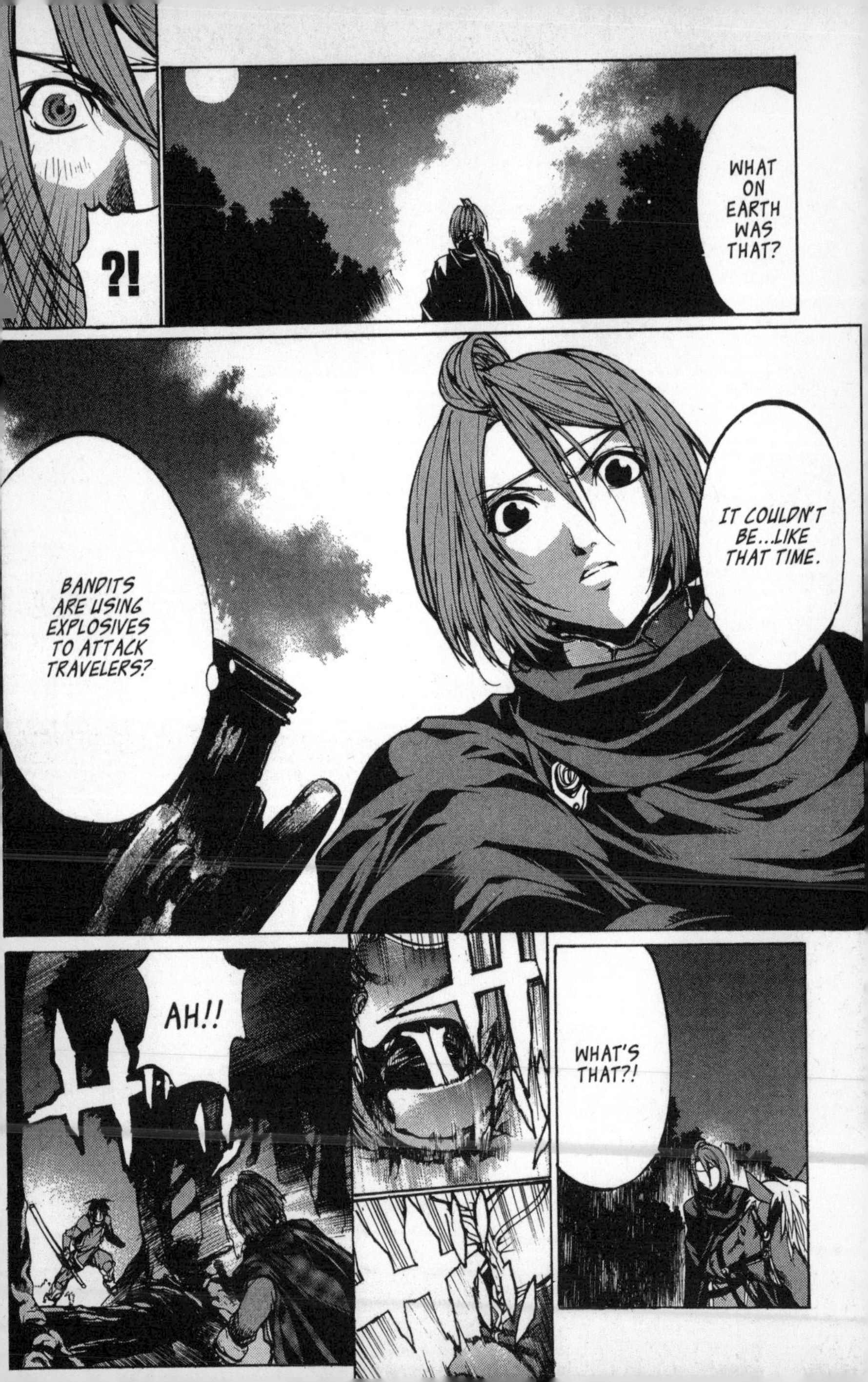
WHAT ON EARTH WAS THAT?
?!
IT COULDN'T BE...LIKE THAT TIME.
BANDITS ARE USING EXPLOSIVES TO ATTACK TRAVELERS?
WHAT'S THAT?!
AH!!

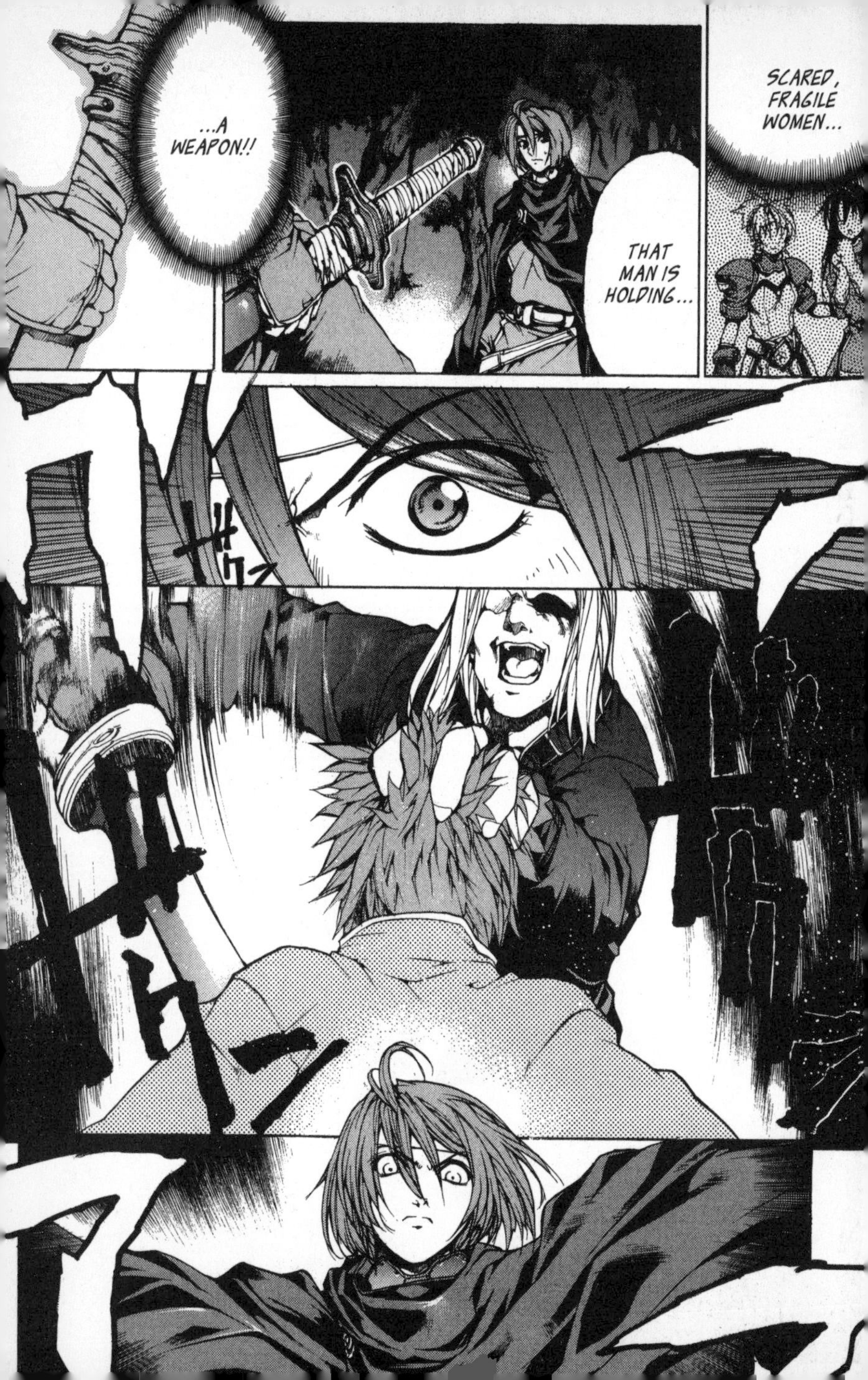
SCARED, FRAGILE WOMEN...
THAT MAN IS HOLDING...
...A WEAPON!!

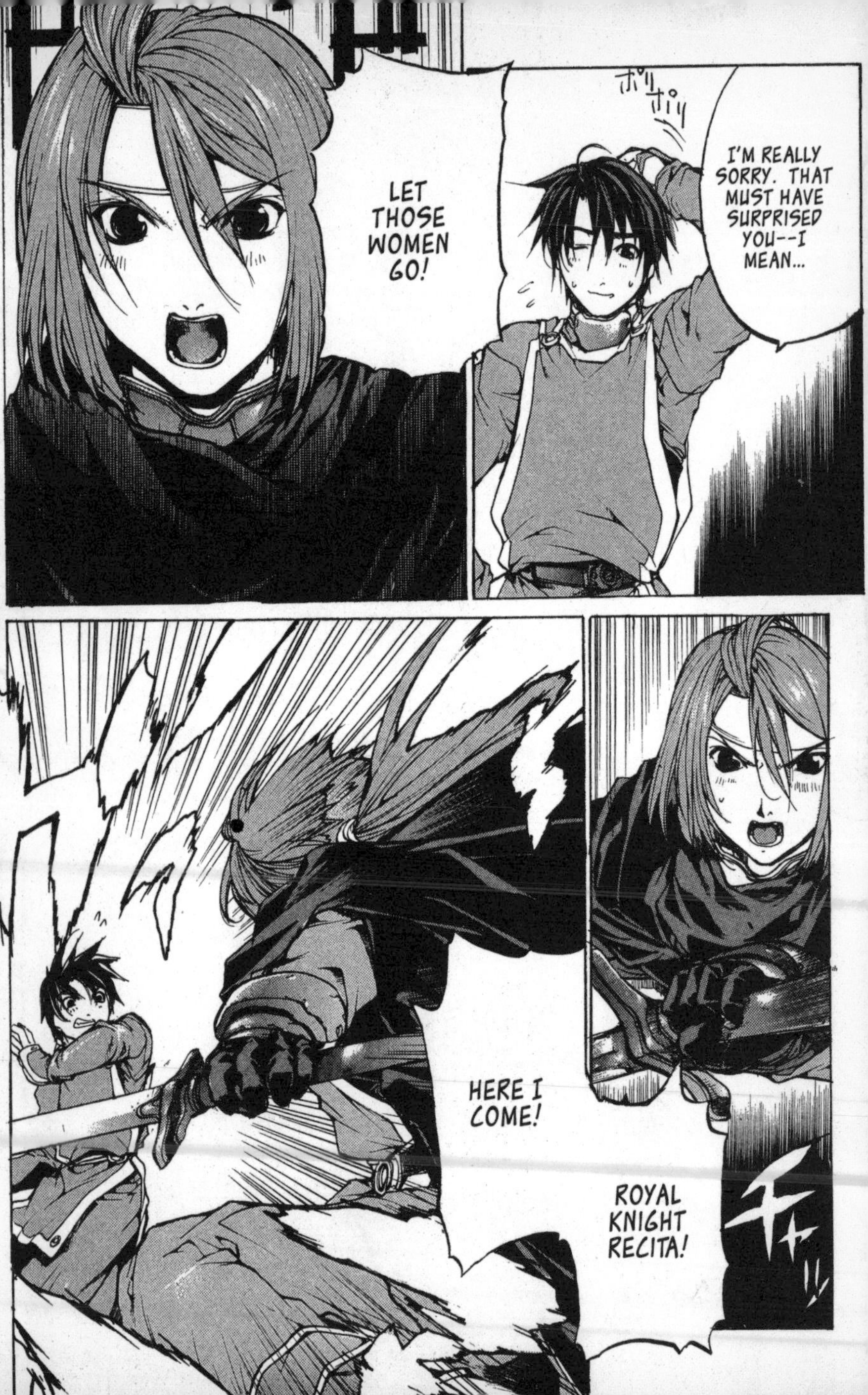
ポリポリ
I'M REALLY SORRY. THAT MUST HAVE SURPRISED YOU--I MEAN...
LET THOSE WOMEN GO!
ROYAL KNIGHT RECITA!
HERE I COME!

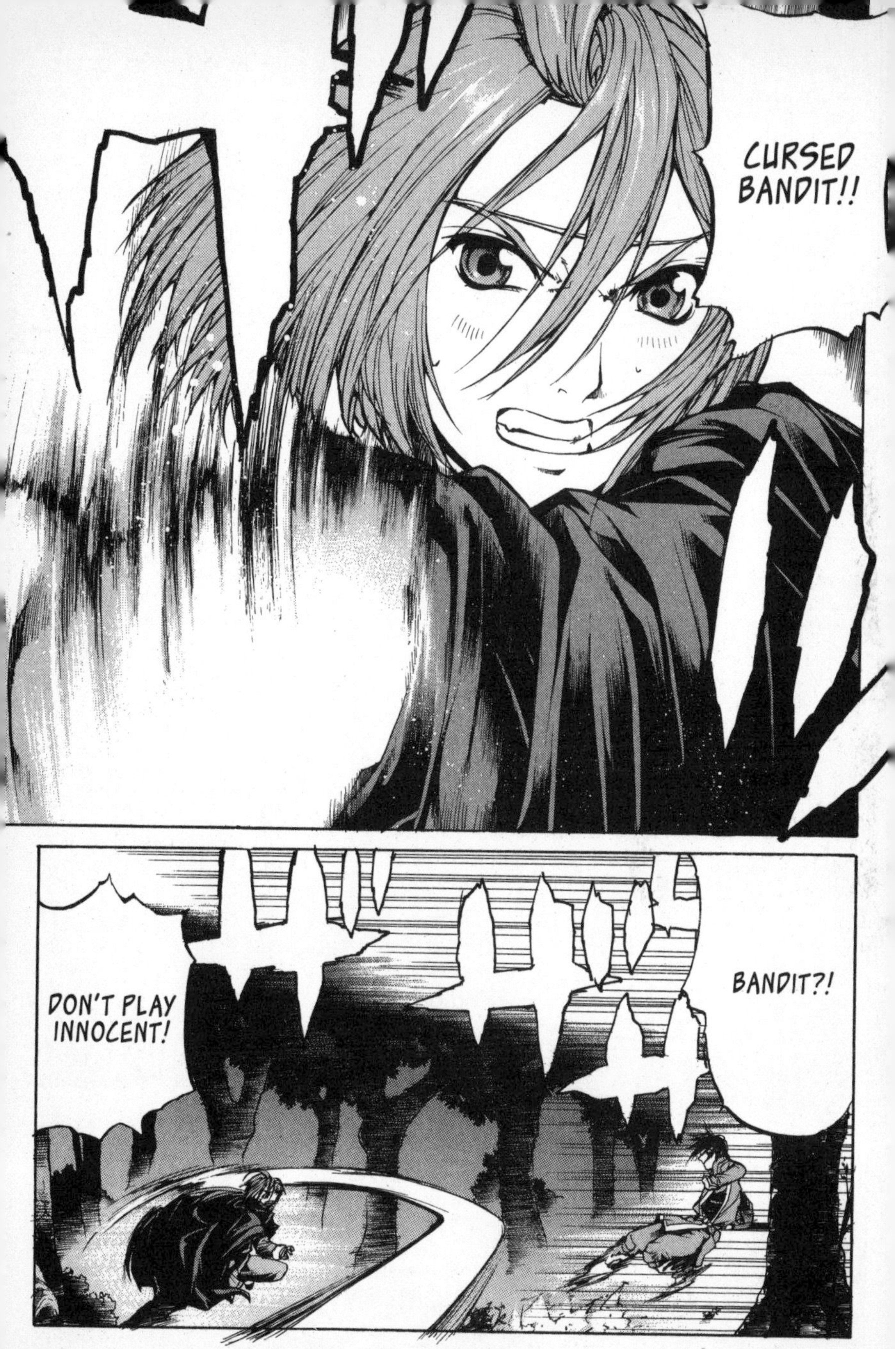
CURSED BANDIT!!
BANDIT?!
DON'T PLAY INNOCENT!

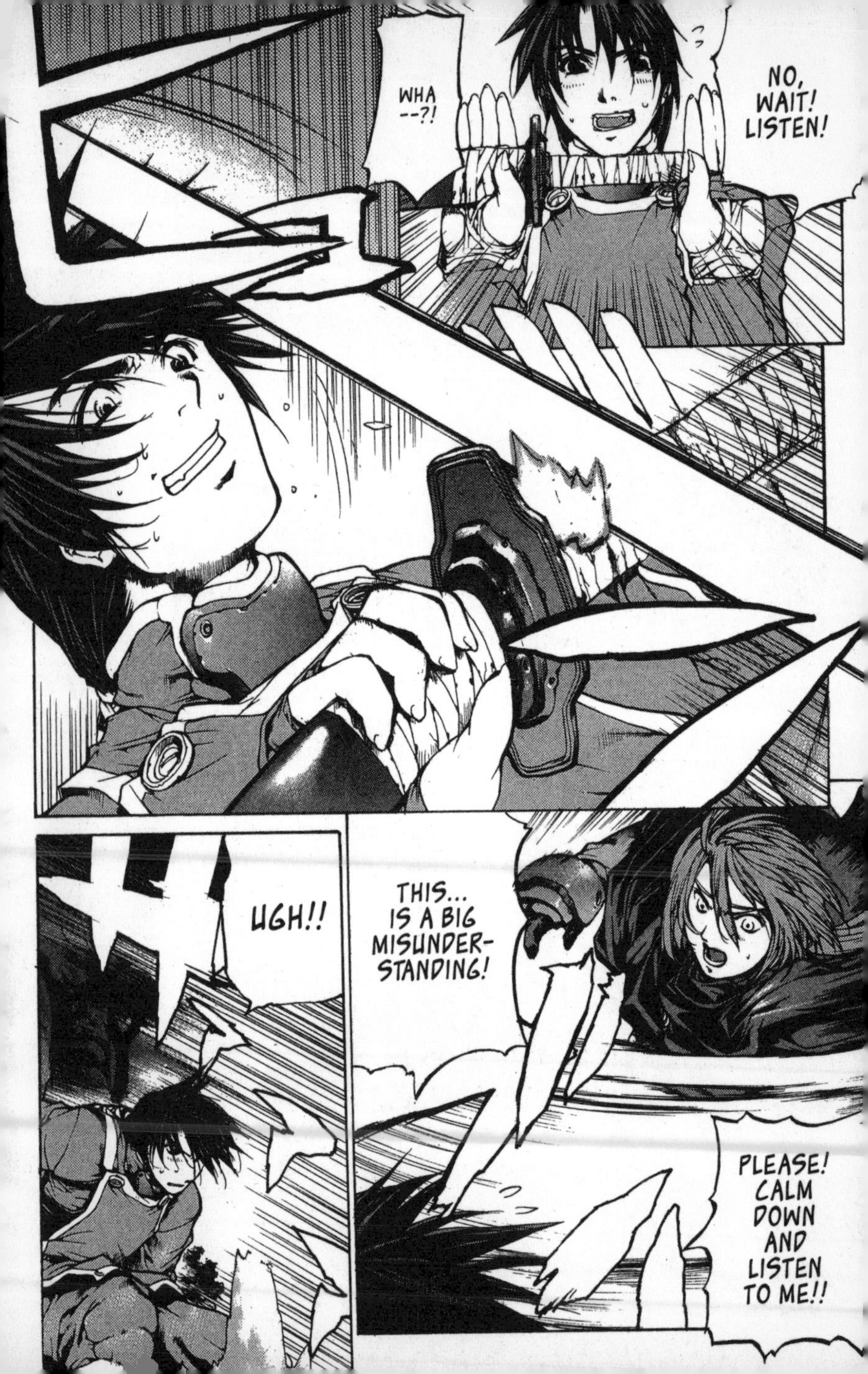
NO, WAIT! LISTEN!
WHA--?!
THIS... IS A BIG MISUNDER-STANDING!
PLEASE! CALM DOWN AND LISTEN TO ME!!
UGH!!

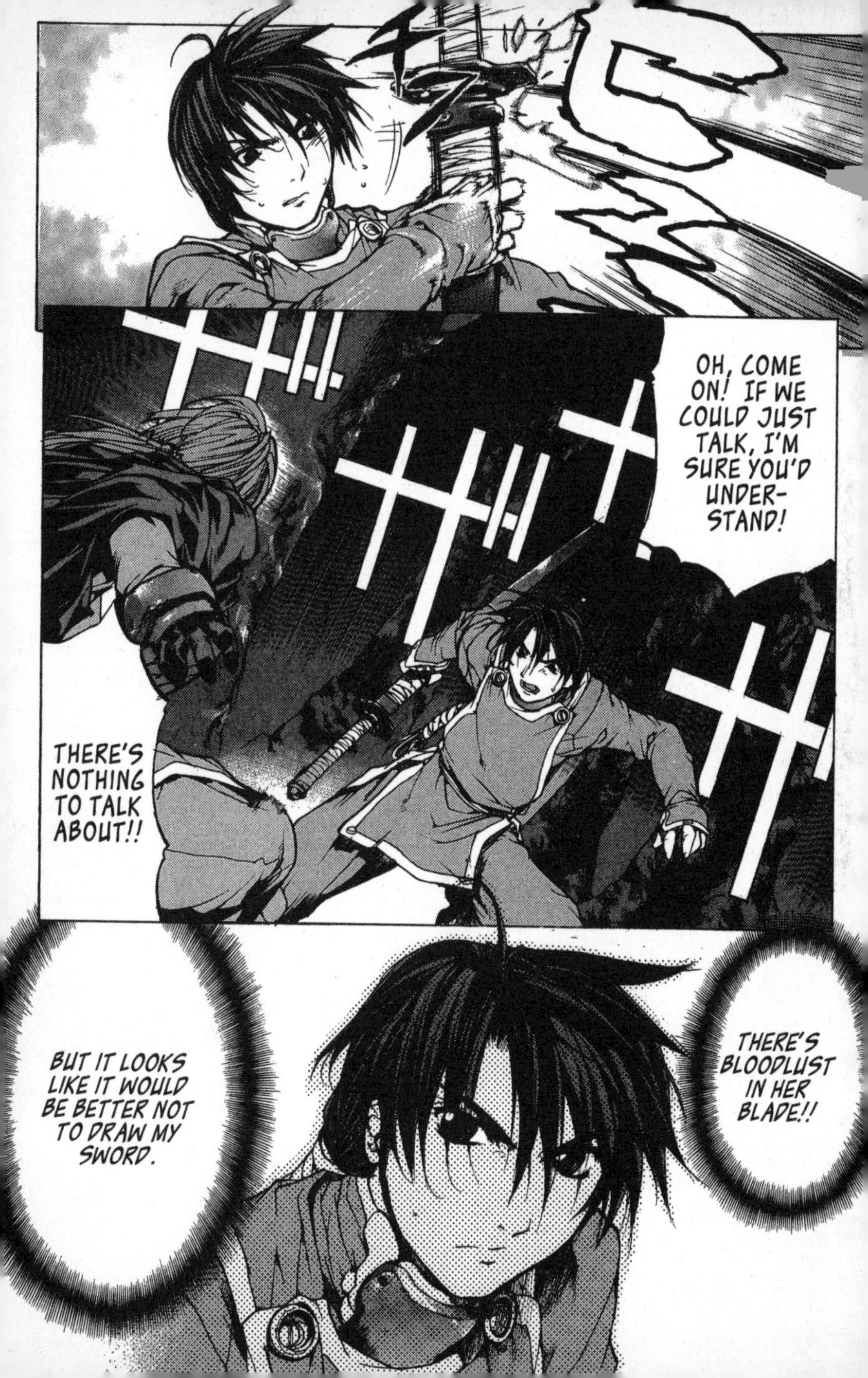
OH, COME ON! IF WE COULD JUST TALK, I'M SURE YOU'D UNDER-STAND!
THERE'S NOTHING TO TALK ABOUT!!
THERE'S BLOODLUST IN HER BLADE!!
BUT IT LOOKS LIKE IT WOULD BE BETTER NOT TO DRAW MY SWORD.

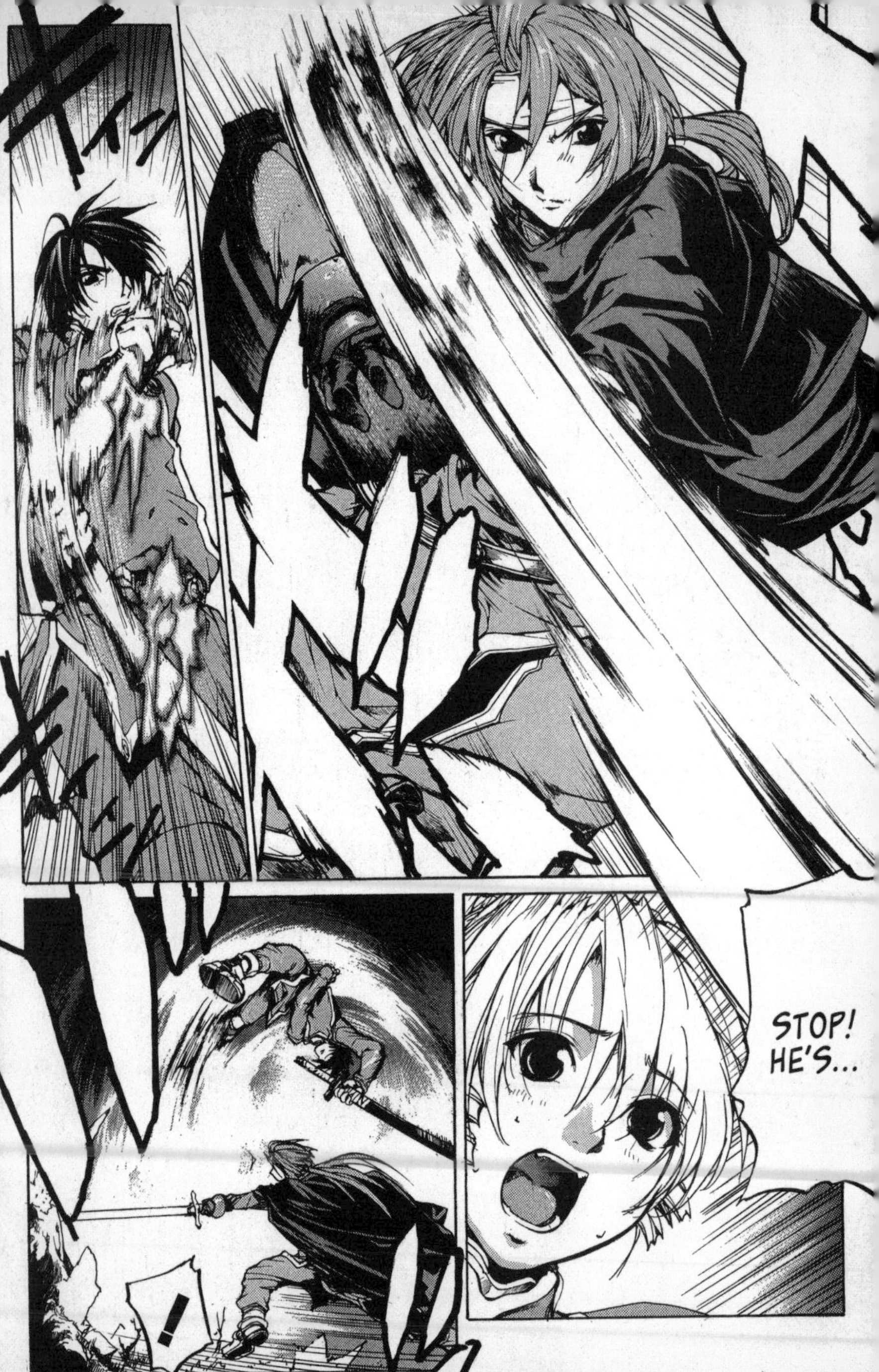
STOP! HE'S...
!

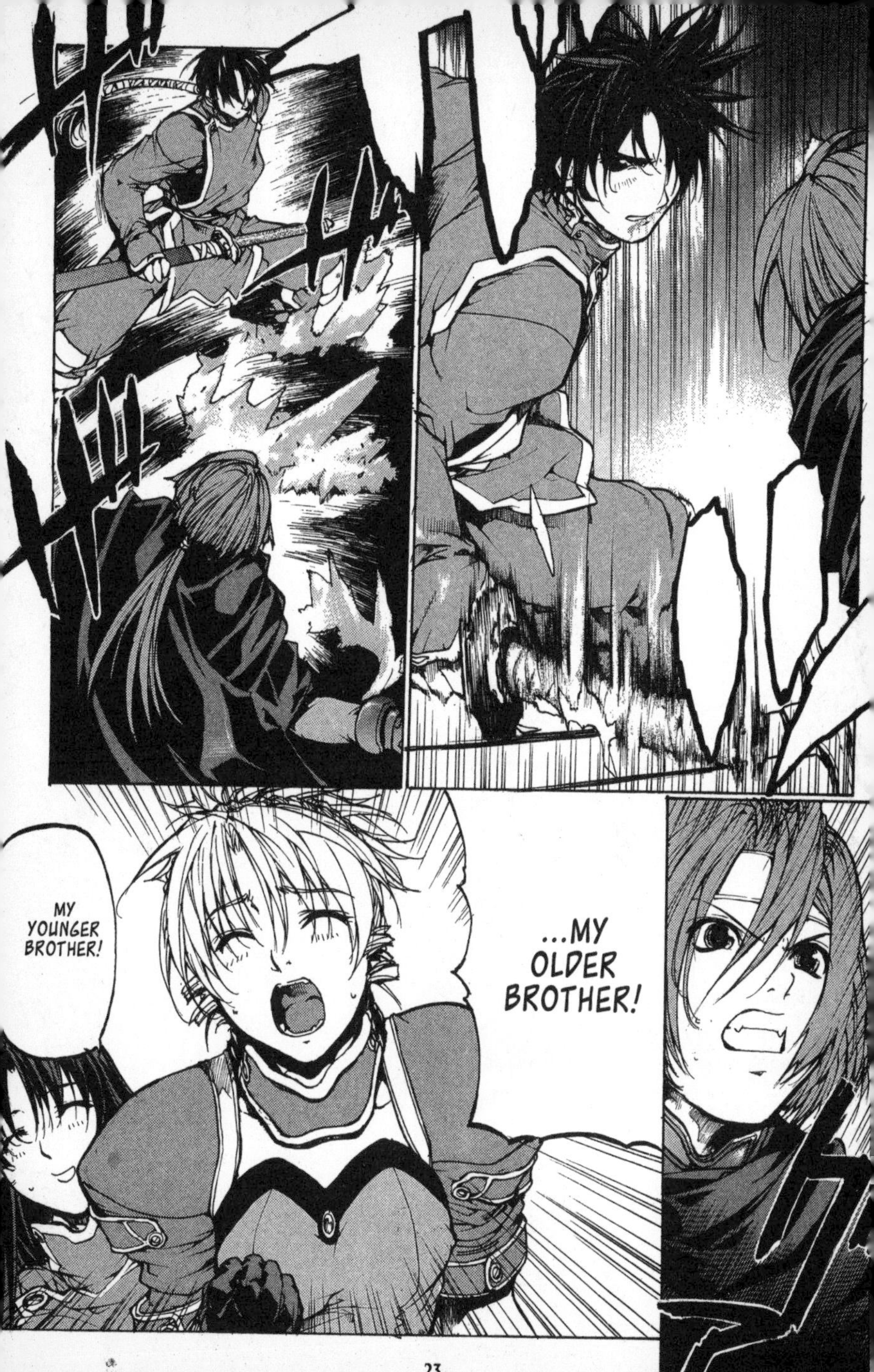
...MY OLDER BROTHER!
MY YOUNGER BROTHER!

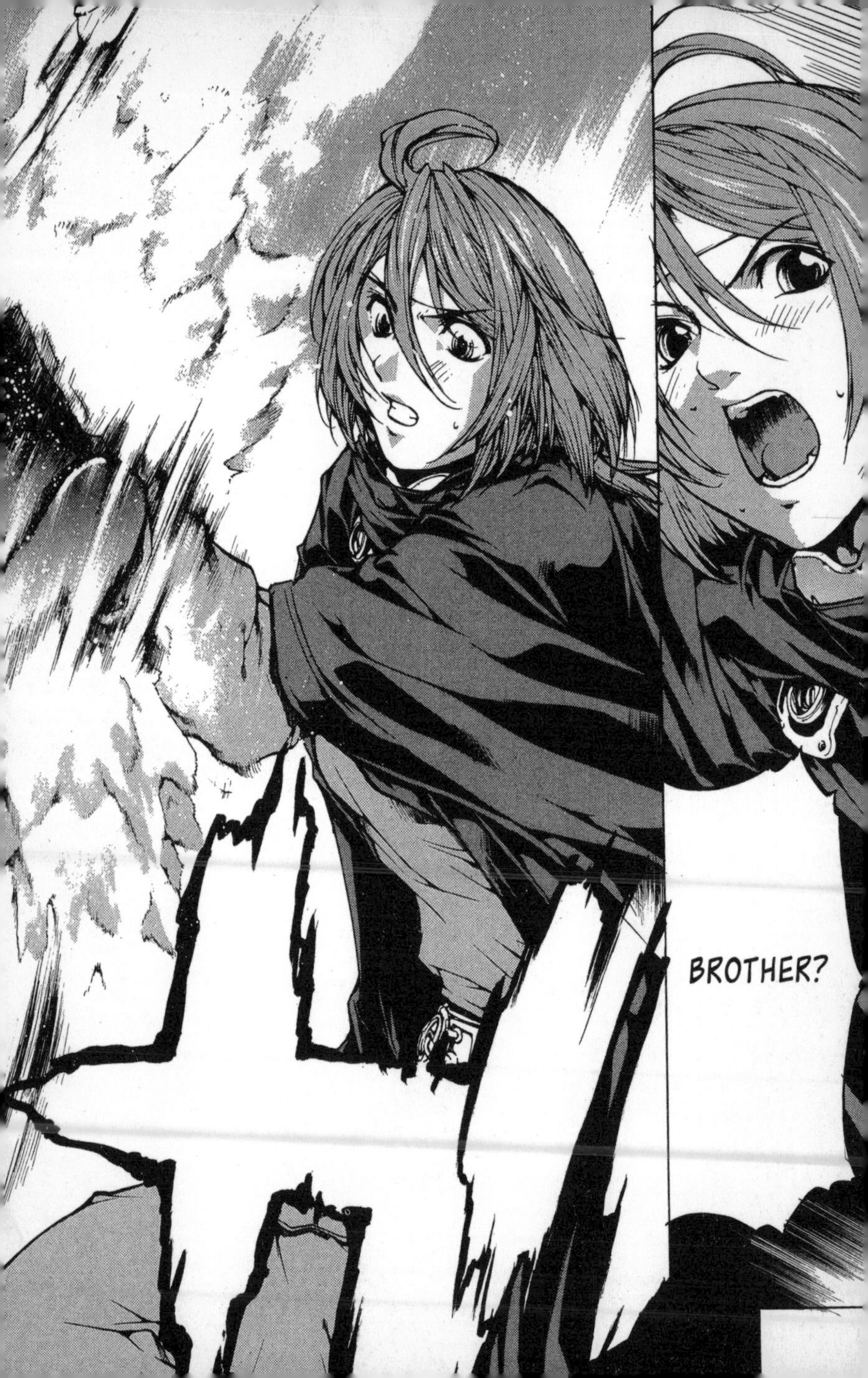
BROTHER?

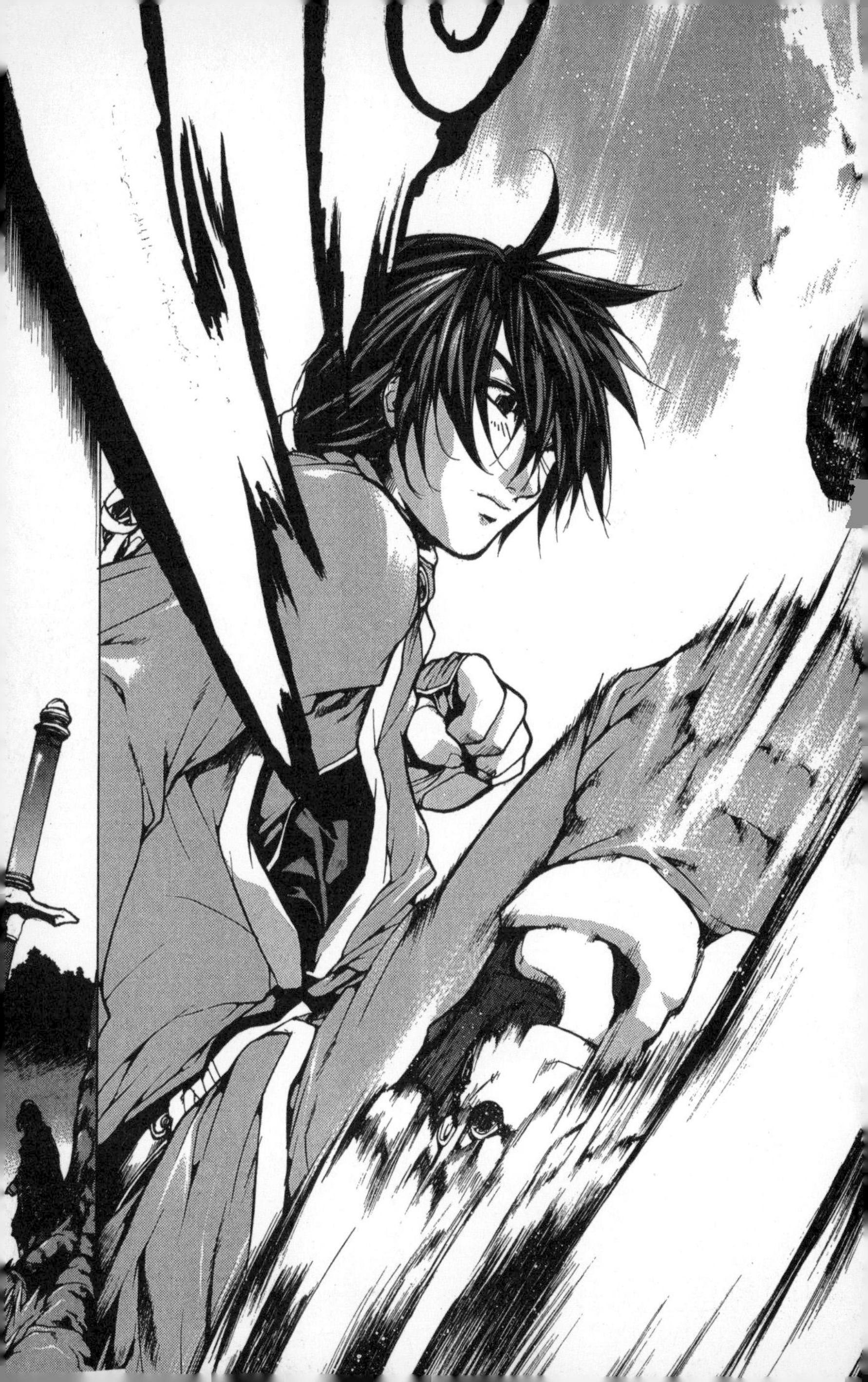

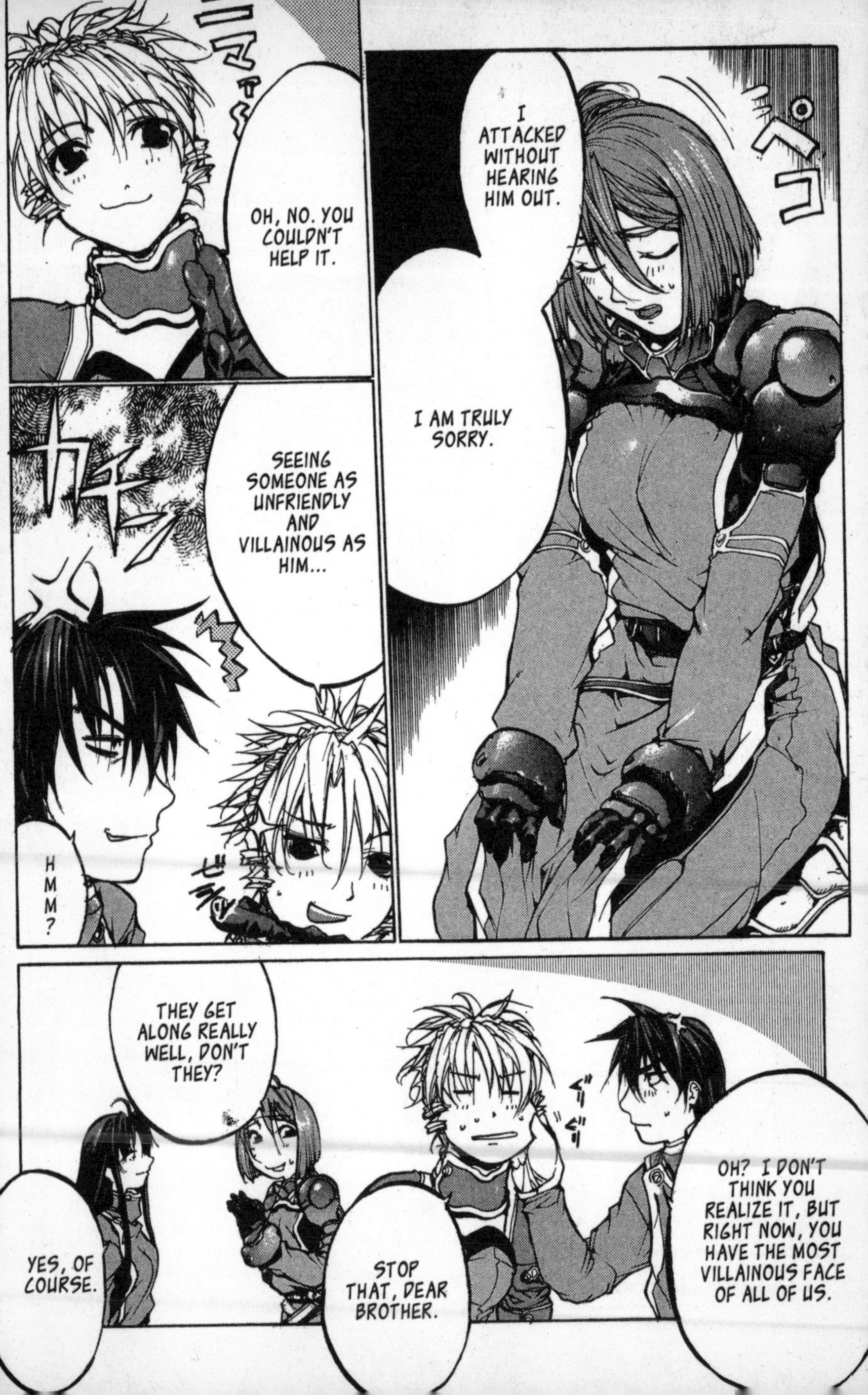
I ATTACKED WITHOUT HEARING HIM OUT.
I AM TRULY SORRY.
OH, NO. YOU COULDN'T HELP IT.
SEEING SOMEONE AS UNFRIENDLY AND VILLAINOUS AS HIM...
HMM?
OH? I DON'T THINK YOU REALIZE IT, BUT RIGHT NOW, YOU HAVE THE MOST VILLAINOUS FACE OF ALL OF US.
STOP THAT, DEAR BROTHER.
THEY GET ALONG REALLY WELL, DON'T THEY?
YES, OF COURSE.

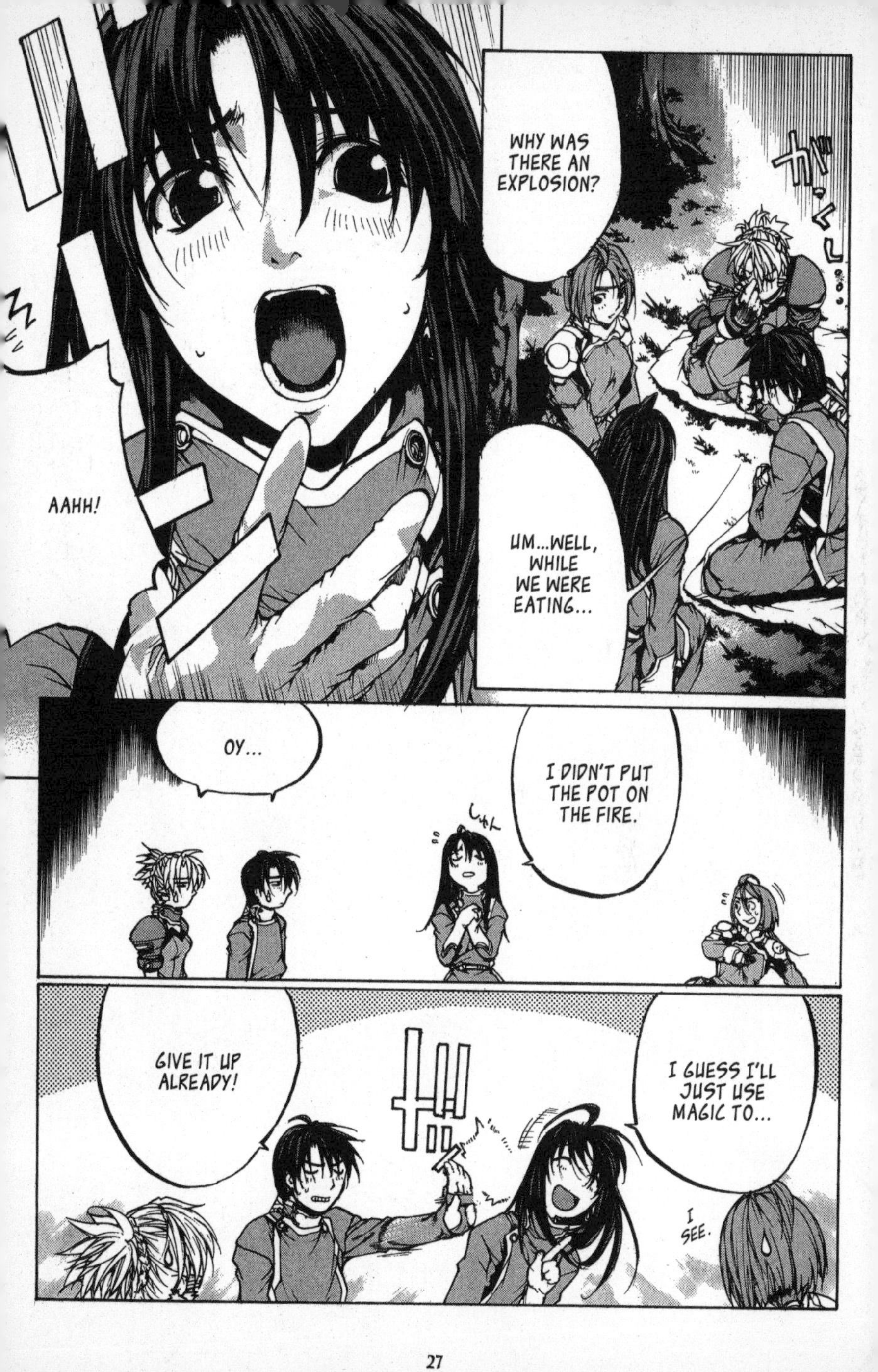
WHY WAS THERE AN EXPLOSION?
UM...WELL, WHILE WE WERE EATING...
AAHH!
I DIDN'T PUT THE POT ON THE FIRE.
OY...
I GUESS I'LL JUST USE MAGIC TO...
I SEE.
GIVE IT UP ALREADY!

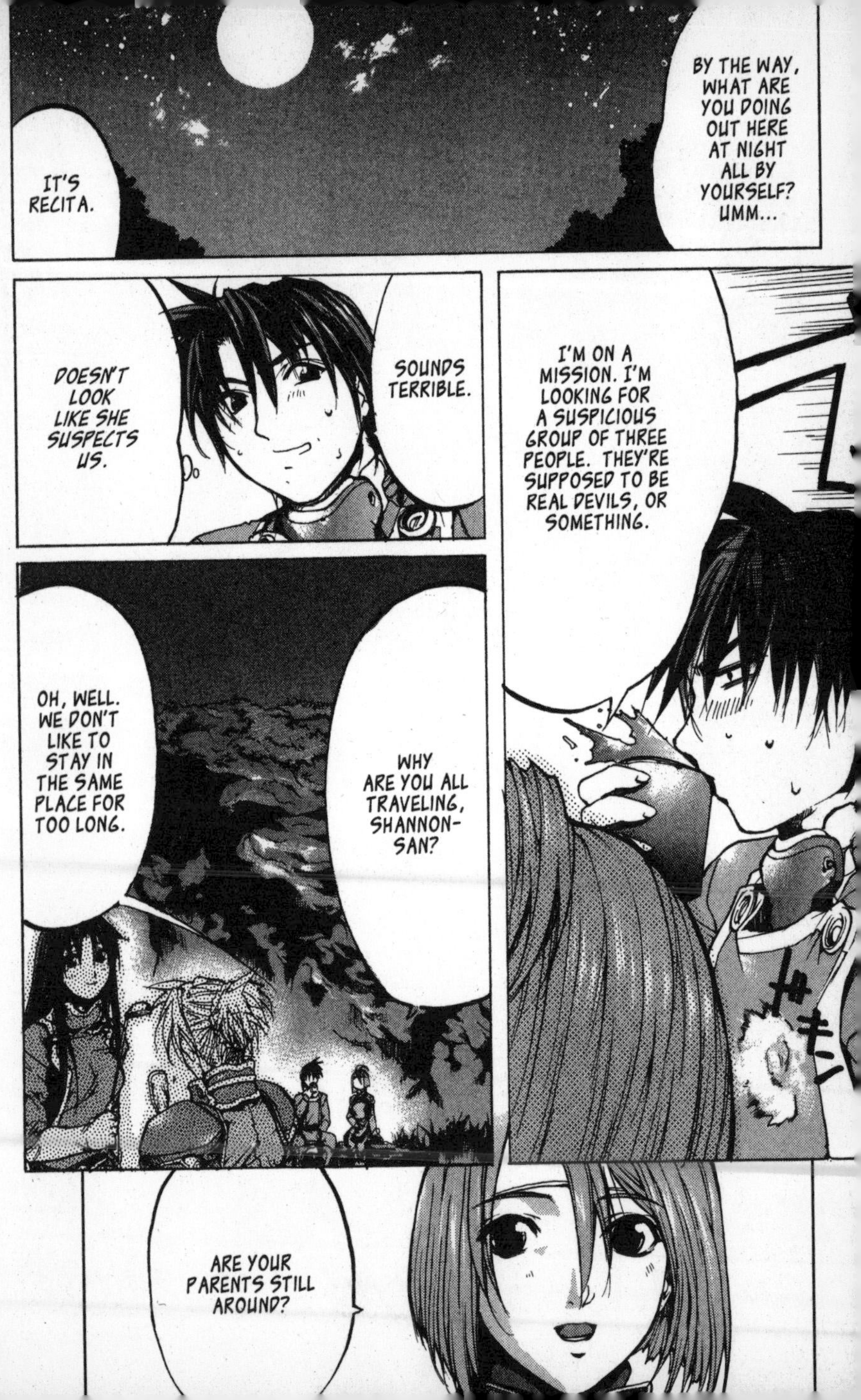
BY THE WAY, WHAT ARE YOU DOING OUT HERE AT NIGHT ALL BY YOURSELF? UMM...
IT'S RECITA.
I'M ON A MISSION. I'M LOOKING FOR A SUSPICIOUS GROUP OF THREE PEOPLE. THEY'RE SUPPOSED TO BE REAL DEVILS, OR SOMETHING.
SOUNDS TERRIBLE.
DOESN'T LOOK LIKE SHE SUSPECTS US.
WHY ARE YOU ALL TRAVELING, SHANNON-SAN?
OH, WELL. WE DON'T LIKE TO STAY IN THE SAME PLACE FOR TOO LONG.
ARE YOUR PARENTS STILL AROUND?

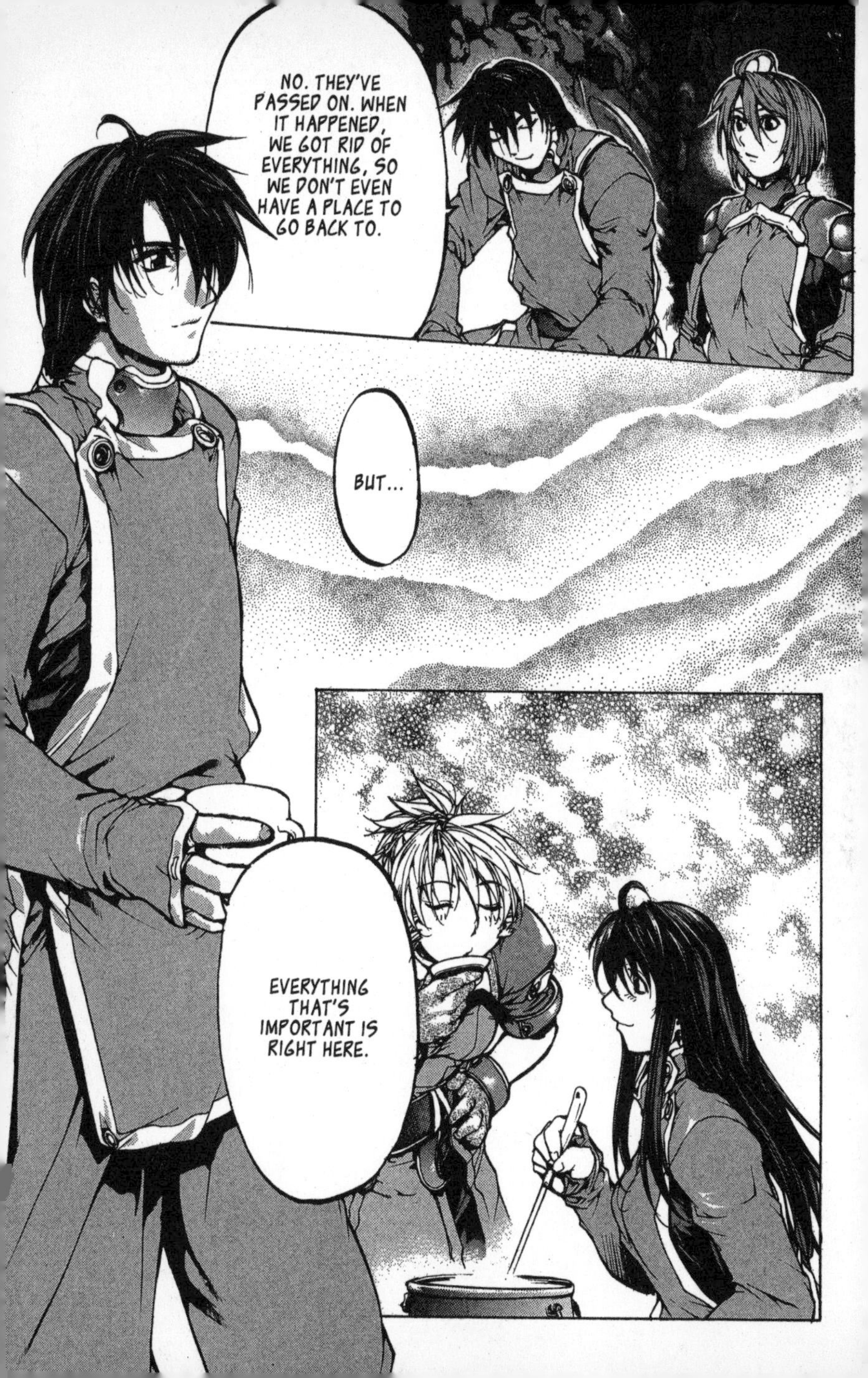
NO. THEY'VE PASSED ON. WHEN IT HAPPENED, WE GOT RID OF EVERYTHING, SO WE DON'T EVEN HAVE A PLACE TO GO BACK TO.
BUT...
EVERYTHING THAT'S IMPORTANT IS RIGHT HERE.

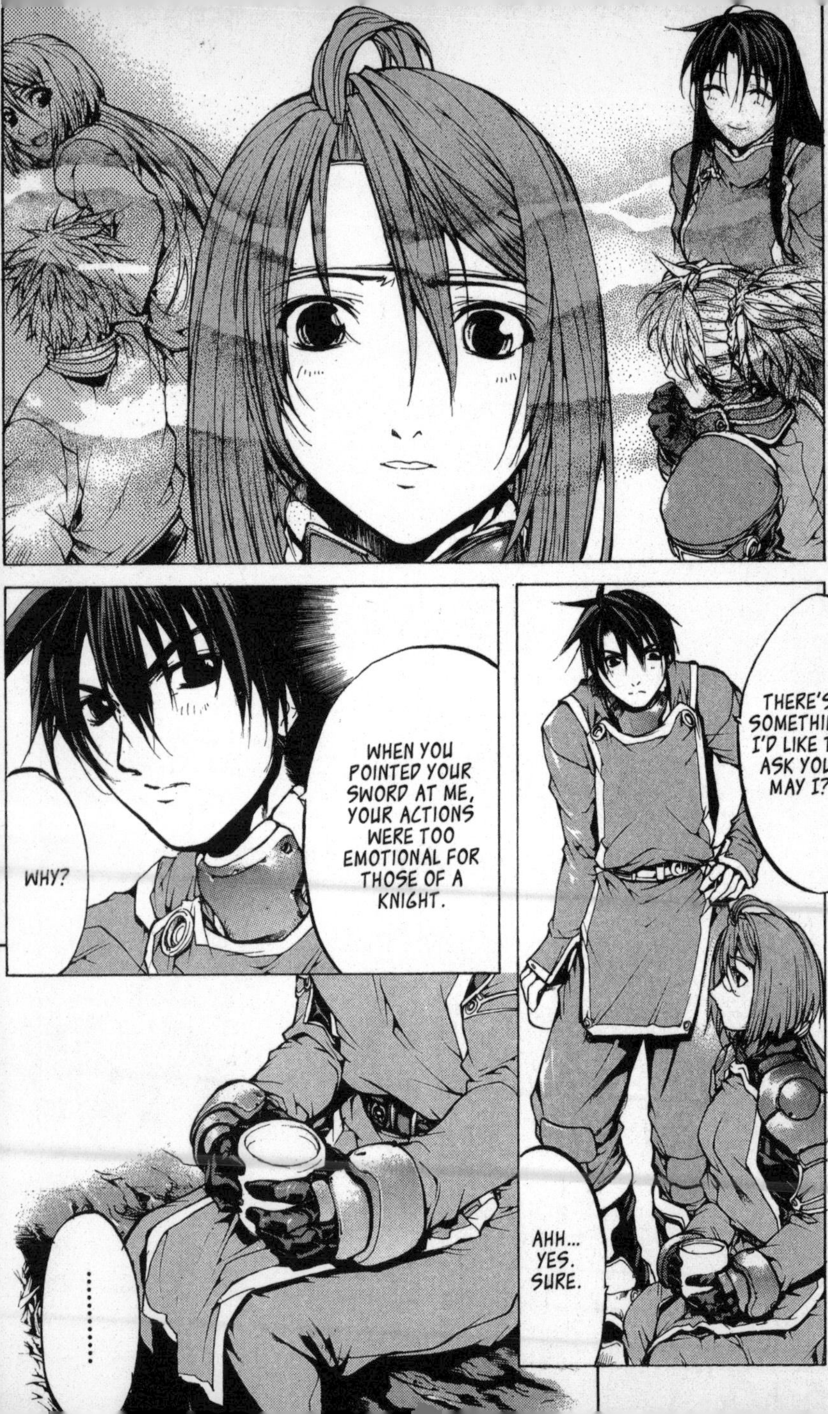
THERE'S SOMETHING I'D LIKE TO ASK YOU. MAY I?
AHH... YES. SURE.
WHEN YOU POINTED YOUR SWORD AT ME, YOUR ACTIONS WERE TOO EMOTIONAL FOR THOSE OF A KNIGHT.
WHY?
......

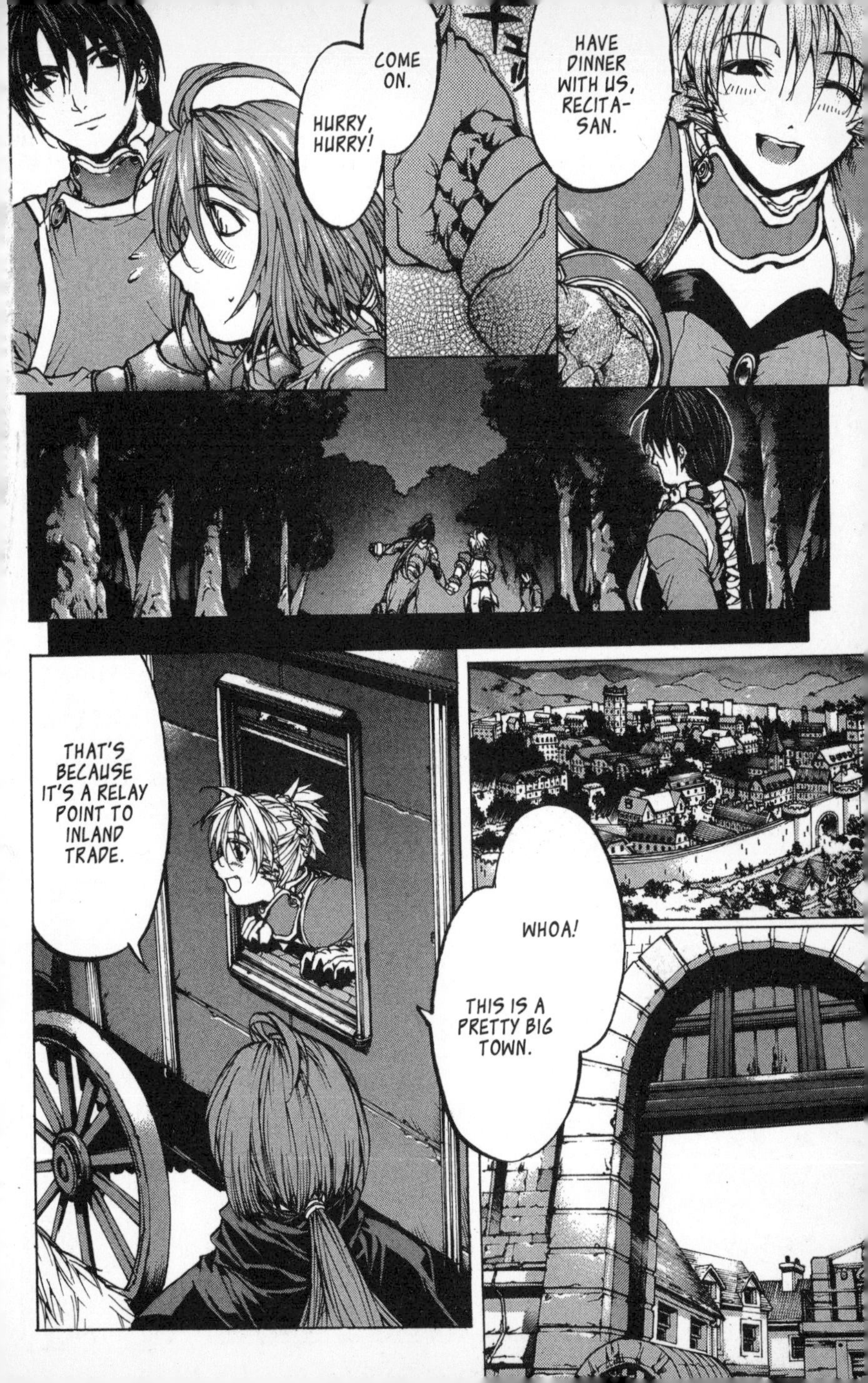
HAVE DINNER WITH US, RECITA-SAN.
COME ON.
HURRY, HURRY!
WHOA!
THIS IS A PRETTY BIG TOWN.
THAT'S BECAUSE IT'S A RELAY POINT TO INLAND TRADE.

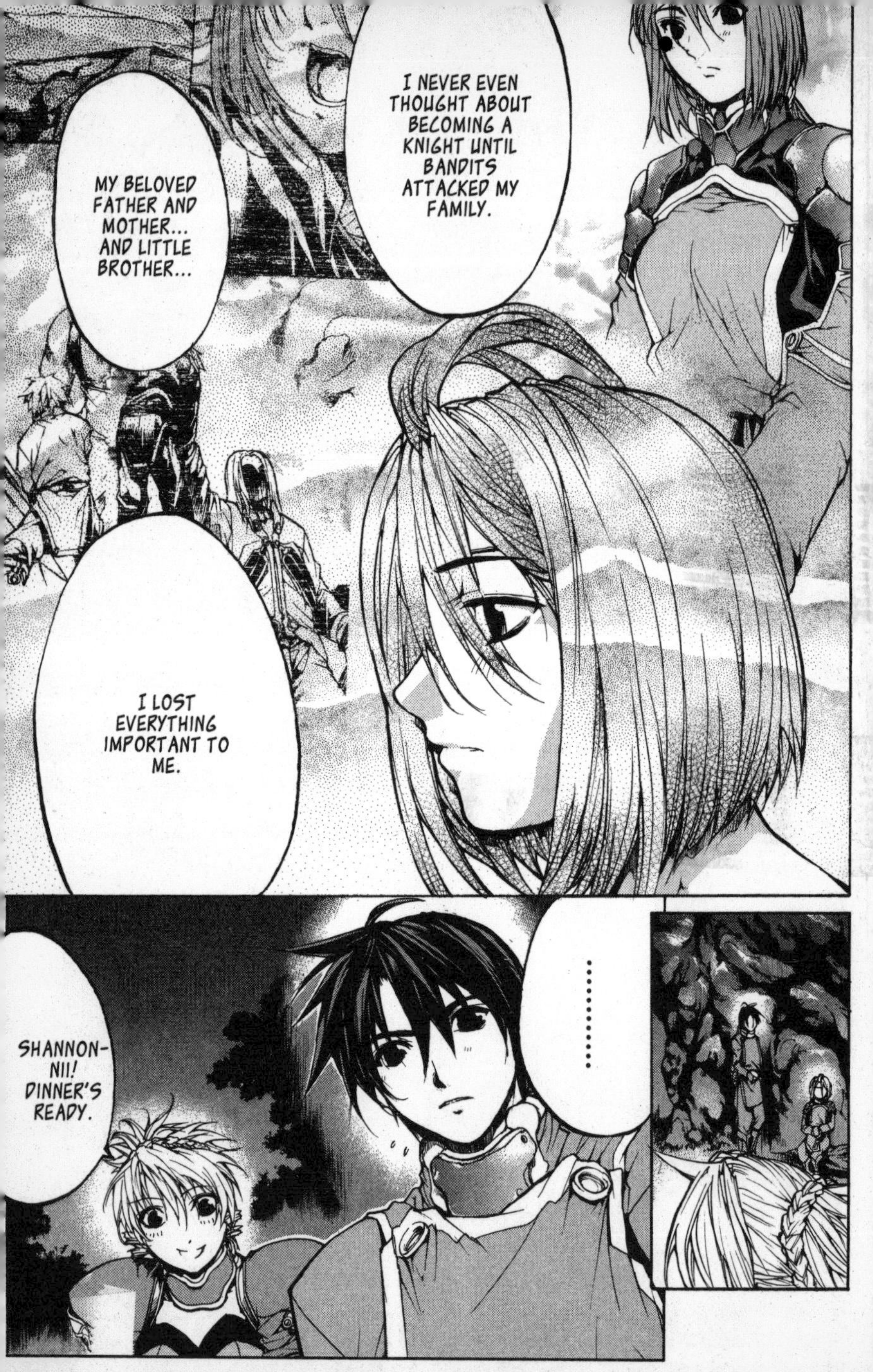
I NEVER EVEN THOUGHT ABOUT BECOMING A KNIGHT UNTIL BANDITS ATTACKED MY FAMILY.
MY BELOVED FATHER AND MOTHER... AND LITTLE BROTHER...
I LOST EVERYTHING IMPORTANT TO ME.
......
SHANNON-NII! DINNER'S READY.

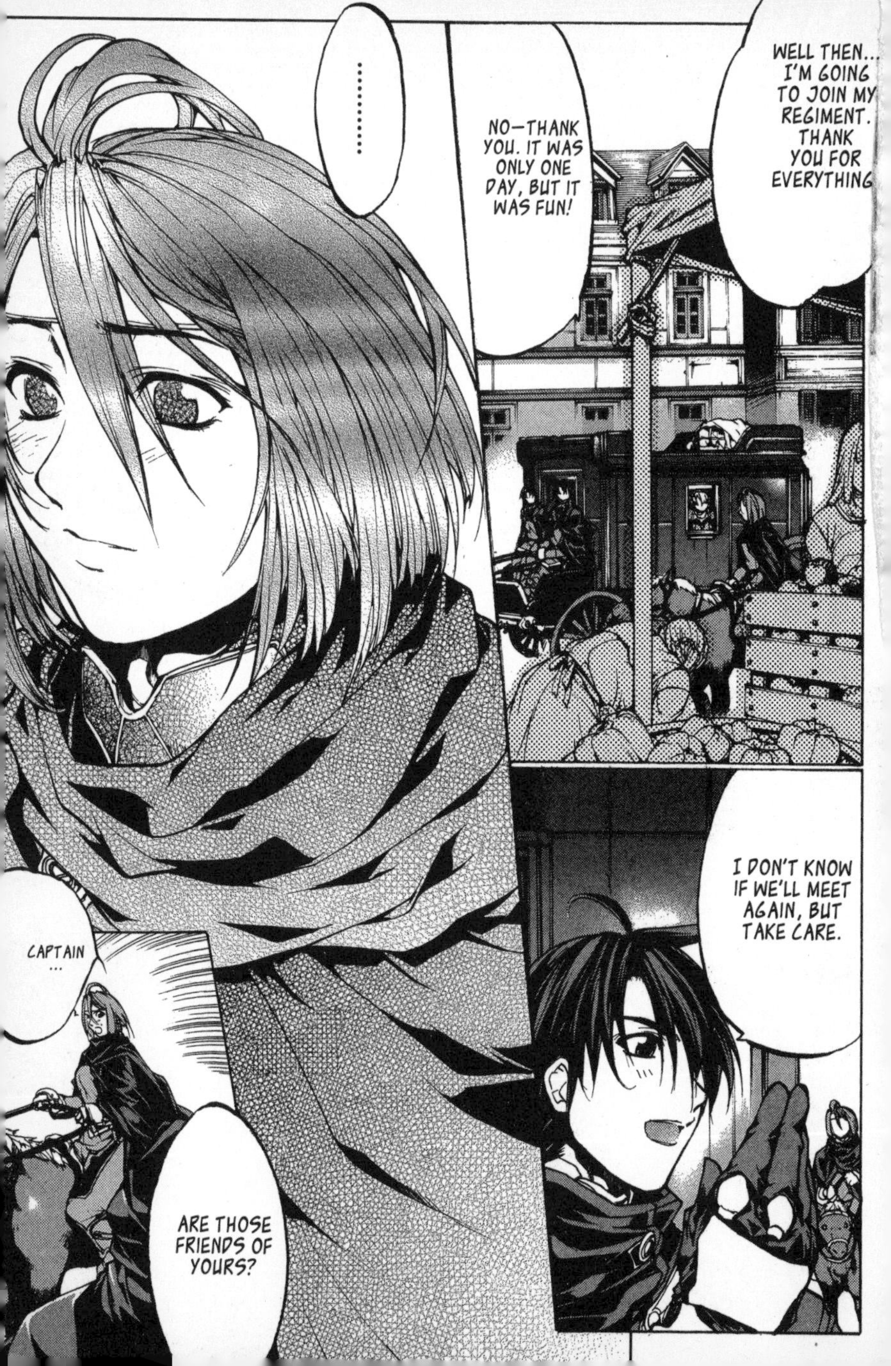
WELL THEN... I'M GOING TO JOIN MY REGIMENT. THANK YOU FOR EVERYTHING
NO—THANK YOU. IT WAS ONLY ONE DAY, BUT IT WAS FUN!
I DON'T KNOW IF WE'LL MEET AGAIN, BUT TAKE CARE.
......
CAPTAIN ...
ARE THOSE FRIENDS OF YOURS?

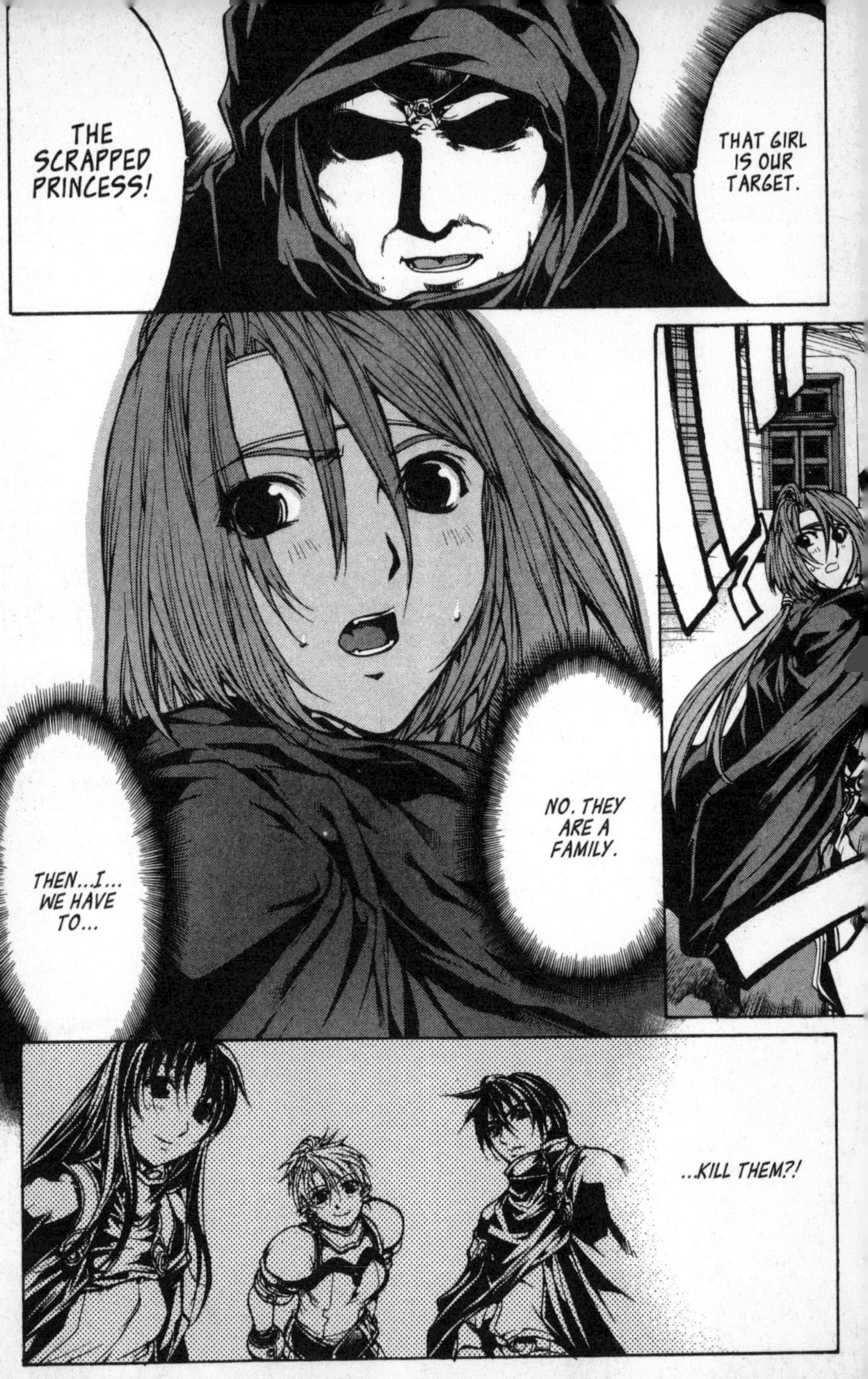
THAT GIRL IS OUR TARGET.
THE SCRAPPED PRINCESS!
NO. THEY ARE A FAMILY.
THEN...I... WE HAVE TO...
...KILL THEM?!

THE THREE PEOPLE YOU WERE JUST TALKING TO...
...ARE OUR TARGETS.
NO. THOSE SIBLINGS ARE THE POISON THAT WILL DESTROY THE WORLD?
THE ONES WE HAVE TO KILL?
THE SCRAPPED PRINCESS?!!

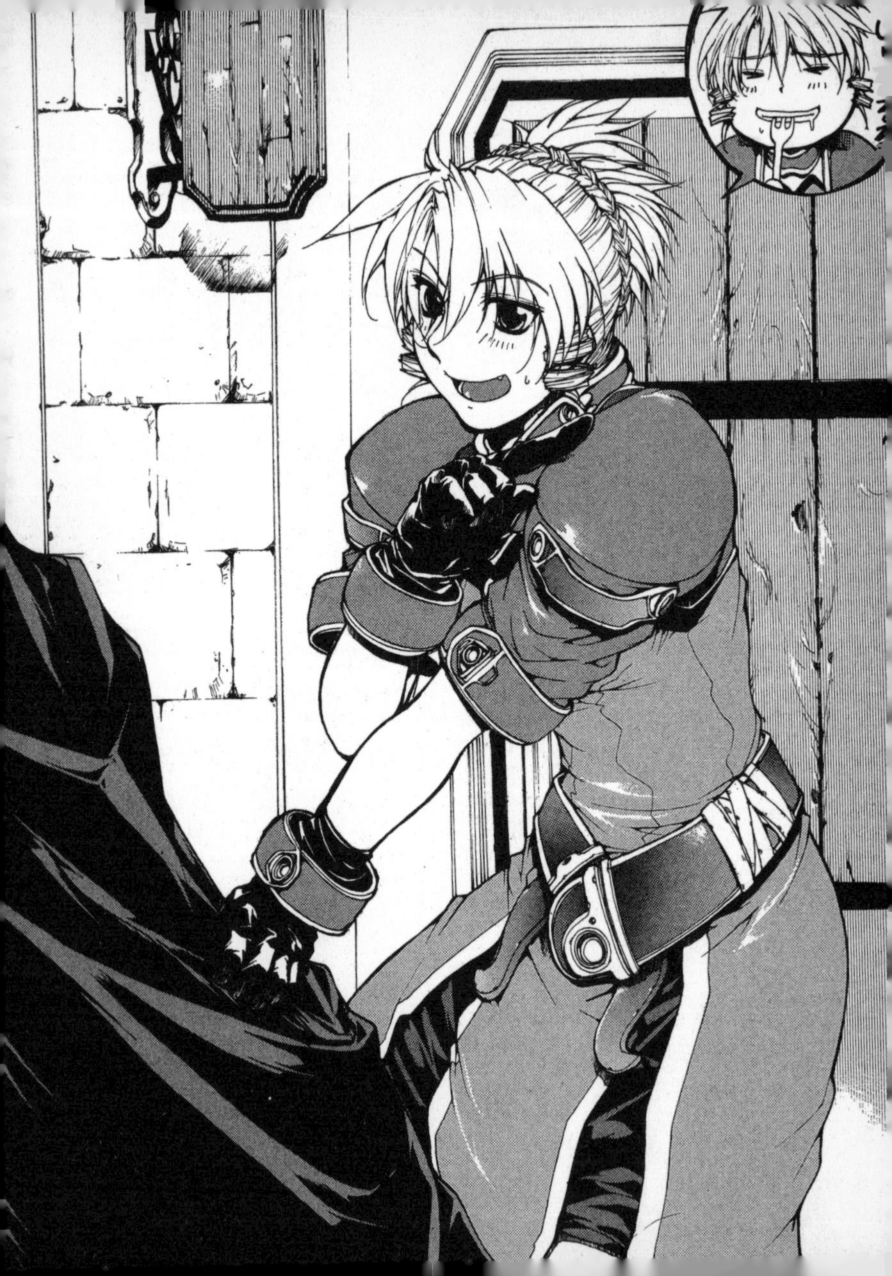

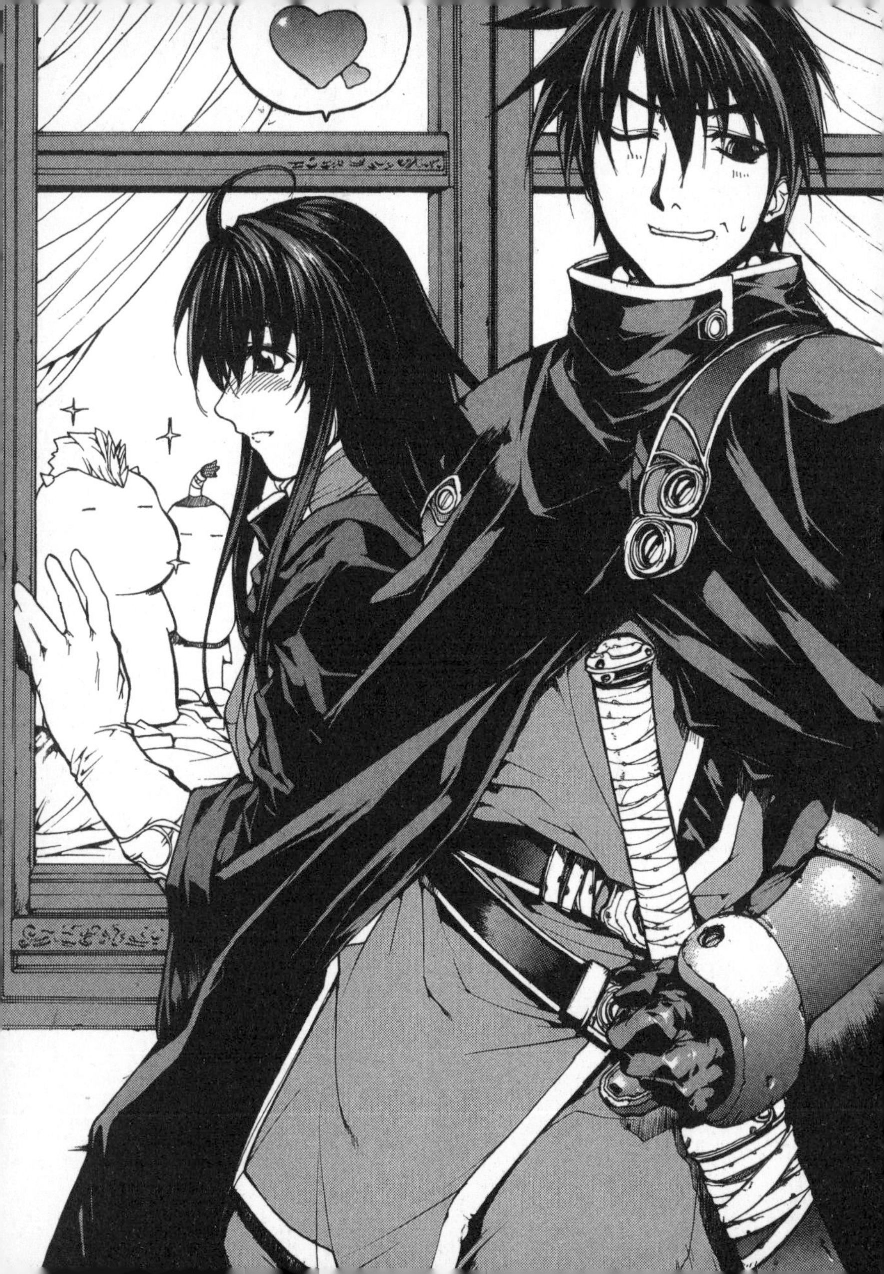

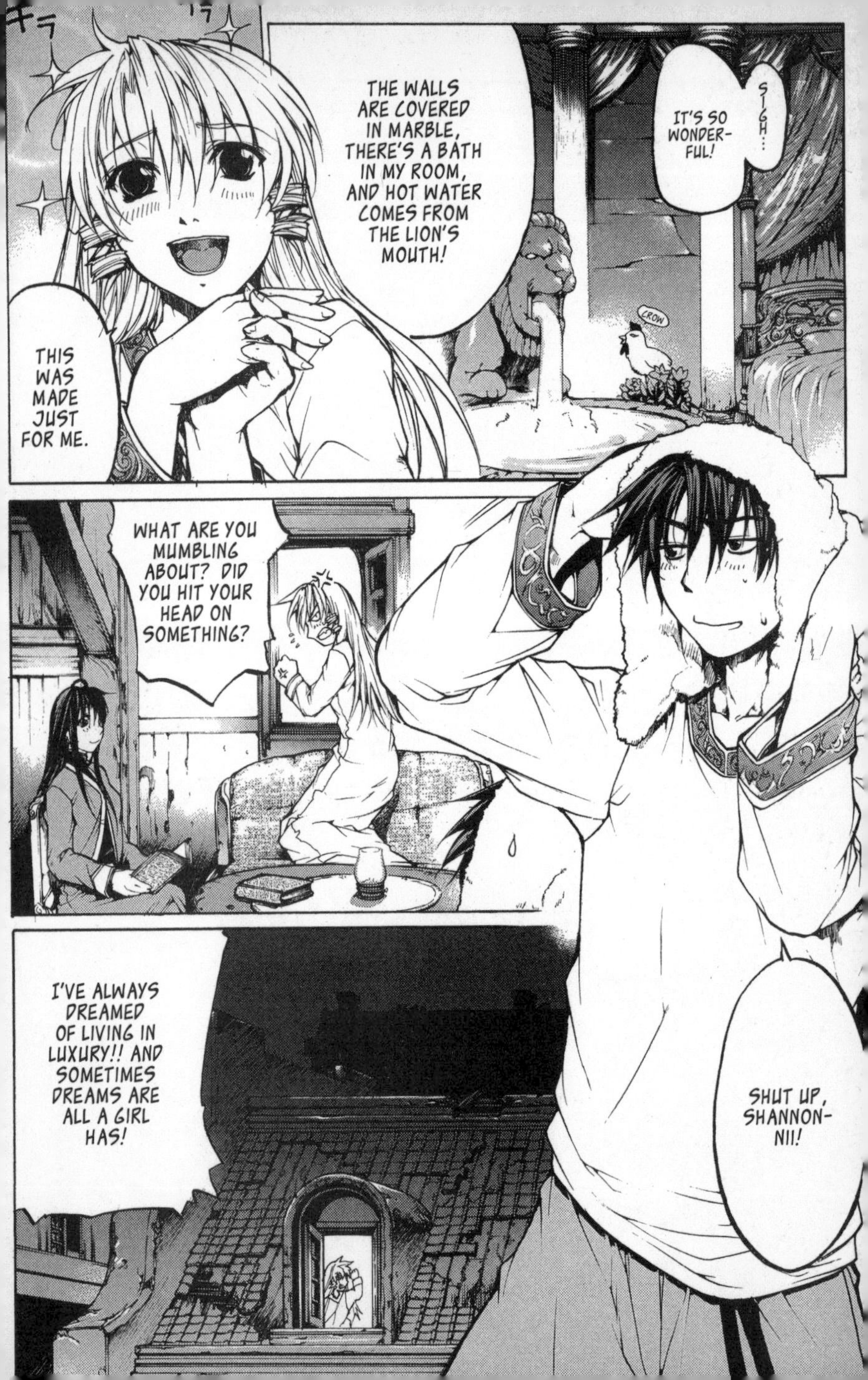
IT'S SO WONDER-FUL!
SIGH...
THE WALLS ARE COVERED IN MARBLE, THERE'S A BATH IN MY ROOM, AND HOT WATER COMES FROM THE LION'S MOUTH!
CROW
THIS WAS MADE JUST FOR ME.
WHAT ARE YOU MUMBLING ABOUT? DID YOU HIT YOUR HEAD ON SOMETHING?
SHUT UP, SHANNON-NII!
I'VE ALWAYS DREAMED OF LIVING IN LUXURY!! AND SOMETIMES DREAMS ARE ALL A GIRL HAS!

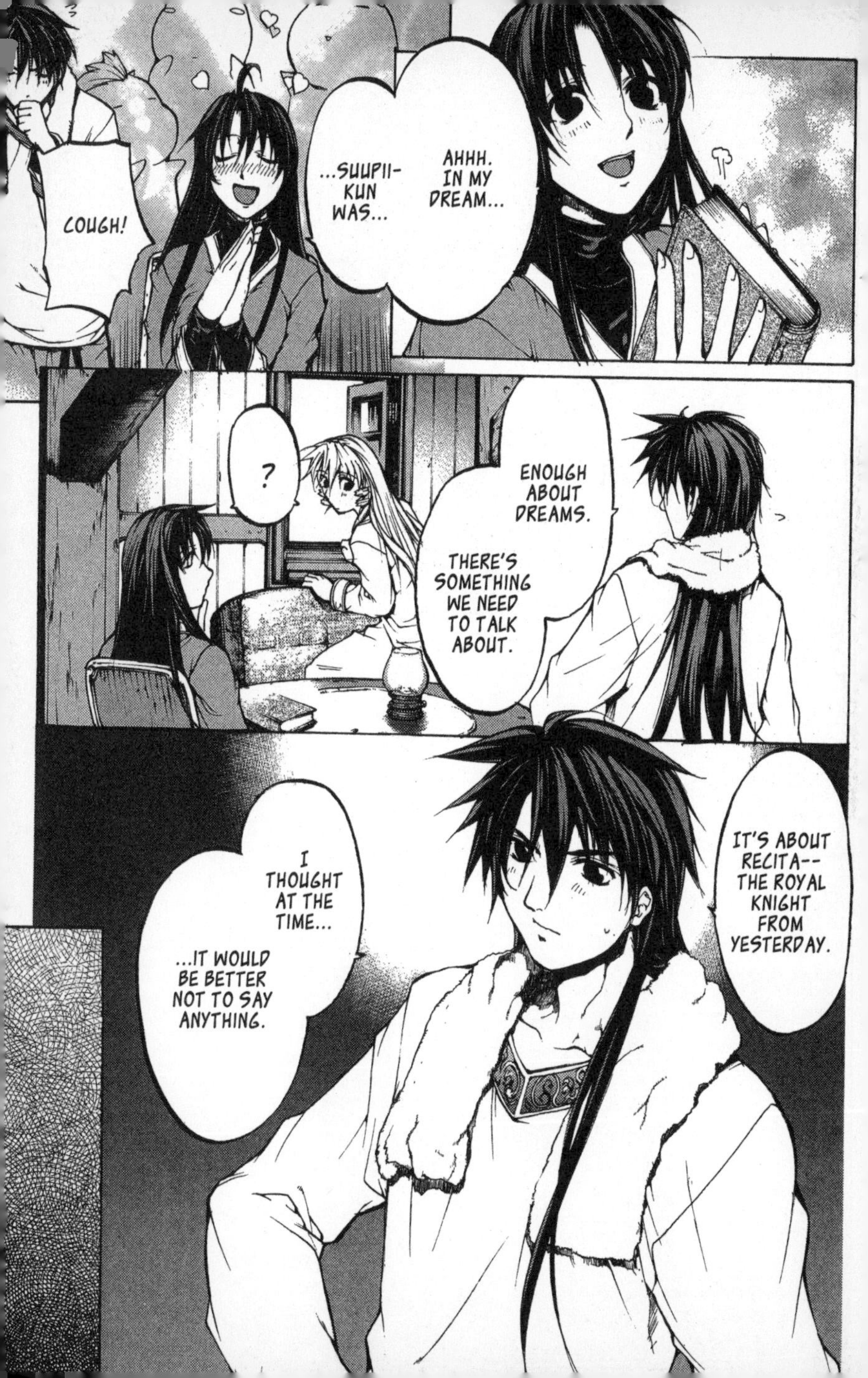
AHHH. IN MY DREAM...
...SUUPII-KUN WAS...
COUGH!
ENOUGH ABOUT DREAMS.
THERE'S SOMETHING WE NEED TO TALK ABOUT.
?
IT'S ABOUT RECITA-- THE ROYAL KNIGHT FROM YESTERDAY.
I THOUGHT AT THE TIME...
...IT WOULD BE BETTER NOT TO SAY ANYTHING.

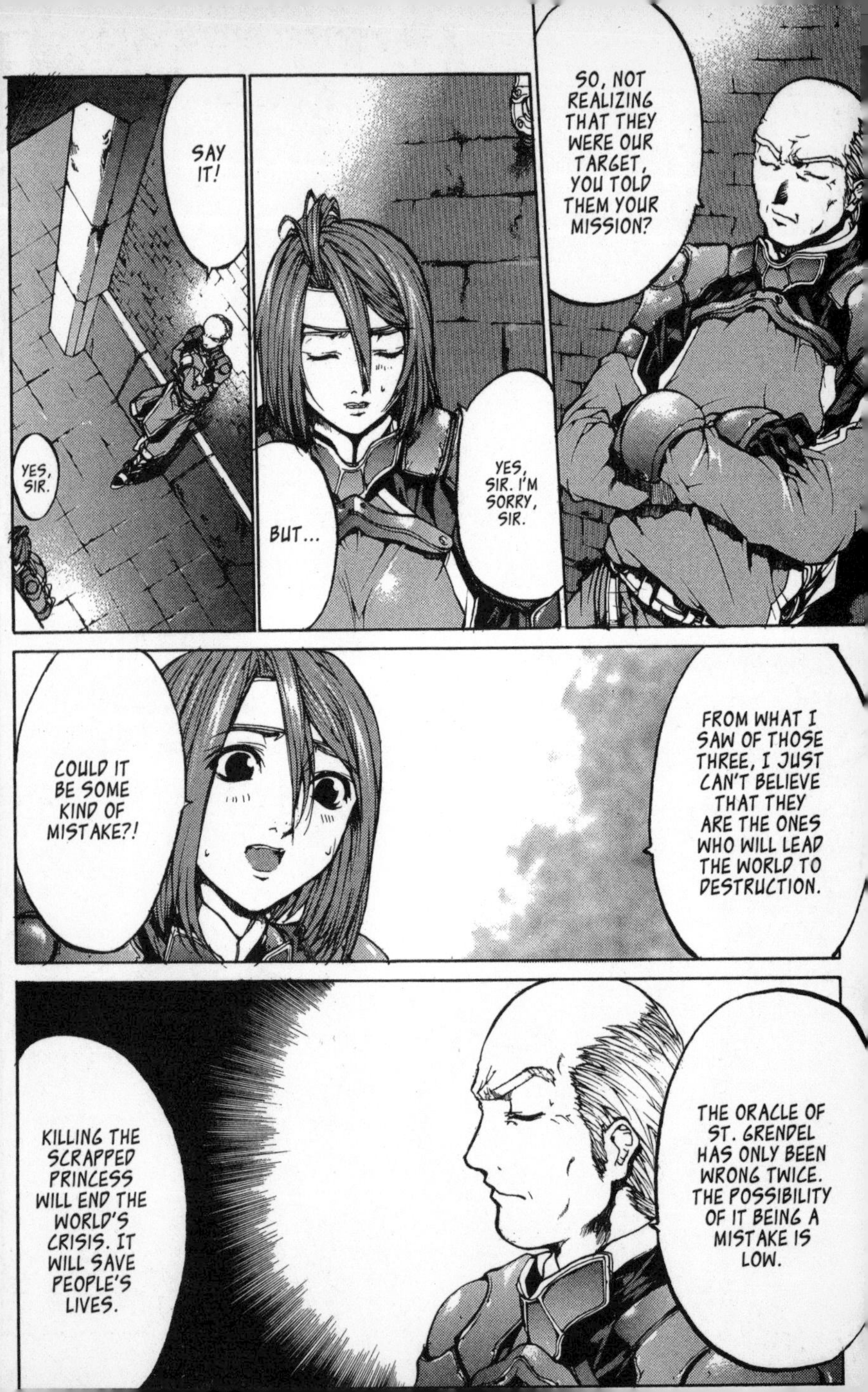
SO, NOT REALIZING THAT THEY WERE OUR TARGET, YOU TOLD THEM YOUR MISSION?
YES, SIR. I'M SORRY, SIR.
BUT...
SAY IT!
YES, SIR.
FROM WHAT I SAW OF THOSE THREE, I JUST CAN'T BELIEVE THAT THEY ARE THE ONES WHO WILL LEAD THE WORLD TO DESTRUCTION.
COULD IT BE SOME KIND OF MISTAKE?!
THE ORACLE OF ST. GRENDEL HAS ONLY BEEN WRONG TWICE. THE POSSIBILITY OF IT BEING A MISTAKE IS LOW.
KILLING THE SCRAPPED PRINCESS WILL END THE WORLD'S CRISIS. IT WILL SAVE PEOPLE'S LIVES.

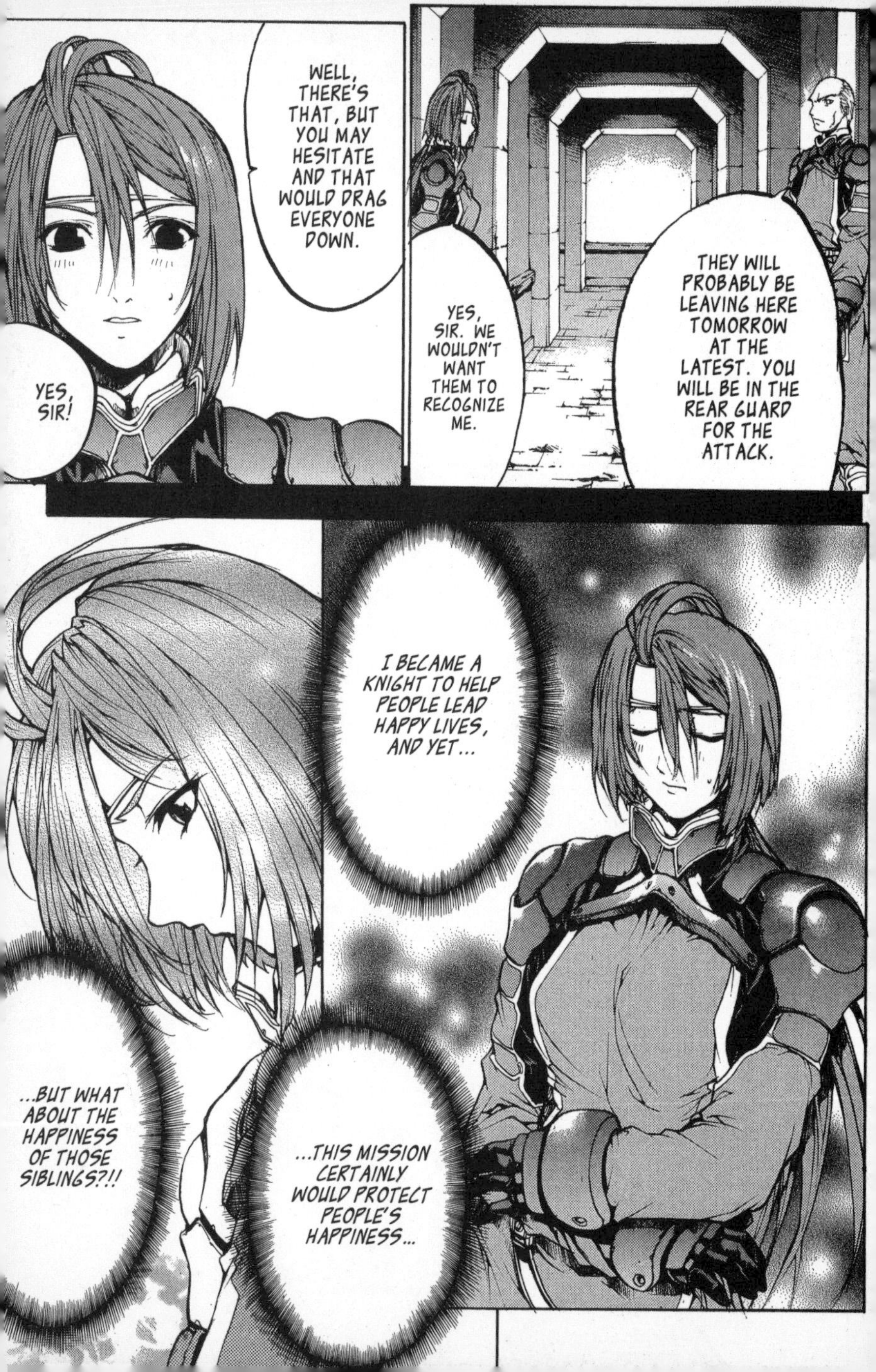
THEY WILL PROBABLY BE LEAVING HERE TOMORROW AT THE LATEST. YOU WILL BE IN THE REAR GUARD FOR THE ATTACK.
YES, SIR. WE WOULDN'T WANT THEM TO RECOGNIZE ME.
WELL, THERE'S THAT, BUT YOU MAY HESITATE AND THAT WOULD DRAG EVERYONE DOWN.
YES, SIR!
I BECAME A KNIGHT TO HELP PEOPLE LEAD HAPPY LIVES, AND YET...
...THIS MISSION CERTAINLY WOULD PROTECT PEOPLE'S HAPPINESS...
...BUT WHAT ABOUT THE HAPPINESS OF THOSE SIBLINGS?!!

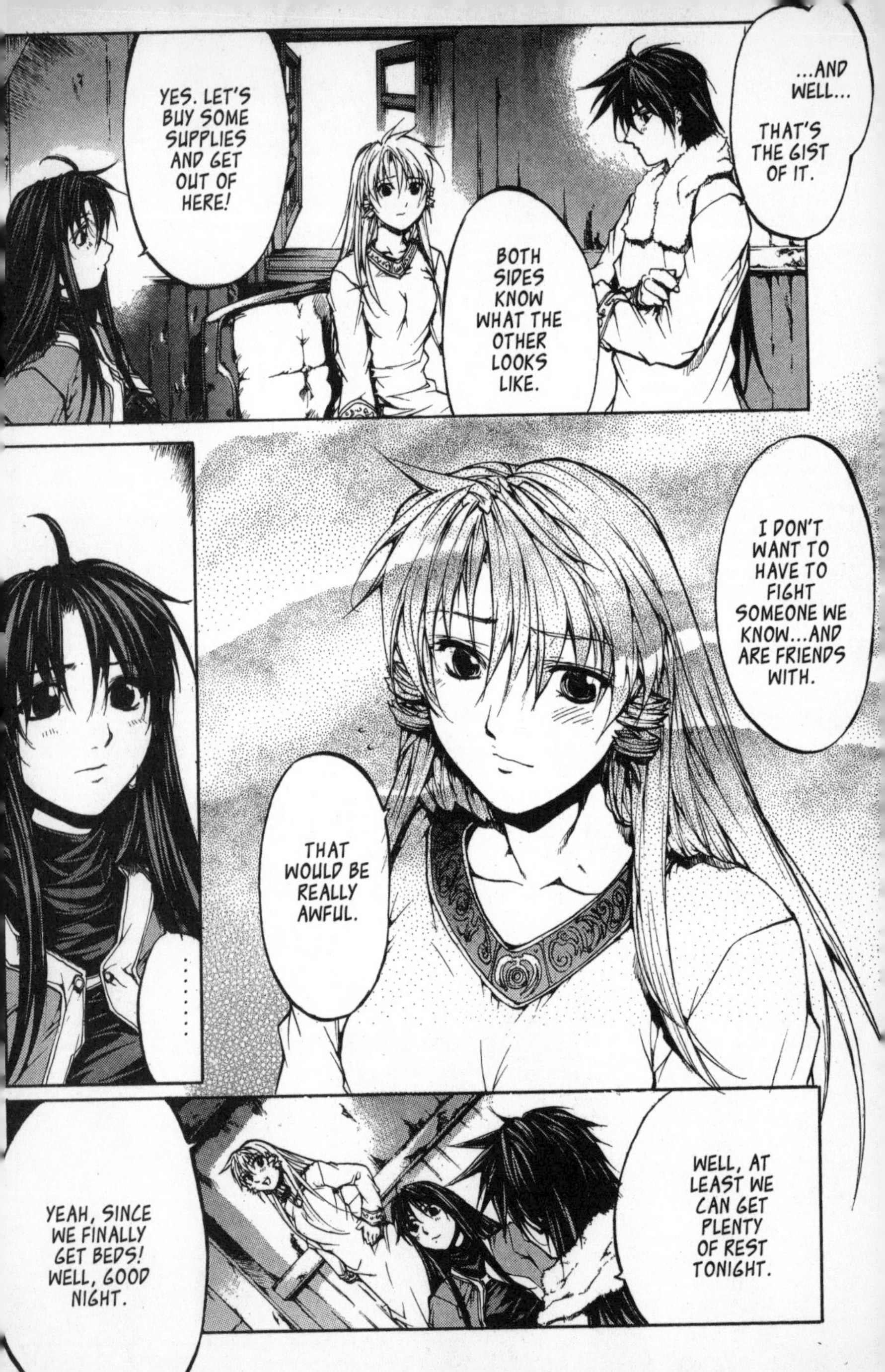
...AND WELL... THAT'S THE GIST OF IT.
BOTH SIDES KNOW WHAT THE OTHER LOOKS LIKE.
YES. LET'S BUY SOME SUPPLIES AND GET OUT OF HERE!
I DON'T WANT TO HAVE TO FIGHT SOMEONE WE KNOW...AND ARE FRIENDS WITH.
THAT WOULD BE REALLY AWFUL.
......
WELL, AT LEAST WE CAN GET PLENTY OF REST TONIGHT.
YEAH, SINCE WE FINALLY GET BEDS! WELL, GOOD NIGHT.

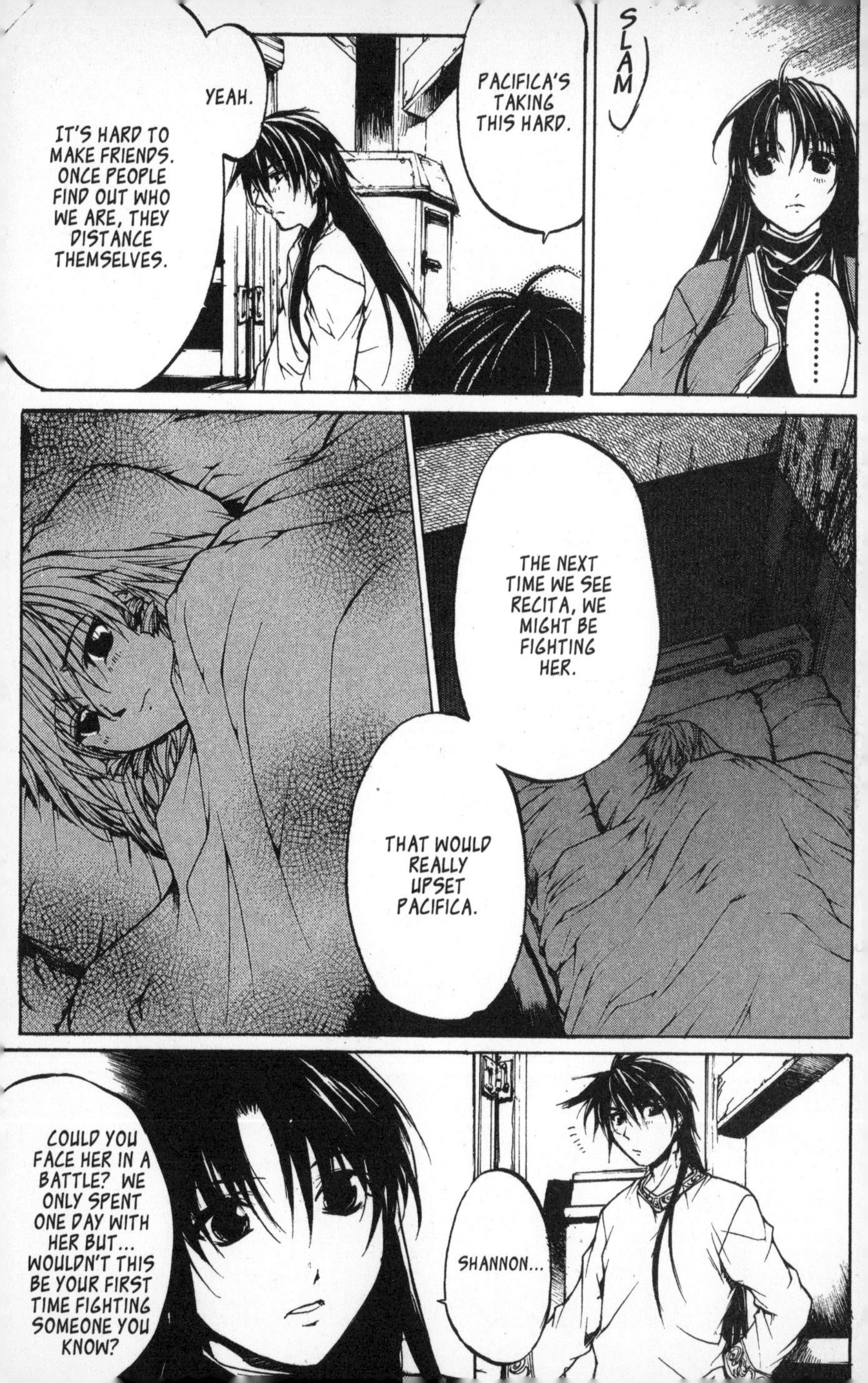
SLAM
......
PACIFICA'S TAKING THIS HARD.
YEAH.
IT'S HARD TO MAKE FRIENDS. ONCE PEOPLE FIND OUT WHO WE ARE, THEY DISTANCE THEMSELVES.
THE NEXT TIME WE SEE RECITA, WE MIGHT BE FIGHTING HER.
THAT WOULD REALLY UPSET PACIFICA.
SHANNON...
COULD YOU FACE HER IN A BATTLE? WE ONLY SPENT ONE DAY WITH HER BUT... WOULDN'T THIS BE YOUR FIRST TIME FIGHTING SOMEONE YOU KNOW?

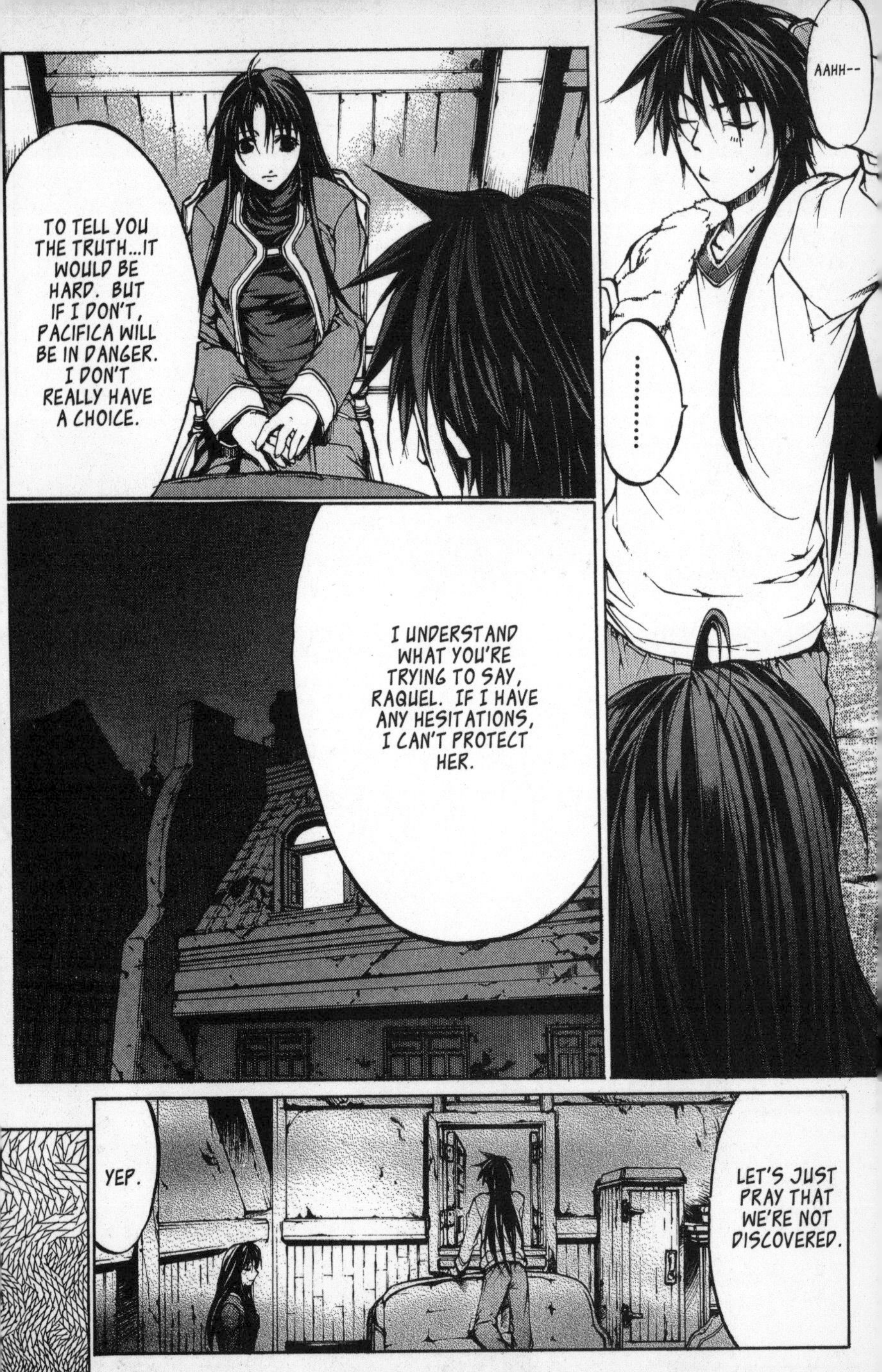
AAHH--
......
TO TELL YOU THE TRUTH...IT WOULD BE HARD. BUT IF I DON'T, PACIFICA WILL BE IN DANGER. I DON'T REALLY HAVE A CHOICE.
I UNDERSTAND WHAT YOU'RE TRYING TO SAY, RAQUEL. IF I HAVE ANY HESITATIONS, I CAN'T PROTECT HER.
LET'S JUST PRAY THAT WE'RE NOT DISCOVERED.
YEP.

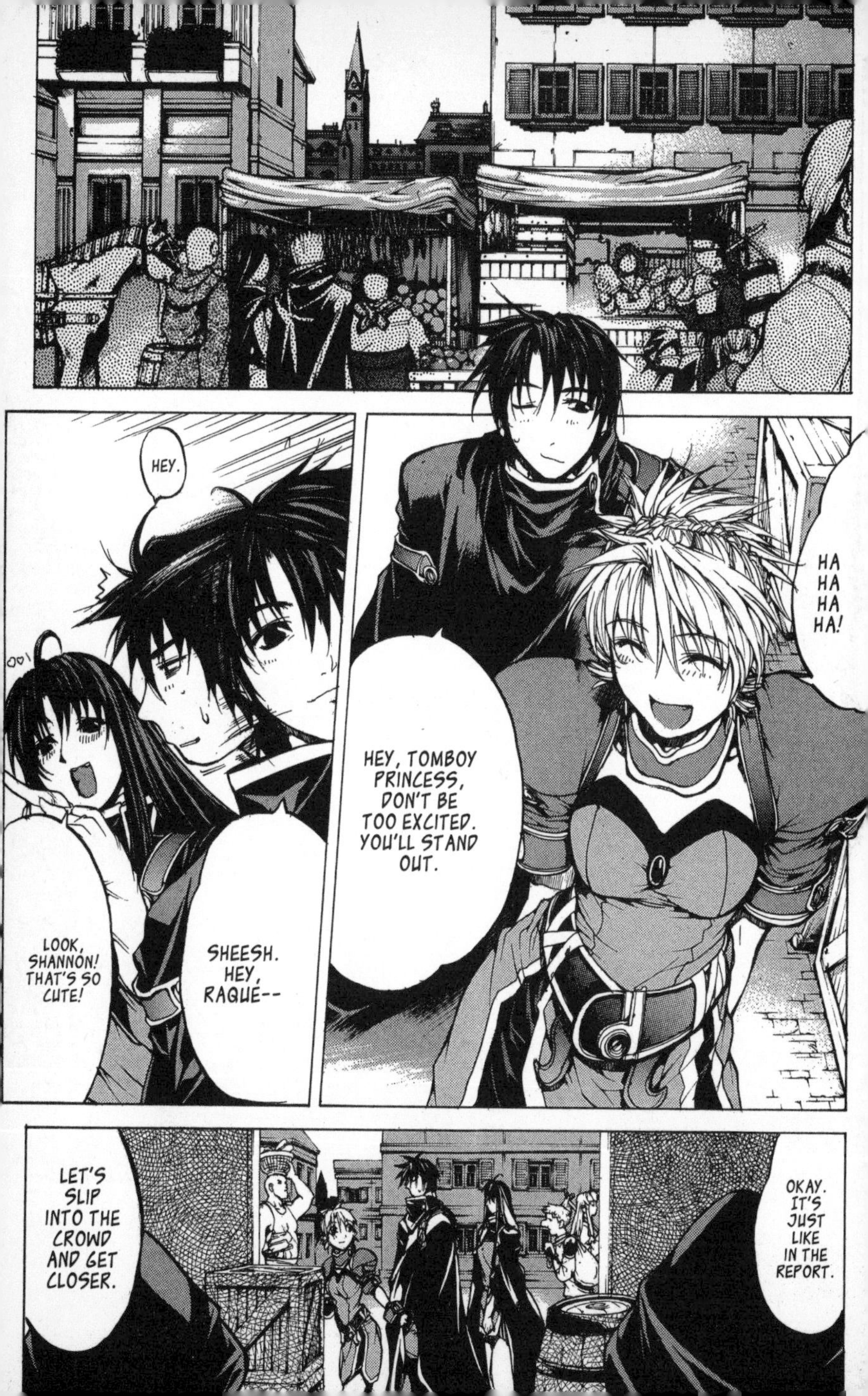
HA HA HA HA!
HEY, TOMBOY PRINCESS, DON'T BE TOO EXCITED. YOU'LL STAND OUT.
HEY.
SHEESH. HEY, RAQUE--
LOOK, SHANNON! THAT'S SO CUTE!
OKAY. IT'S JUST LIKE IN THE REPORT.
LET'S SLIP INTO THE CROWD AND GET CLOSER.

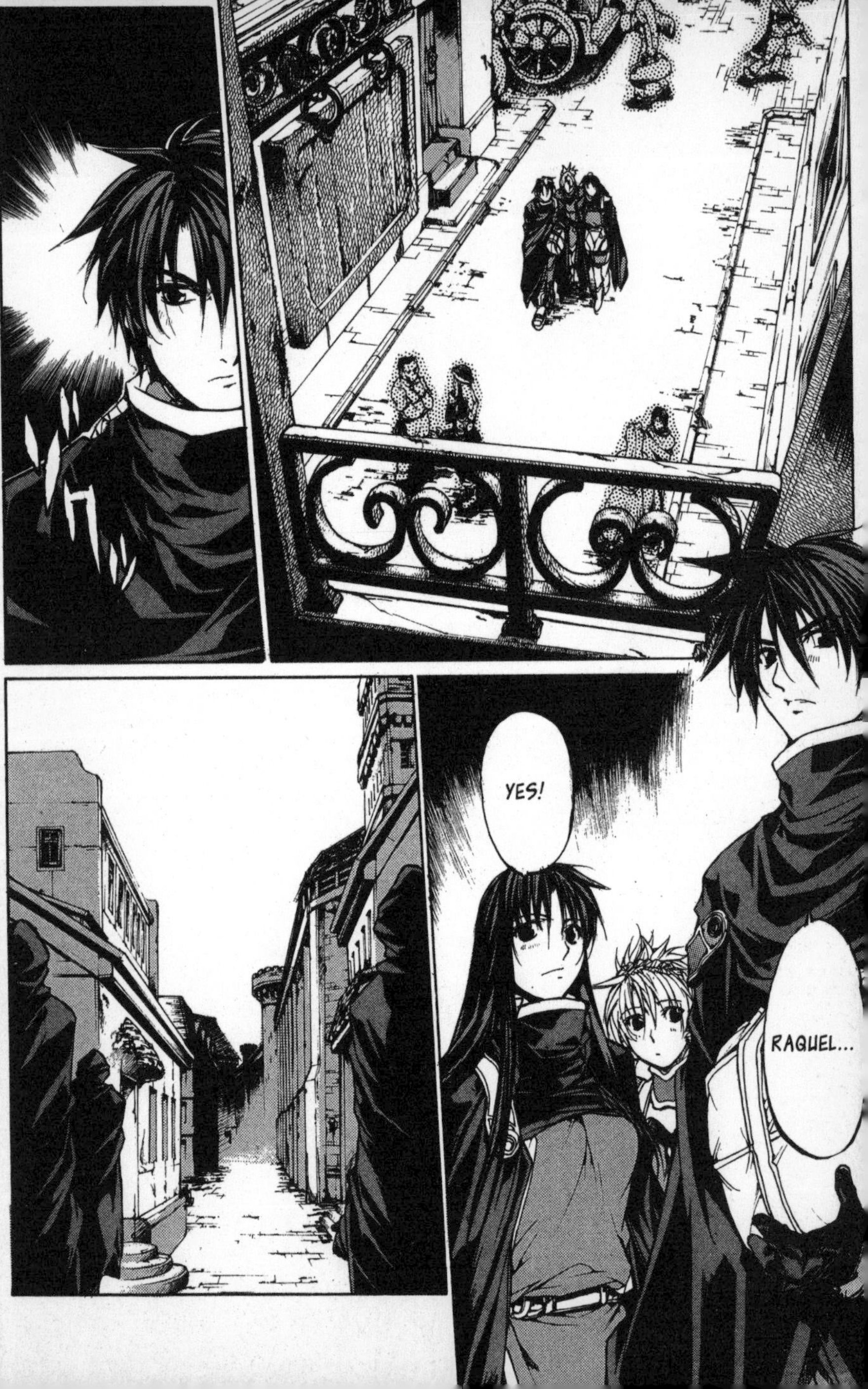
RAQUEL...
YES!

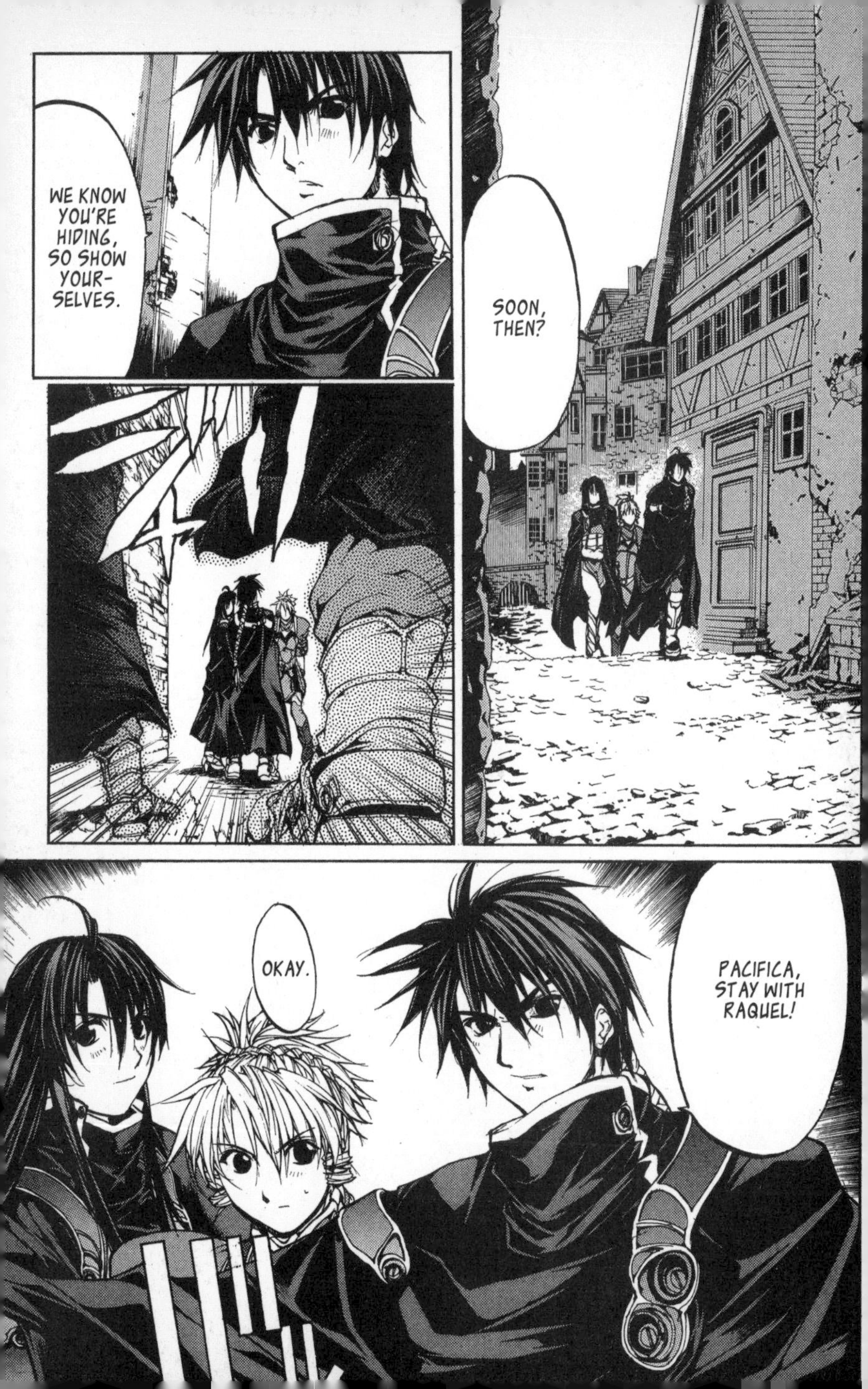
SOON, THEN?
WE KNOW YOU'RE HIDING, SO SHOW YOURSELVES.
PACIFICA, STAY WITH RAQUEL!
OKAY.

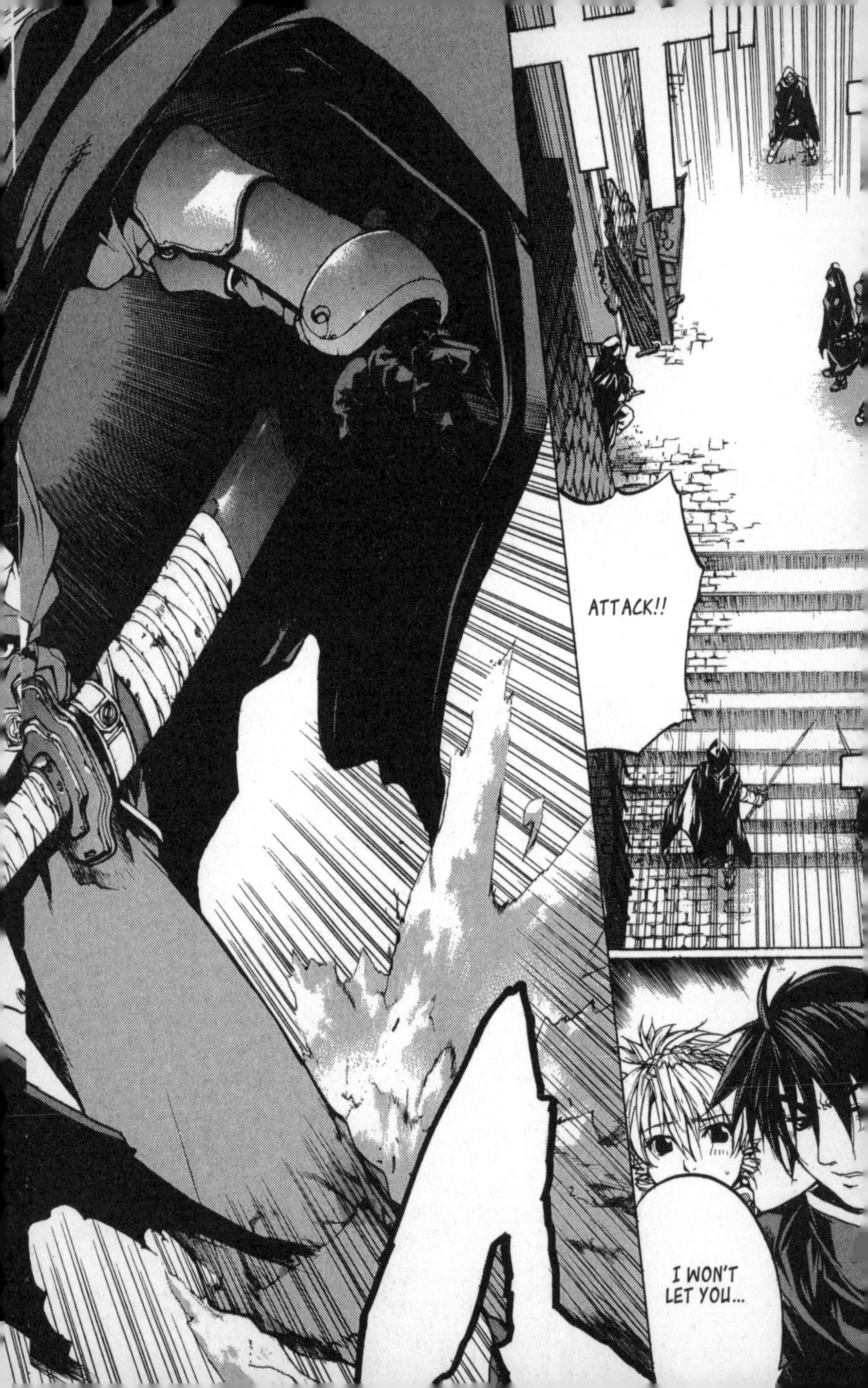
ATTACK!!
I WON'T LET YOU...

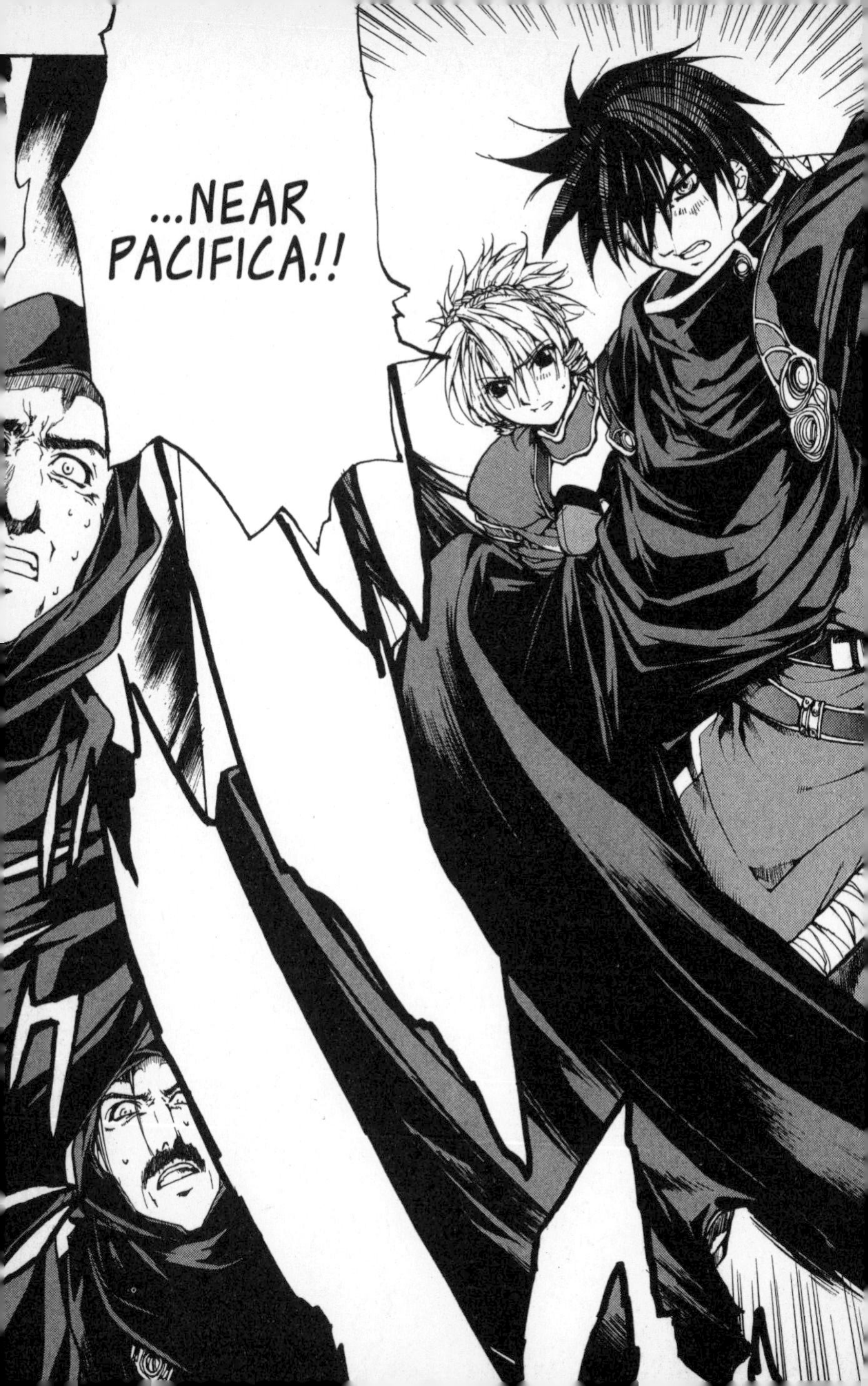
...NEAR PACIFICA!!

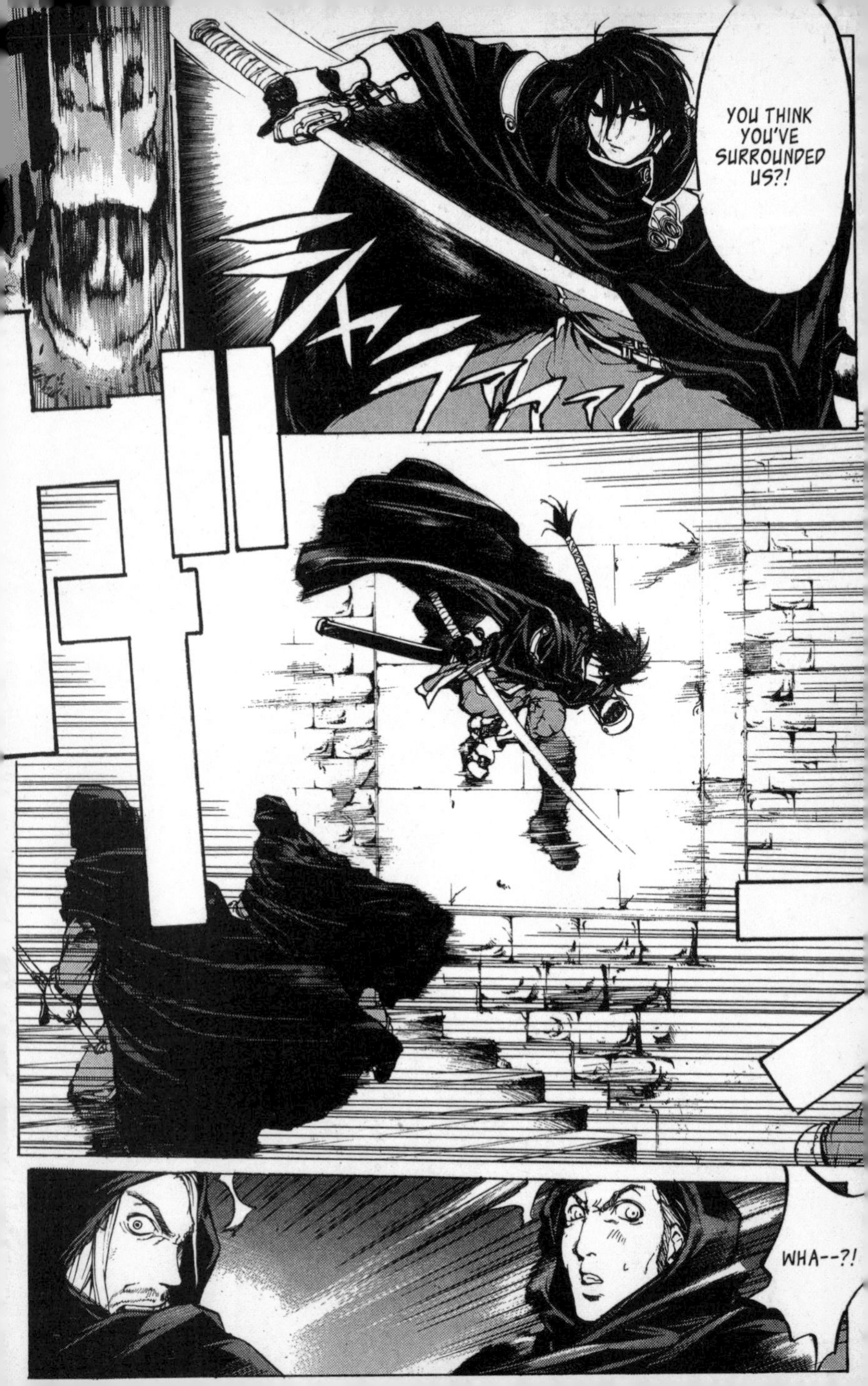
YOU THINK YOU'VE SURROUNDED US?!
WHA--?!

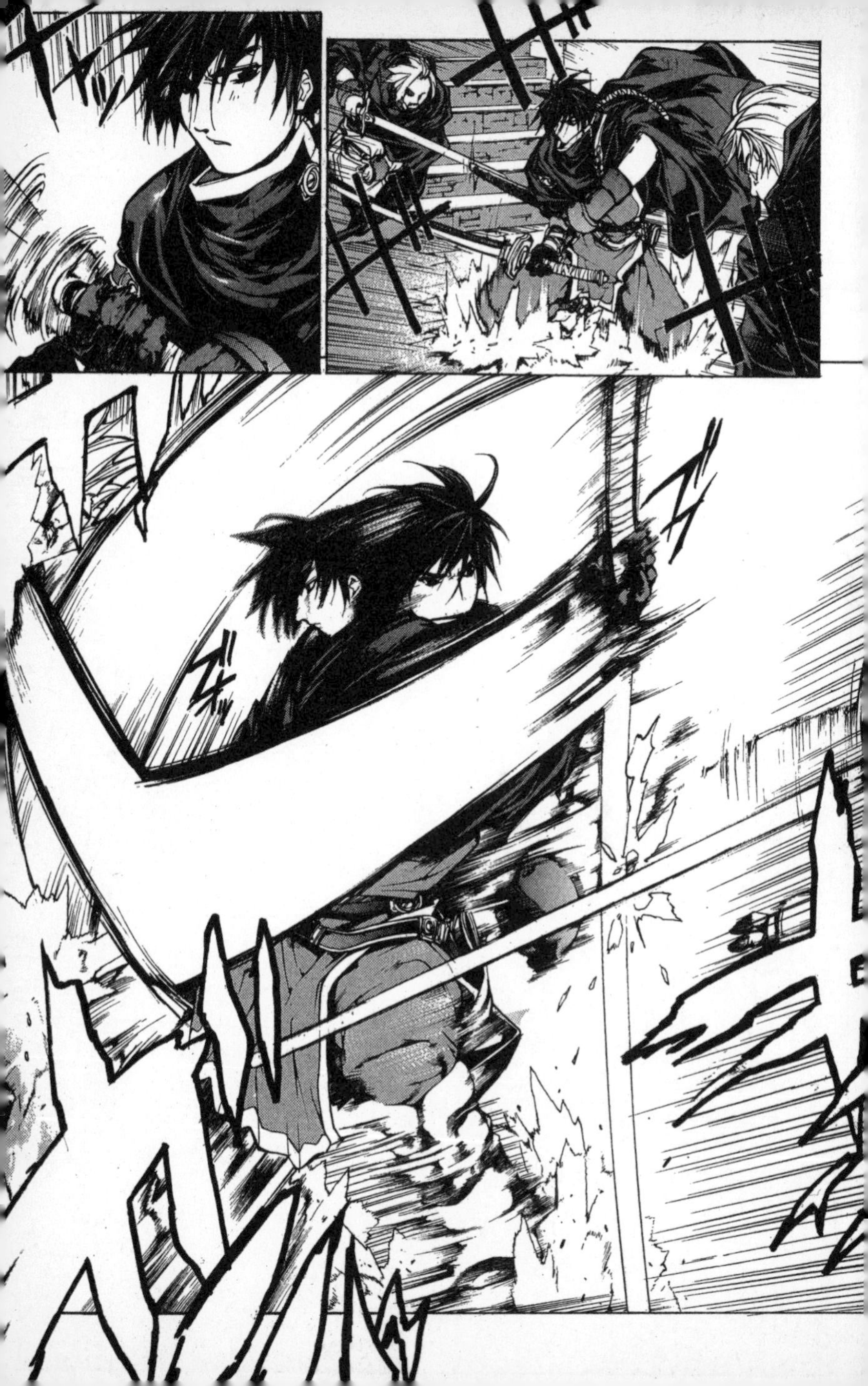

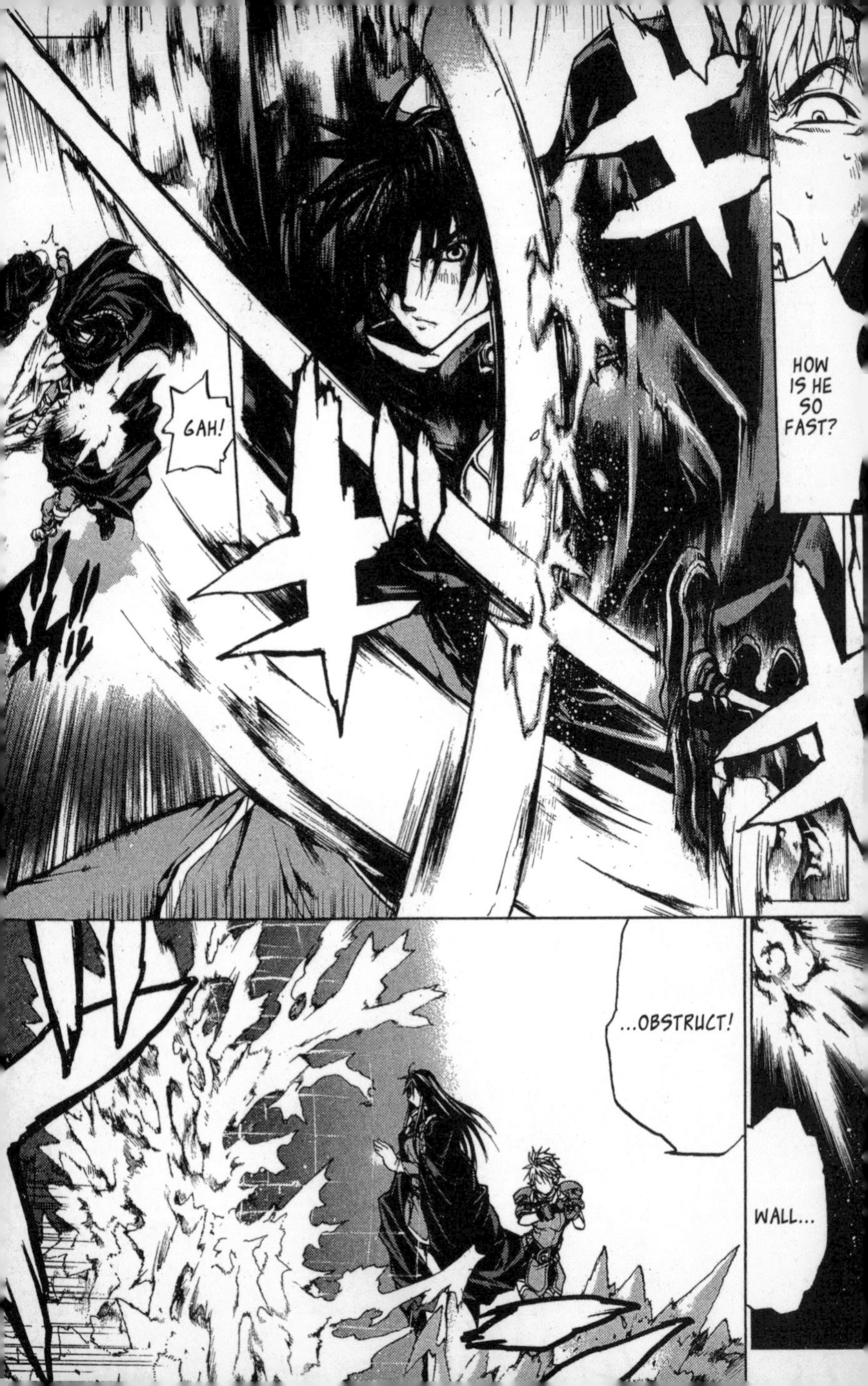
HOW IS HE SO FAST?
GAH!
WALL...
...OBSTRUCT!

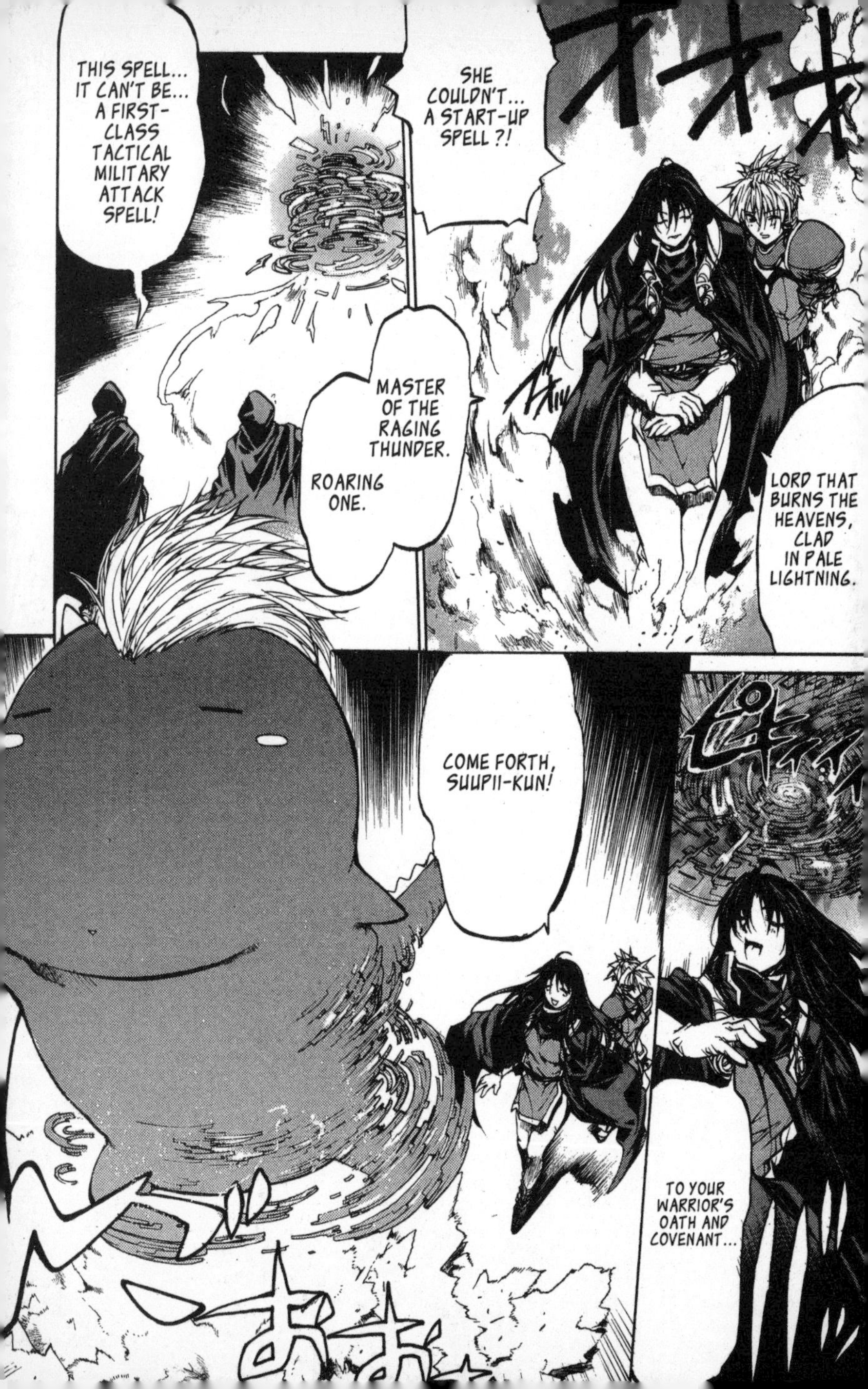
SHE COULDN'T... A START-UP SPELL?!
LORD THAT BURNS THE HEAVENS, CLAD IN PALE LIGHTNING.
MASTER OF THE RAGING THUNDER.
ROARING ONE.
THIS SPELL... IT CAN'T BE... A FIRST-CLASS TACTICAL MILITARY ATTACK SPELL!
TO YOUR WARRIOR'S OATH AND COVENANT...
COME FORTH, SUUPII-KUN!

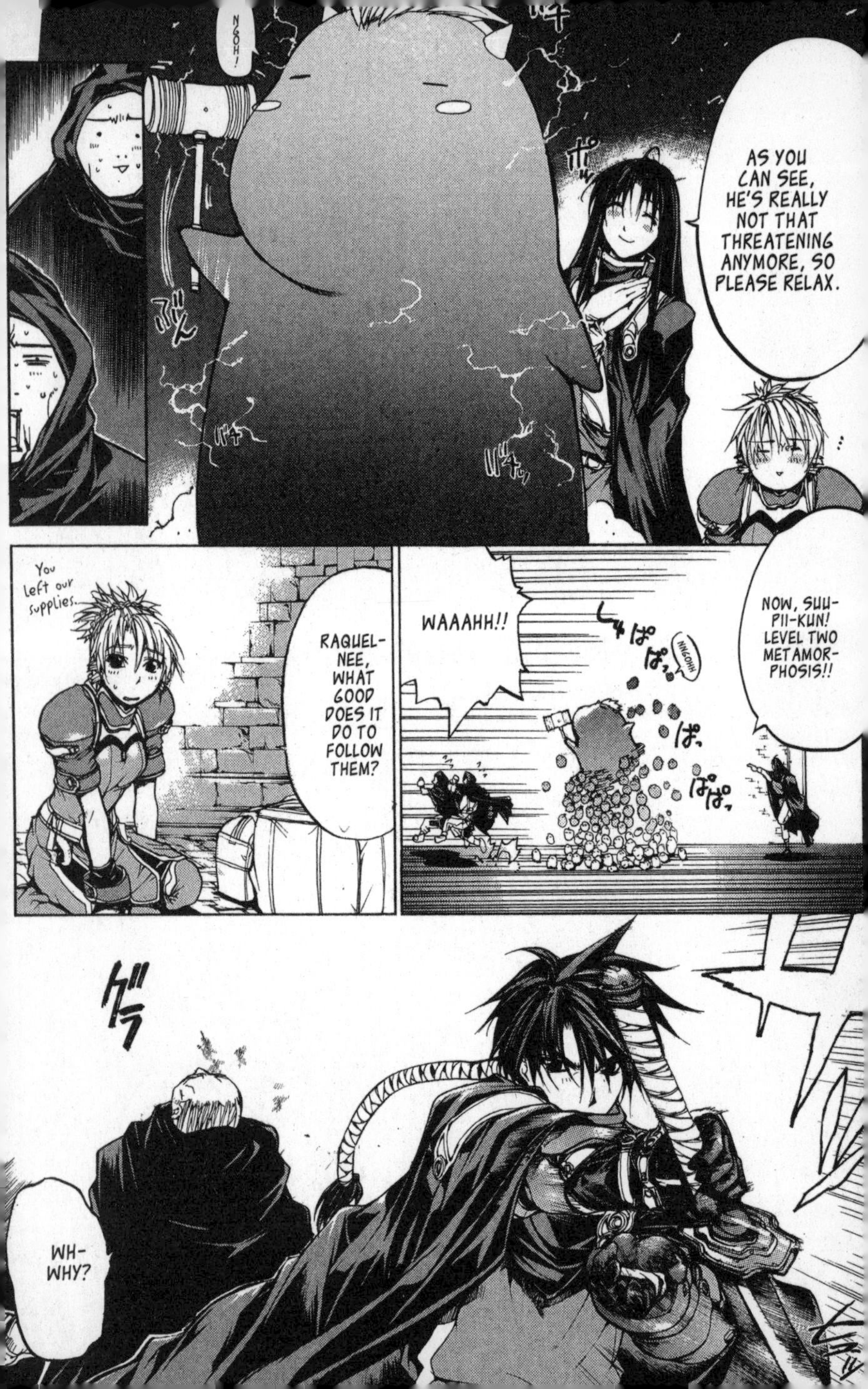
AS YOU CAN SEE, HE'S REALLY NOT THAT THREATENING ANYMORE, SO PLEASE RELAX.
...
NGOH!
NOW, SUU-PII-KUN! LEVEL TWO METAMORPHOSIS!!
NNGOHH
WAAAHH!!
RAQUEL-NEE, WHAT GOOD DOES IT DO TO FOLLOW THEM?
You left our supplies.
WH-WHY?

IF ONLY I COULD HAVE HAD A STRONG HEART LIKE THEM...
I'M SORRY!!
BUT NOW...

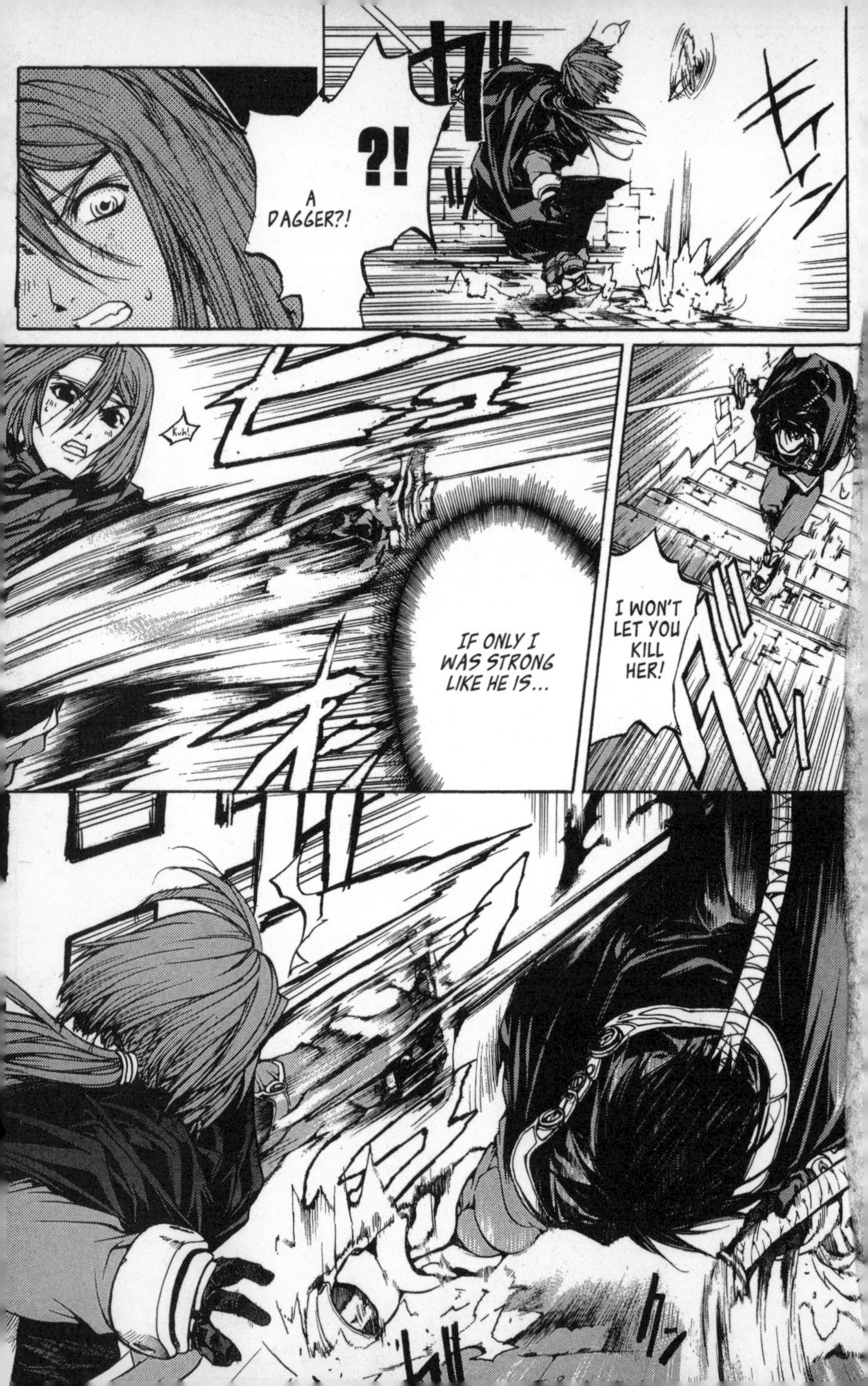
?!
A DAGGER?!
I WON'T LET YOU KILL HER!
Kuh!
IF ONLY I WAS STRONG LIKE HE IS...

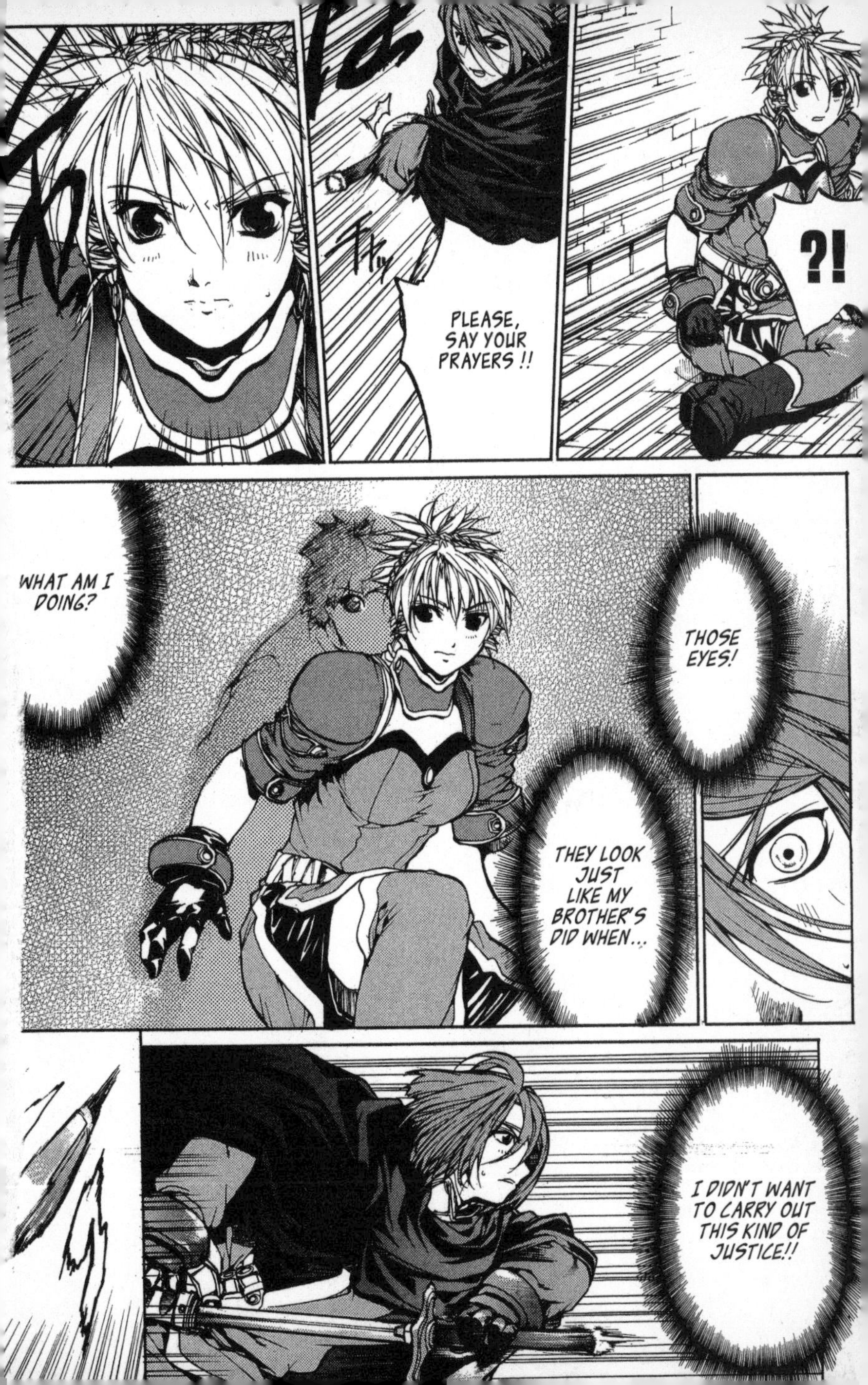
?!
PLEASE, SAY YOUR PRAYERS !!
THOSE EYES!
THEY LOOK JUST LIKE MY BROTHER'S DID WHEN...
WHAT AM I DOING?
I DIDN'T WANT TO CARRY OUT THIS KIND OF JUSTICE!!

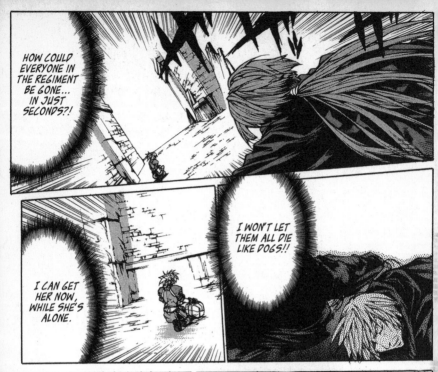

HOW COULD EVERYONE IN THE REGIMENT BE GONE... IN JUST SECONDS?!

I WON'T LET THEM ALL DIE LIKE DOGS!!

I CAN GET HER NOW, WHILE SHE'S ALONE.

DAMN!

THEN I ALONE SHALL FINISH THE TASK!

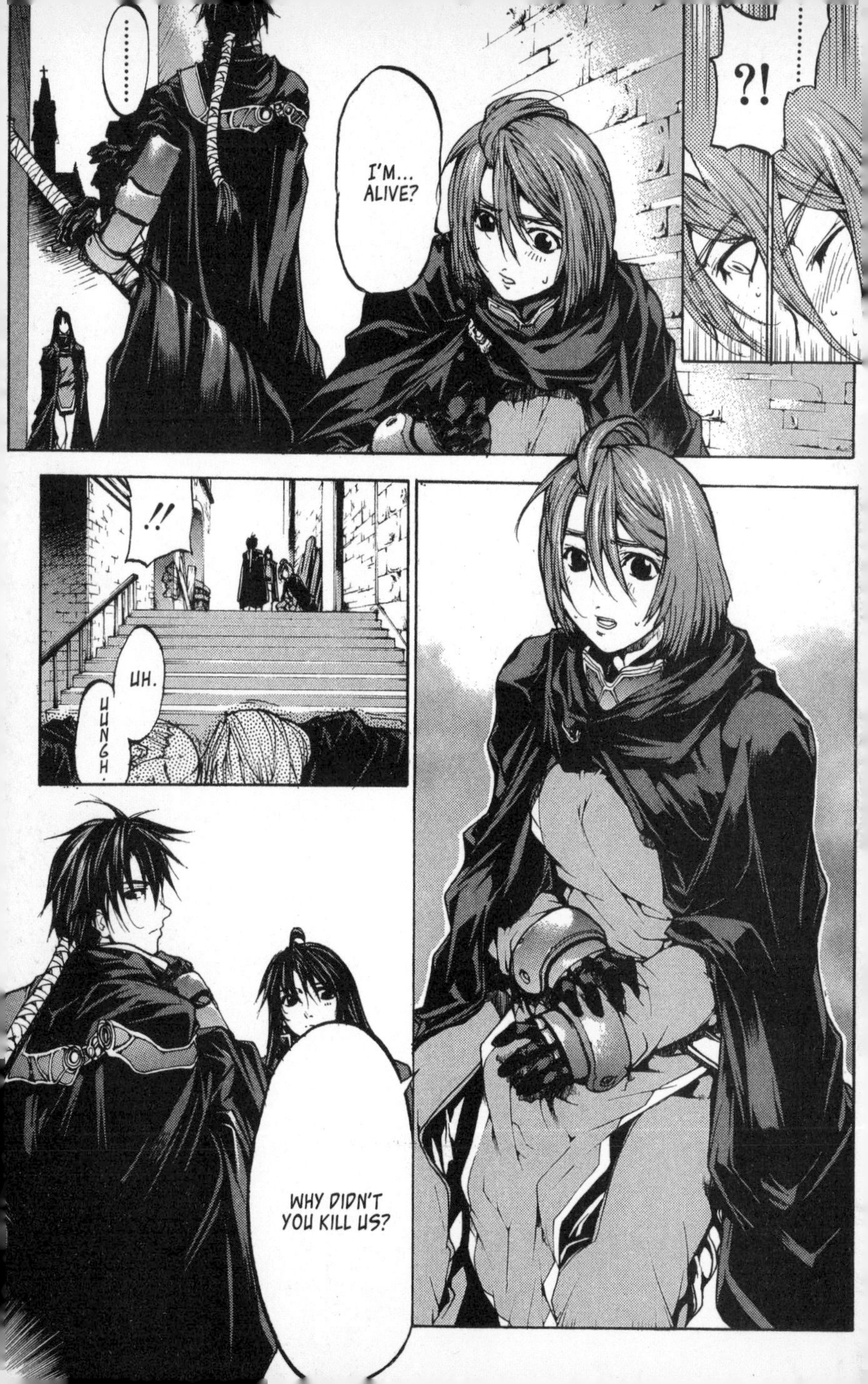

......
?!
I'M... ALIVE?
......
!!
UH.
HUNGH.
WHY DIDN'T YOU KILL US?

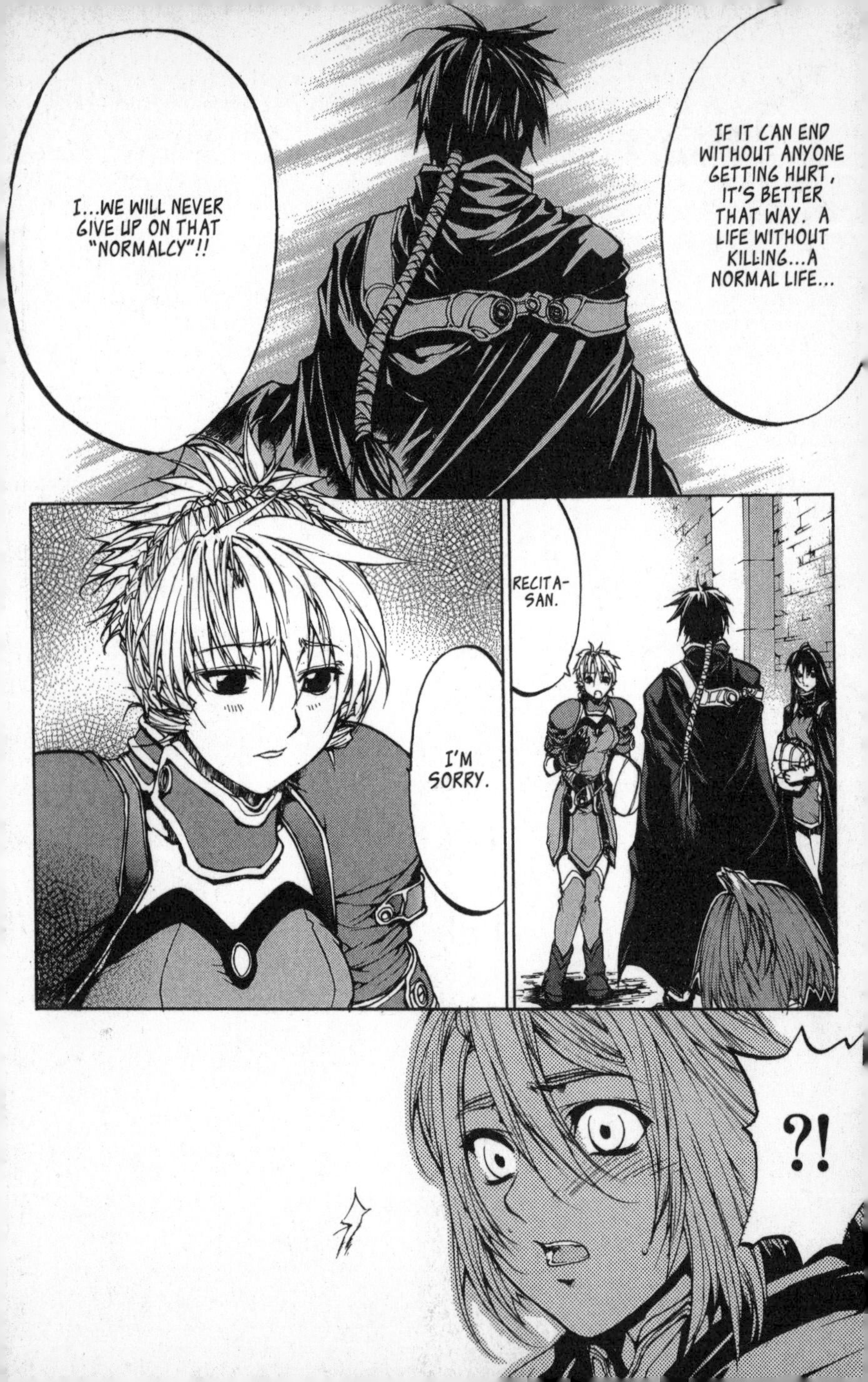
IF IT CAN END WITHOUT ANYONE GETTING HURT, IT'S BETTER THAT WAY. A LIFE WITHOUT KILLING...A NORMAL LIFE...
I...WE WILL NEVER GIVE UP ON THAT "NORMALCY"!!
RECITA-SAN.
I'M SORRY.
?!

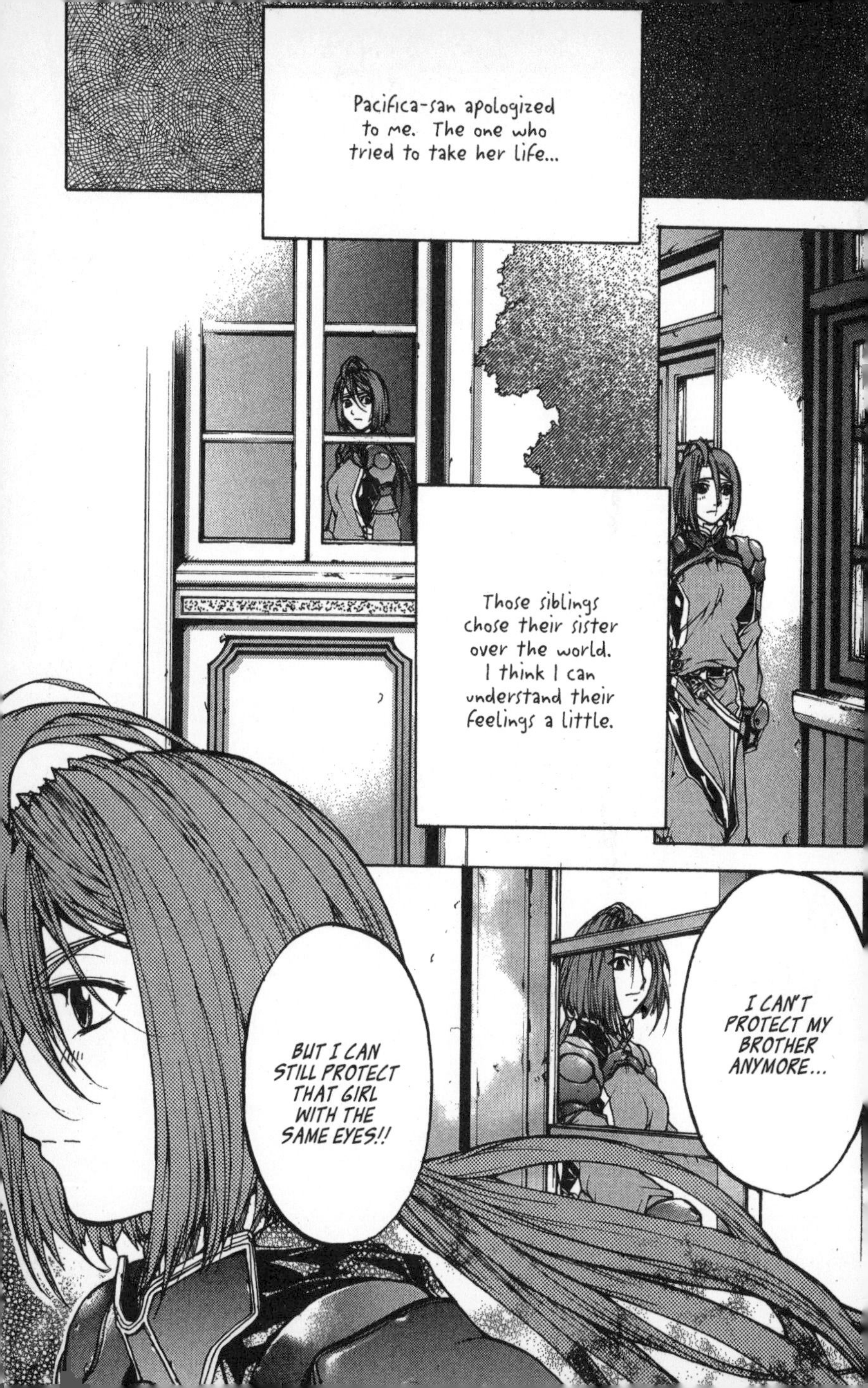
Pacifica-san apologized to me. The one who tried to take her life...
Those siblings chose their sister over the world. I think I can understand their feelings a little.
I CAN'T PROTECT MY BROTHER ANYMORE...
BUT I CAN STILL PROTECT THAT GIRL WITH THE SAME EYES!!

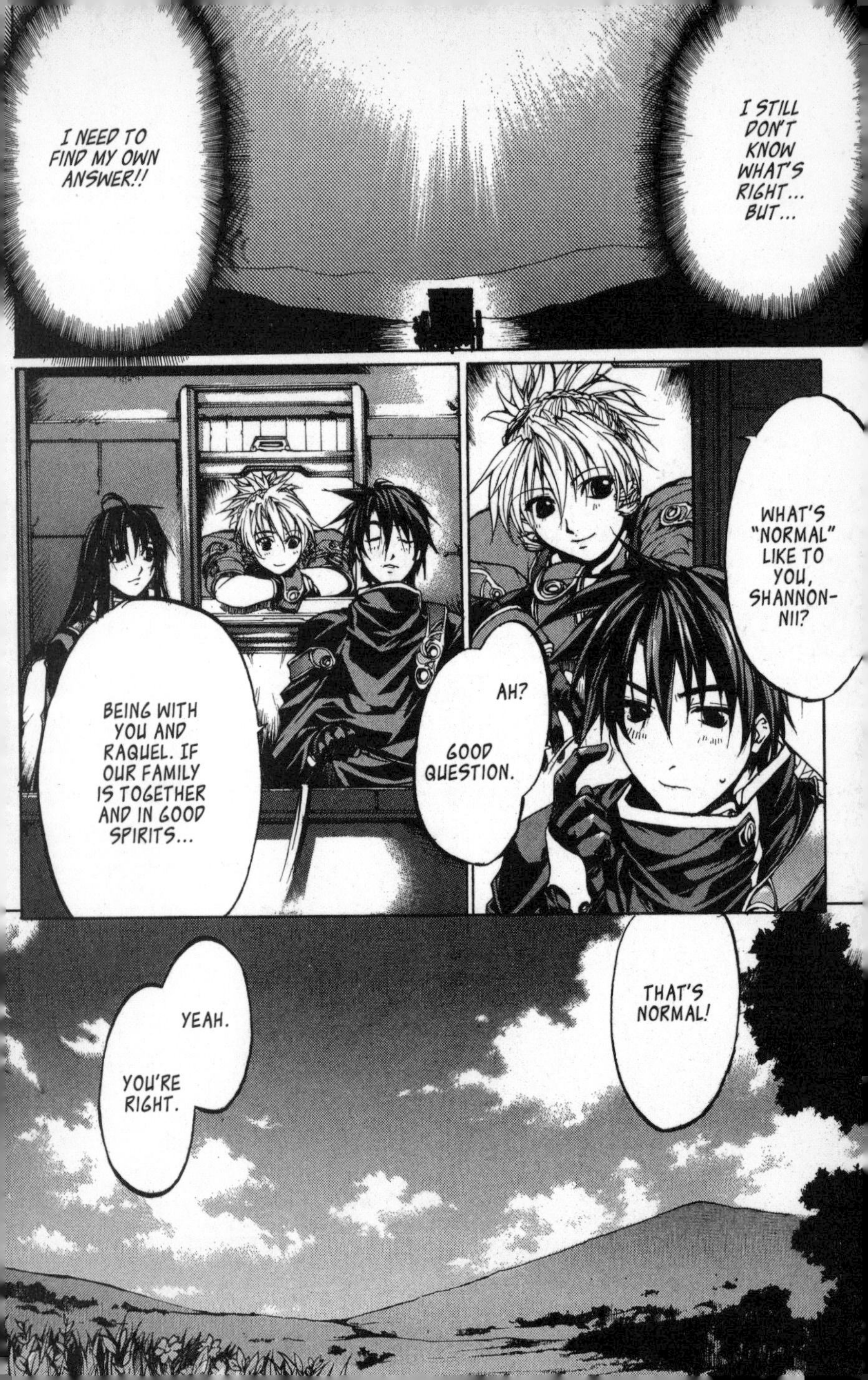
I STILL DON'T KNOW WHAT'S RIGHT... BUT...
I NEED TO FIND MY OWN ANSWER!!
WHAT'S "NORMAL" LIKE TO YOU, SHANNON-NII?
AH?
GOOD QUESTION.
BEING WITH YOU AND RAQUEL. IF OUR FAMILY IS TOGETHER AND IN GOOD SPIRITS...
THAT'S NORMAL!
YEAH.
YOU'RE RIGHT.

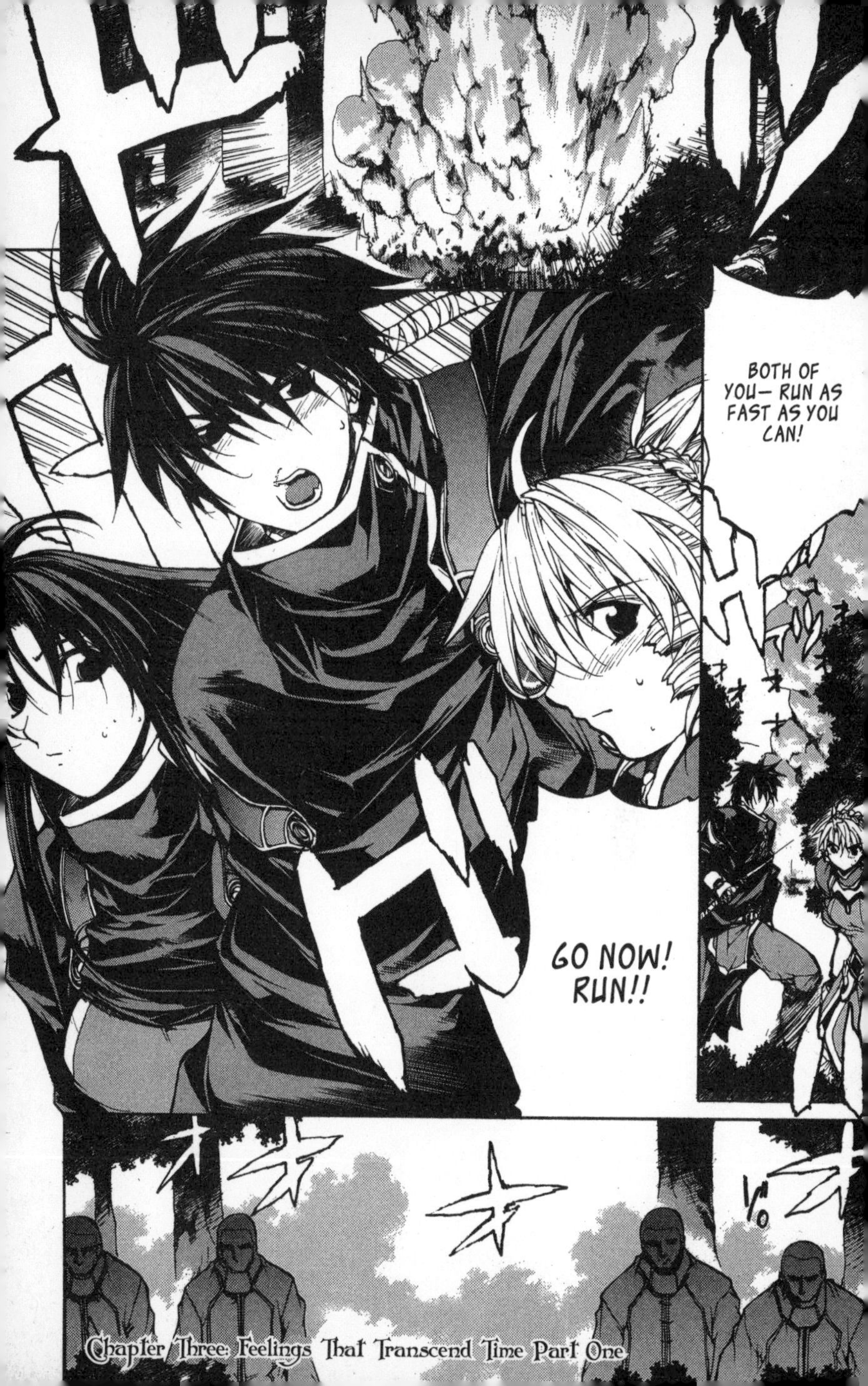
BOTH OF YOU— RUN AS FAST AS YOU CAN!
GO NOW! RUN!!
Chapter Three: Feelings That Transcend Time Part One

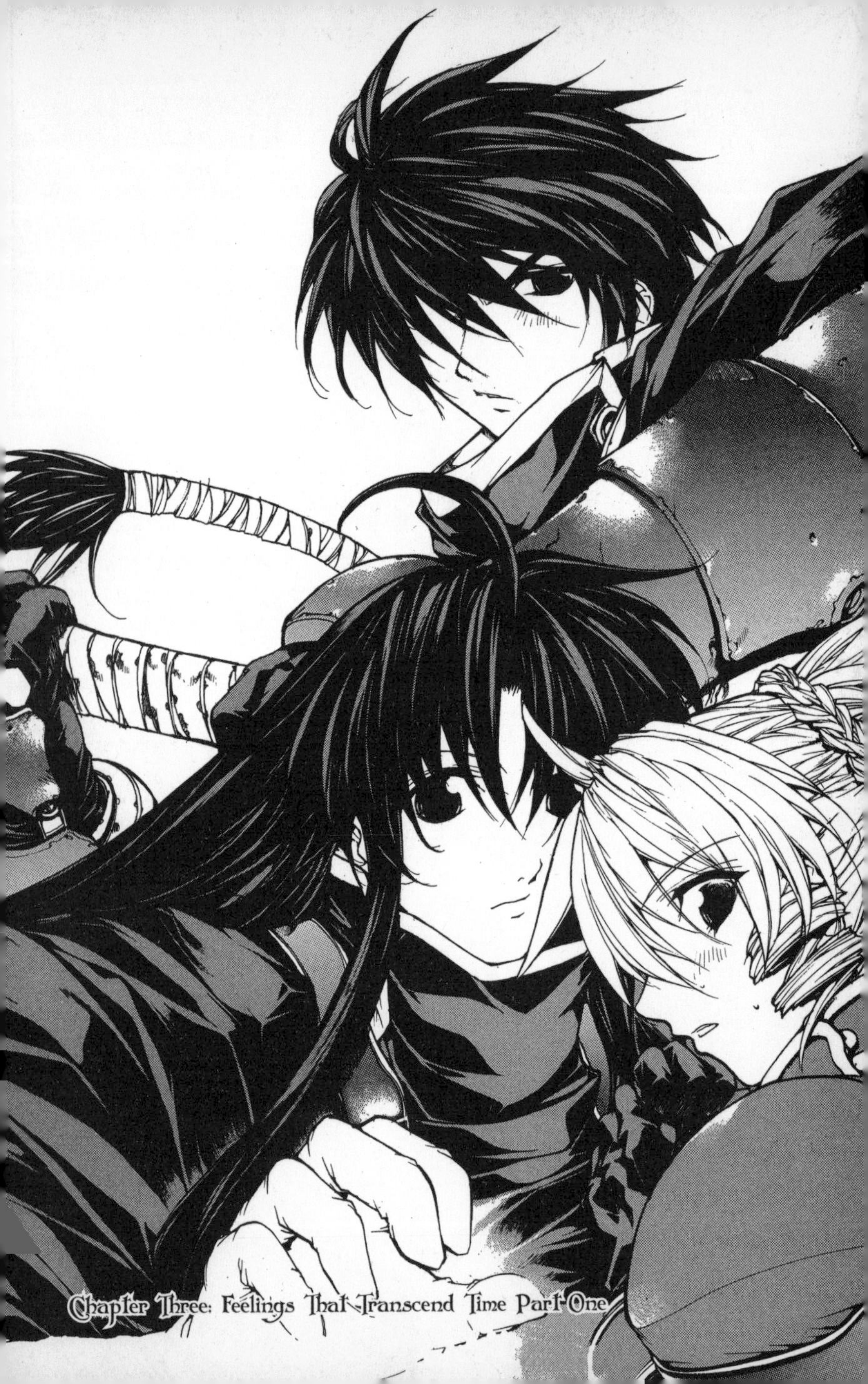
Chapter Three: Feelings That Transcend Time Part One

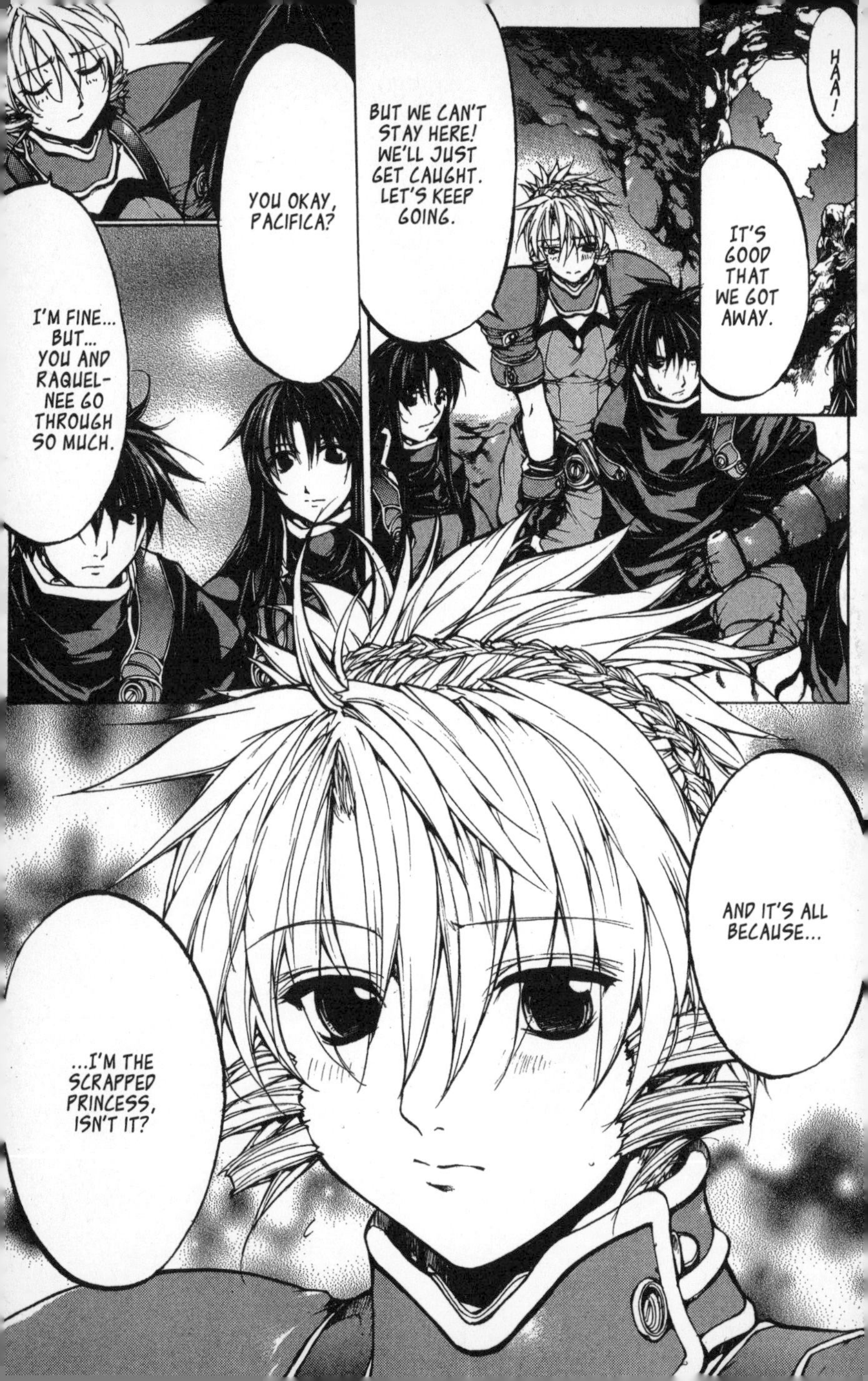
HAA!
IT'S GOOD THAT WE GOT AWAY.
BUT WE CAN'T STAY HERE! WE'LL JUST GET CAUGHT. LET'S KEEP GOING.
YOU OKAY, PACIFICA?
I'M FINE... BUT... YOU AND RAQUEL-NEE GO THROUGH SO MUCH.
AND IT'S ALL BECAUSE...
...I'M THE SCRAPPED PRINCESS, ISN'T IT?

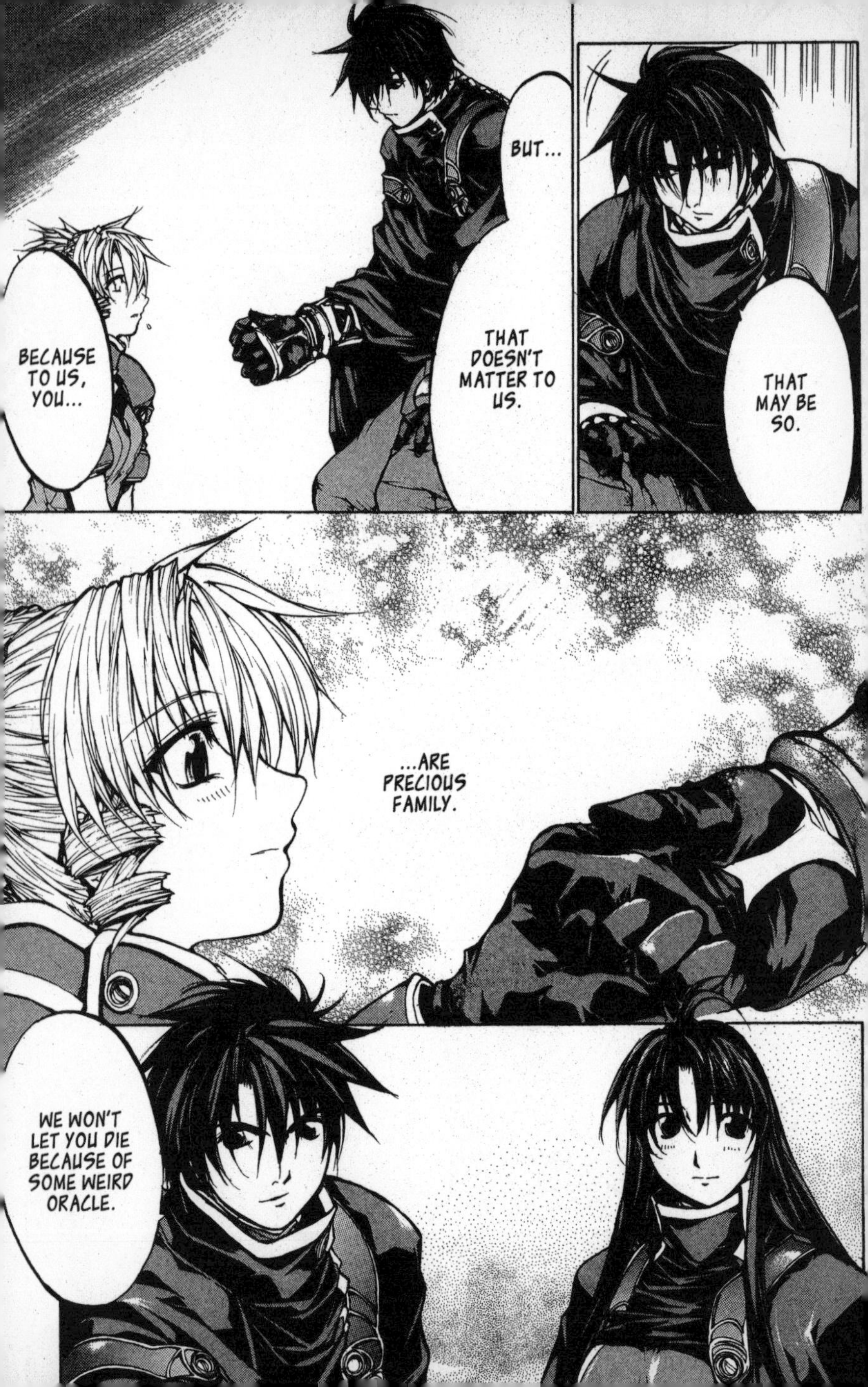
THAT MAY BE SO.
BUT...
THAT DOESN'T MATTER TO US.
BECAUSE TO US, YOU...
...ARE PRECIOUS FAMILY.
WE WON'T LET YOU DIE BECAUSE OF SOME WEIRD ORACLE.

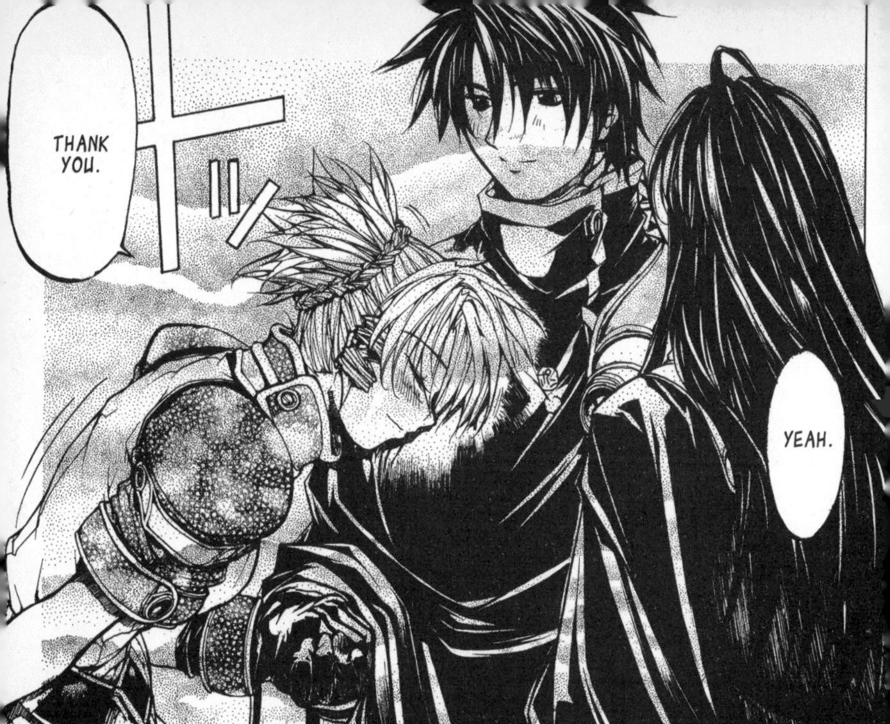
THANK YOU.
YEAH.
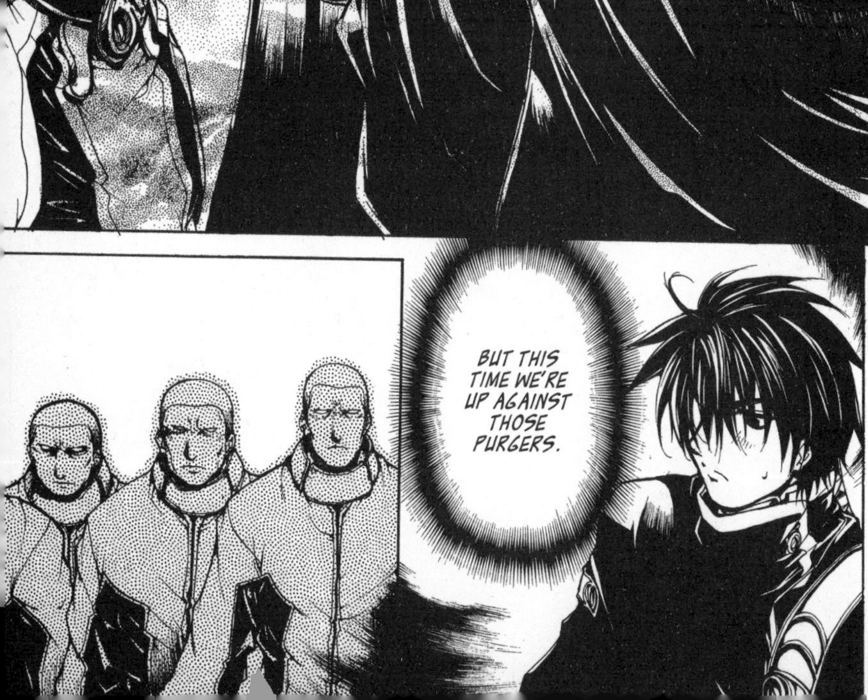
BUT THIS TIME WE'RE UP AGAINST THOSE PURGERS.

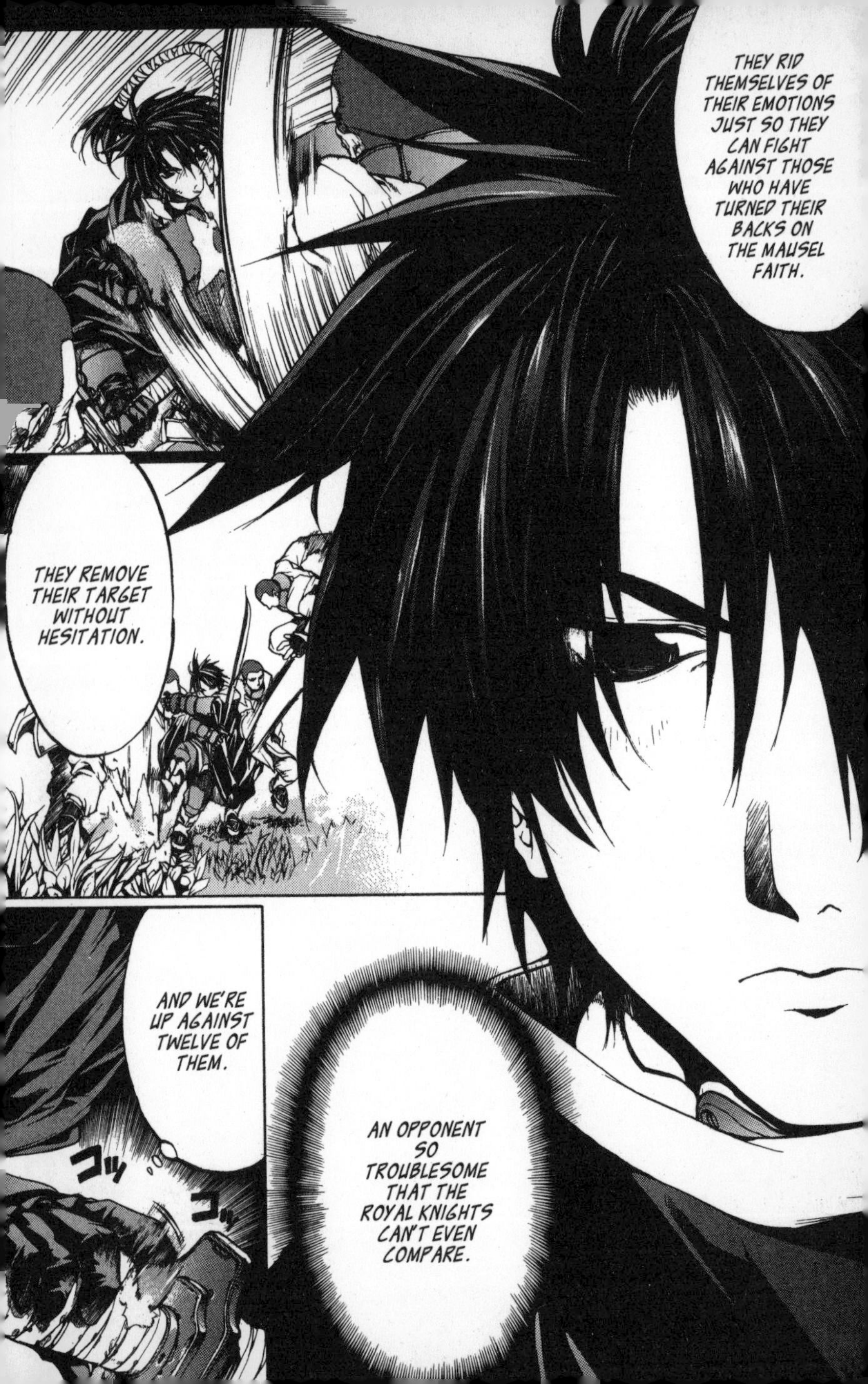
THEY RID THEMSELVES OF THEIR EMOTIONS JUST SO THEY CAN FIGHT AGAINST THOSE WHO HAVE TURNED THEIR BACKS ON THE MAUSEL FAITH.
THEY REMOVE THEIR TARGET WITHOUT HESITATION.
AND WE'RE UP AGAINST TWELVE OF THEM.
コッ
コッ
AN OPPONENT SO TROUBLESOME THAT THE ROYAL KNIGHTS CAN'T EVEN COMPARE.

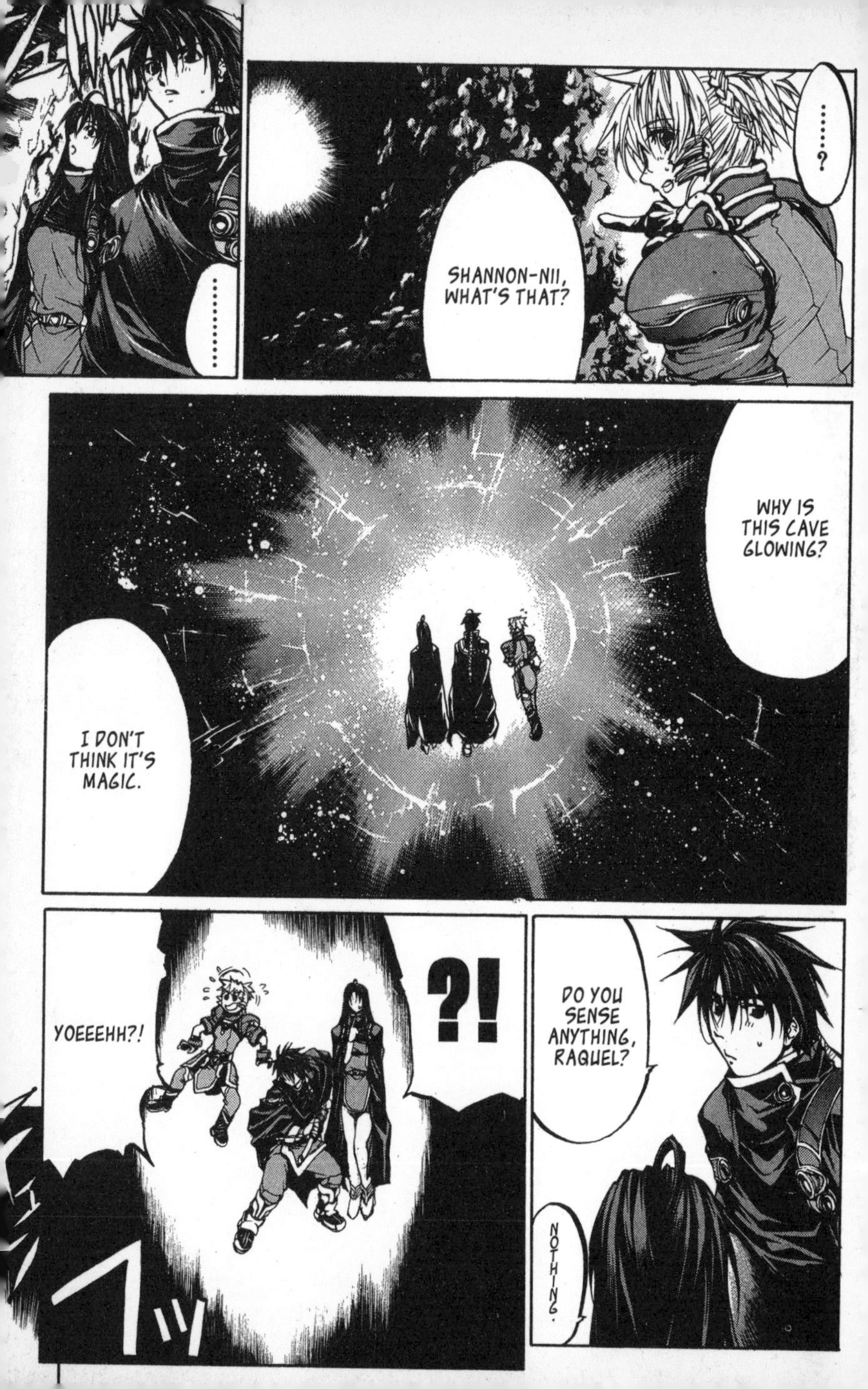
......?
SHANNON-NII, WHAT'S THAT?
....
WHY IS THIS CAVE GLOWING?
I DON'T THINK IT'S MAGIC.
DO YOU SENSE ANYTHING, RAQUEL?
NOTHING.
?!
YOEEEHH?!
フッ

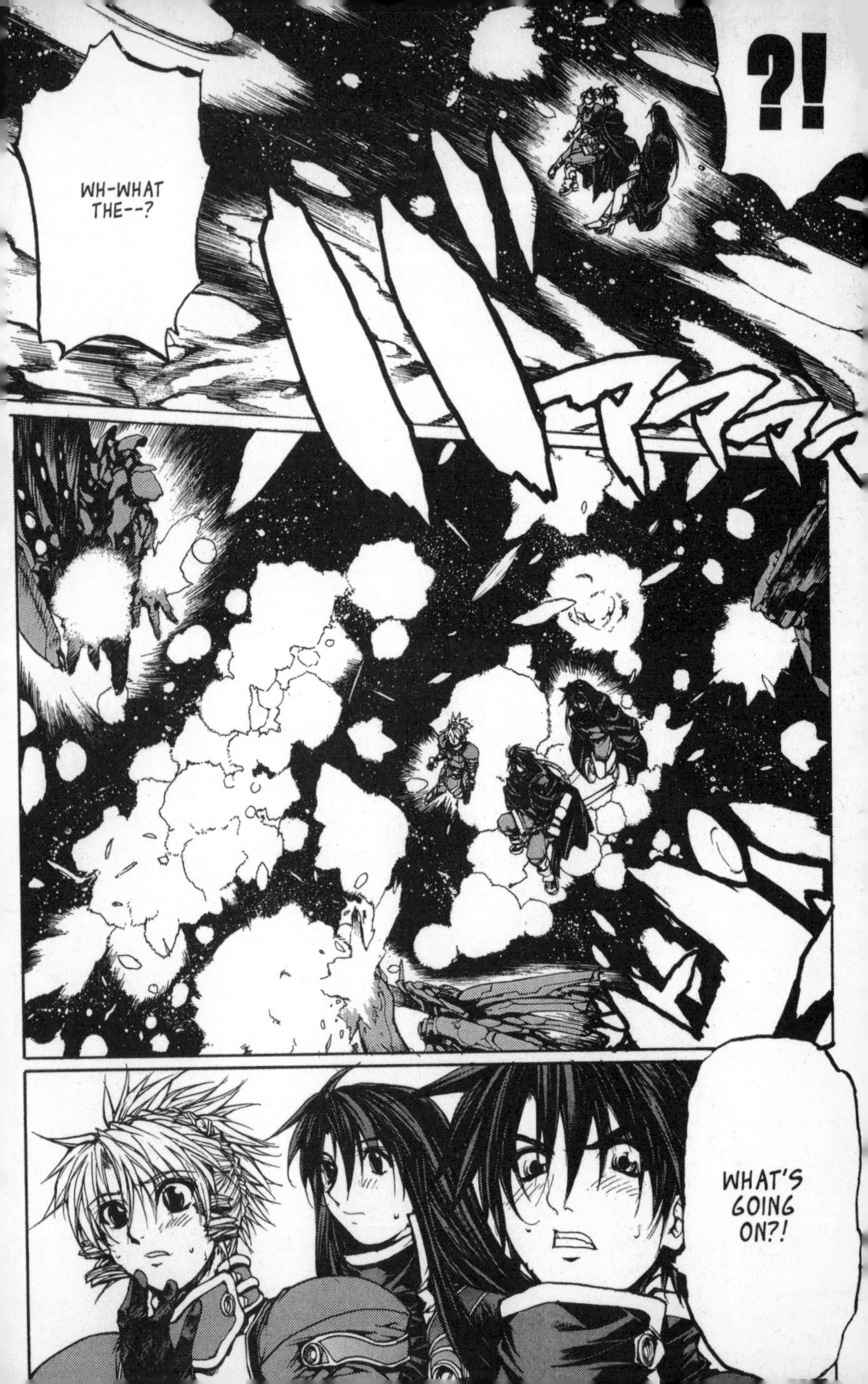
?!
WH-WHAT THE--?
WHAT'S GOING ON?!

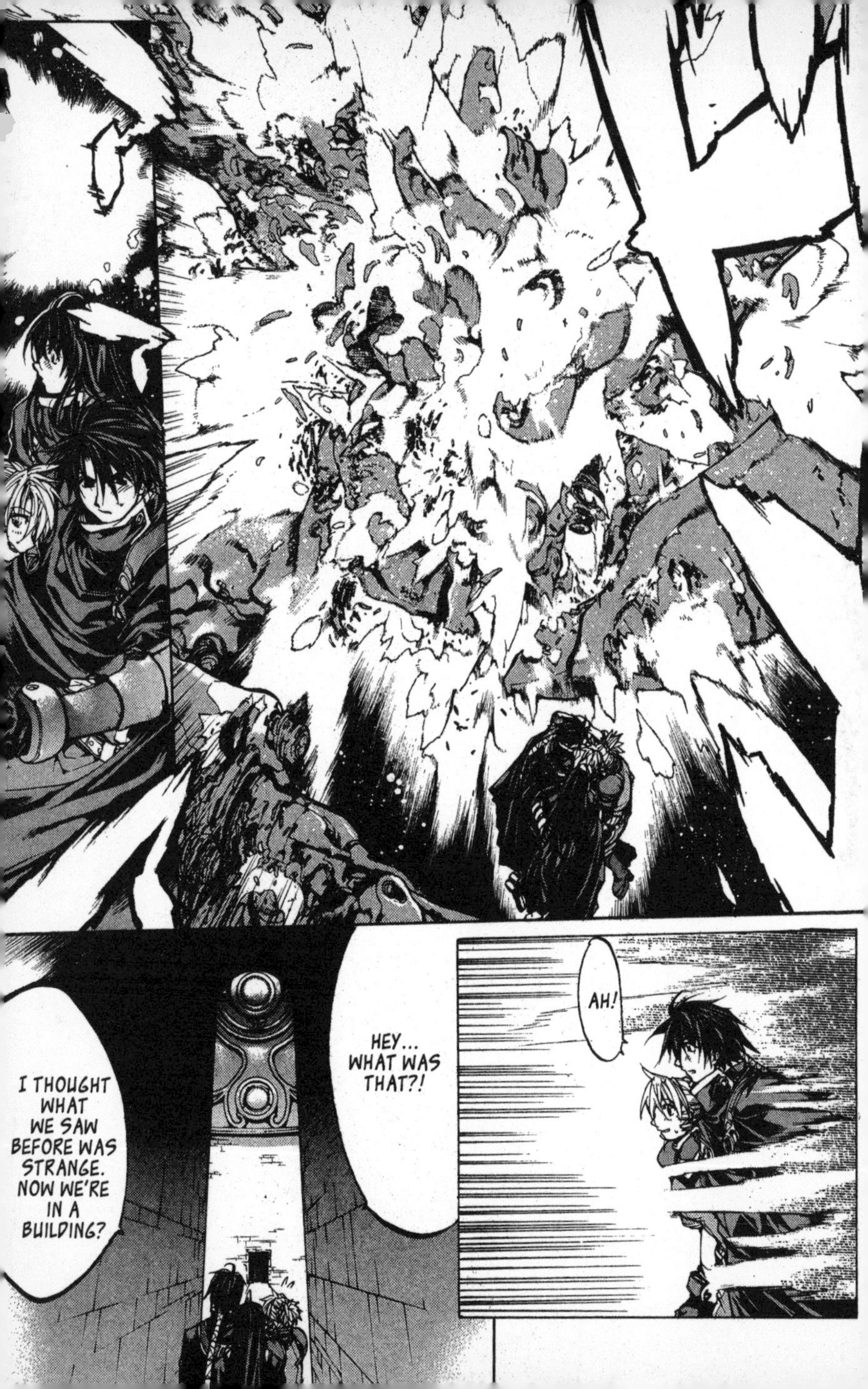
AH!
HEY... WHAT WAS THAT?!
I THOUGHT WHAT WE SAW BEFORE WAS STRANGE. NOW WE'RE IN A BUILDING?

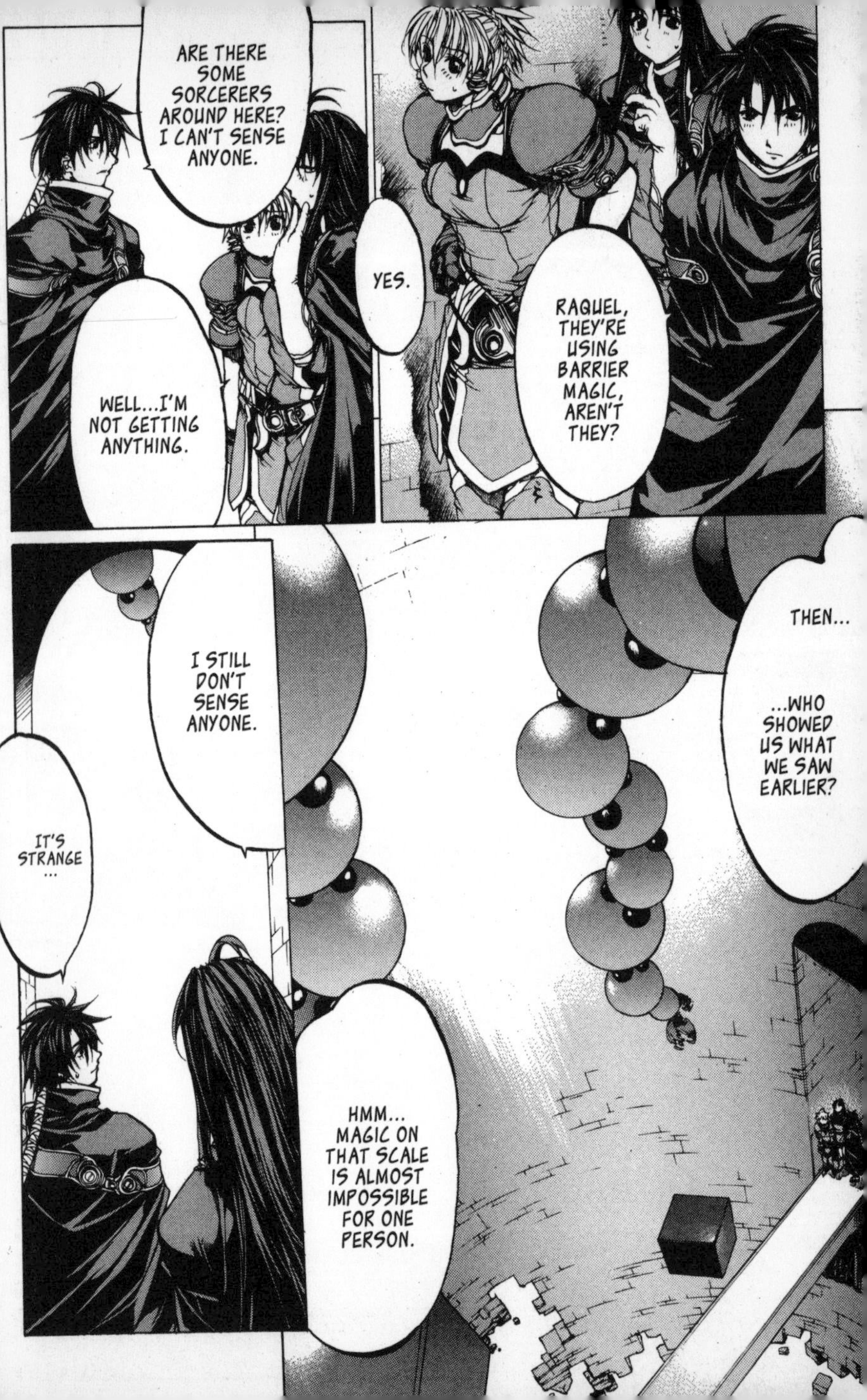
RAQUEL, THEY'RE USING BARRIER MAGIC, AREN'T THEY?
YES.
ARE THERE SOME SORCERERS AROUND HERE? I CAN'T SENSE ANYONE.
WELL...I'M NOT GETTING ANYTHING.
THEN...
...WHO SHOWED US WHAT WE SAW EARLIER?
I STILL DON'T SENSE ANYONE.
IT'S STRANGE...
HMM... MAGIC ON THAT SCALE IS ALMOST IMPOSSIBLE FOR ONE PERSON.

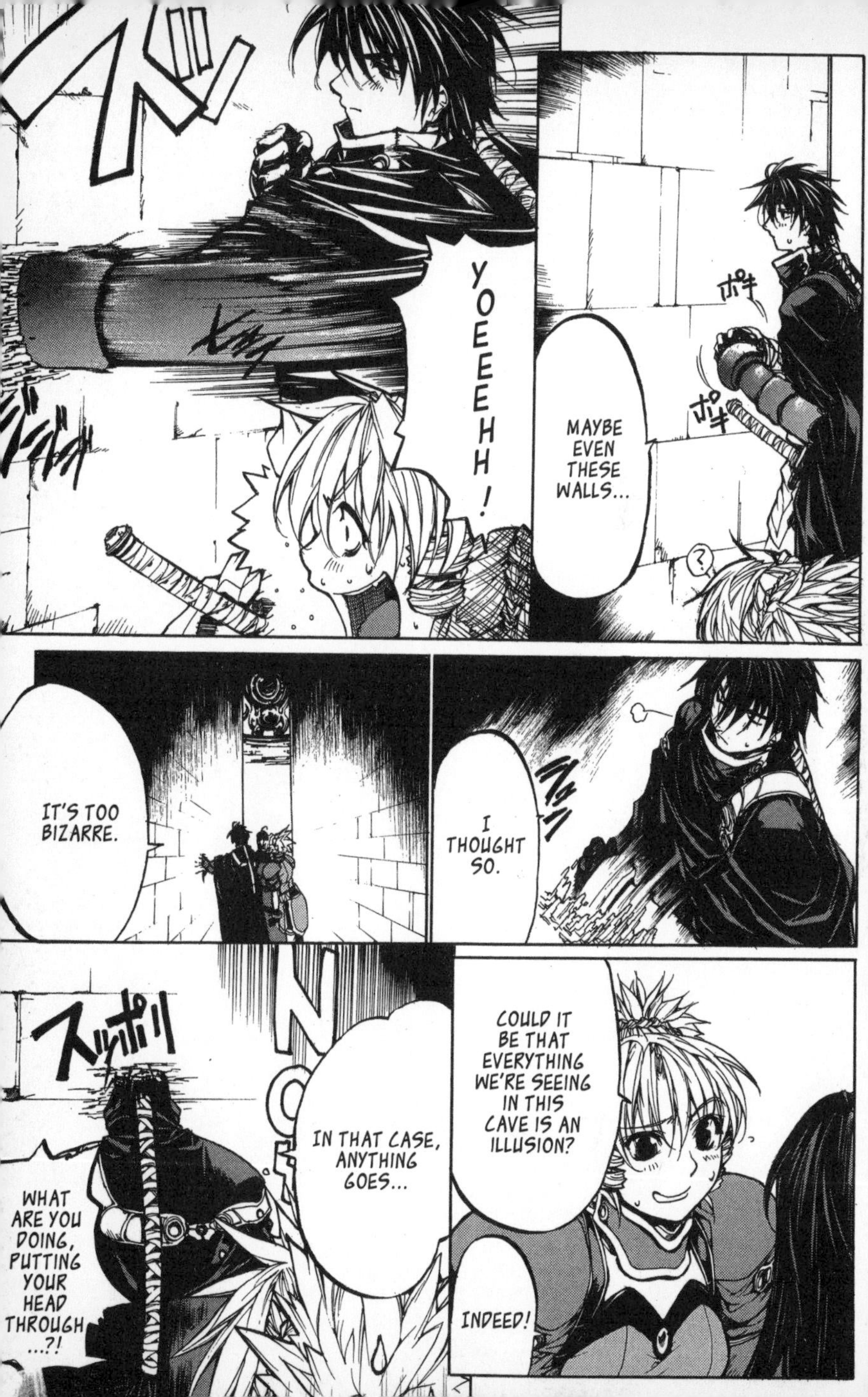
ポキ
MAYBE EVEN THESE WALLS...
ポキ
?
YOEEEEHH!
I THOUGHT SO.
IT'S TOO BIZARRE.
COULD IT BE THAT EVERYTHING WE'RE SEEING IN THIS CAVE IS AN ILLUSION?
INDEED!
IN THAT CASE, ANYTHING GOES...
スッポリ
WHAT ARE YOU DOING, PUTTING YOUR HEAD THROUGH ...?!

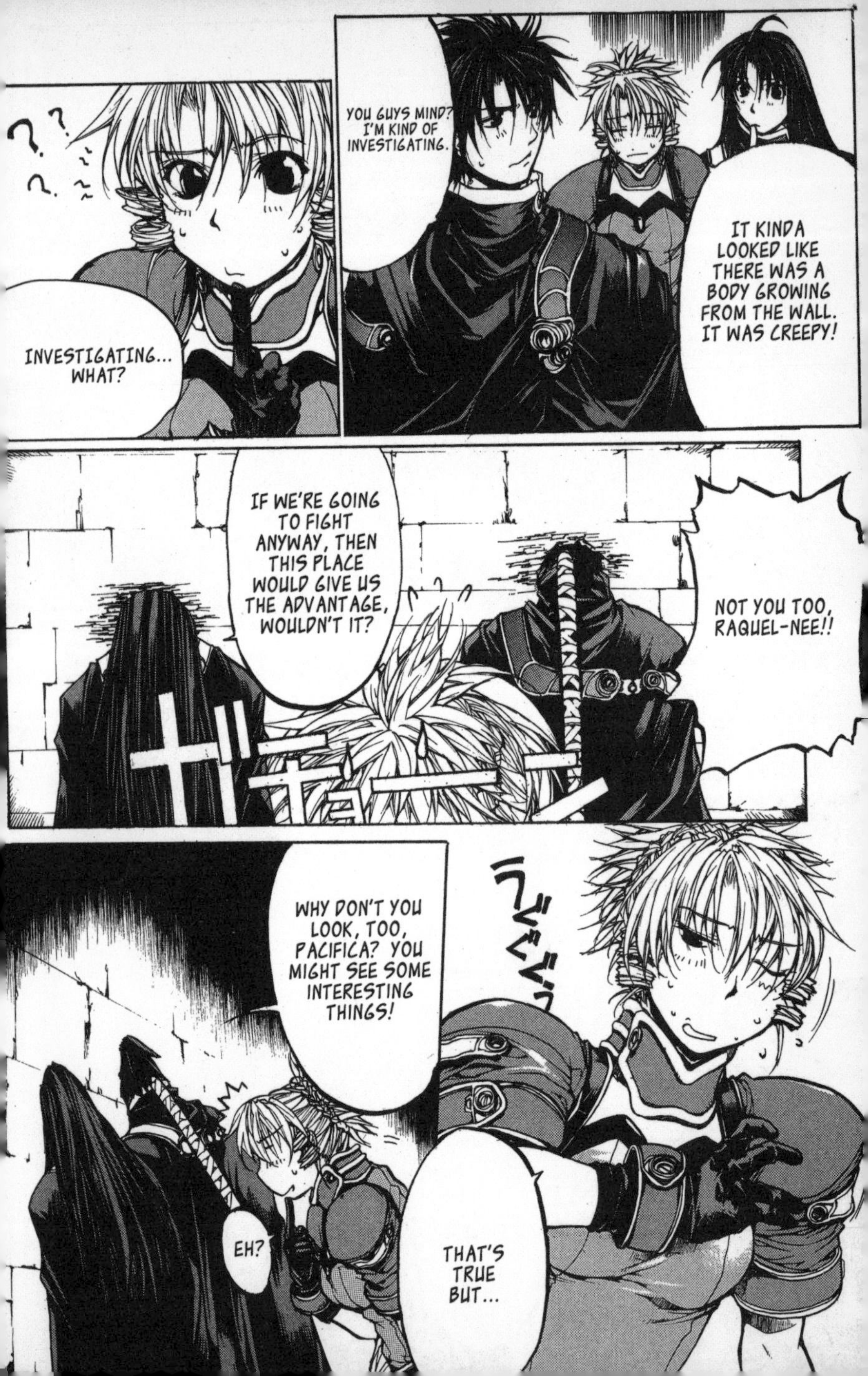

YOU GUYS MIND? I'M KIND OF INVESTIGATING.
IT KINDA LOOKED LIKE THERE WAS A BODY GROWING FROM THE WALL. IT WAS CREEPY!
INVESTIGATING... WHAT?
IF WE'RE GOING TO FIGHT ANYWAY, THEN THIS PLACE WOULD GIVE US THE ADVANTAGE, WOULDN'T IT?
NOT YOU TOO, RAQUEL-NEE!!
WHY DON'T YOU LOOK, TOO, PACIFICA? YOU MIGHT SEE SOME INTERESTING THINGS!
THAT'S TRUE BUT...
EH?

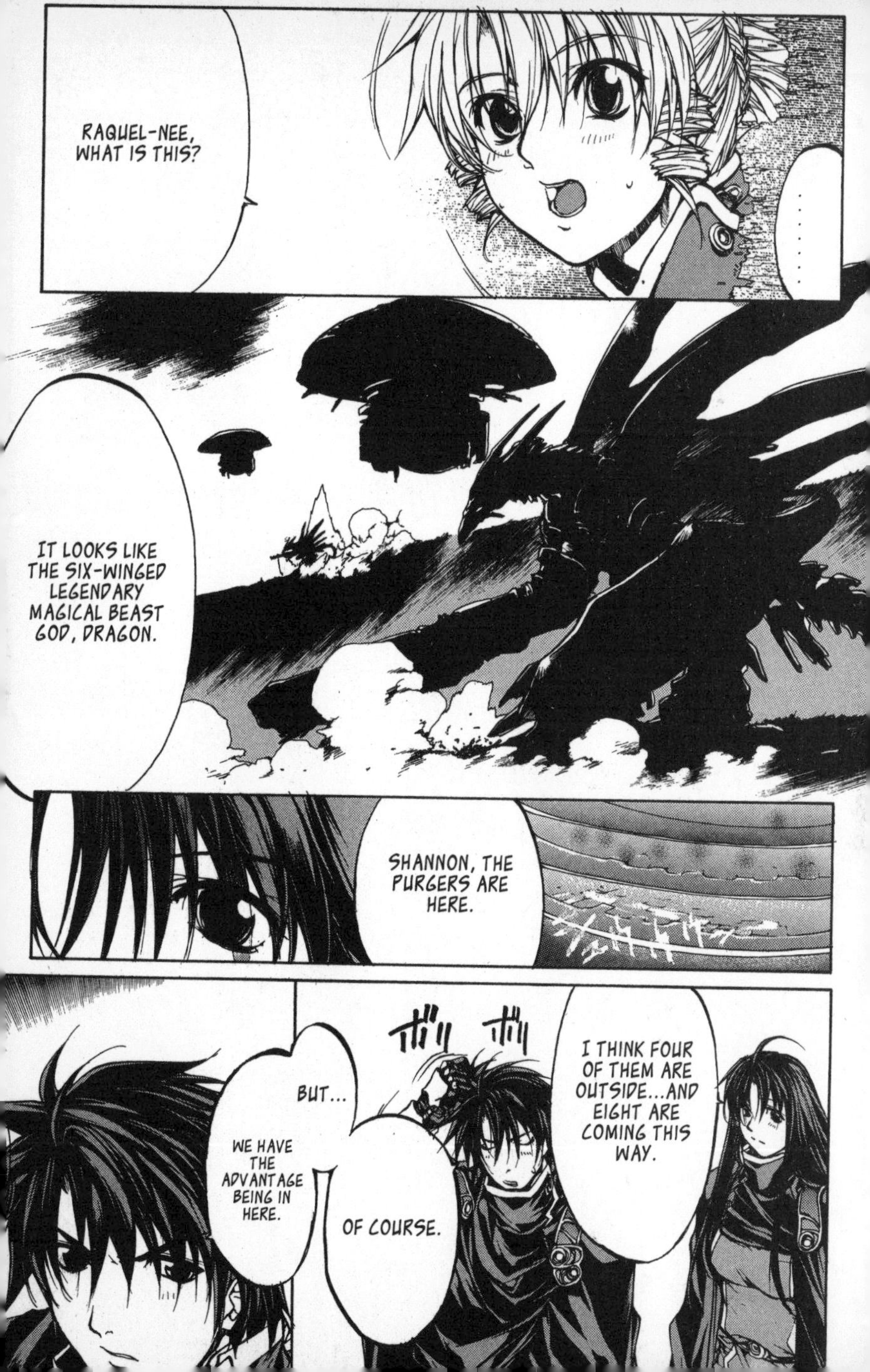
RAQUEL-NEE, WHAT IS THIS?
......
IT LOOKS LIKE THE SIX-WINGED LEGENDARY MAGICAL BEAST GOD, DRAGON.
SHANNON, THE PURGERS ARE HERE.
I THINK FOUR OF THEM ARE OUTSIDE...AND EIGHT ARE COMING THIS WAY.
ボリ ボリ
OF COURSE.
BUT...
WE HAVE THE ADVANTAGE BEING IN HERE.

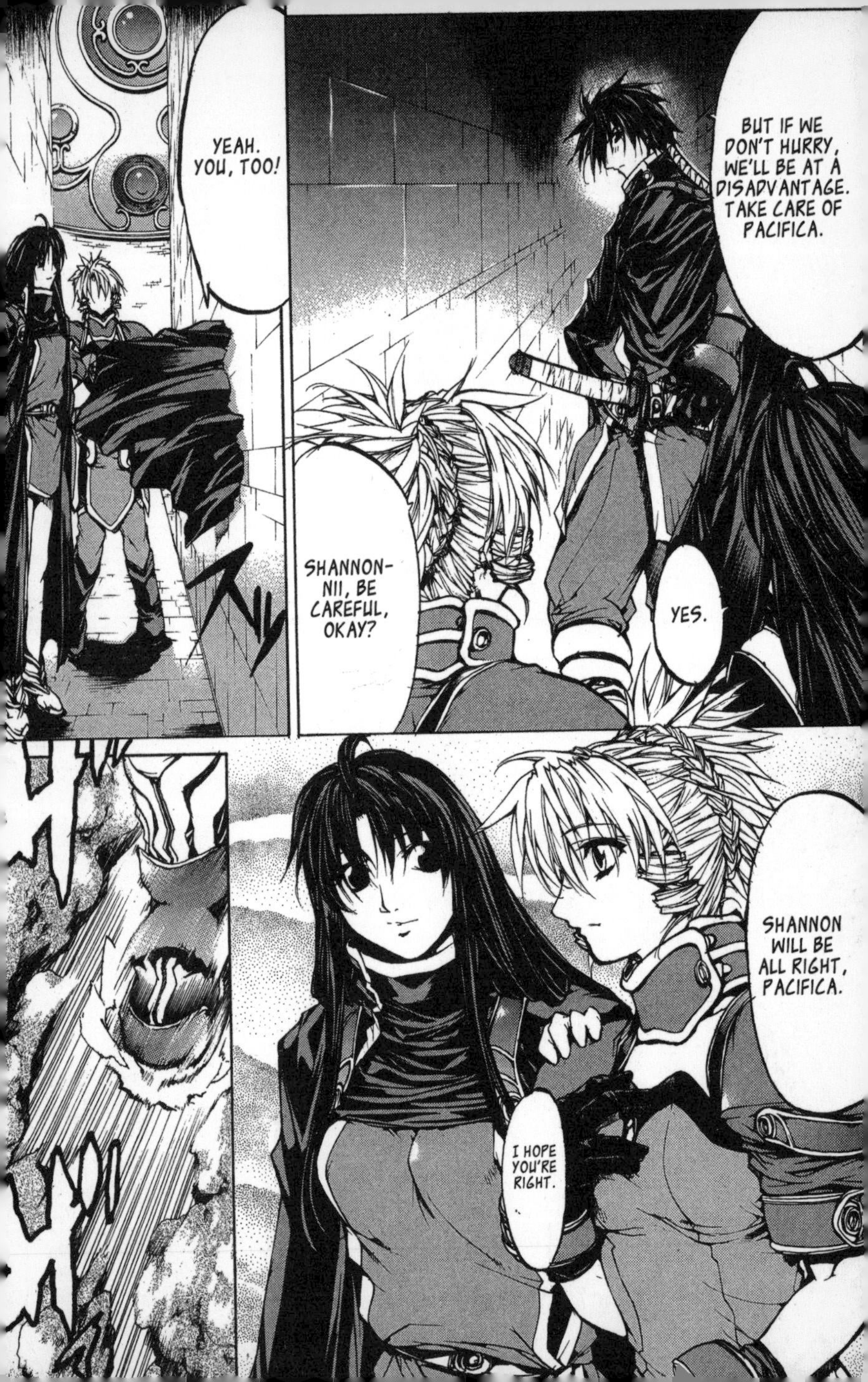
BUT IF WE DON'T HURRY, WE'LL BE AT A DISADVANTAGE. TAKE CARE OF PACIFICA.
SHANNON-NII, BE CAREFUL, OKAY?
YES.
YEAH. YOU, TOO!
SHANNON WILL BE ALL RIGHT, PACIFICA.
I HOPE YOU'RE RIGHT.

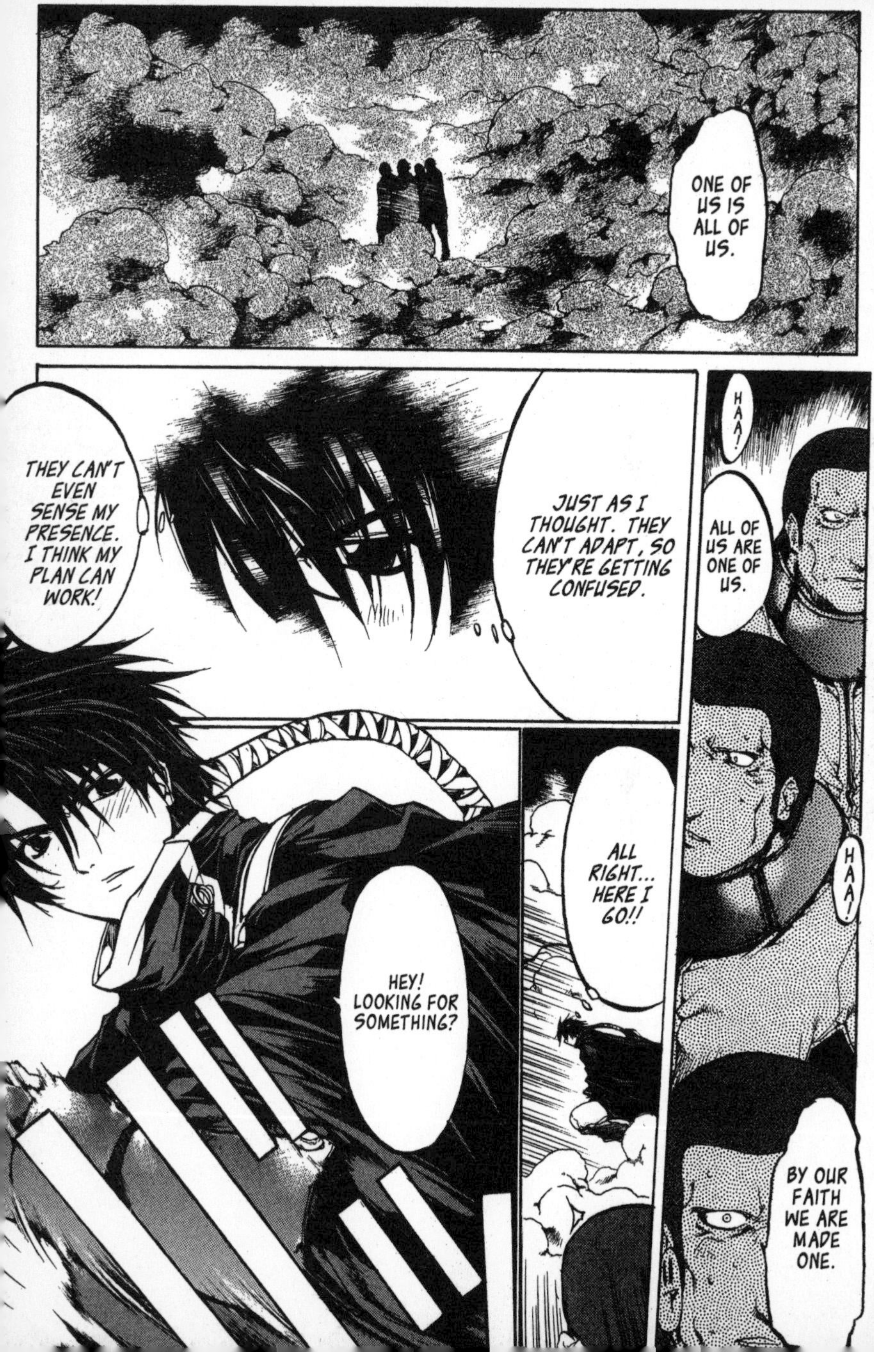
ONE OF US IS ALL OF US.
HAA!
ALL OF US ARE ONE OF US.
HAA!
BY OUR FAITH WE ARE MADE ONE.
JUST AS I THOUGHT. THEY CAN'T ADAPT, SO THEY'RE GETTING CONFUSED.
THEY CAN'T EVEN SENSE MY PRESENCE. I THINK MY PLAN CAN WORK!
ALL RIGHT... HERE I GO!!
HEY! LOOKING FOR SOMETHING?

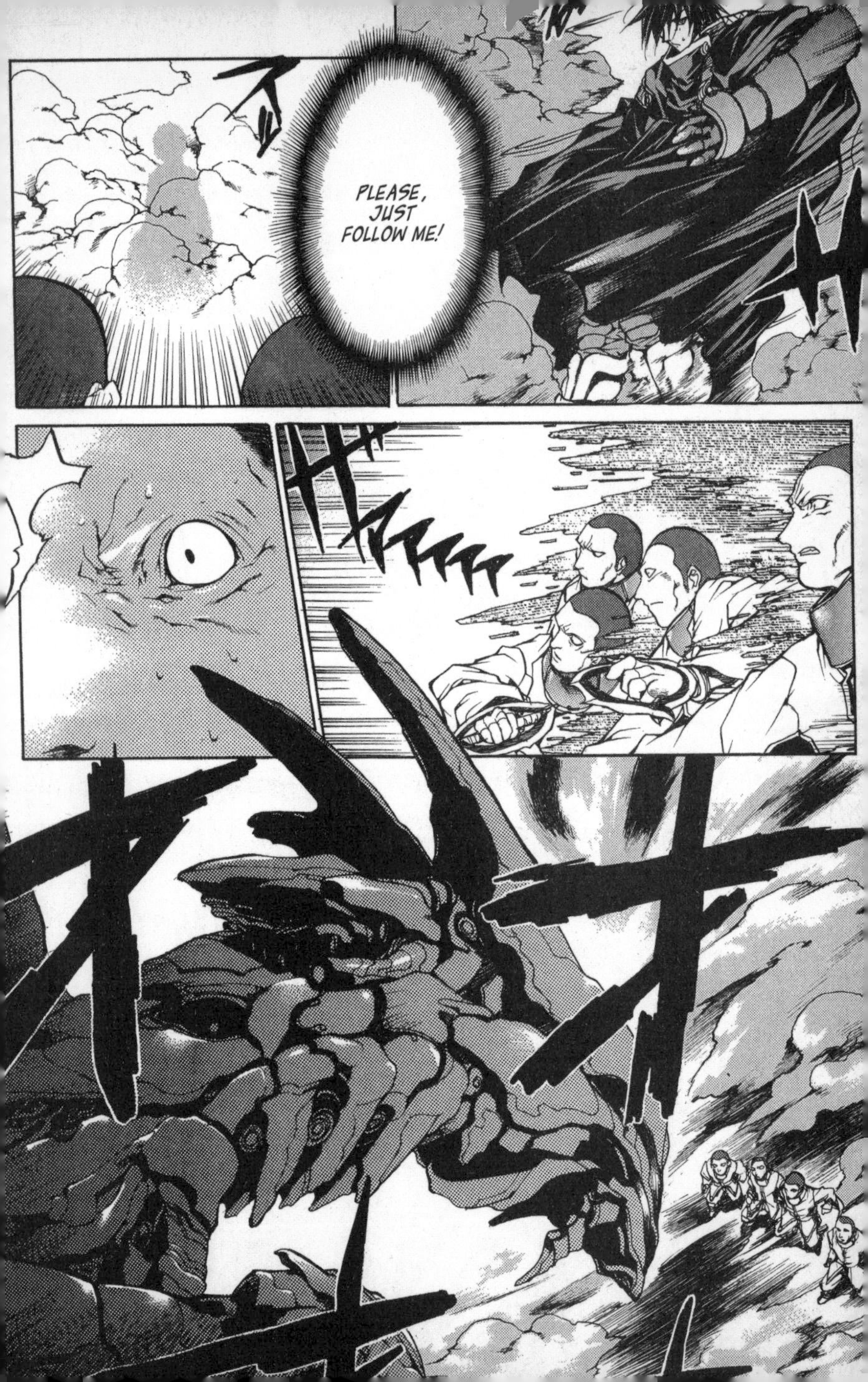
PLEASE, JUST FOLLOW ME!

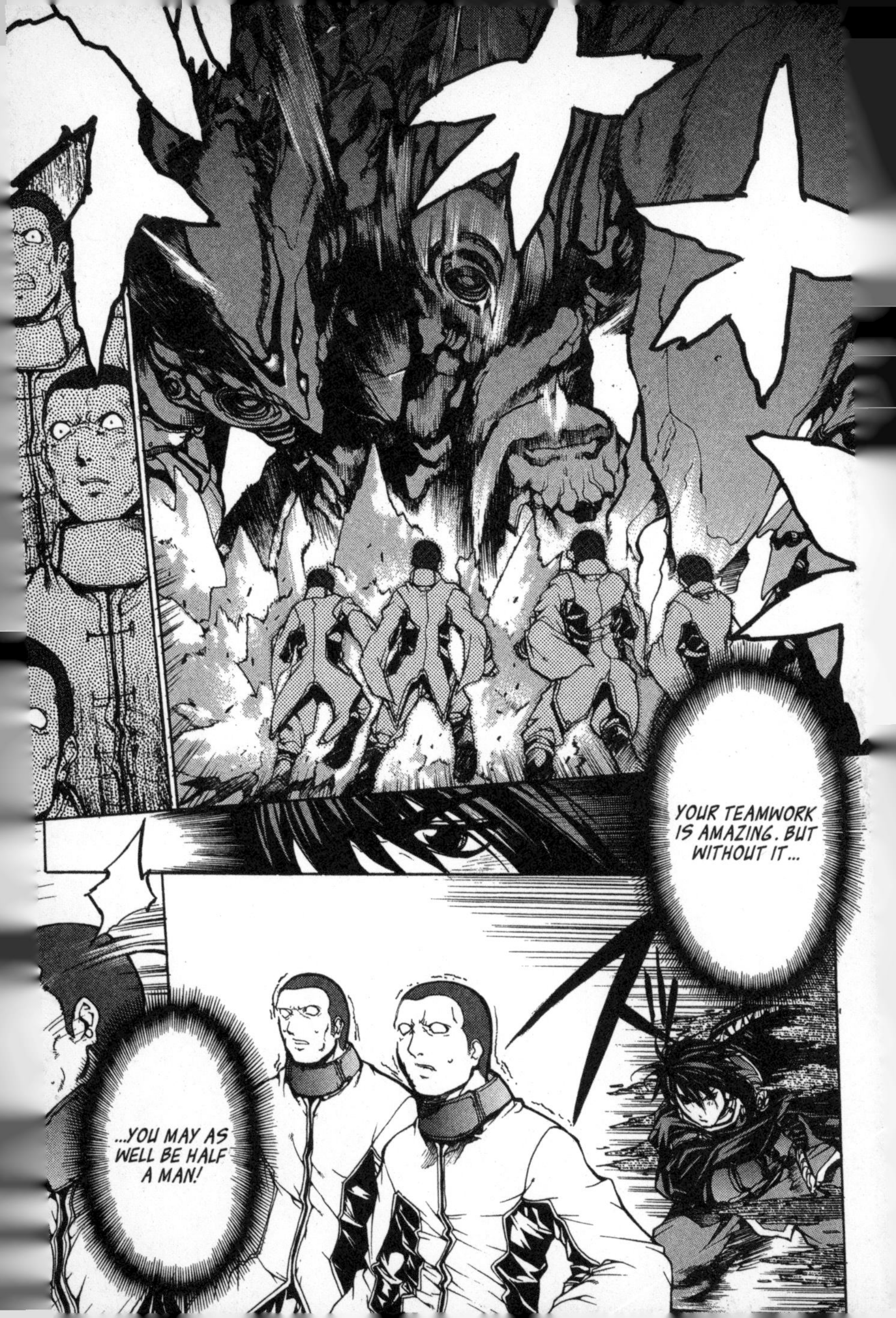
YOUR TEAMWORK IS AMAZING. BUT WITHOUT IT...
...YOU MAY AS WELL BE HALF A MAN!

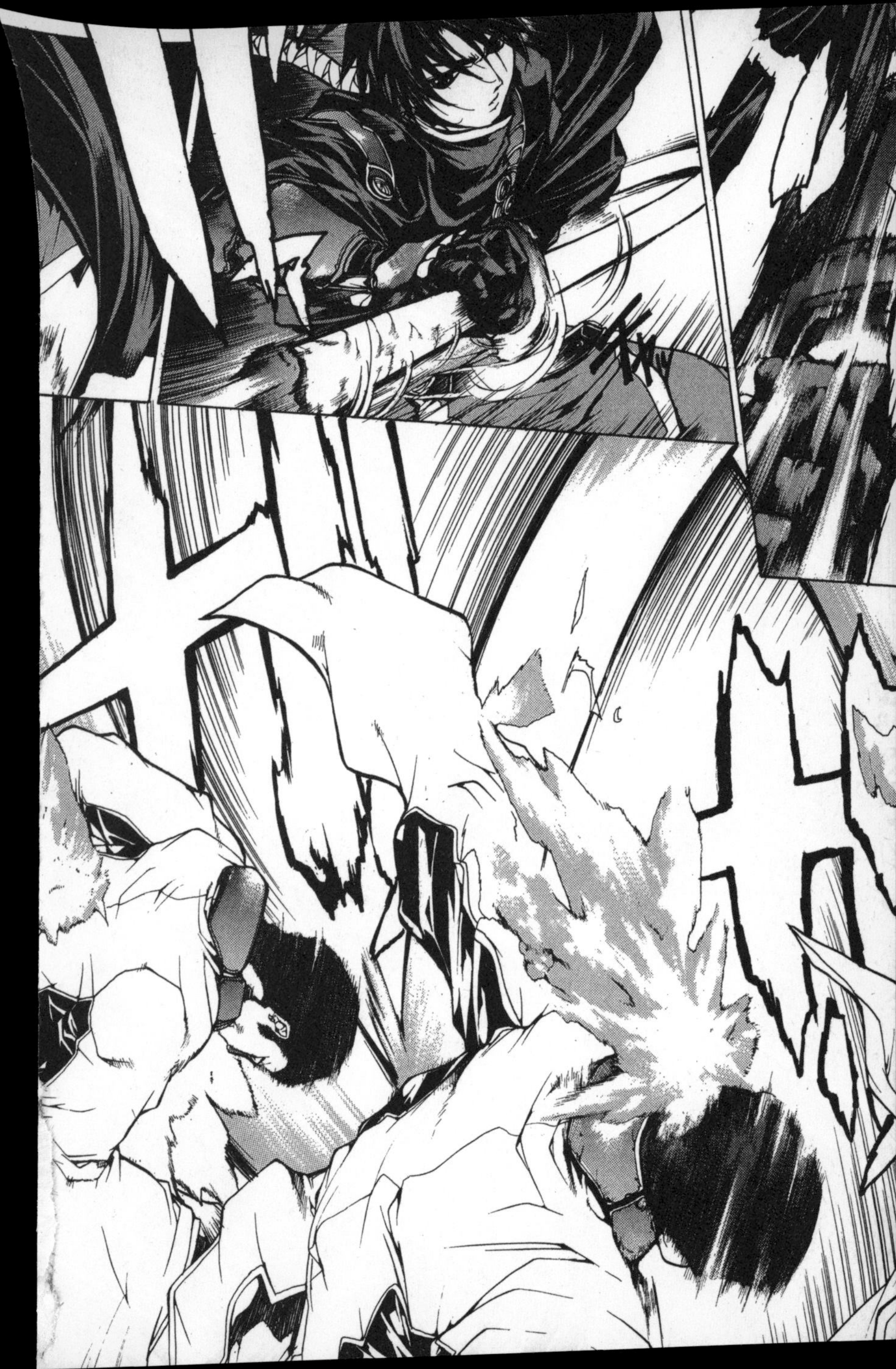

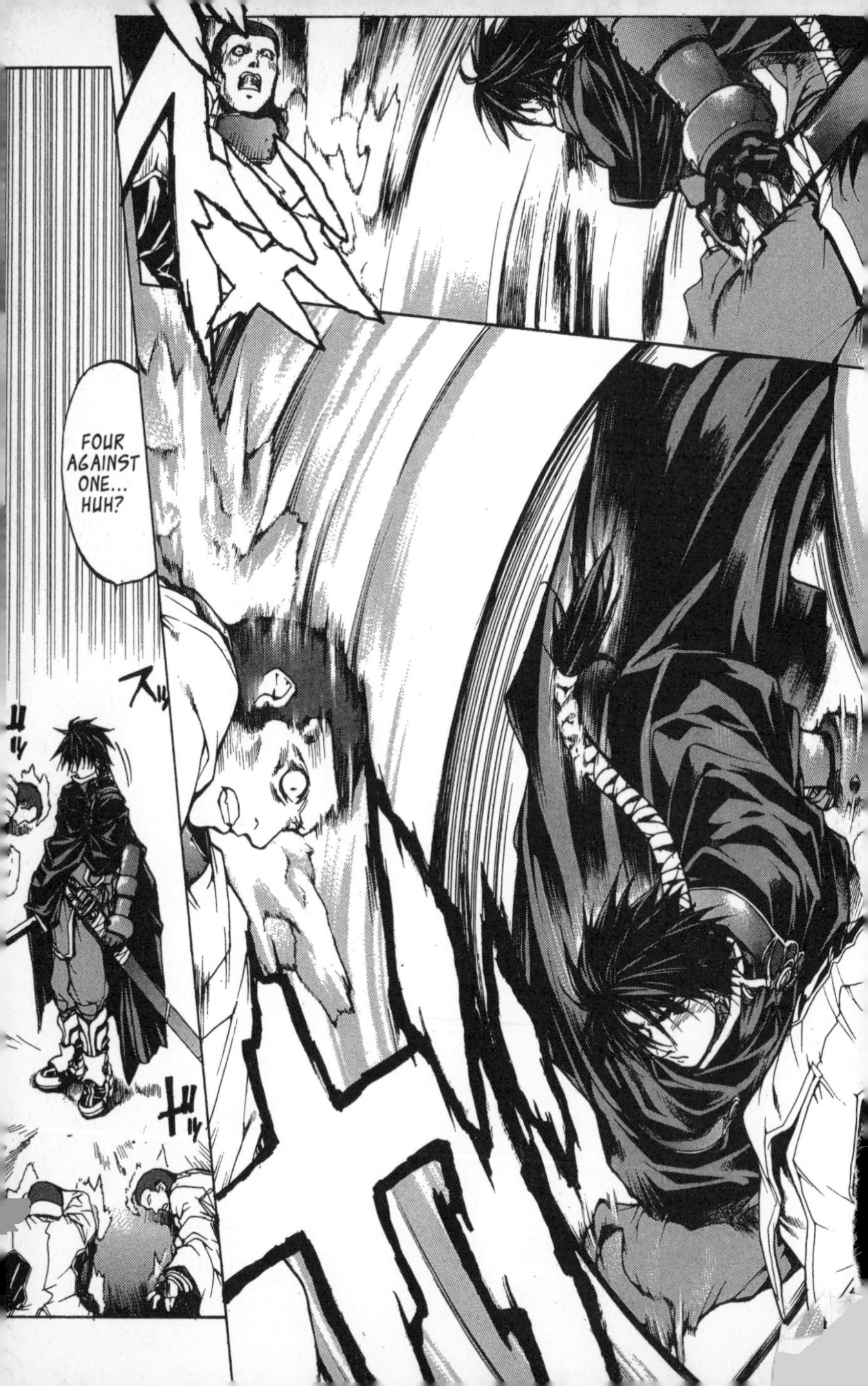
FOUR AGAINST ONE... HUH?

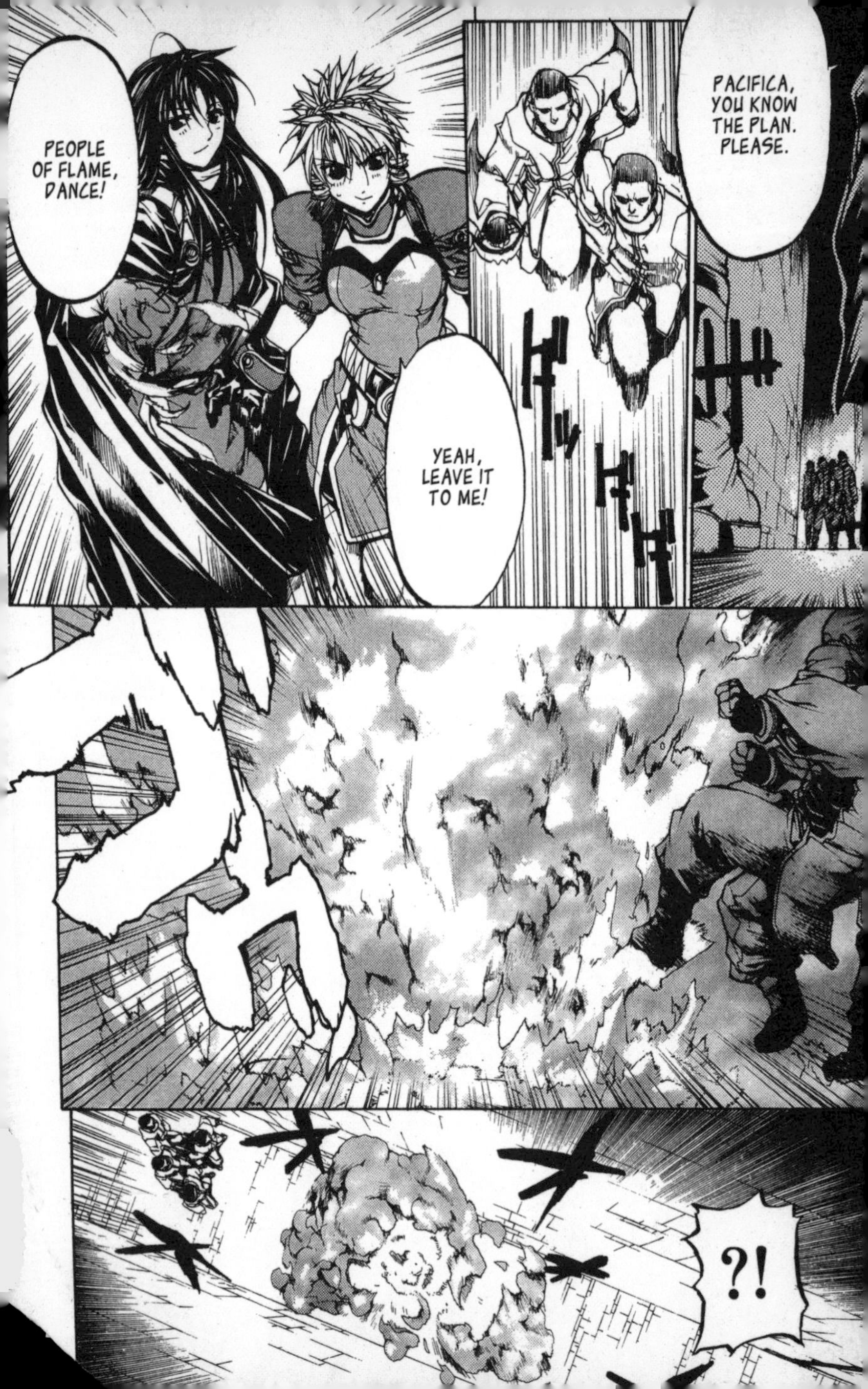
PACIFICA, YOU KNOW THE PLAN. PLEASE.
PEOPLE OF FLAME, DANCE!
YEAH, LEAVE IT TO ME!
?!

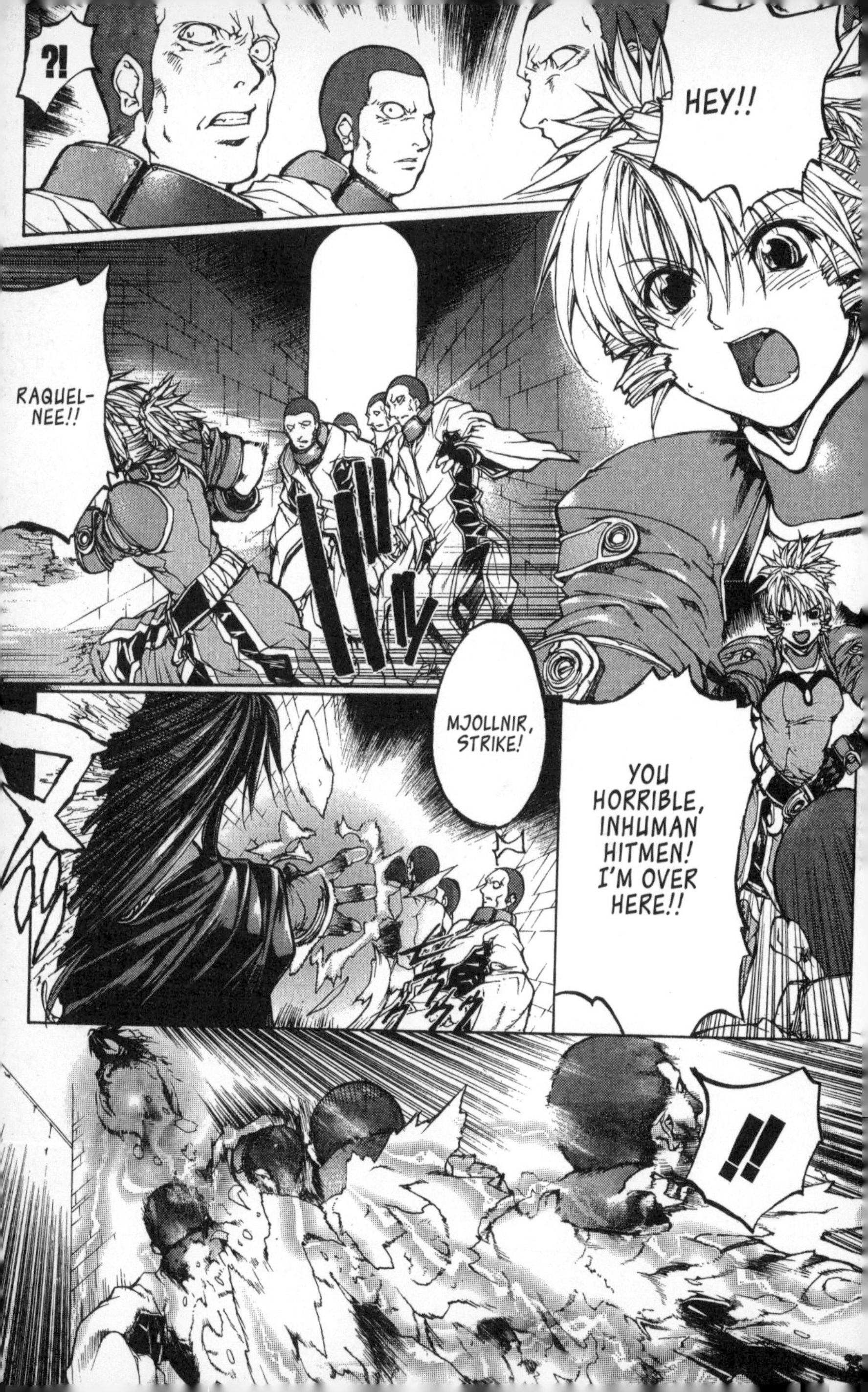
HEY!!
?!
RAQUEL-NEE!!
YOU HORRIBLE, INHUMAN HITMEN! I'M OVER HERE!!
MJOLLNIR, STRIKE!
!!

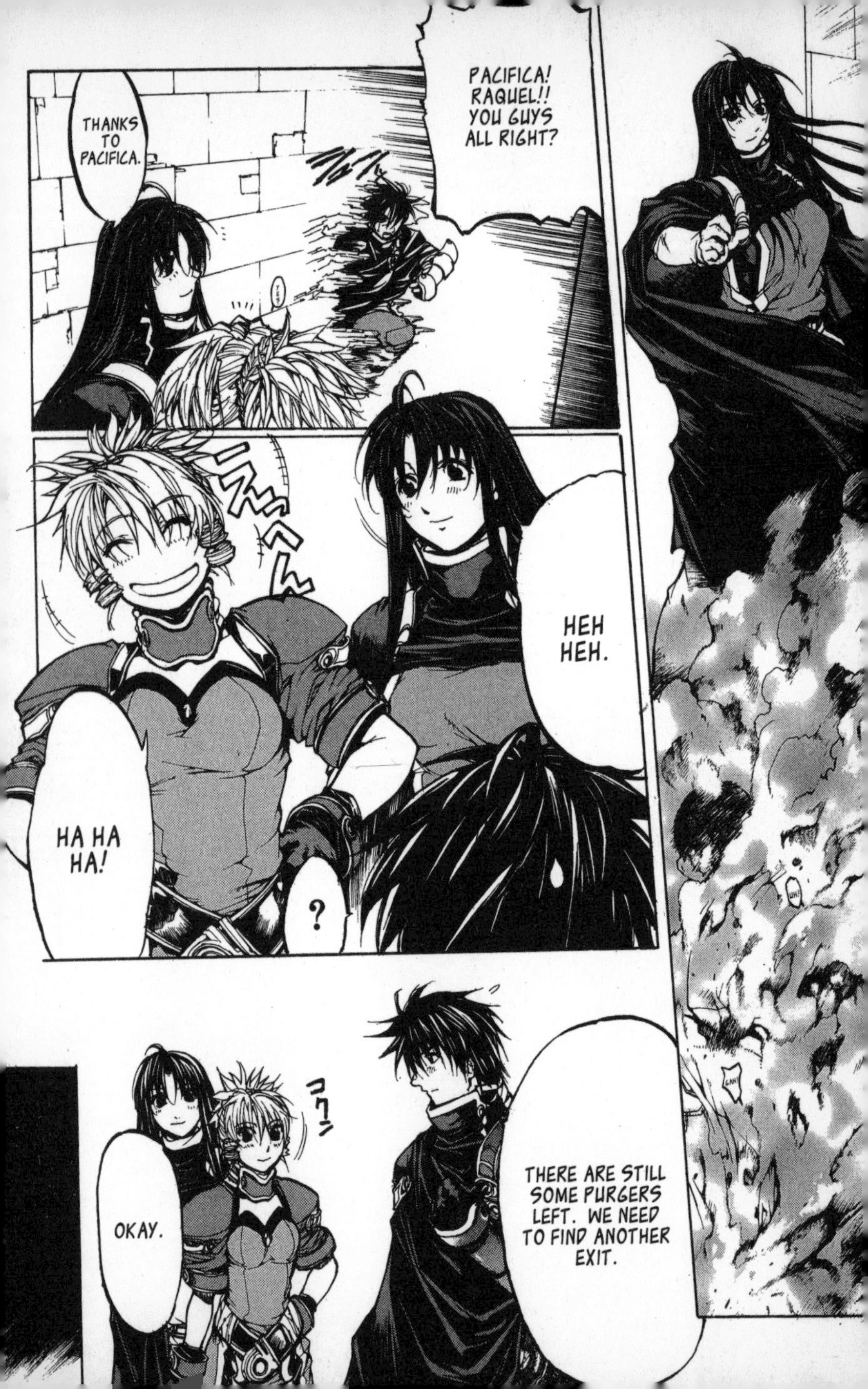
UH!
GAH!
PACIFICA! RAQUEL!! YOU GUYS ALL RIGHT?
THANKS TO PACIFICA.
YES!
HEH HEH.
HA HA HA!
?
THERE ARE STILL SOME PURGERS LEFT. WE NEED TO FIND ANOTHER EXIT.
OKAY.

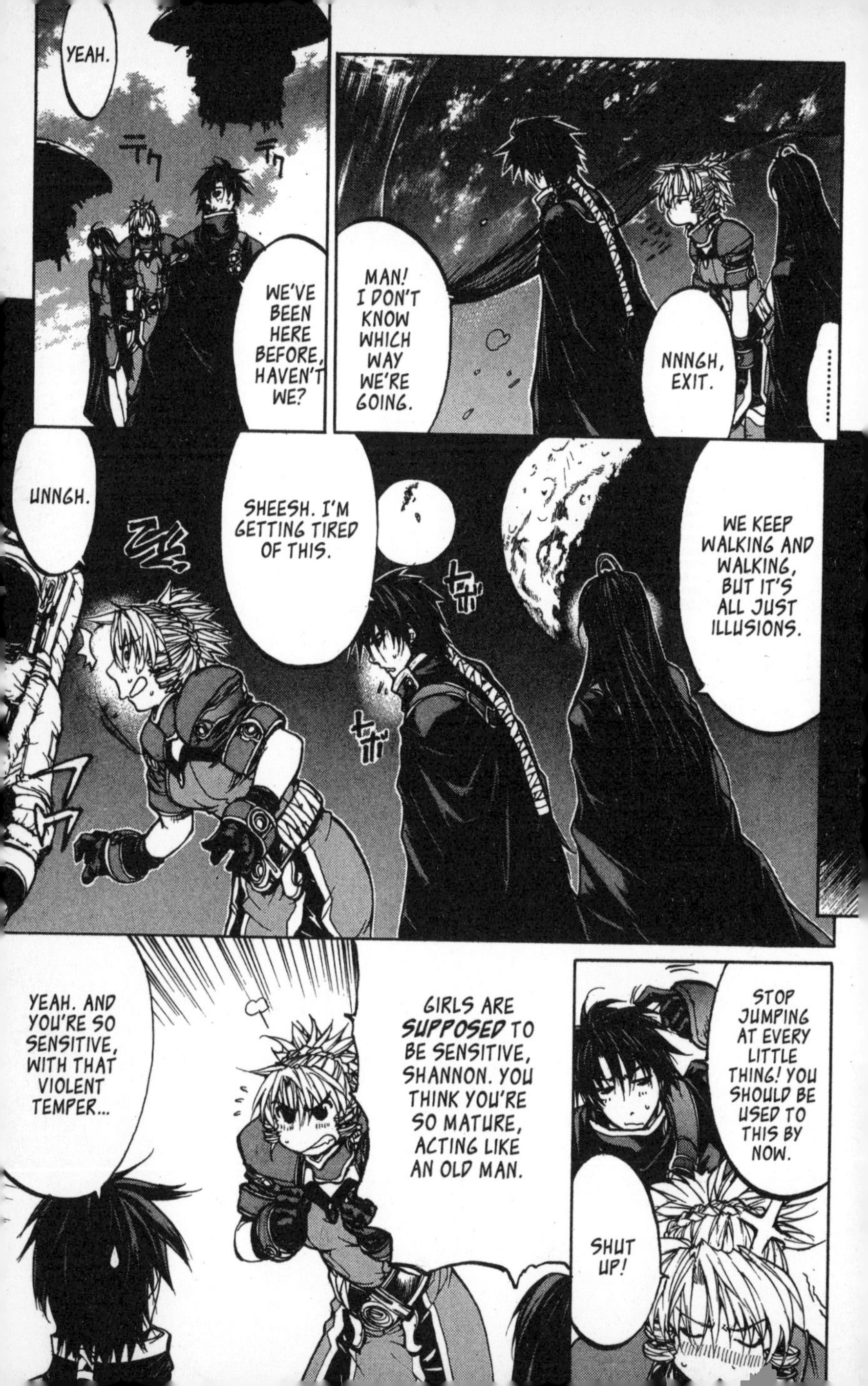

......
NNNGH, EXIT.
MAN! I DON'T KNOW WHICH WAY WE'RE GOING.
YEAH.
WE'VE BEEN HERE BEFORE, HAVEN'T WE?
WE KEEP WALKING AND WALKING, BUT IT'S ALL JUST ILLUSIONS.
SHEESH. I'M GETTING TIRED OF THIS.
UNNGH.
STOP JUMPING AT EVERY LITTLE THING! YOU SHOULD BE USED TO THIS BY NOW.
SHUT UP!
GIRLS ARE **SUPPOSED** TO BE SENSITIVE, SHANNON. YOU THINK YOU'RE SO MATURE, ACTING LIKE AN OLD MAN.
YEAH. AND YOU'RE SO SENSITIVE, WITH THAT VIOLENT TEMPER...

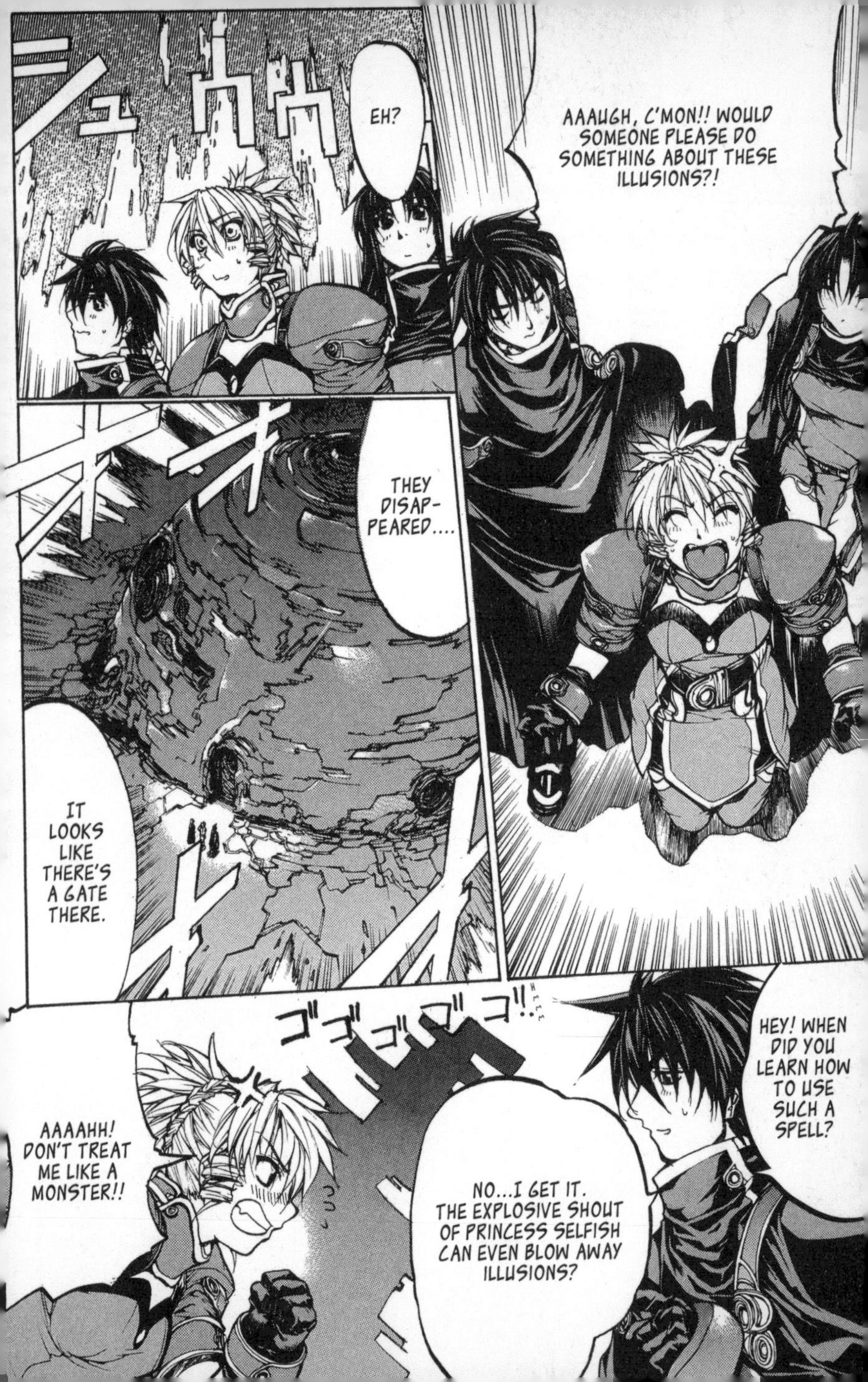
AAAUGH, C'MON!! WOULD SOMEONE PLEASE DO SOMETHING ABOUT THESE ILLUSIONS?!
EH?
THEY DISAP-PEARED....
IT LOOKS LIKE THERE'S A GATE THERE.
HEY! WHEN DID YOU LEARN HOW TO USE SUCH A SPELL?
NO...I GET IT. THE EXPLOSIVE SHOUT OF PRINCESS SELFISH CAN EVEN BLOW AWAY ILLUSIONS?
AAAAHH! DON'T TREAT ME LIKE A MONSTER!!

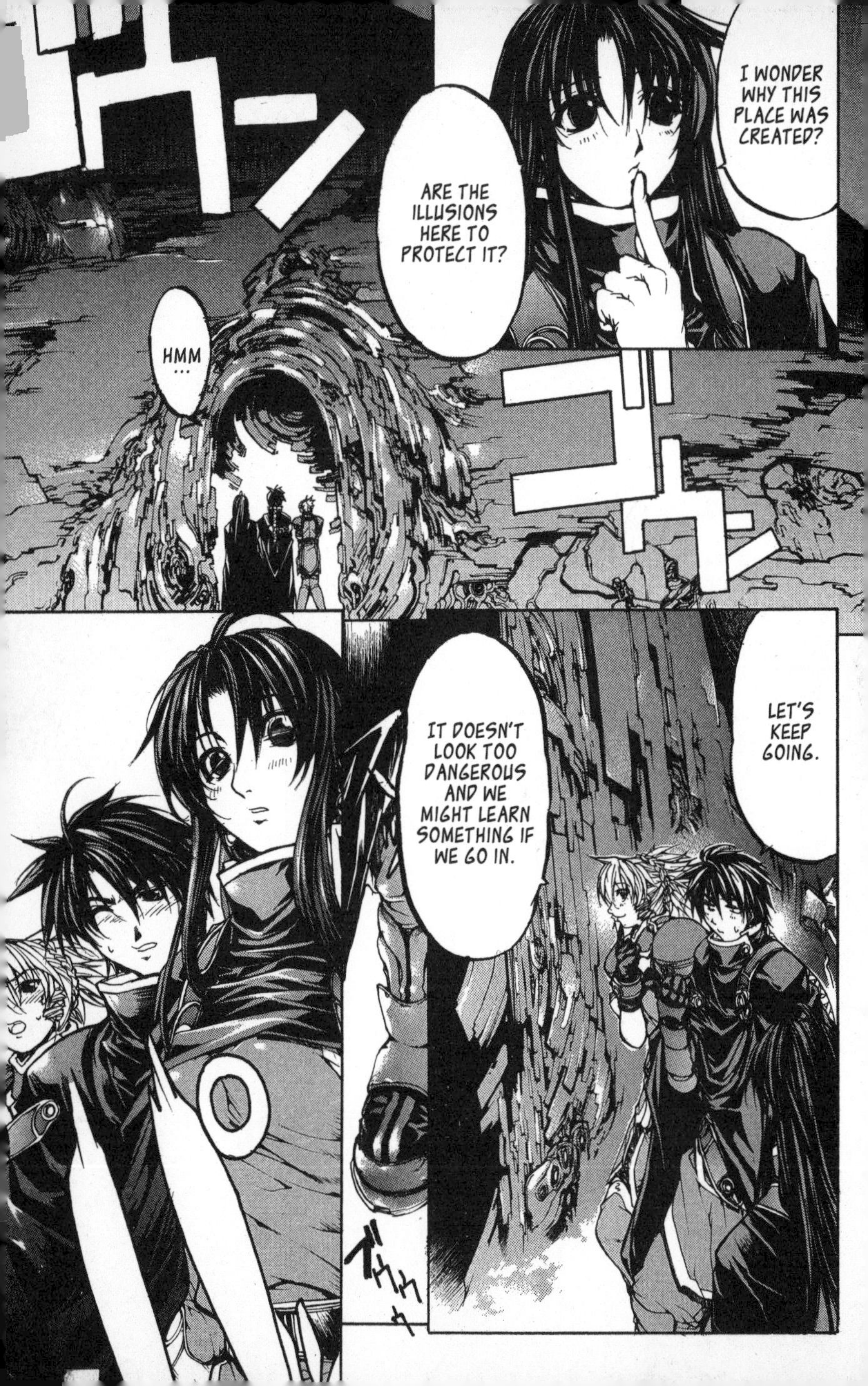
I WONDER WHY THIS PLACE WAS CREATED?
ARE THE ILLUSIONS HERE TO PROTECT IT?
HMM...
LET'S KEEP GOING.
IT DOESN'T LOOK TOO DANGEROUS AND WE MIGHT LEARN SOMETHING IF WE GO IN.

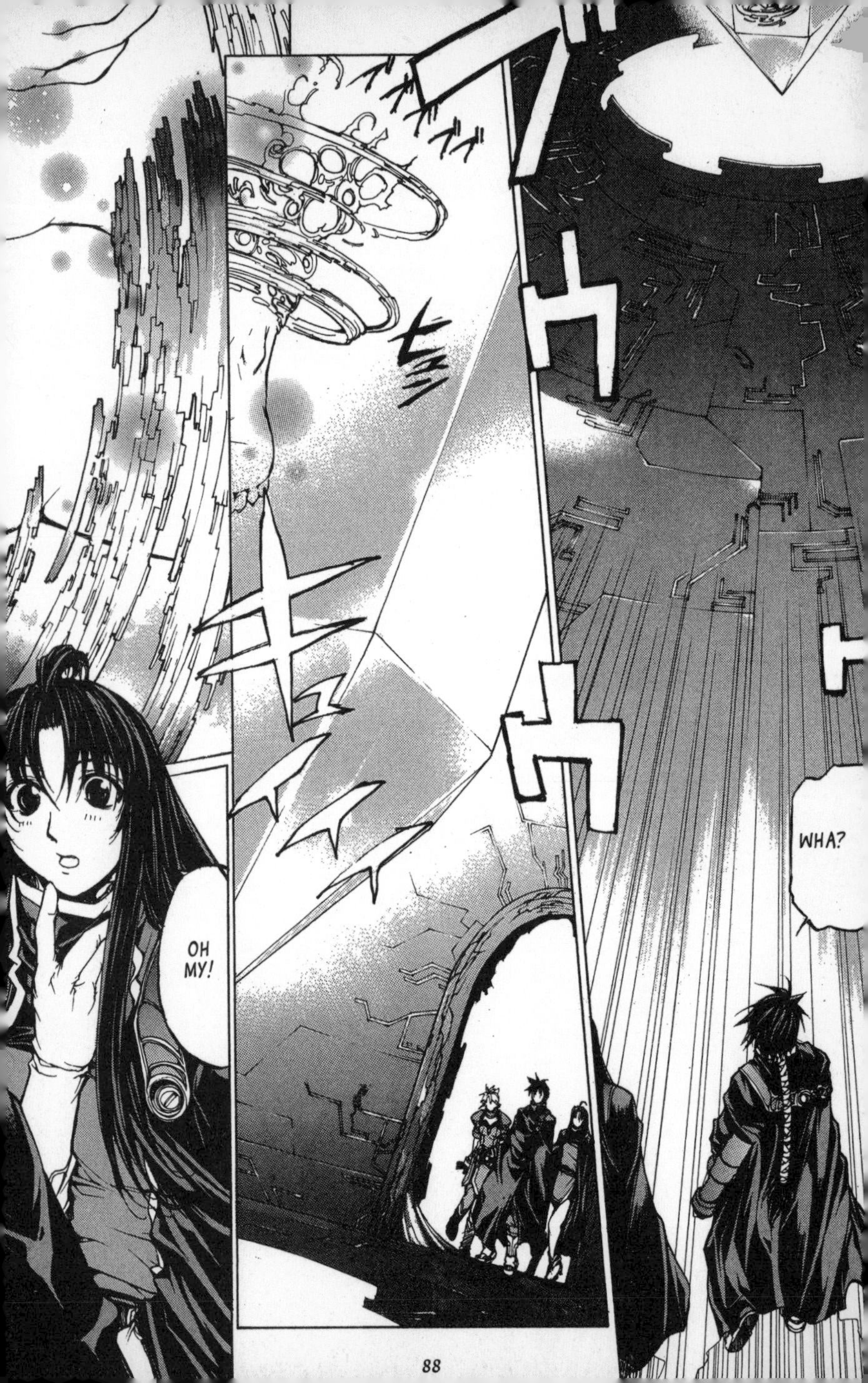
WHA?
OH MY!

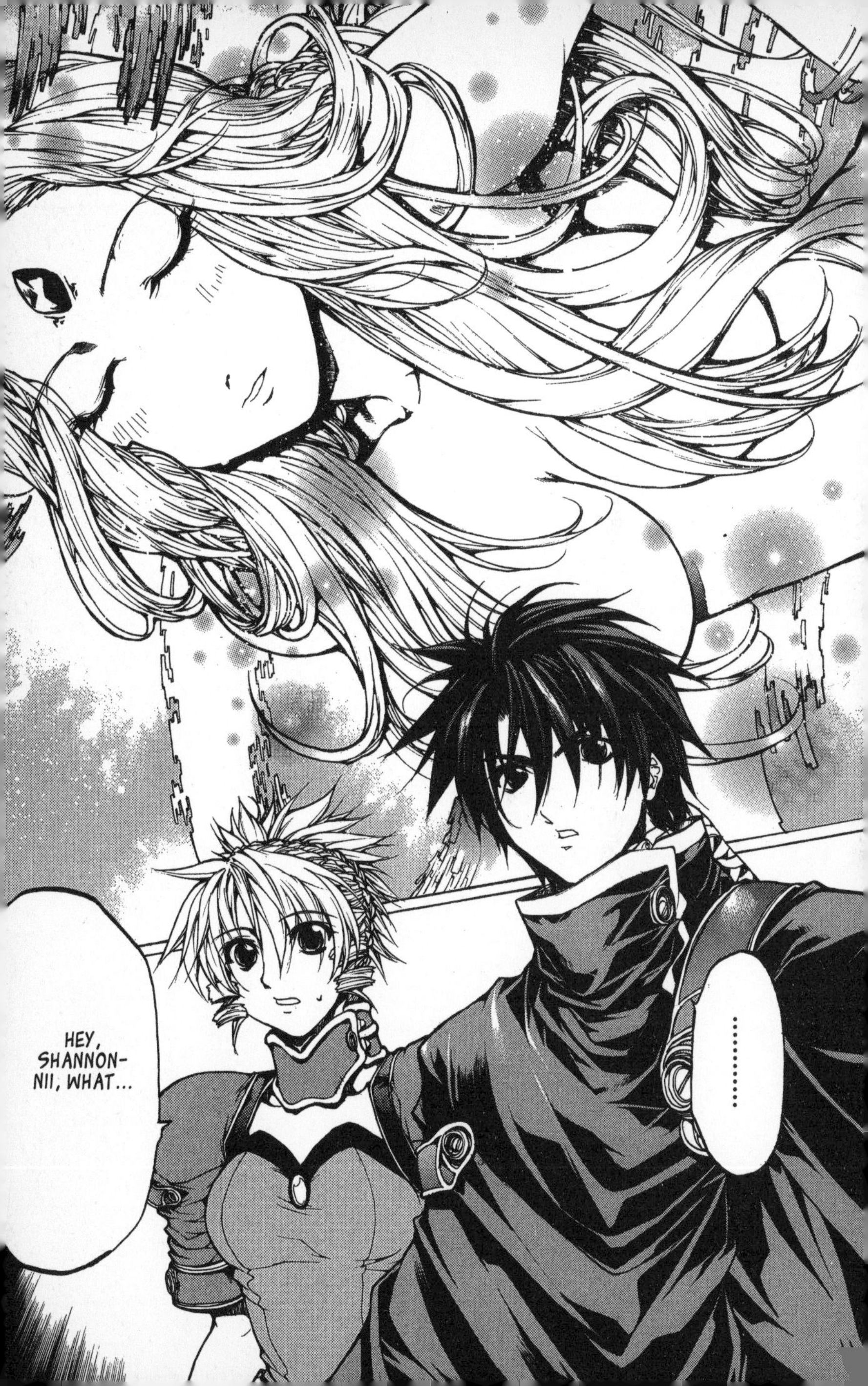
....
HEY, SHANNON-NII, WHAT...

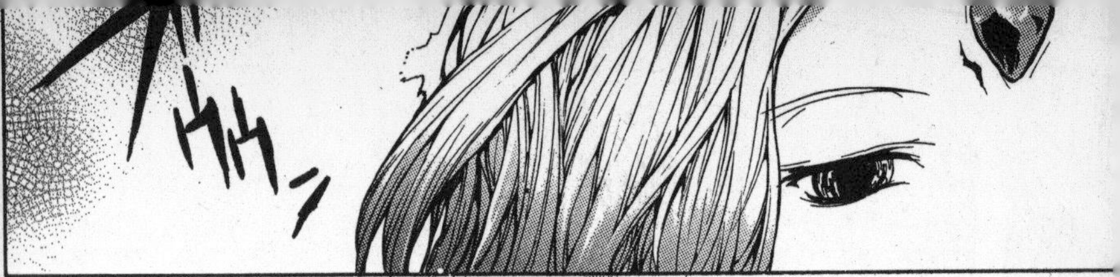
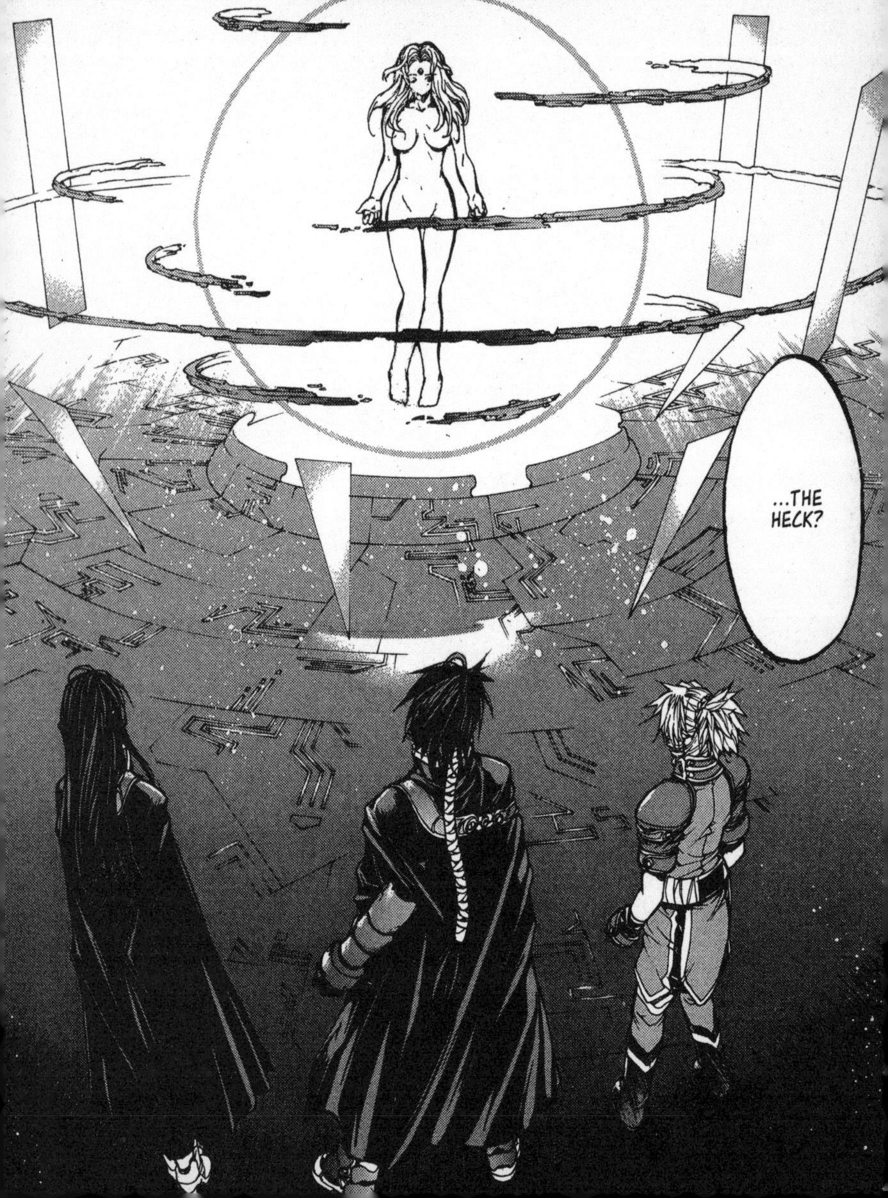
...THE
HECK?

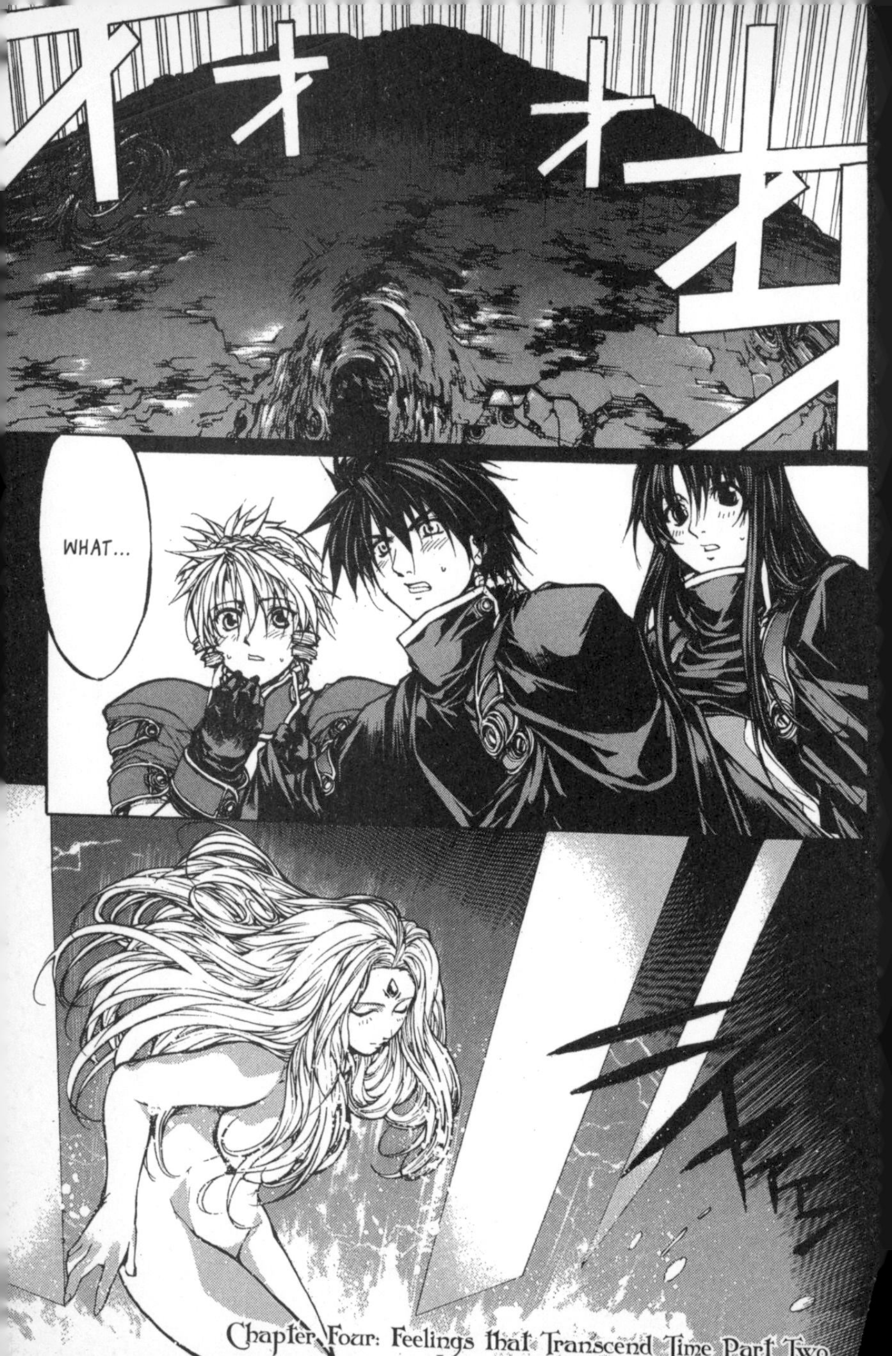
イオオオ
WHAT...

Chapter Four: Feelings that Transcend Time Part Two

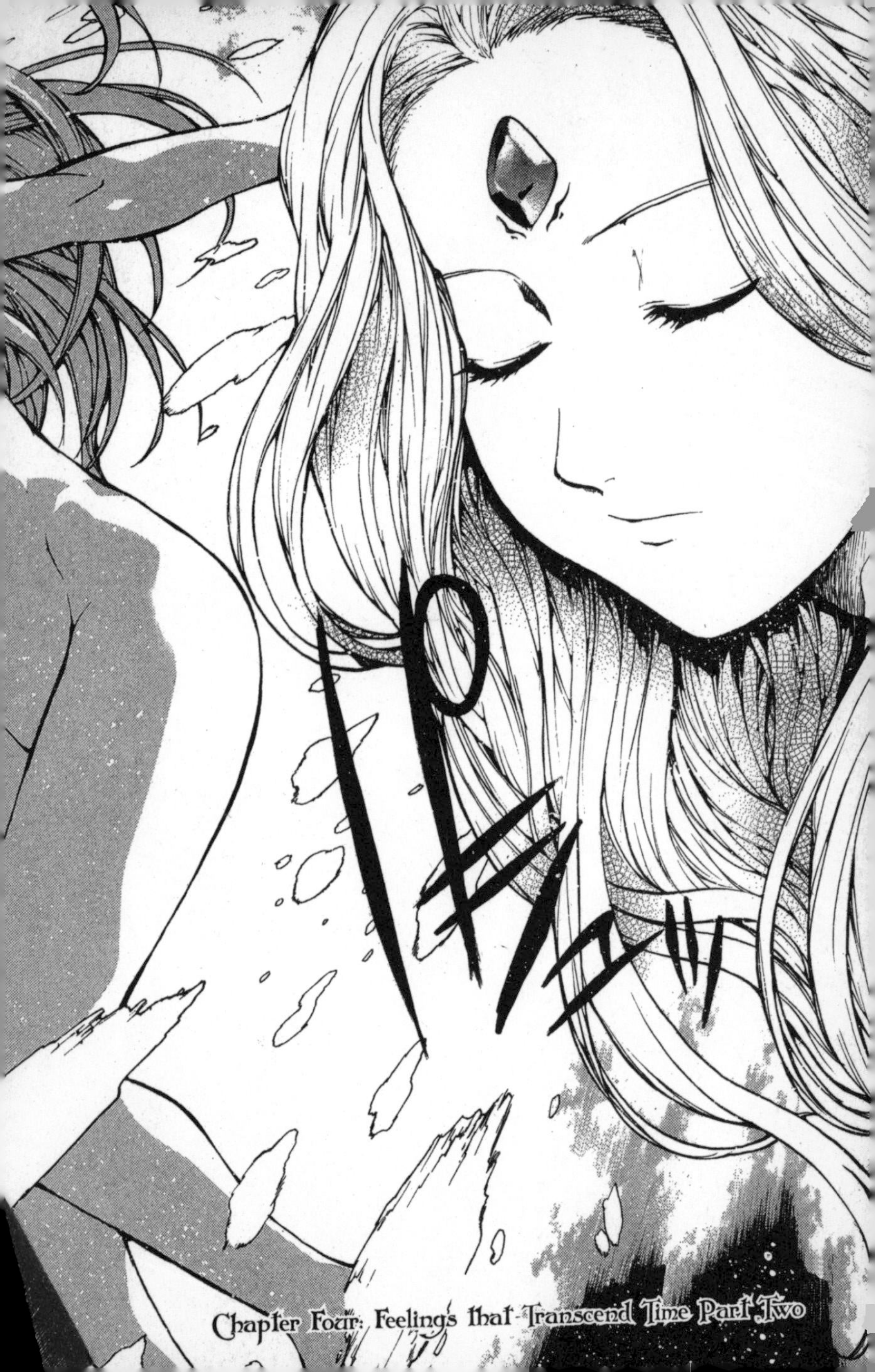

Chapter Four: Feelings that Transcend Time Part Two

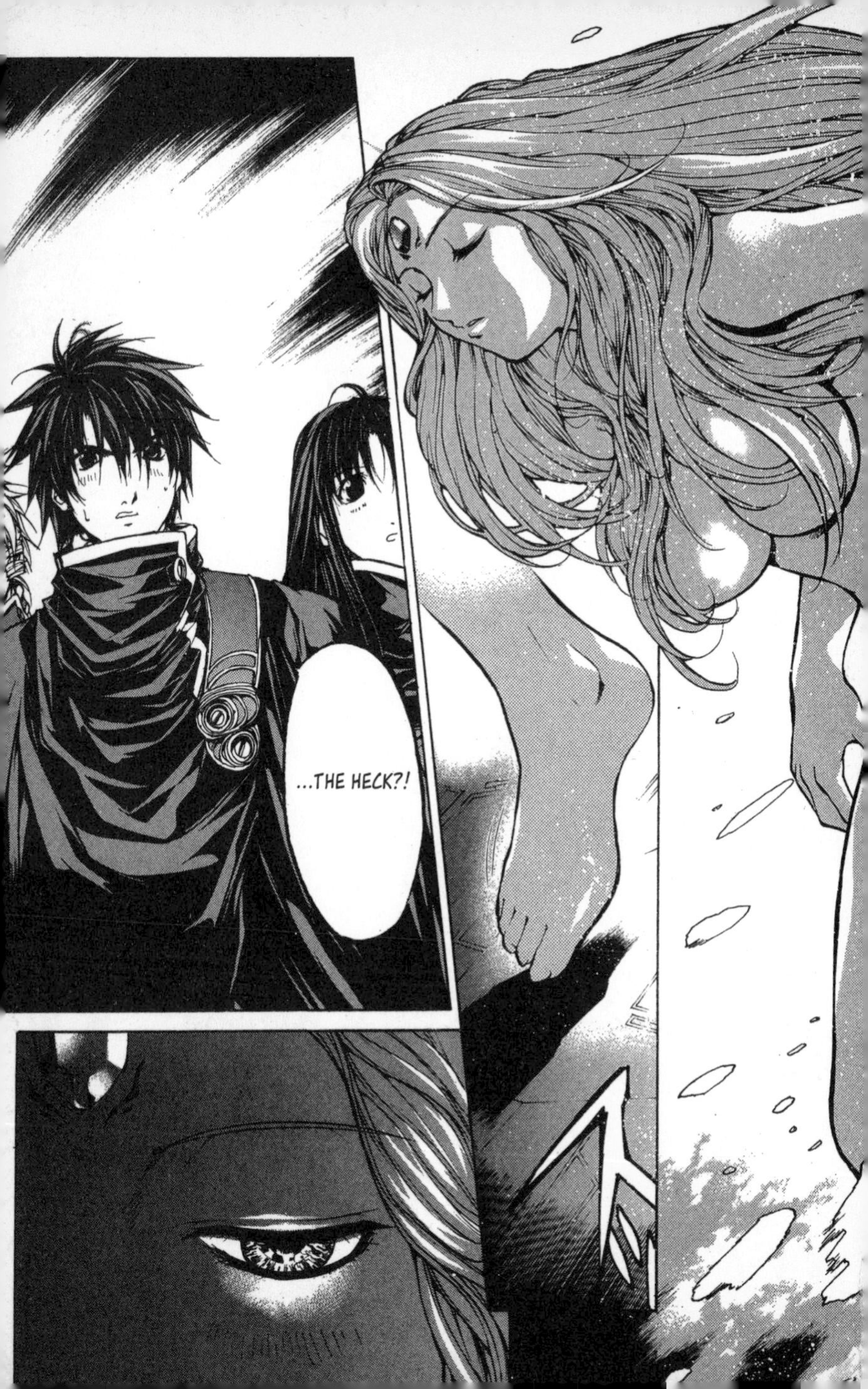
...THE HECK?!

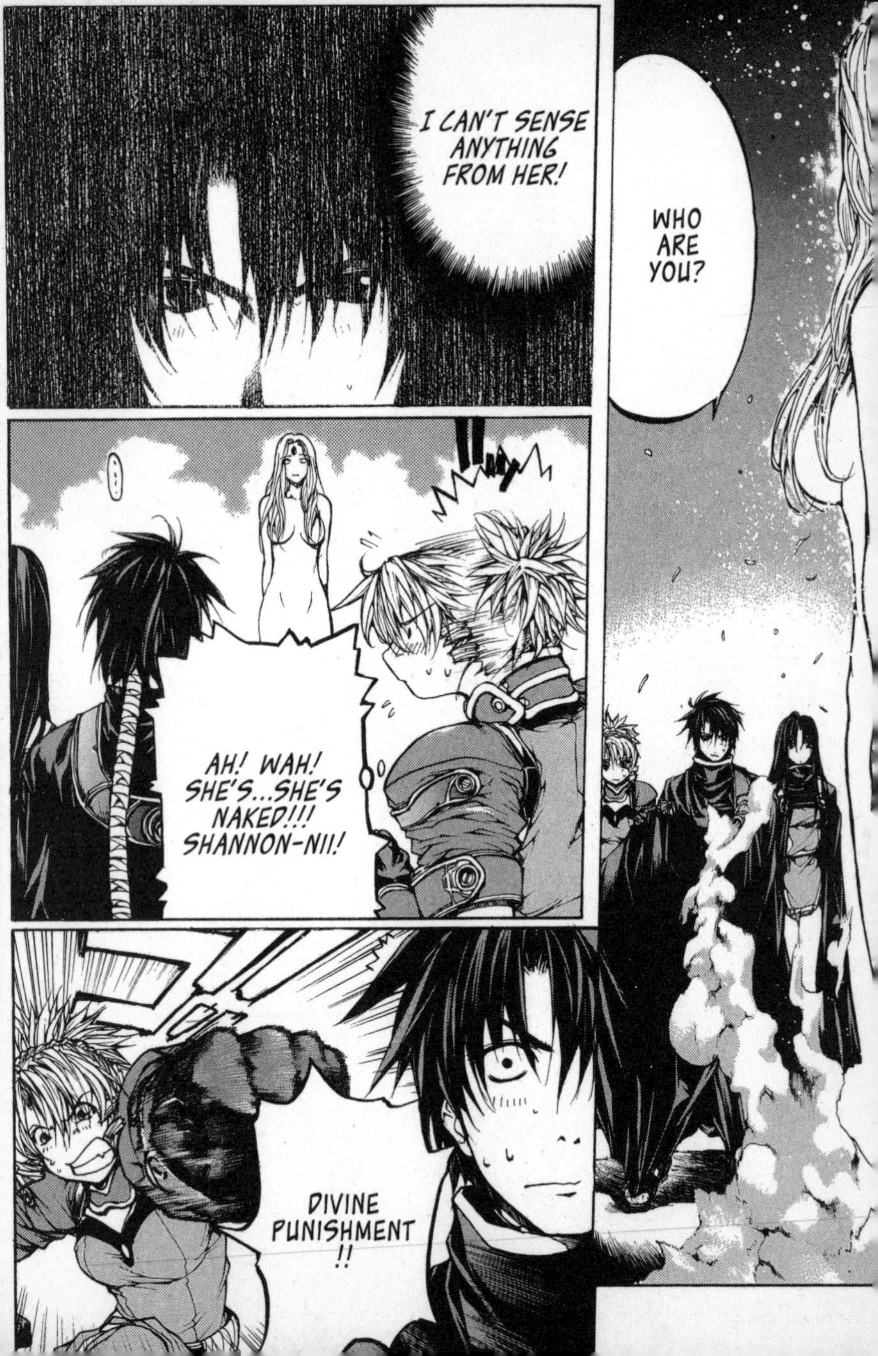
WHO ARE YOU?
I CAN'T SENSE ANYTHING FROM HER!
...
AH! WAH! SHE'S...SHE'S NAKED!!! SHANNON-NII!
DIVINE PUNISHMENT !!

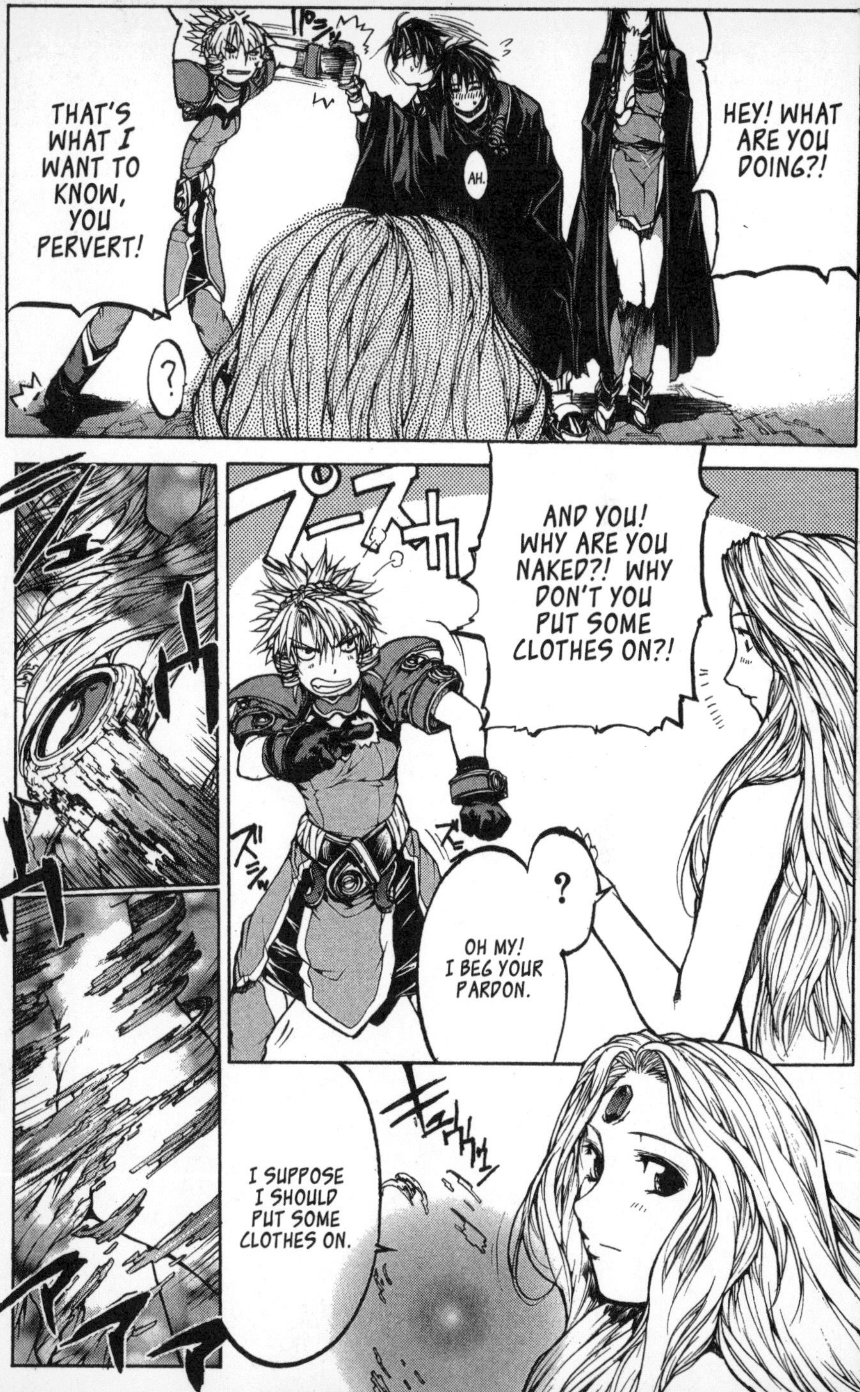
HEY! WHAT ARE YOU DOING?!
AH.
THAT'S WHAT I WANT TO KNOW, YOU PERVERT!
?
AND YOU! WHY ARE YOU NAKED?! WHY DON'T YOU PUT SOME CLOTHES ON?!
?
OH MY! I BEG YOUR PARDON.
I SUPPOSE I SHOULD PUT SOME CLOTHES ON.

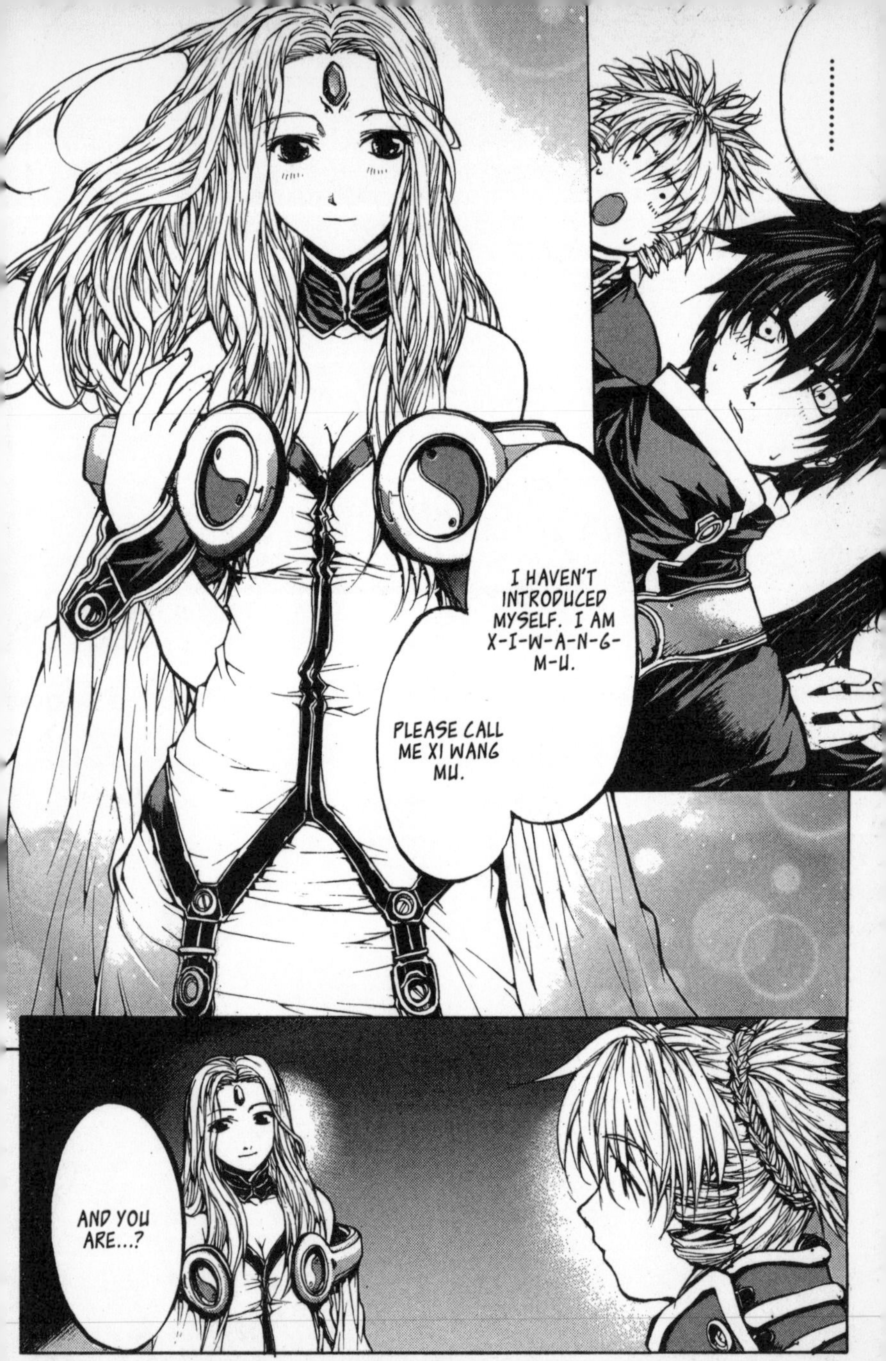
......
I HAVEN'T INTRODUCED MYSELF. I AM X-I-W-A-N-G-M-U.
PLEASE CALL ME XI WANG MU.
AND YOU ARE...?

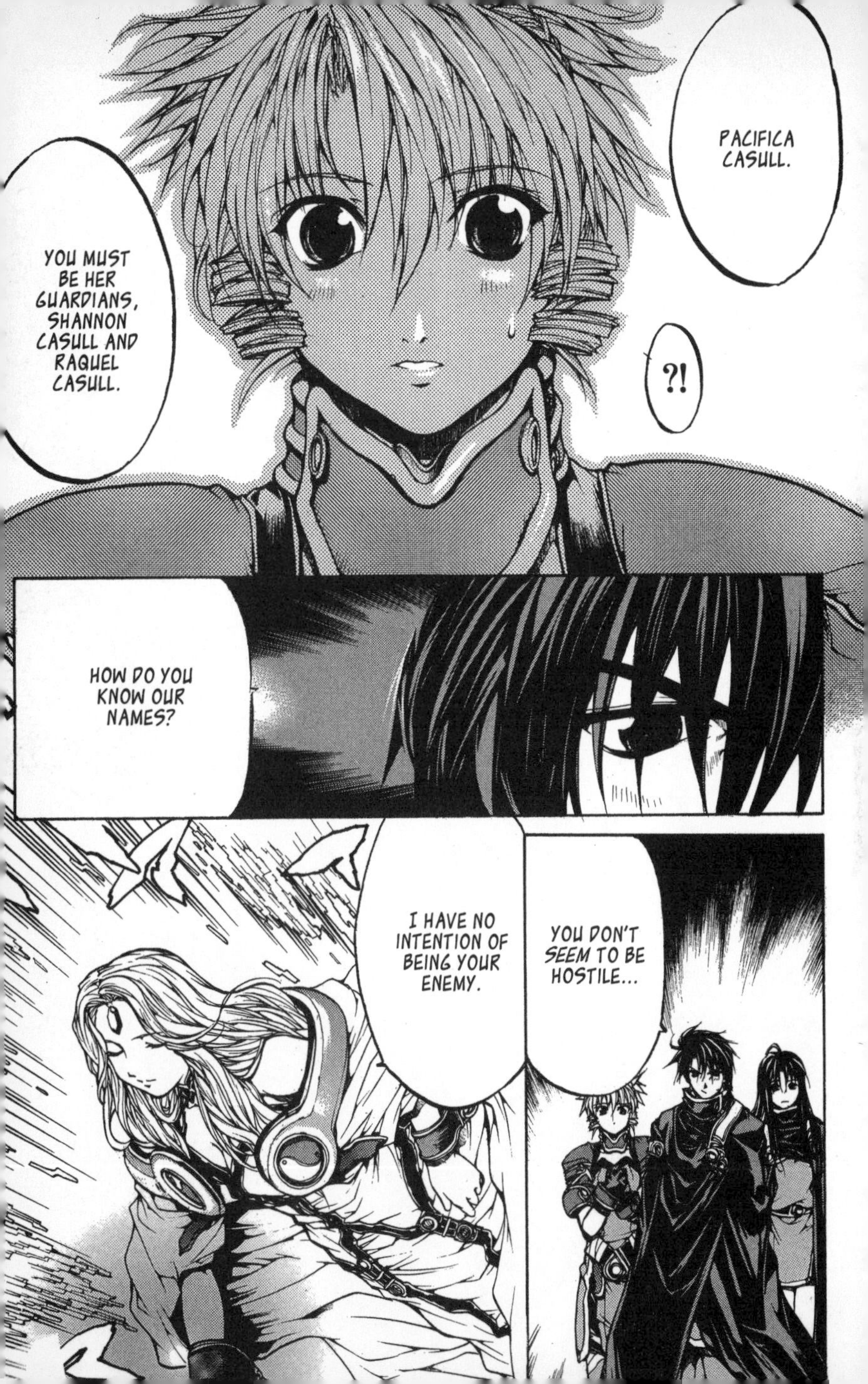
PACIFICA CASULL.
?!
YOU MUST BE HER GUARDIANS, SHANNON CASULL AND RAQUEL CASULL.
HOW DO YOU KNOW OUR NAMES?
YOU DON'T SEEM TO BE HOSTILE...
I HAVE NO INTENTION OF BEING YOUR ENEMY.

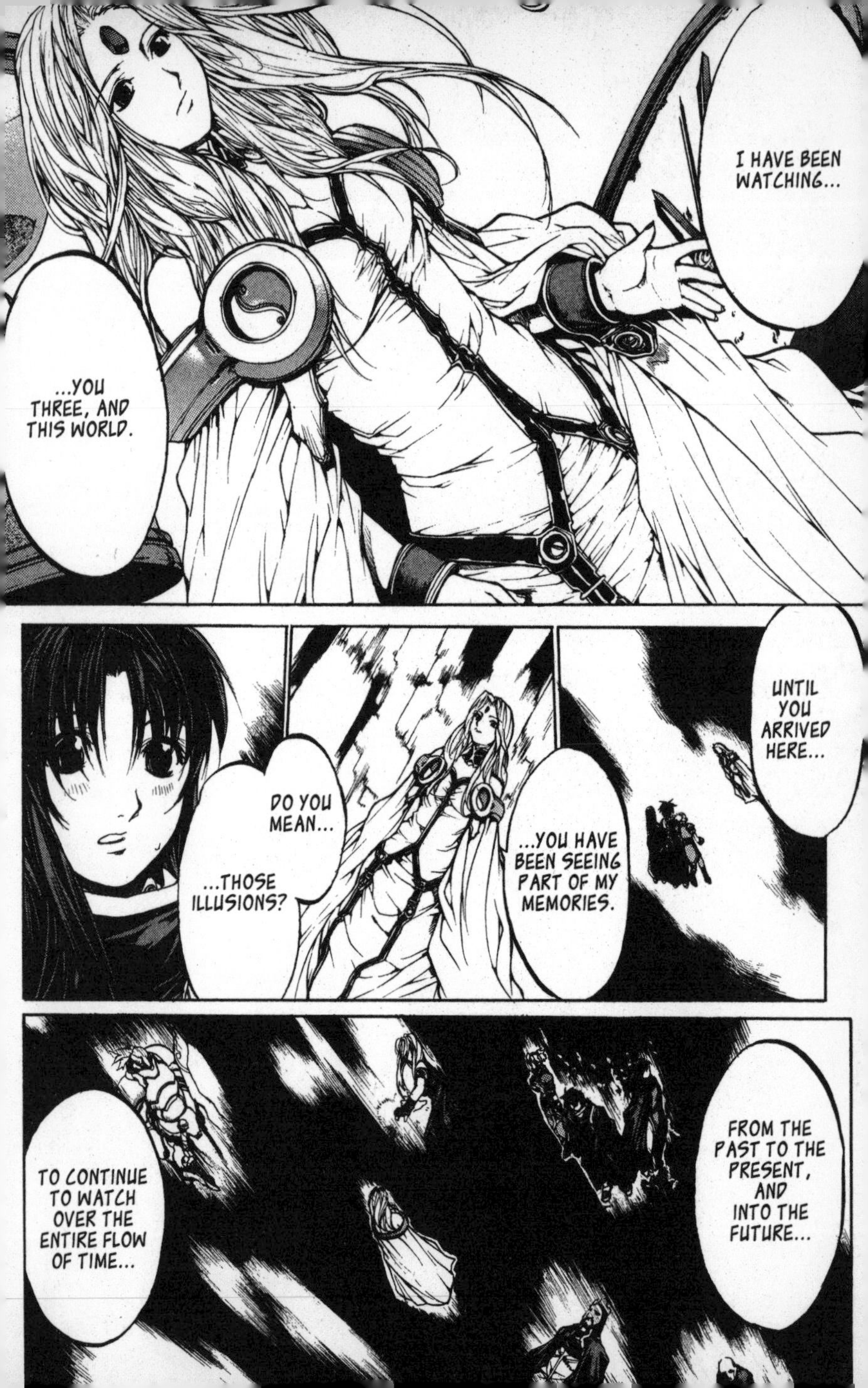
I HAVE BEEN WATCHING...
...YOU THREE, AND THIS WORLD.
UNTIL YOU ARRIVED HERE...
...YOU HAVE BEEN SEEING PART OF MY MEMORIES.
DO YOU MEAN...
...THOSE ILLUSIONS?
FROM THE PAST TO THE PRESENT, AND INTO THE FUTURE...
TO CONTINUE TO WATCH OVER THE ENTIRE FLOW OF TIME...

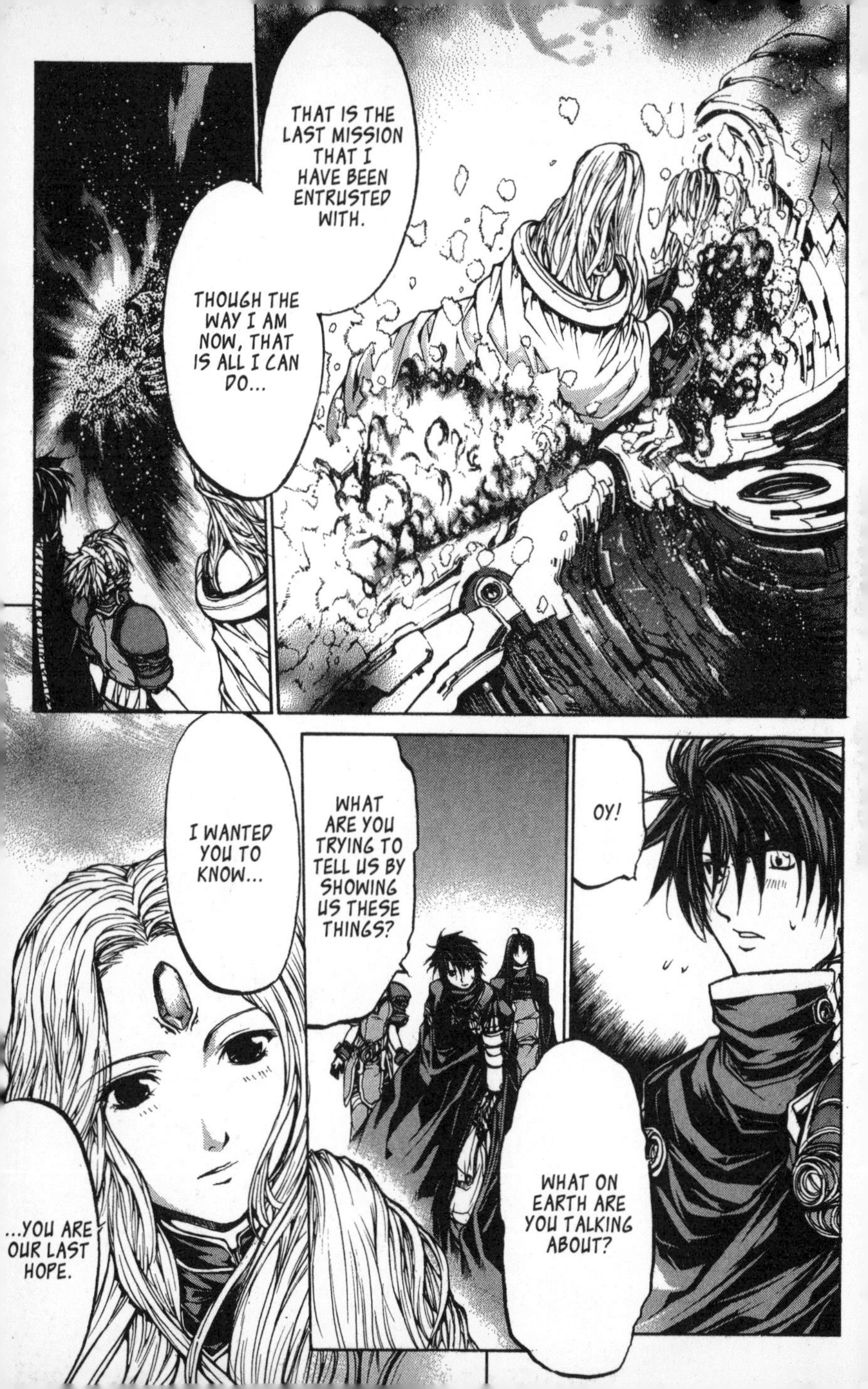
THAT IS THE LAST MISSION THAT I HAVE BEEN ENTRUSTED WITH.
THOUGH THE WAY I AM NOW, THAT IS ALL I CAN DO...
OY!
WHAT ARE YOU TRYING TO TELL US BY SHOWING US THESE THINGS?
I WANTED YOU TO KNOW...
...YOU ARE OUR LAST HOPE.
WHAT ON EARTH ARE YOU TALKING ABOUT?

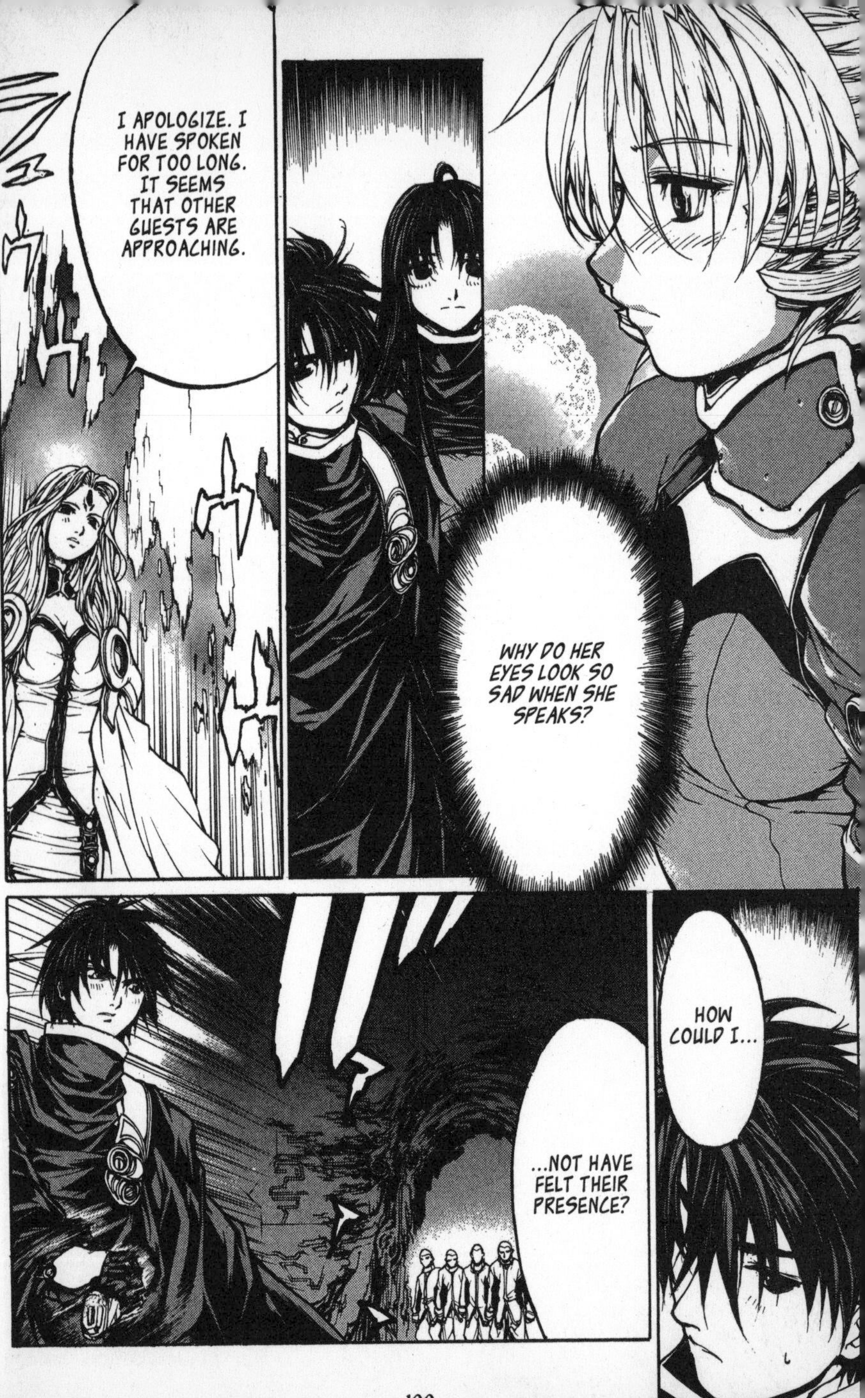
WHY DO HER EYES LOOK SO SAD WHEN SHE SPEAKS?
I APOLOGIZE. I HAVE SPOKEN FOR TOO LONG. IT SEEMS THAT OTHER GUESTS ARE APPROACHING.
HOW COULD I...
...NOT HAVE FELT THEIR PRESENCE?

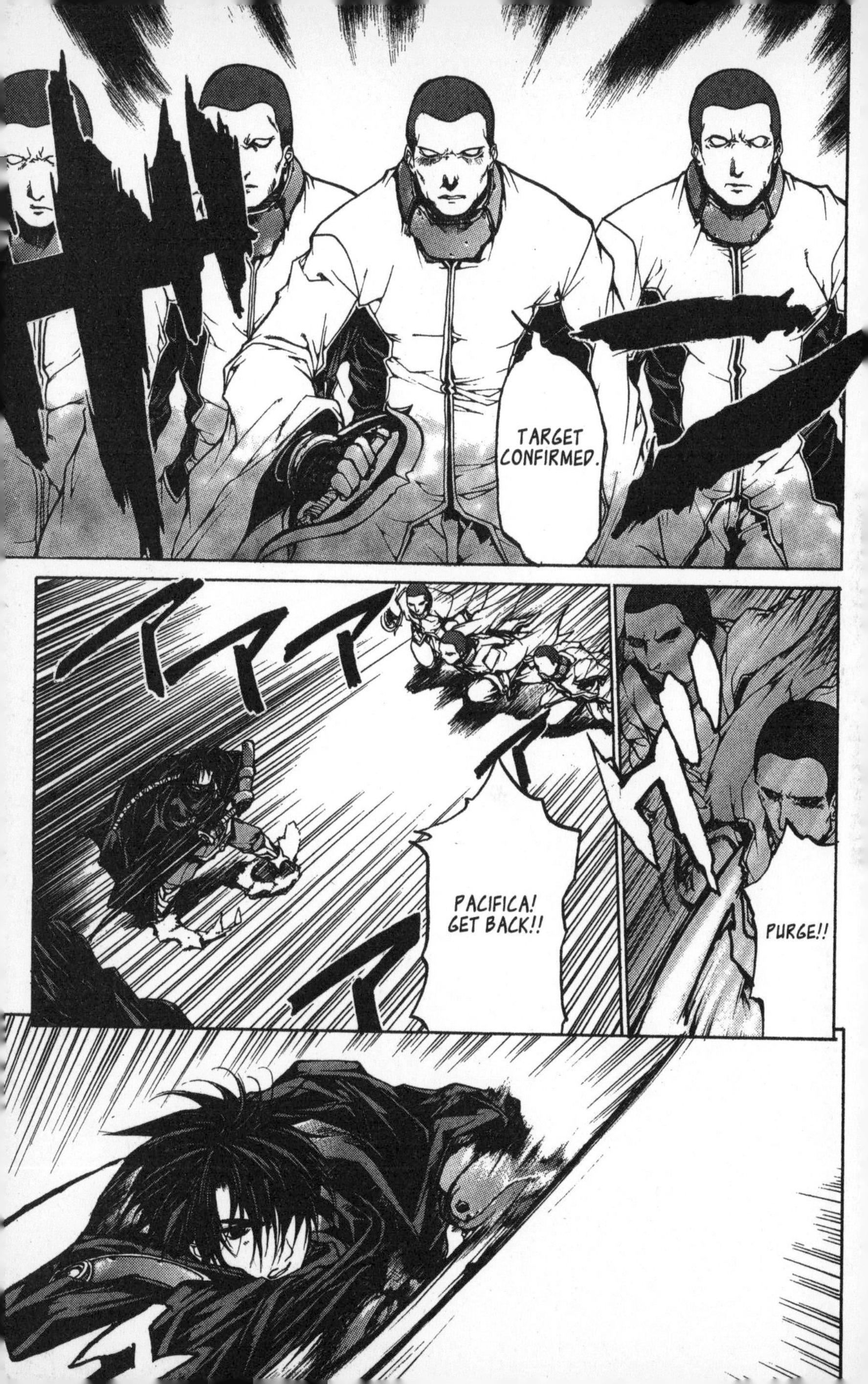
TARGET CONFIRMED.
PURGE!!
PACIFICA! GET BACK!!

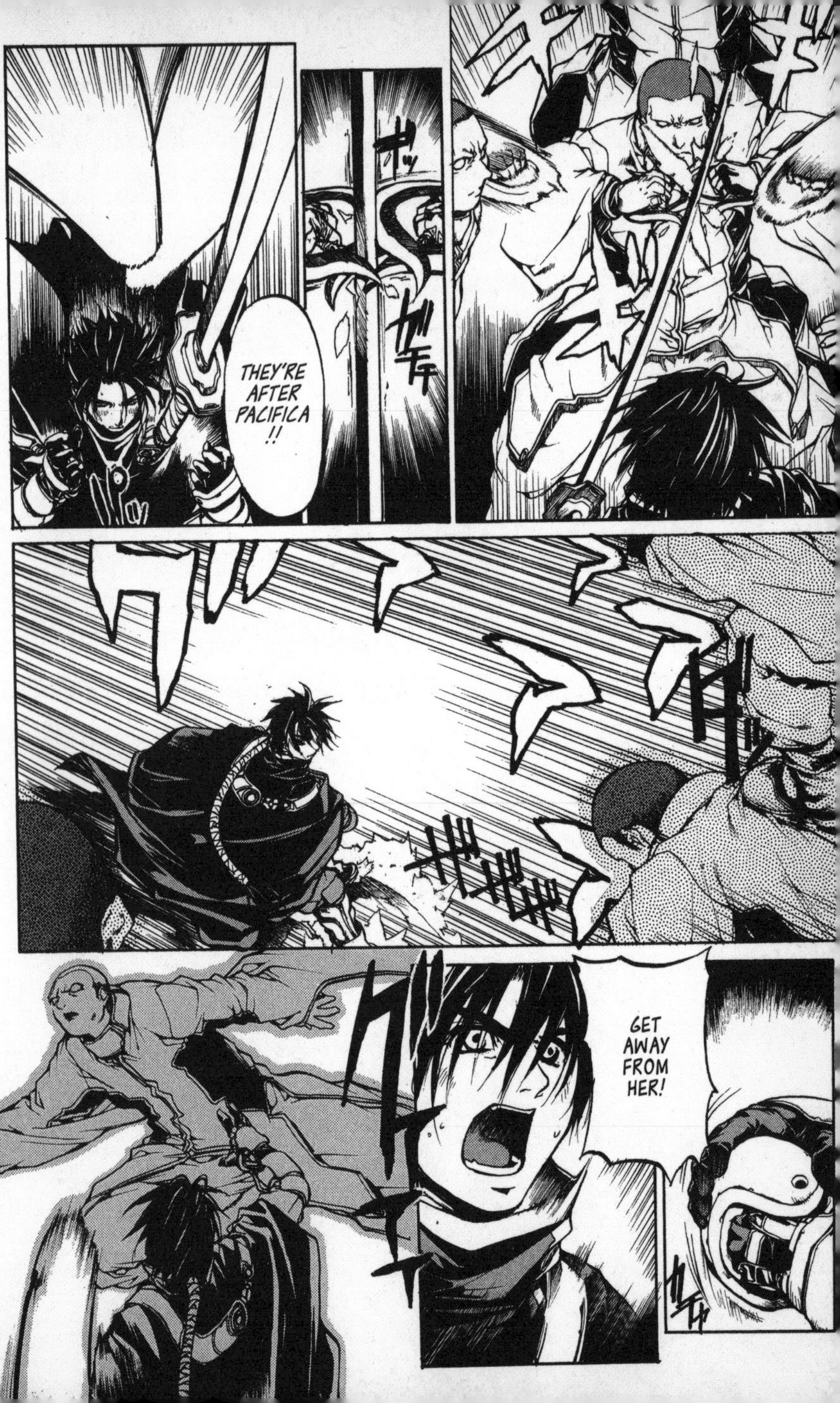
THEY'RE AFTER PACIFICA !!
GET AWAY FROM HER!

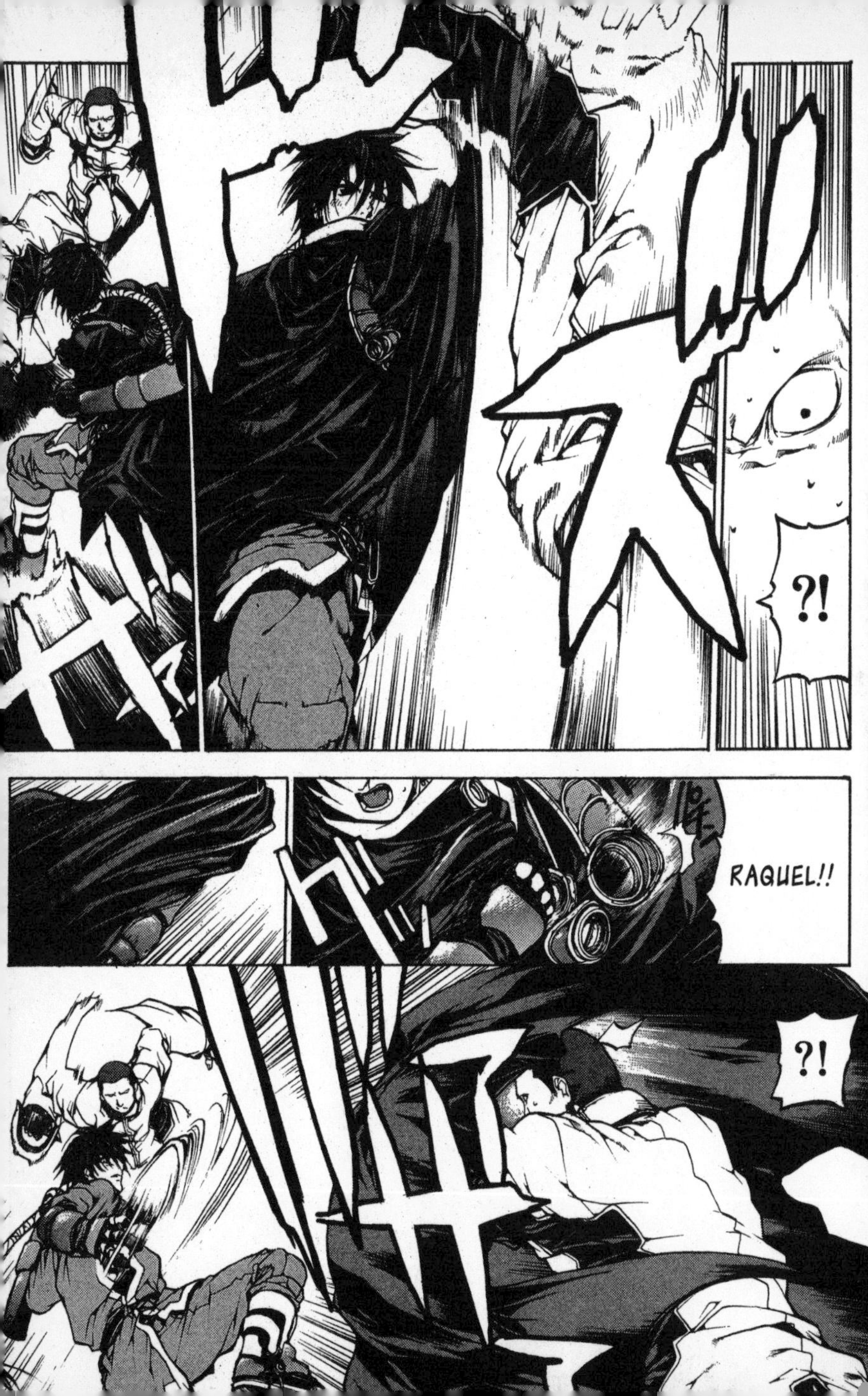
?!
RAQUEL!!
?!

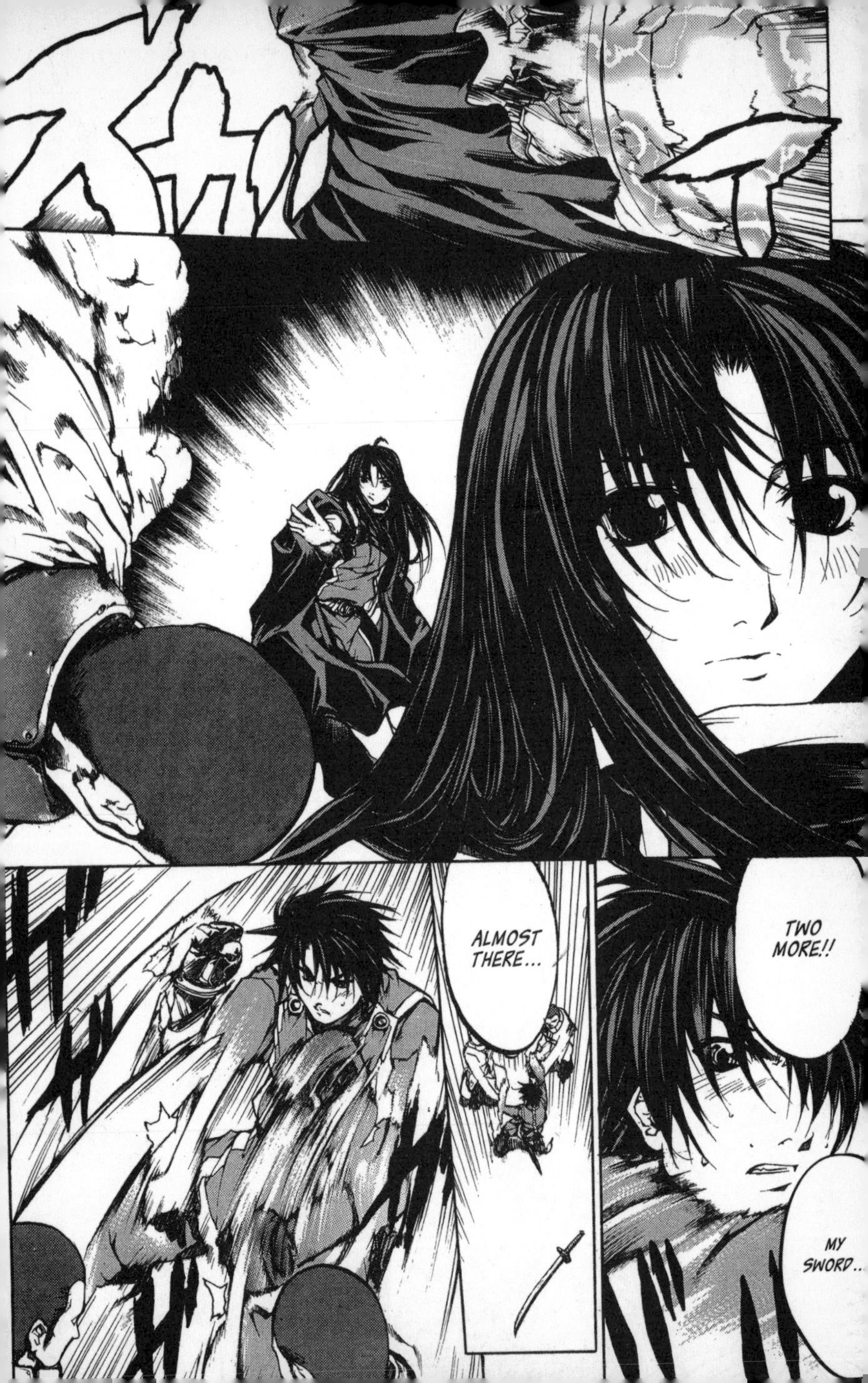
TWO MORE!!
MY SWORD...
ALMOST THERE...

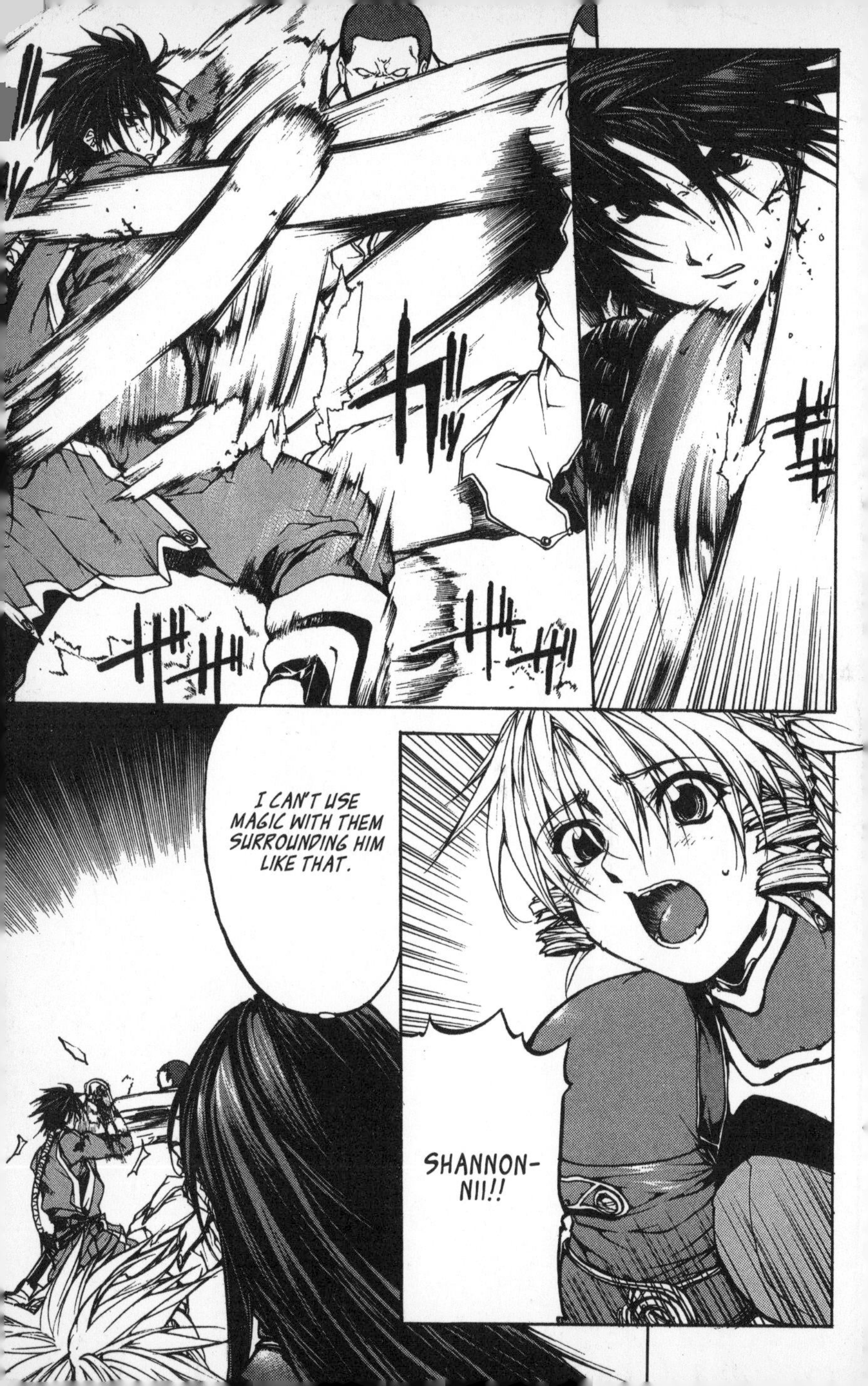
I CAN'T USE MAGIC WITH THEM SURROUNDING HIM LIKE THAT.
SHANNON-NII!!

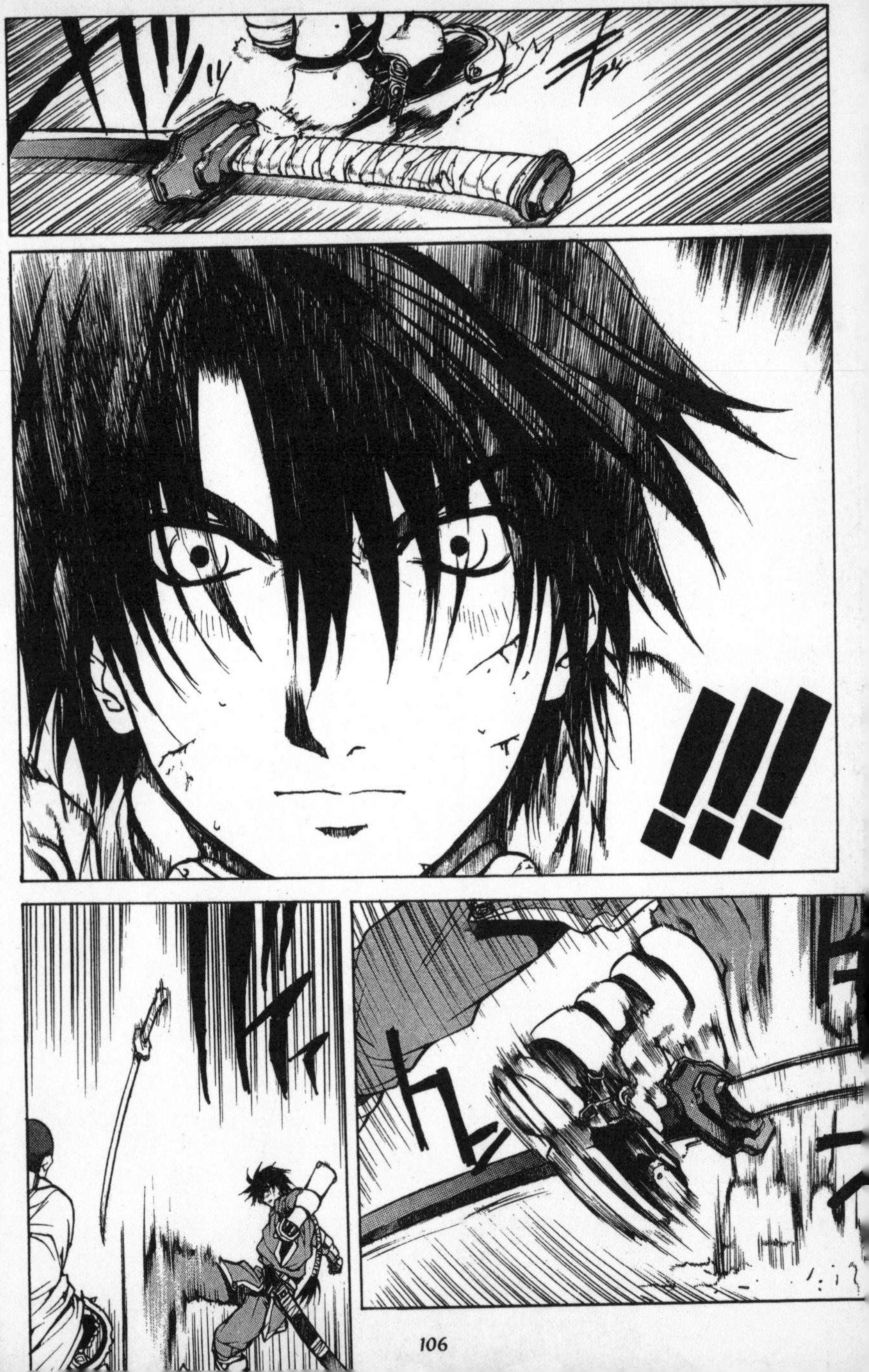
!!!!

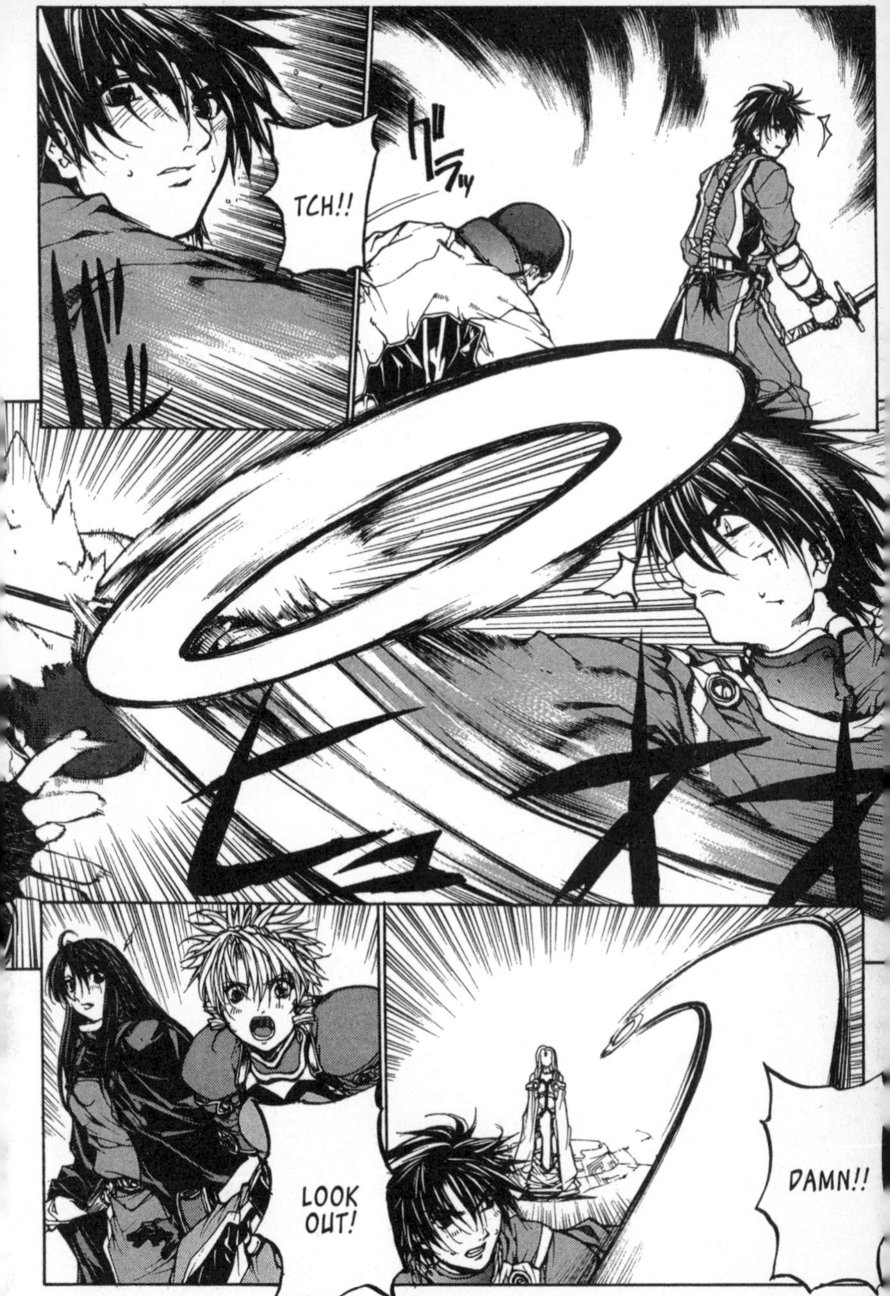
TCH!!
DAMN!!
LOOK OUT!

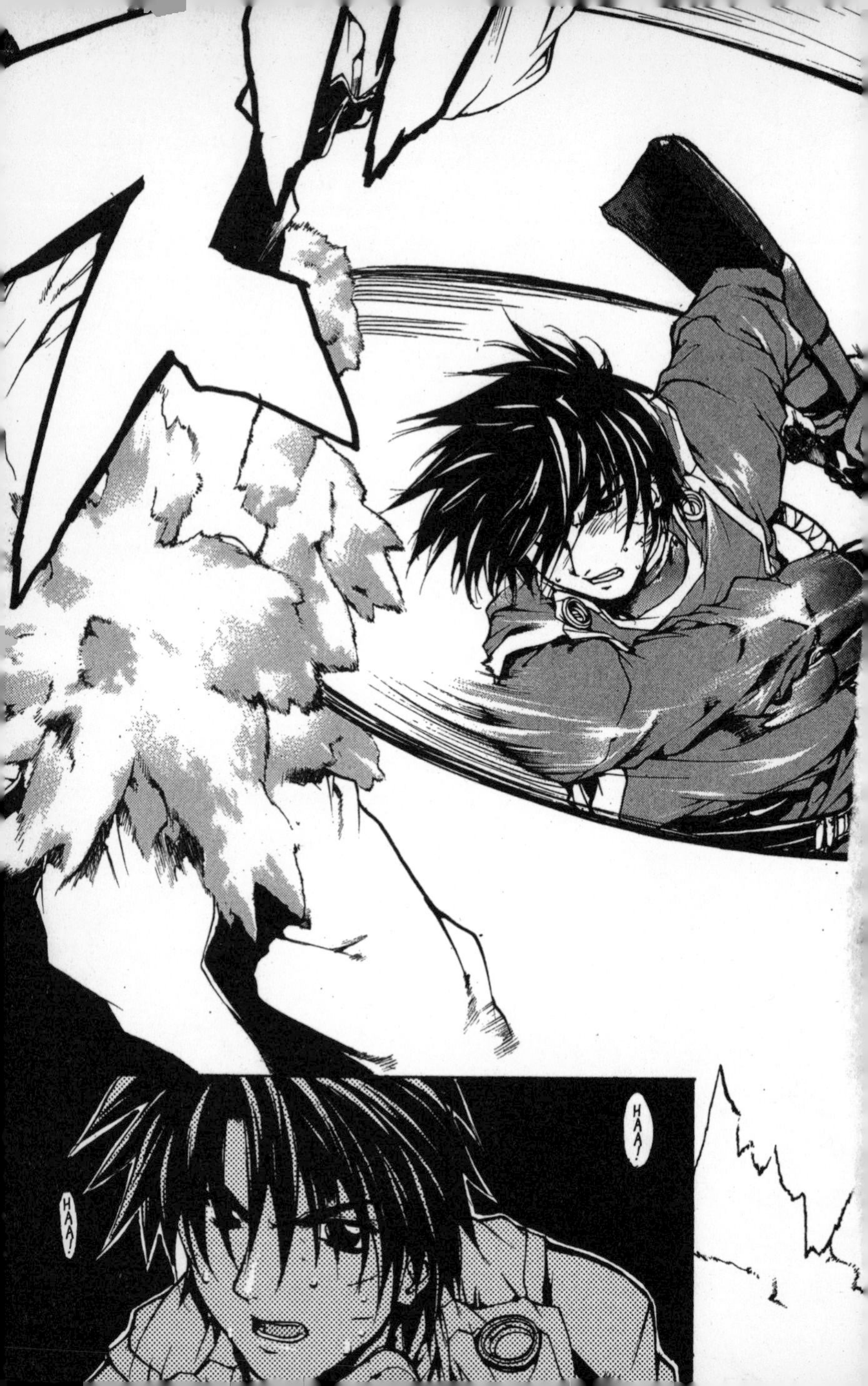
HAA!
HAA!

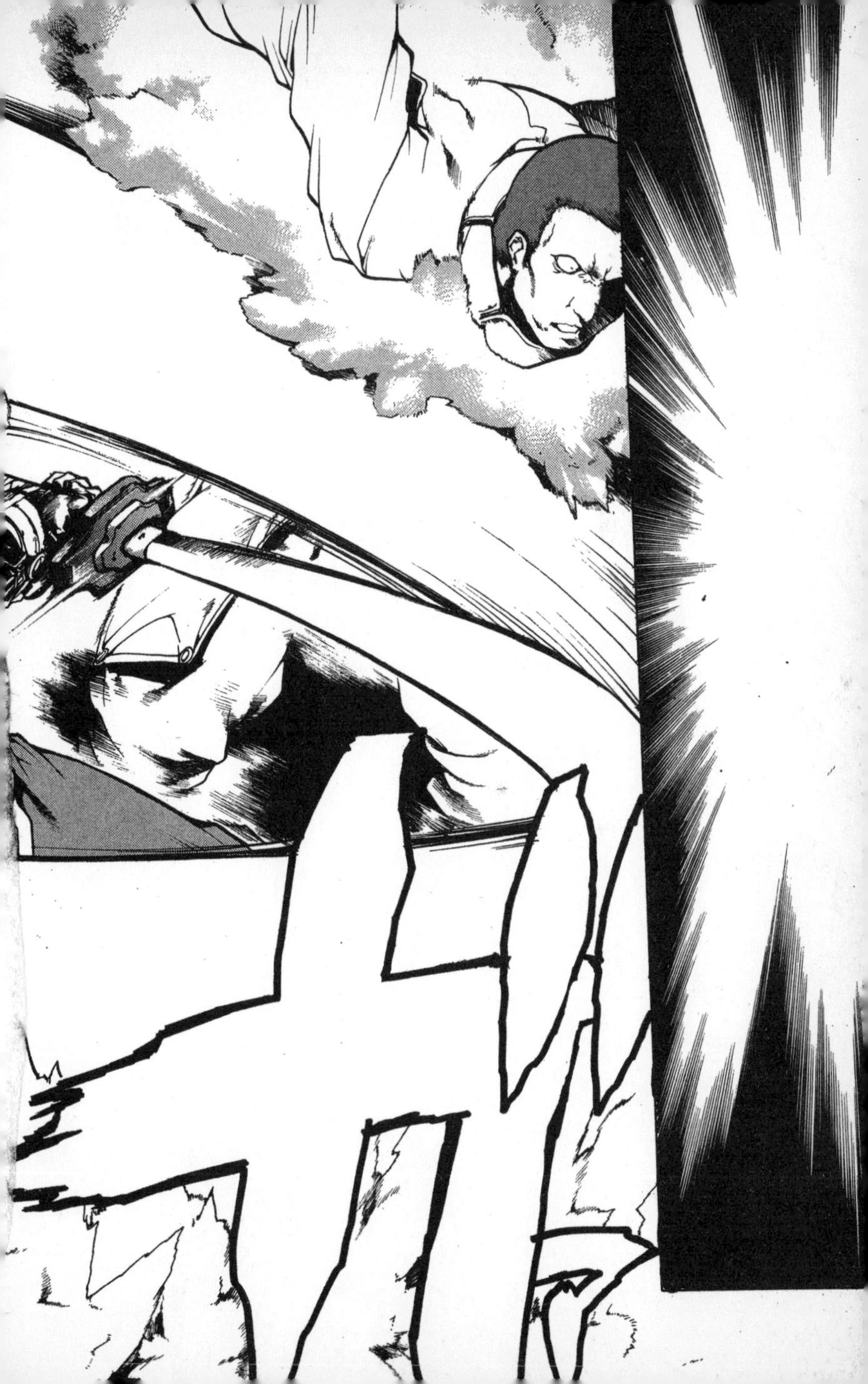

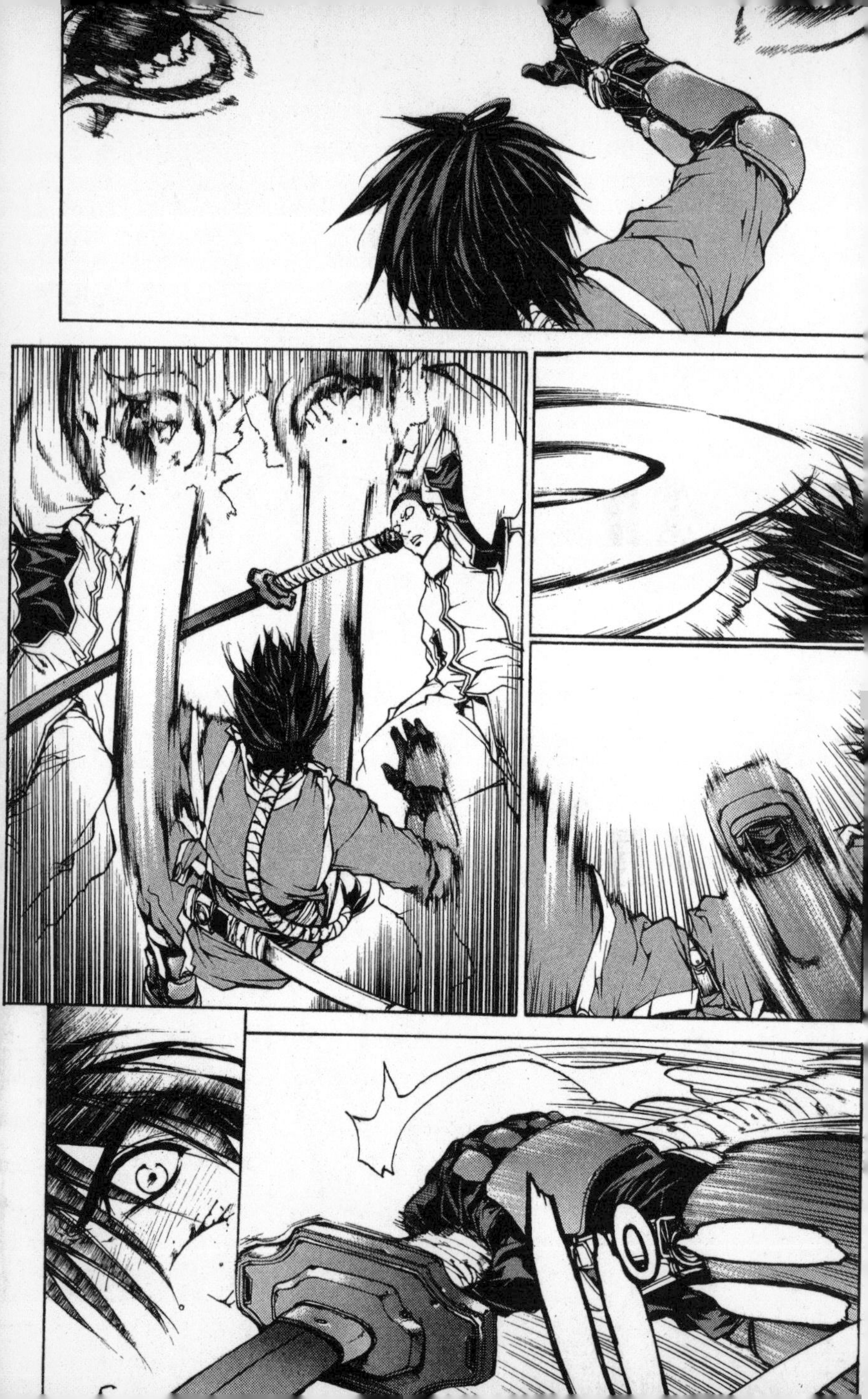

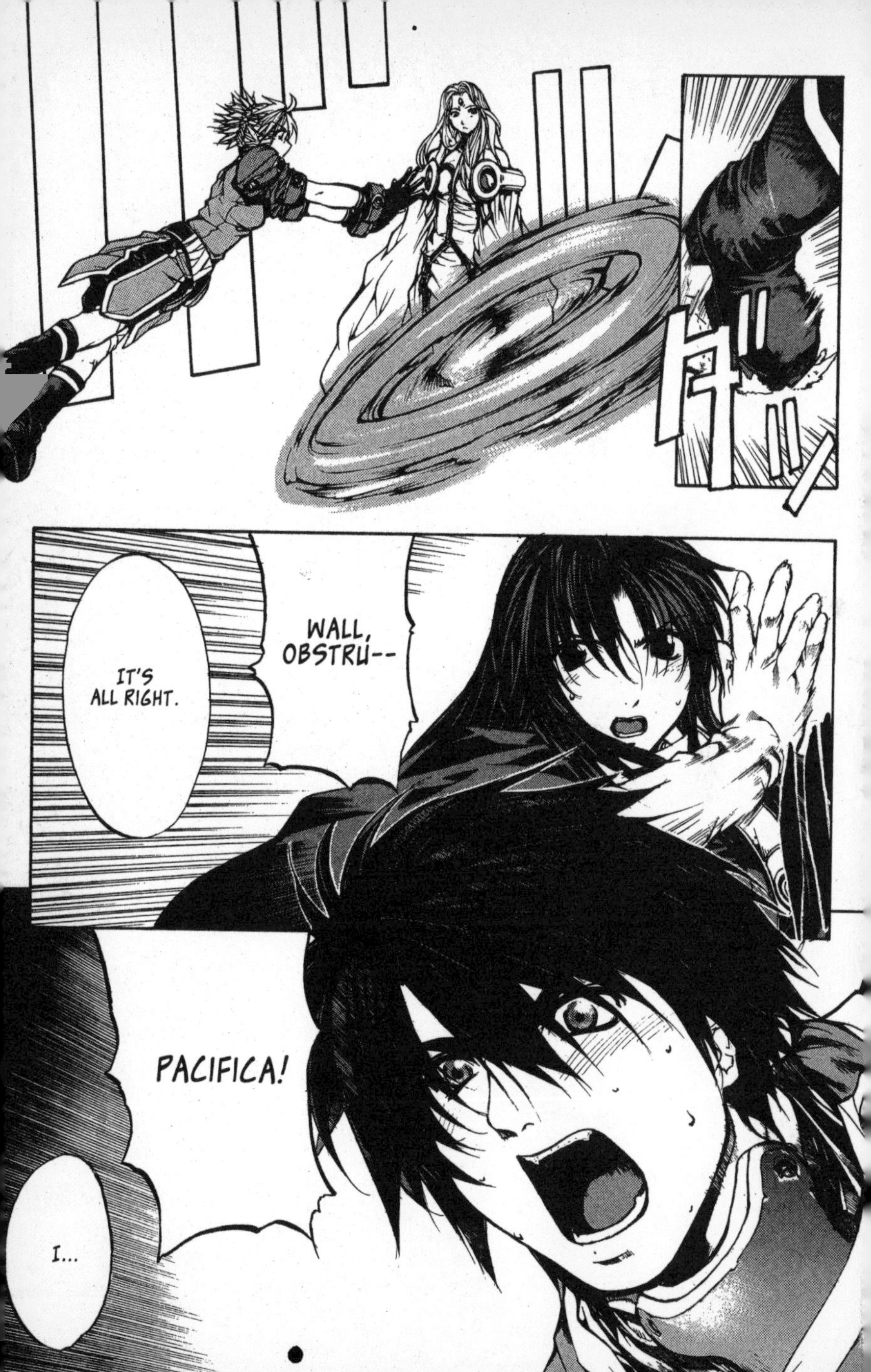
WALL, OBSTRU--
IT'S ALL RIGHT.
PACIFICA!
I...

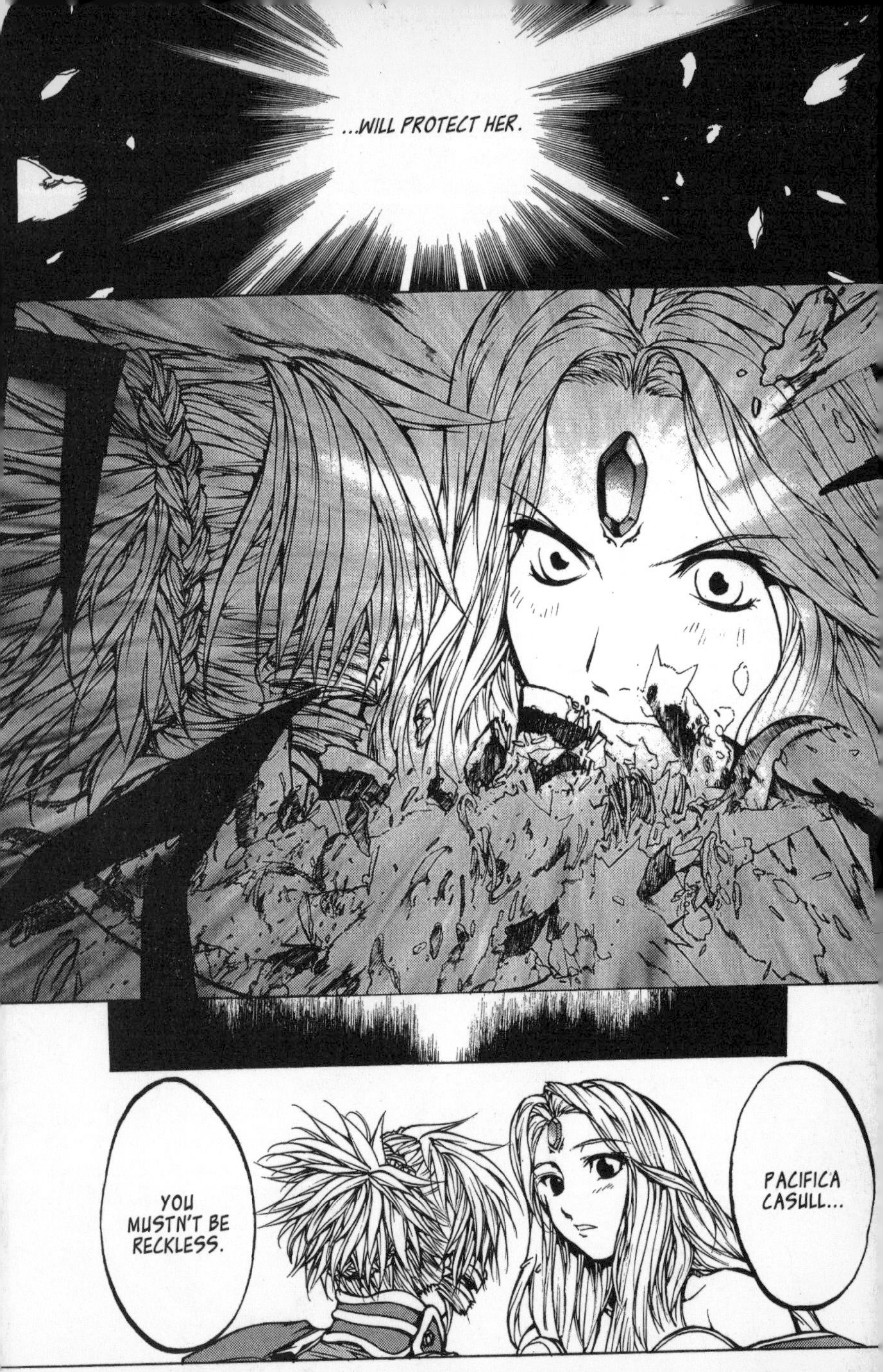
...WILL PROTECT HER.
PACIFICA CASULL...
YOU MUSTN'T BE RECKLESS.

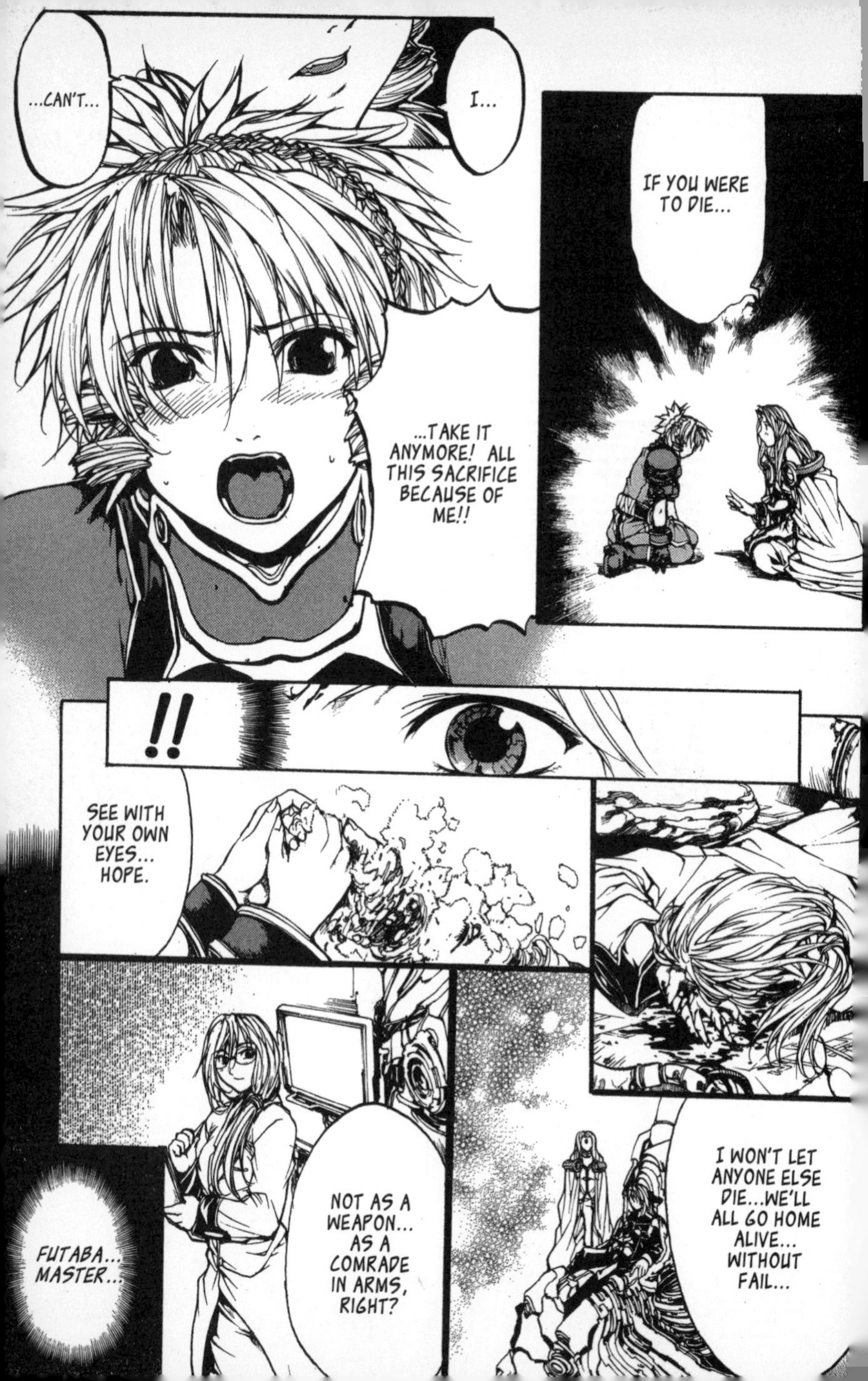
IF YOU WERE TO DIE...
I...
...CAN'T...
...TAKE IT ANYMORE! ALL THIS SACRIFICE BECAUSE OF ME!!
!!
SEE WITH YOUR OWN EYES... HOPE.
I WON'T LET ANYONE ELSE DIE...WE'LL ALL GO HOME ALIVE... WITHOUT FAIL...
NOT AS A WEAPON... AS A COMRADE IN ARMS, RIGHT?
FUTABA... MASTER...

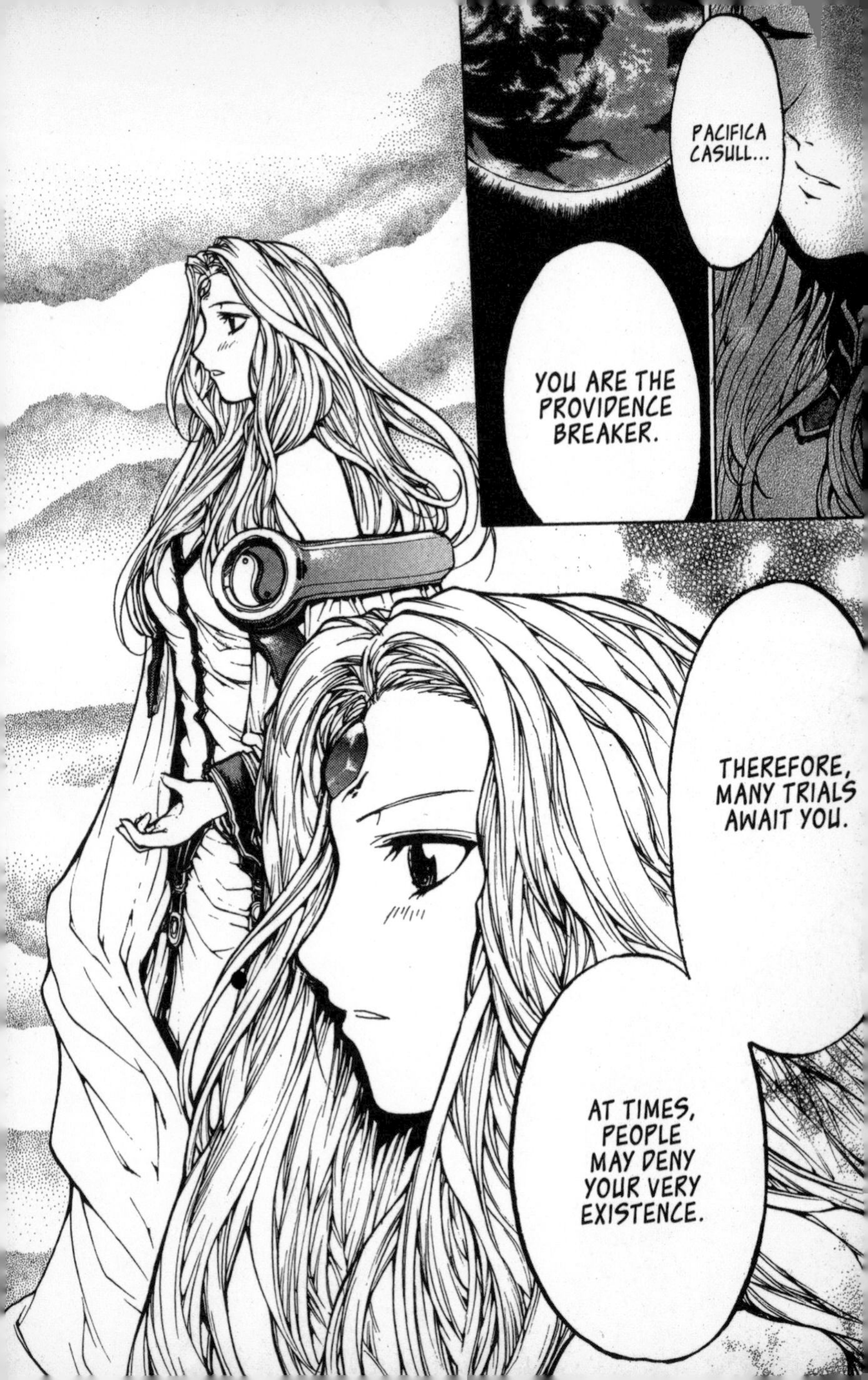
PACIFICA CASULL...
YOU ARE THE PROVIDENCE BREAKER.
THEREFORE, MANY TRIALS AWAIT YOU.
AT TIMES, PEOPLE MAY DENY YOUR VERY EXISTENCE.

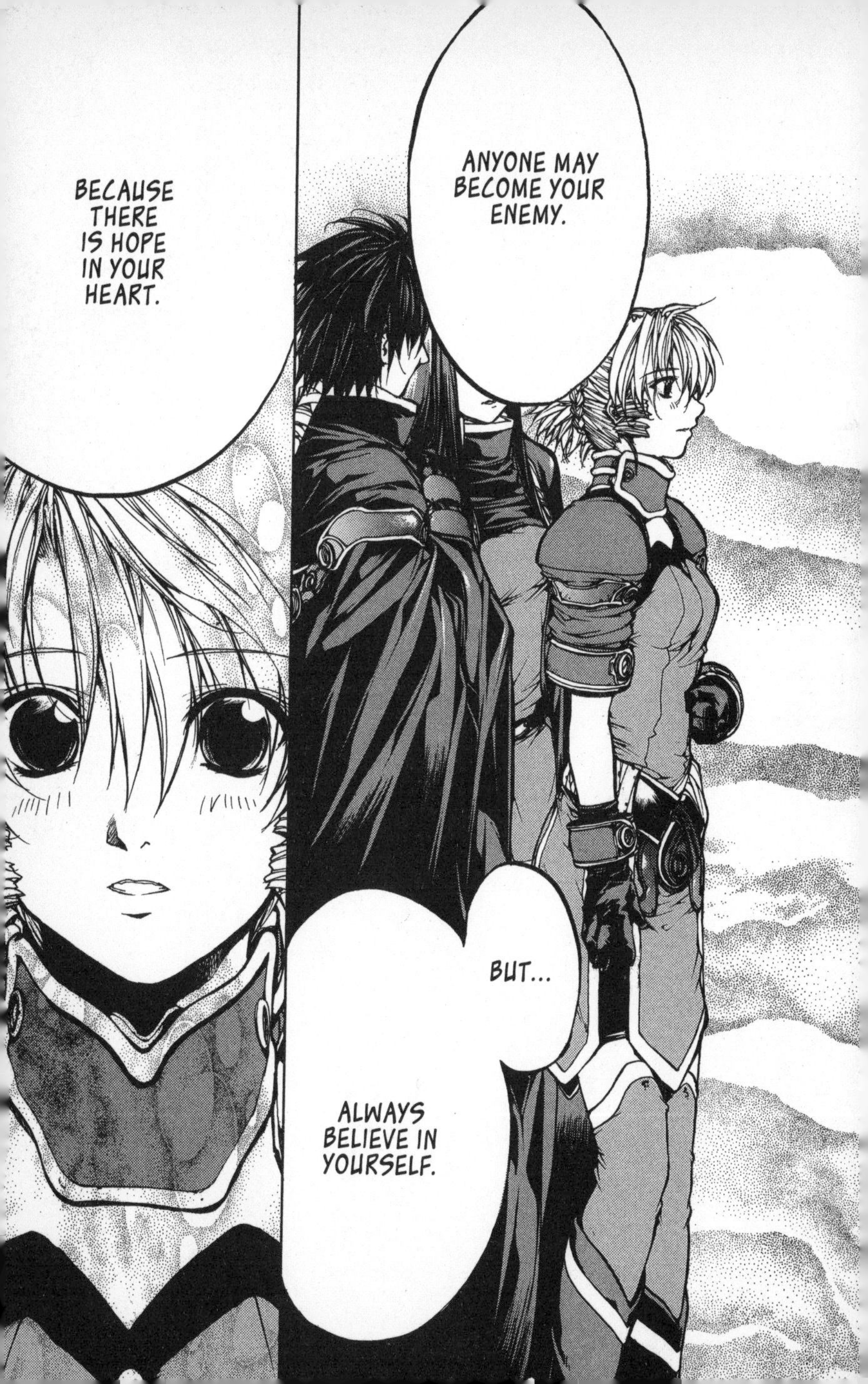
ANYONE MAY BECOME YOUR ENEMY.
BUT...
ALWAYS BELIEVE IN YOURSELF.
BECAUSE THERE IS HOPE IN YOUR HEART.

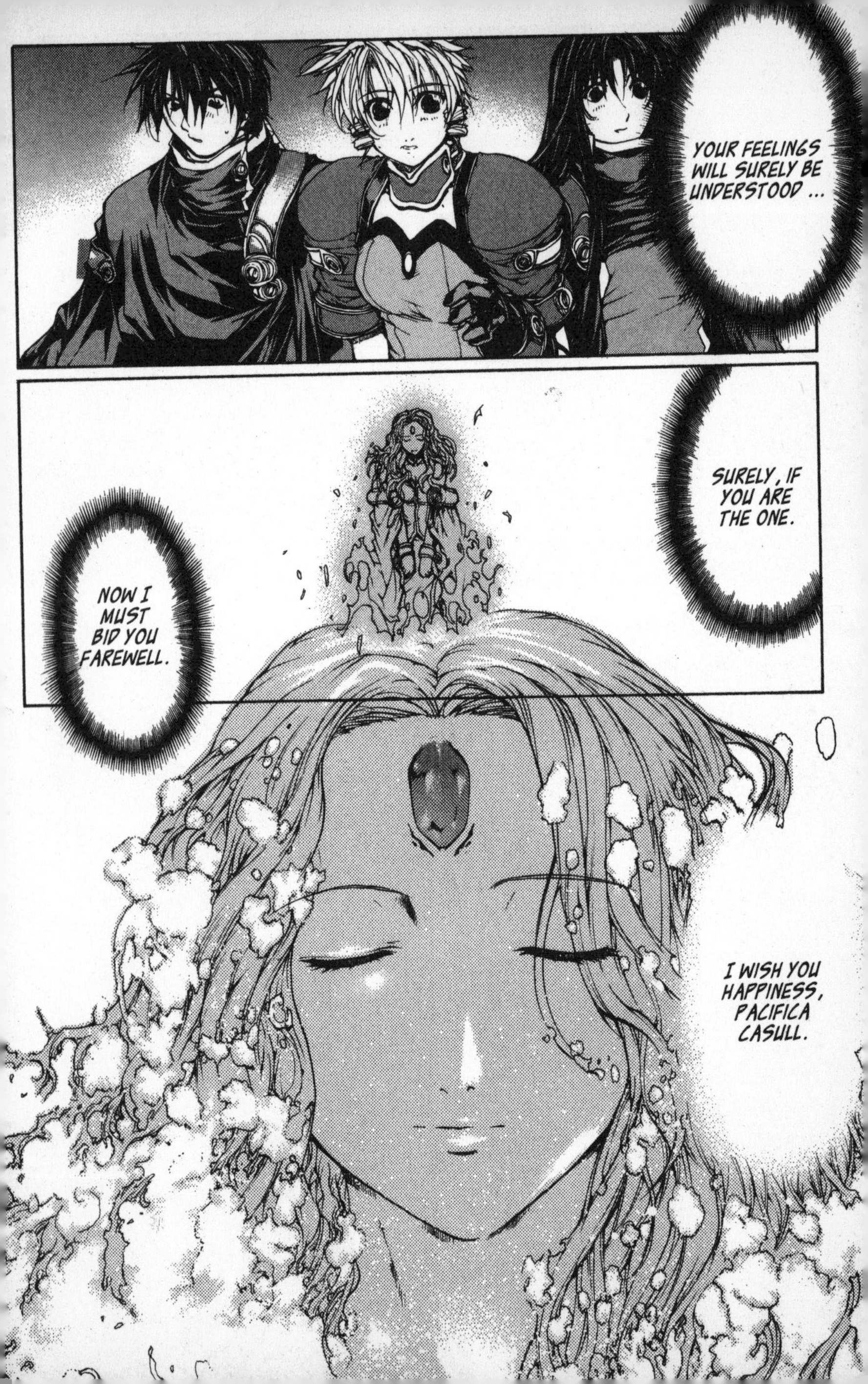
YOUR FEELINGS WILL SURELY BE UNDERSTOOD ...
SURELY, IF YOU ARE THE ONE.
NOW I MUST BID YOU FAREWELL.
I WISH YOU HAPPINESS, PACIFICA CASULL.

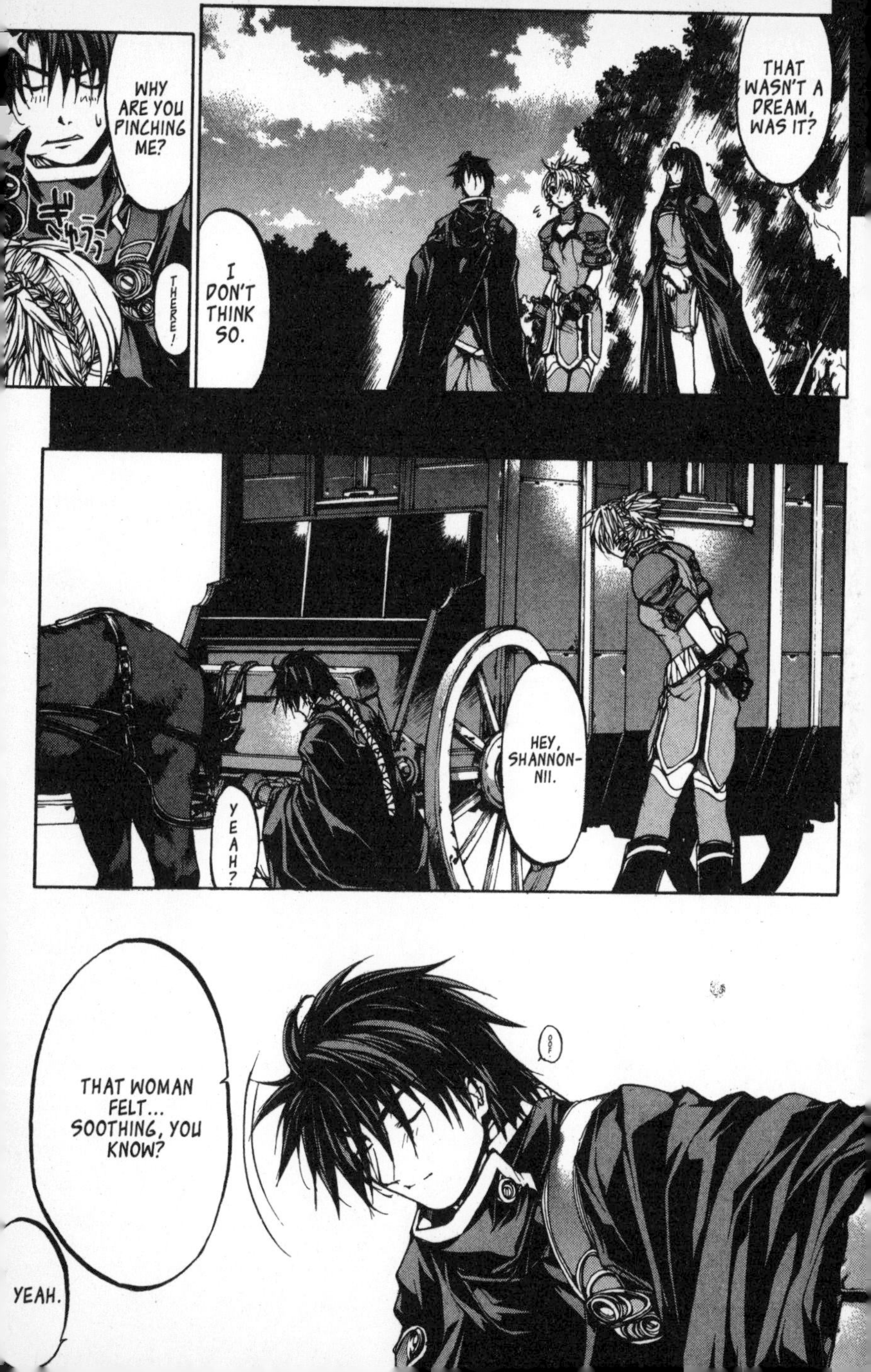
THAT WASN'T A DREAM, WAS IT?
I DON'T THINK SO.
WHY ARE YOU PINCHING ME?
THERE!
HEY, SHANNON-NII.
YEAH?
OOF.
THAT WOMAN FELT... SOOTHING, YOU KNOW?
YEAH.

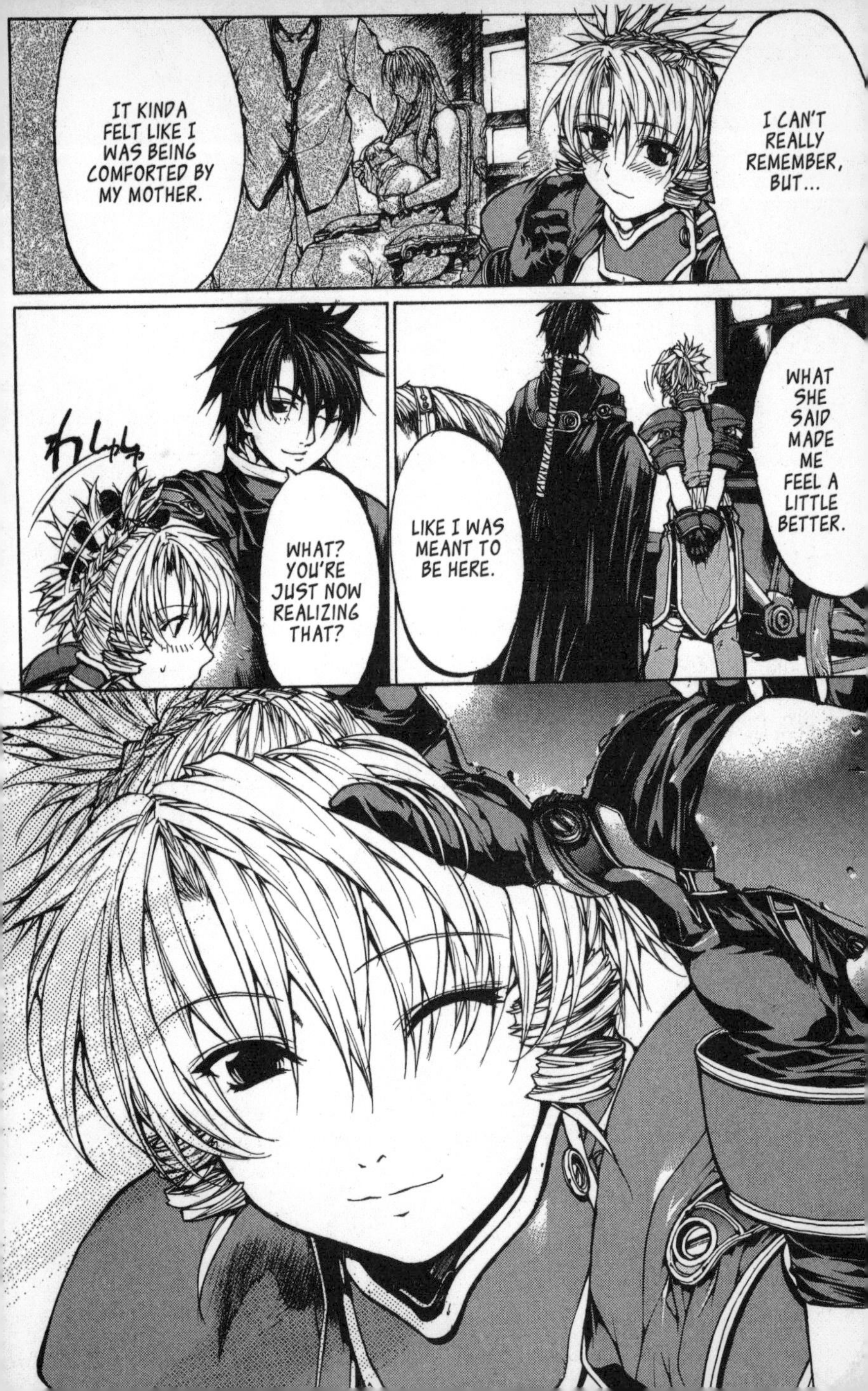
I CAN'T REALLY REMEMBER, BUT...
IT KINDA FELT LIKE I WAS BEING COMFORTED BY MY MOTHER.
WHAT SHE SAID MADE ME FEEL A LITTLE BETTER.
LIKE I WAS MEANT TO BE HERE.
WHAT? YOU'RE JUST NOW REALIZING THAT?

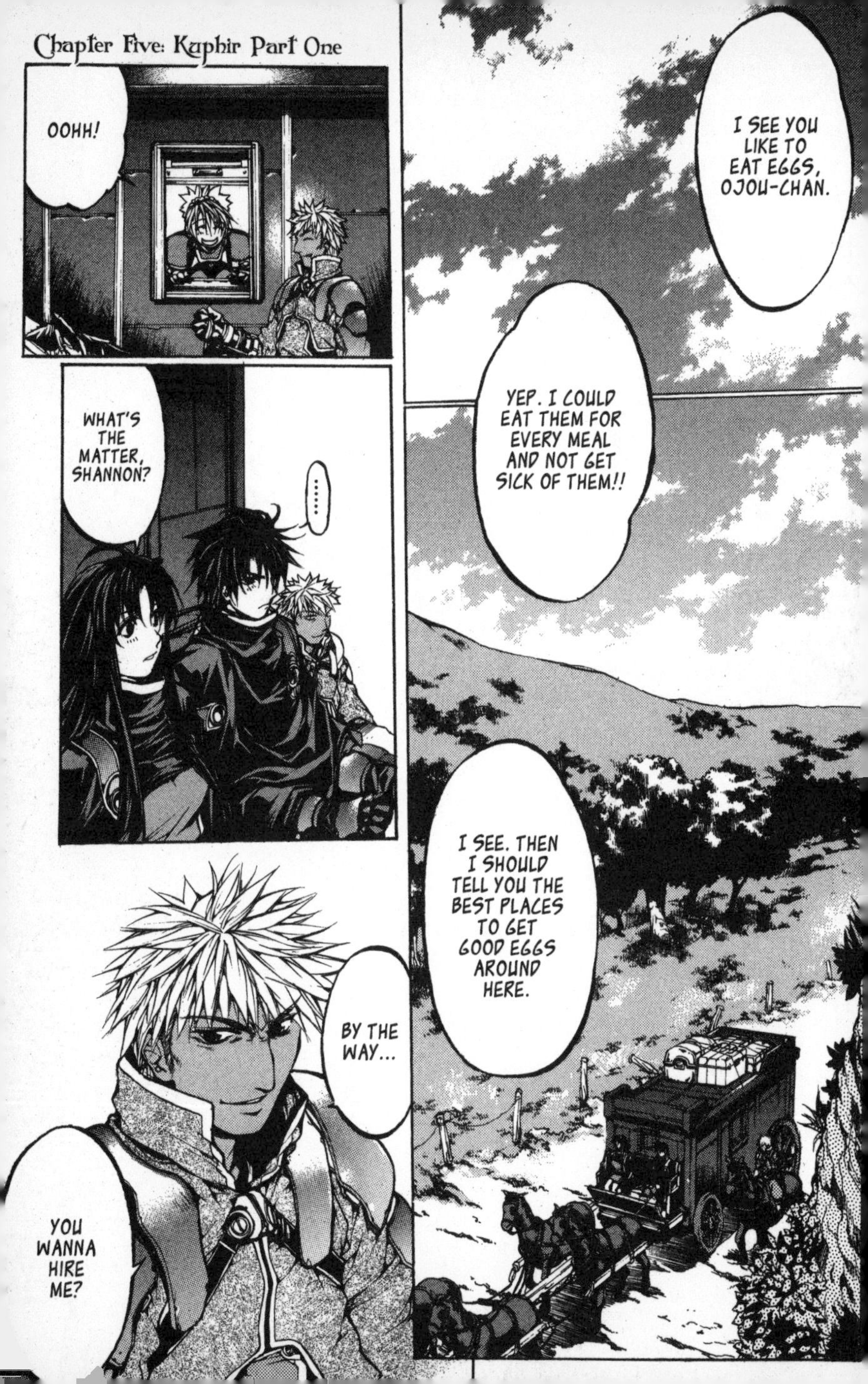
I SEE YOU LIKE TO EAT EGGS, OJOU-CHAN.
YEP. I COULD EAT THEM FOR EVERY MEAL AND NOT GET SICK OF THEM!!
I SEE. THEN I SHOULD TELL YOU THE BEST PLACES TO GET GOOD EGGS AROUND HERE.
OOHH!
WHAT'S THE MATTER, SHANNON?
......
BY THE WAY...
YOU WANNA HIRE ME?

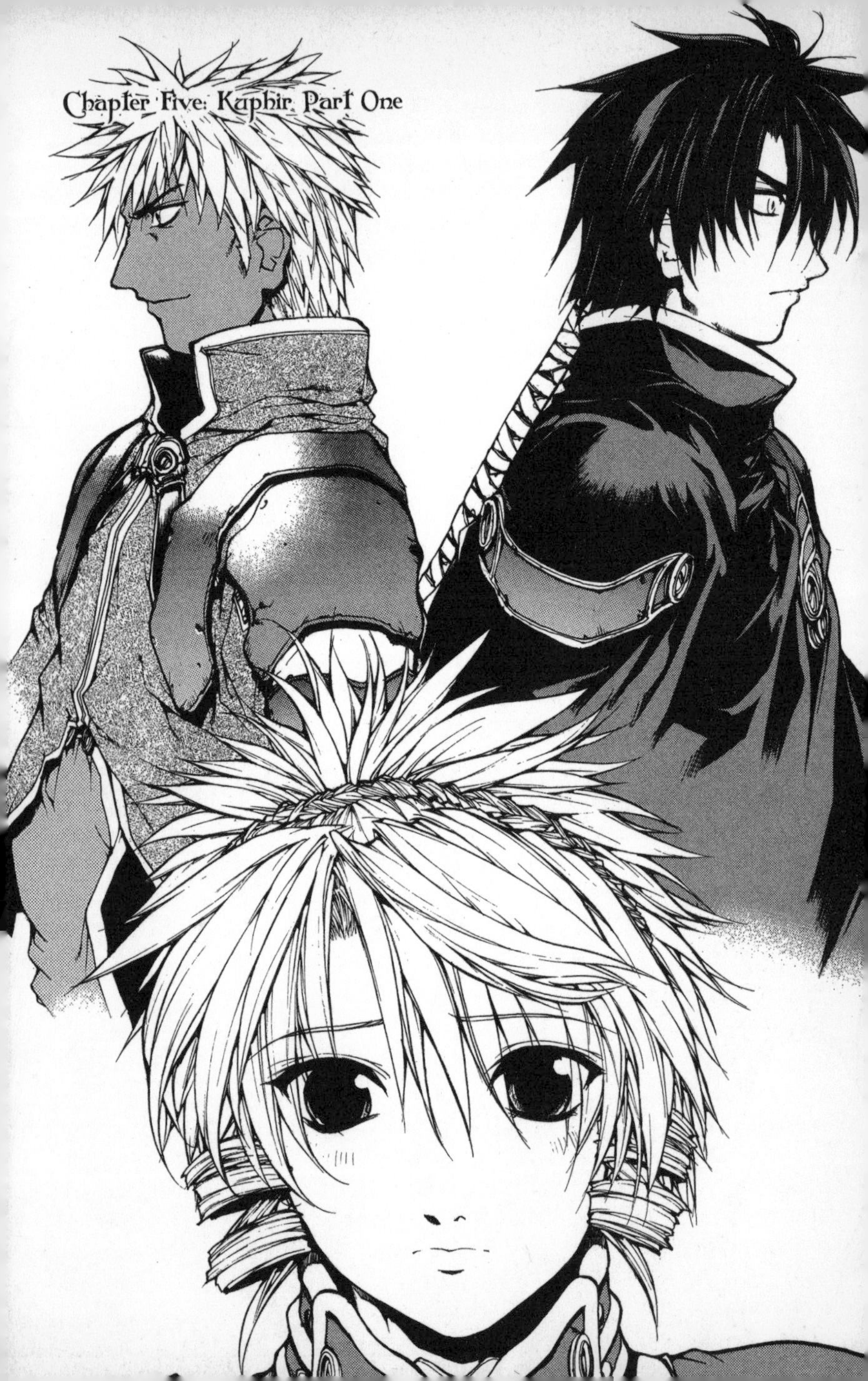
Chapter Five: Kuphir Part One

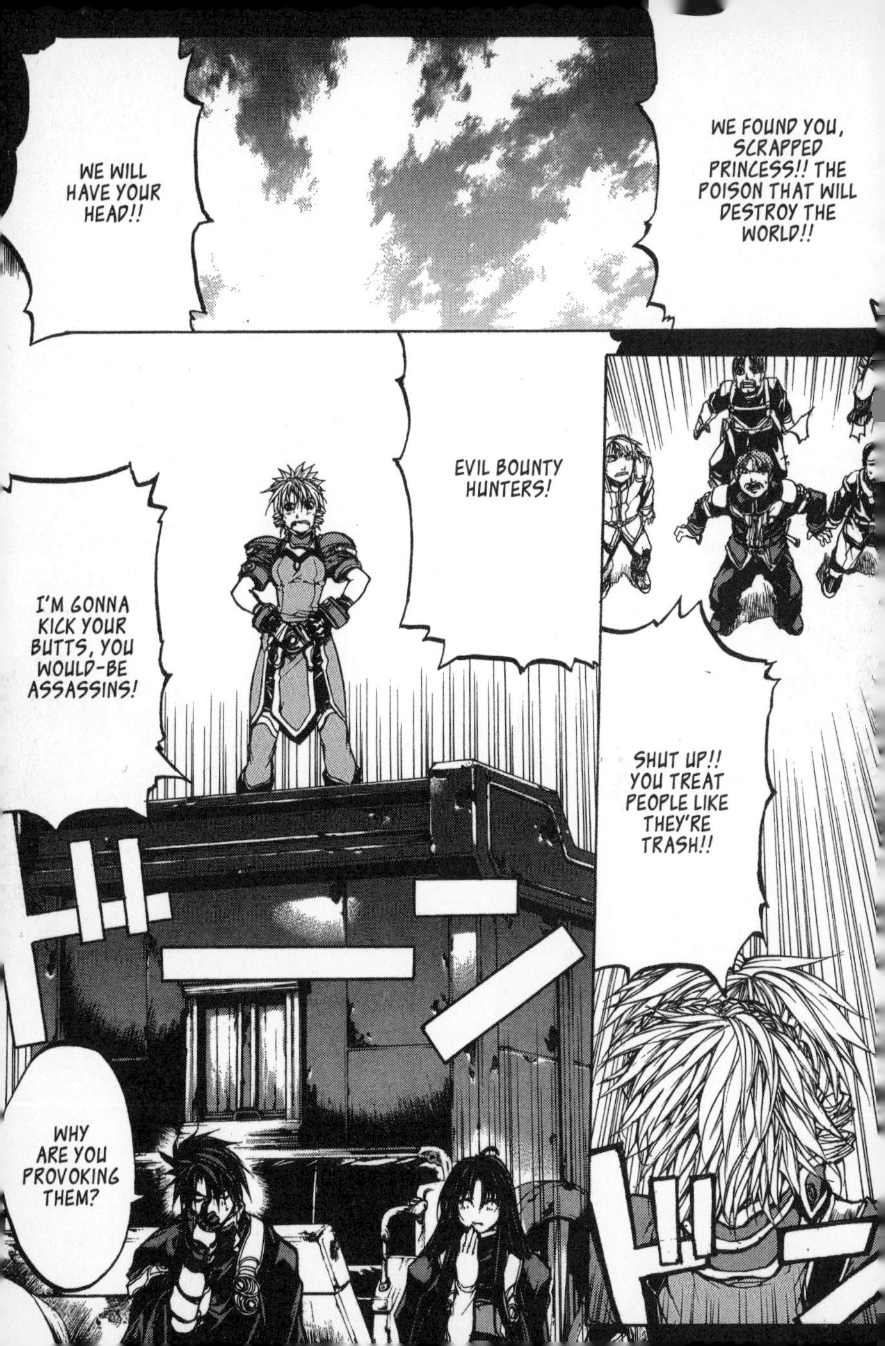
WE FOUND YOU, SCRAPPED PRINCESS!! THE POISON THAT WILL DESTROY THE WORLD!!
WE WILL HAVE YOUR HEAD!!
SHUT UP!! YOU TREAT PEOPLE LIKE THEY'RE TRASH!!
EVIL BOUNTY HUNTERS!
I'M GONNA KICK YOUR BUTTS, YOU WOULD-BE ASSASSINS!
WHY ARE YOU PROVOKING THEM?

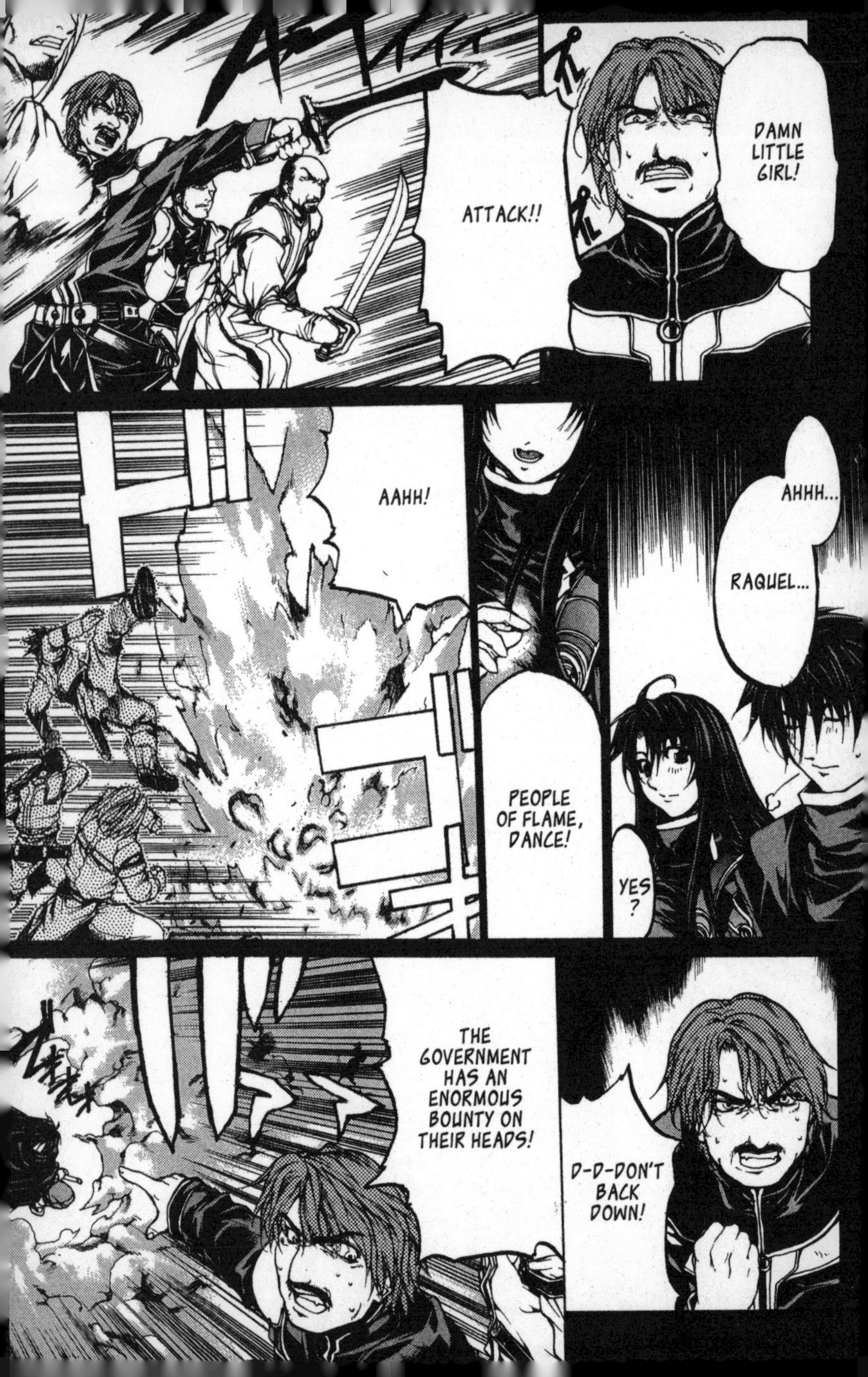
DAMN LITTLE GIRL!
ATTACK!!
AHHH...
RAQUEL...
YES?
PEOPLE OF FLAME, DANCE!
AAHH!
D-D-DON'T BACK DOWN!
THE GOVERNMENT HAS AN ENORMOUS BOUNTY ON THEIR HEADS!

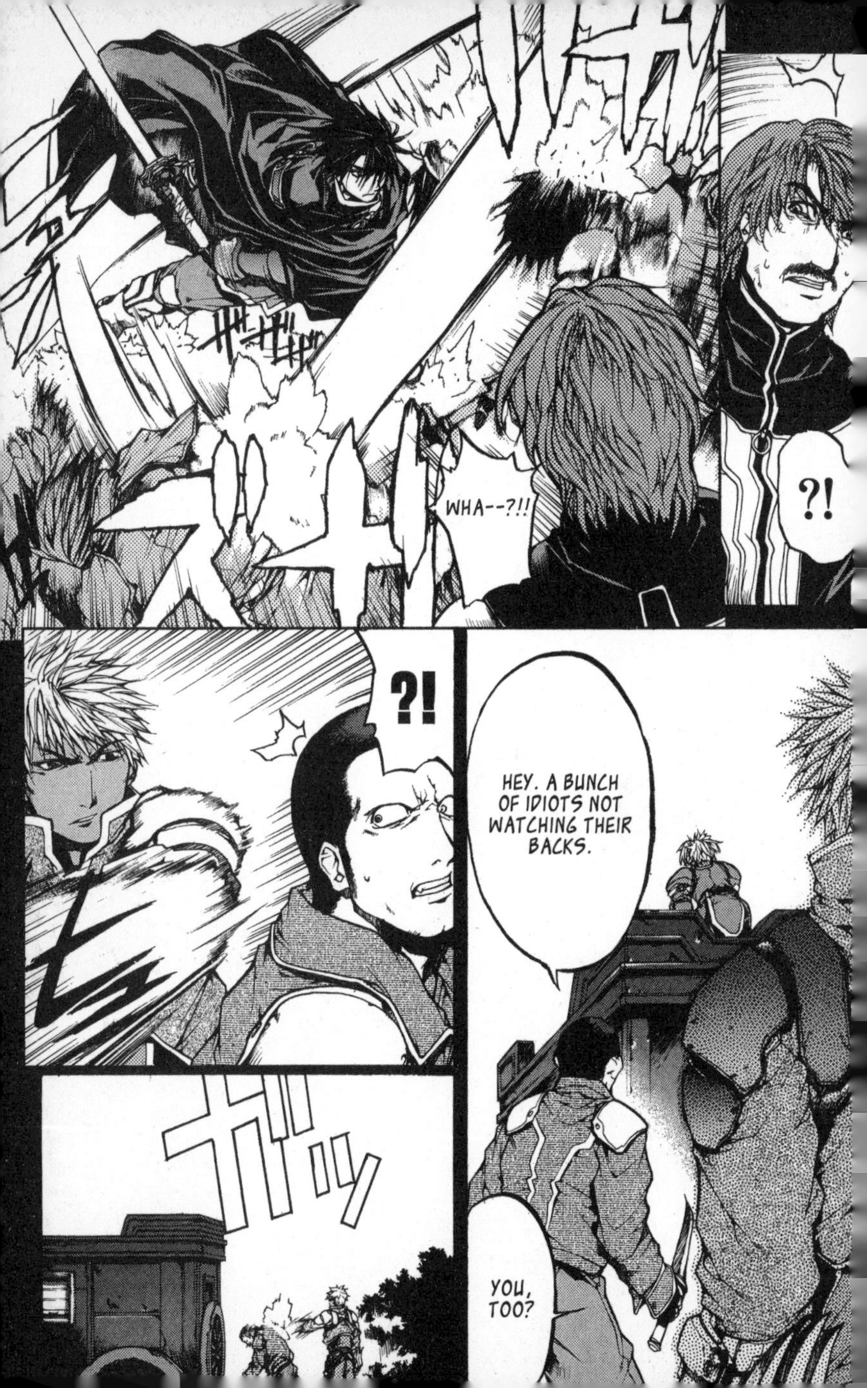
?!
WHA--?!!
HEY. A BUNCH OF IDIOTS NOT WATCHING THEIR BACKS.
YOU, TOO?
?!

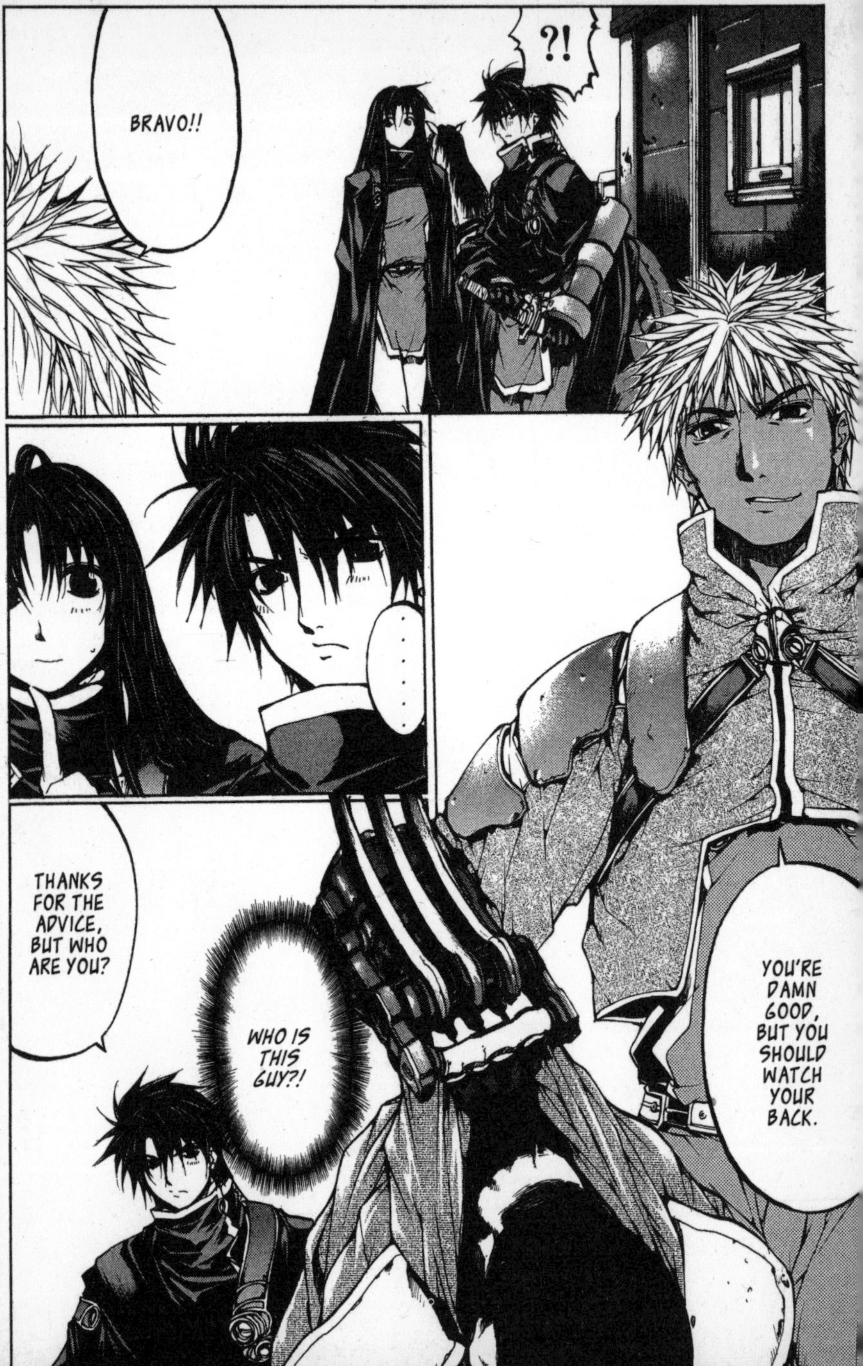
?!
BRAVO!!
YOU'RE DAMN GOOD, BUT YOU SHOULD WATCH YOUR BACK.
......
THANKS FOR THE ADVICE, BUT WHO ARE YOU?
WHO IS THIS GUY?!

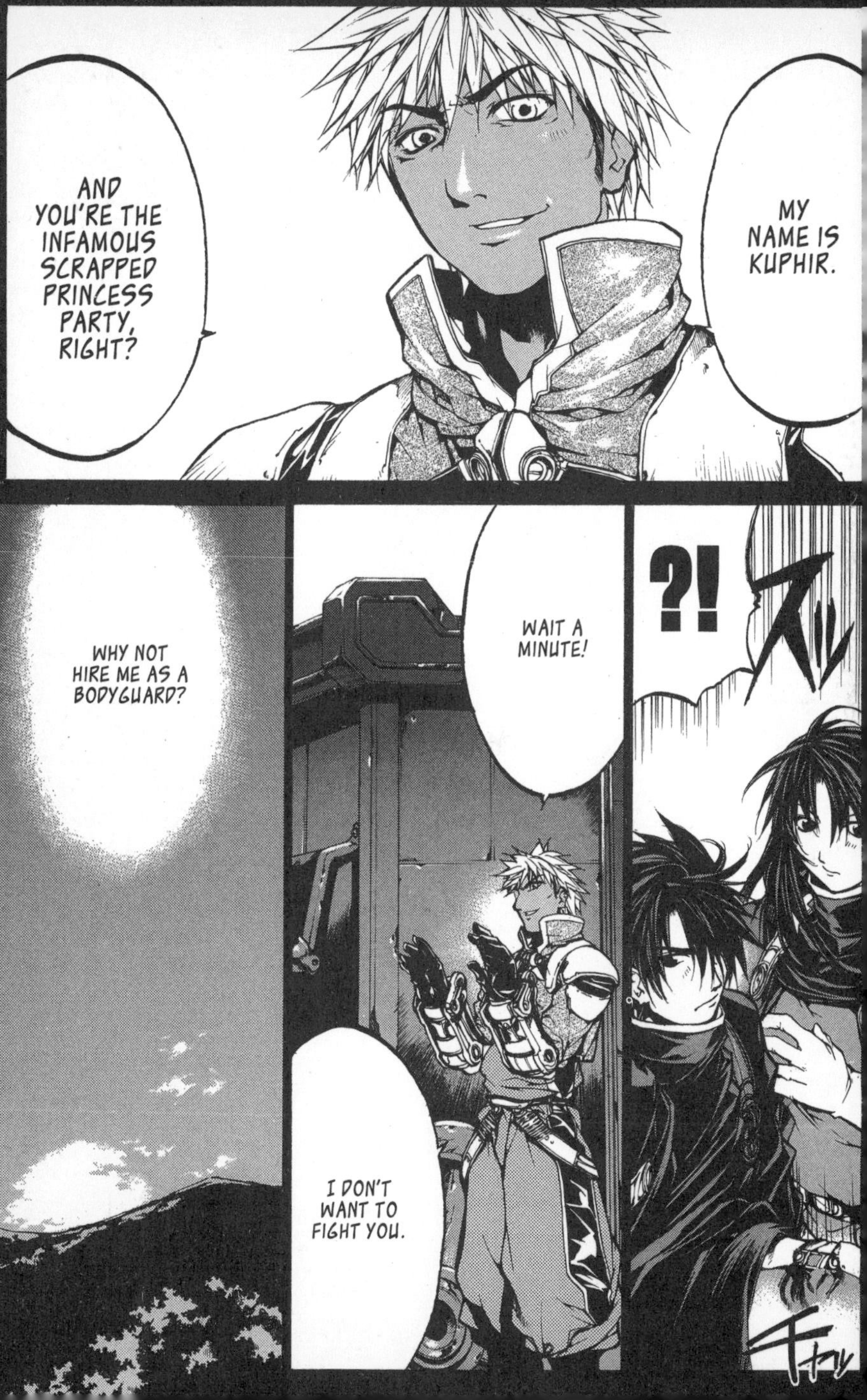
MY NAME IS KUPHIR.
AND YOU'RE THE INFAMOUS SCRAPPED PRINCESS PARTY, RIGHT?
?!
WAIT A MINUTE!
I DON'T WANT TO FIGHT YOU.
WHY NOT HIRE ME AS A BODYGUARD?

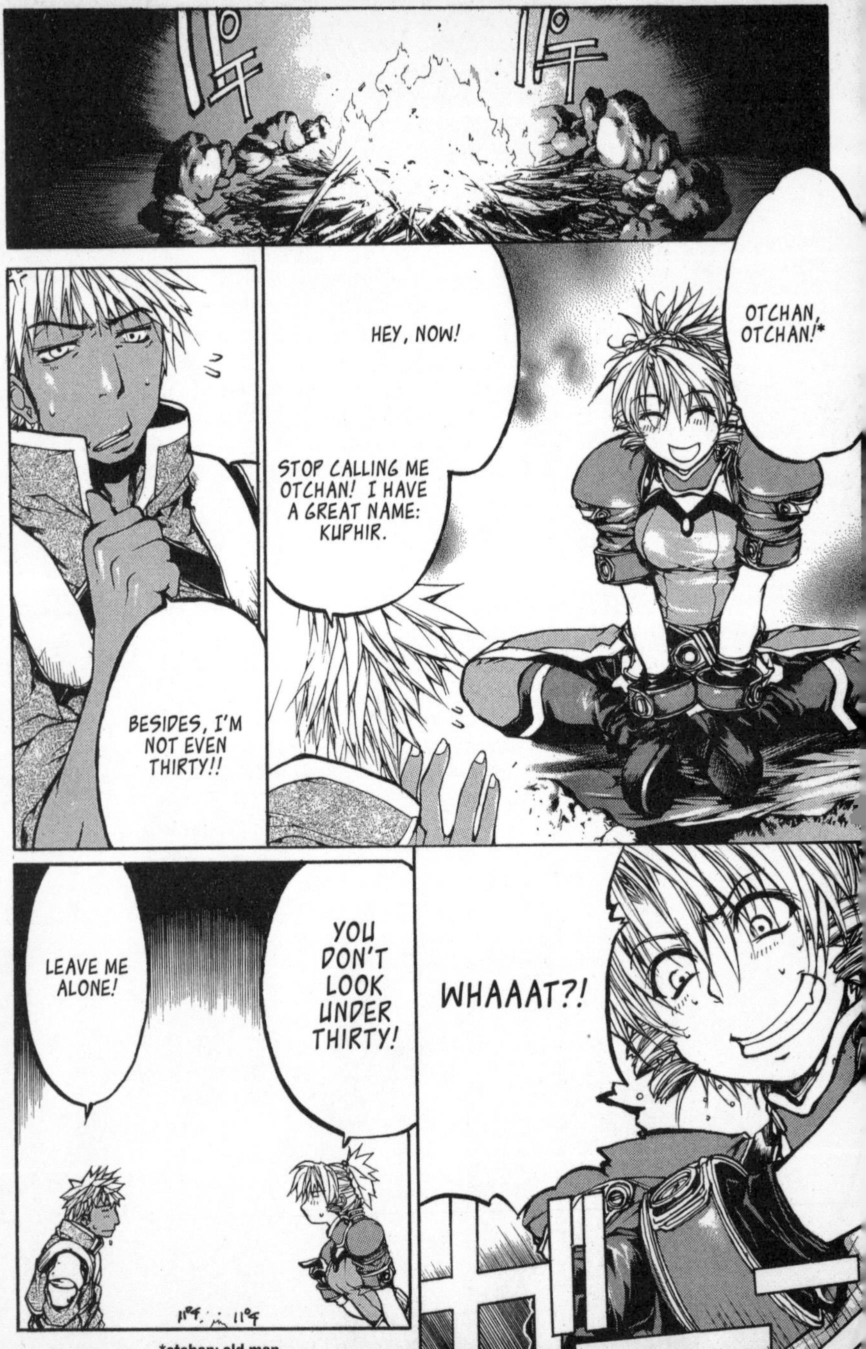
パチ
パチ
OTCHAN, OTCHAN!*
HEY, NOW!
STOP CALLING ME OTCHAN! I HAVE A GREAT NAME: KUPHIR.
BESIDES, I'M NOT EVEN THIRTY!!
WHAAAT?!
YOU DON'T LOOK UNDER THIRTY!
LEAVE ME ALONE!

*otchan: old man

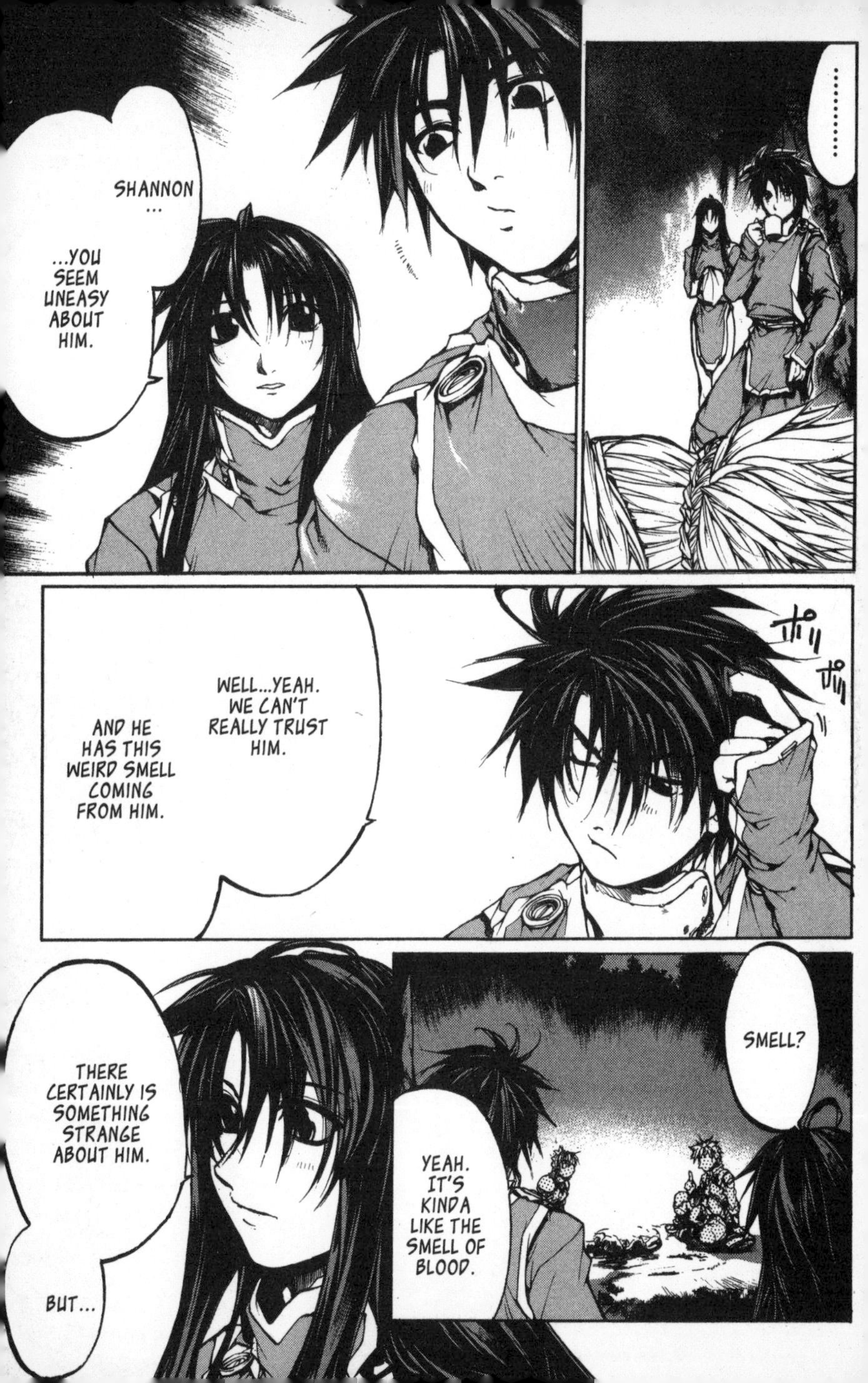
......
SHANNON...
...YOU SEEM UNEASY ABOUT HIM.
ポリ
ポリ
WELL...YEAH. WE CAN'T REALLY TRUST HIM.
AND HE HAS THIS WEIRD SMELL COMING FROM HIM.
SMELL?
YEAH. IT'S KINDA LIKE THE SMELL OF BLOOD.
THERE CERTAINLY IS SOMETHING STRANGE ABOUT HIM.
BUT...

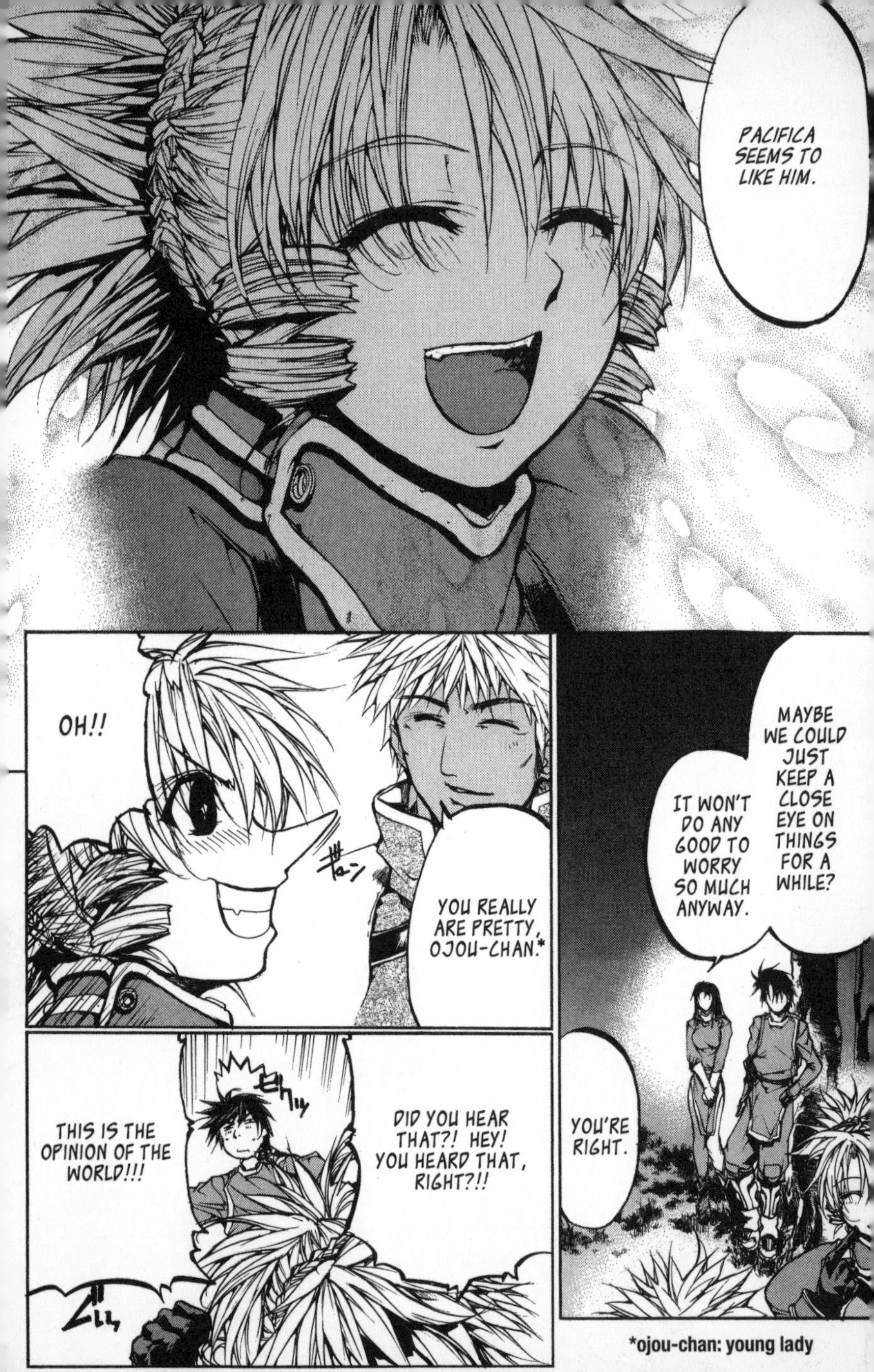
PACIFICA SEEMS TO LIKE HIM.
MAYBE WE COULD JUST KEEP A CLOSE EYE ON THINGS FOR A WHILE?
IT WON'T DO ANY GOOD TO WORRY SO MUCH ANYWAY.
YOU'RE RIGHT.
YOU REALLY ARE PRETTY, OJOU-CHAN.*
OH!!
DID YOU HEAR THAT?! HEY! YOU HEARD THAT, RIGHT?!!
THIS IS THE OPINION OF THE WORLD!!!

*ojou-chan: young lady

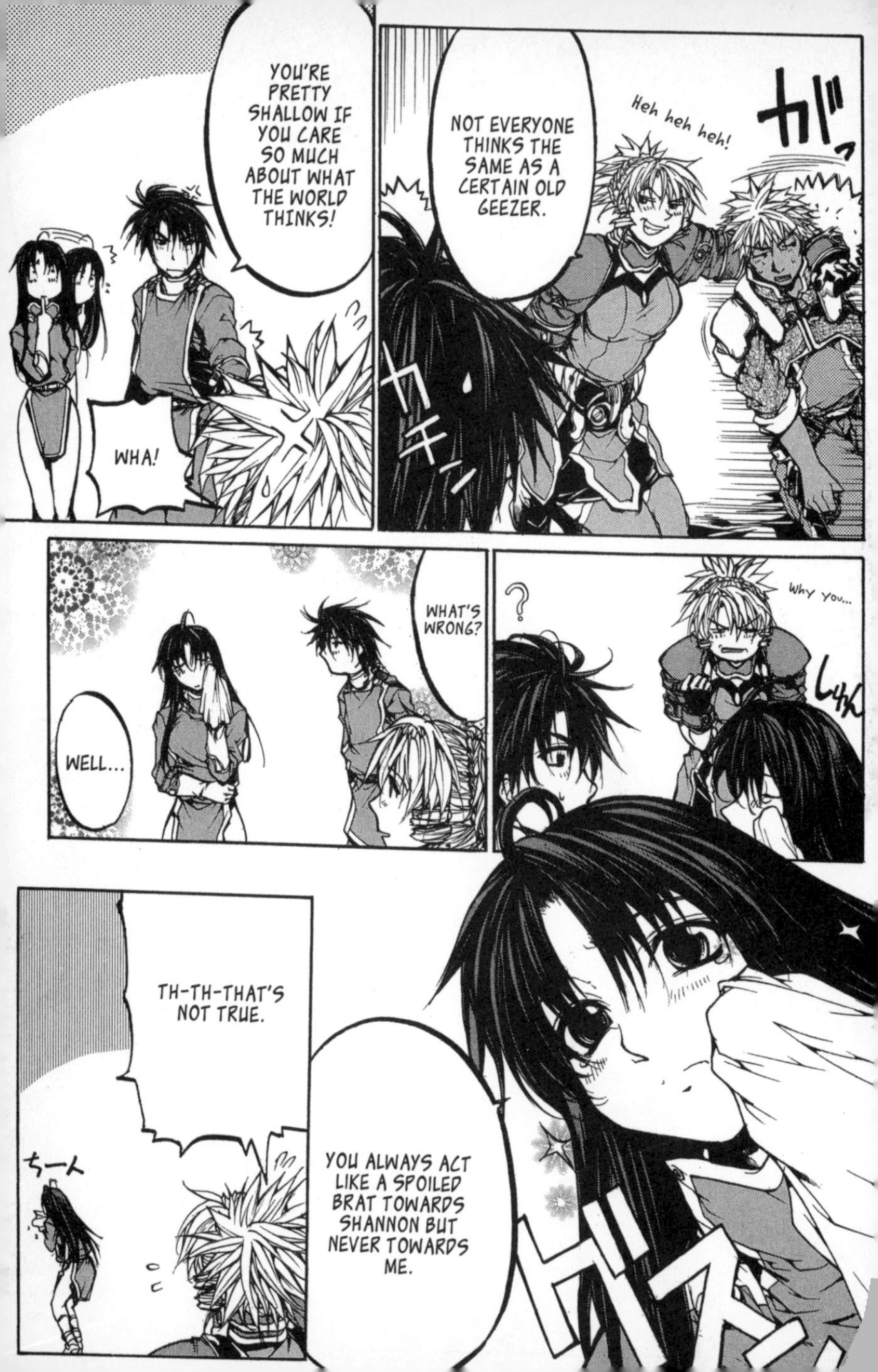
ガッ
Heh heh heh!
NOT EVERYONE THINKS THE SAME AS A CERTAIN OLD GEEZER.
YOU'RE PRETTY SHALLOW IF YOU CARE SO MUCH ABOUT WHAT THE WORLD THINKS!
WHA!
Why you...
?
WHAT'S WRONG?
WELL...
YOU ALWAYS ACT LIKE A SPOILED BRAT TOWARDS SHANNON BUT NEVER TOWARDS ME.
TH-TH-THAT'S NOT TRUE.
ちーん

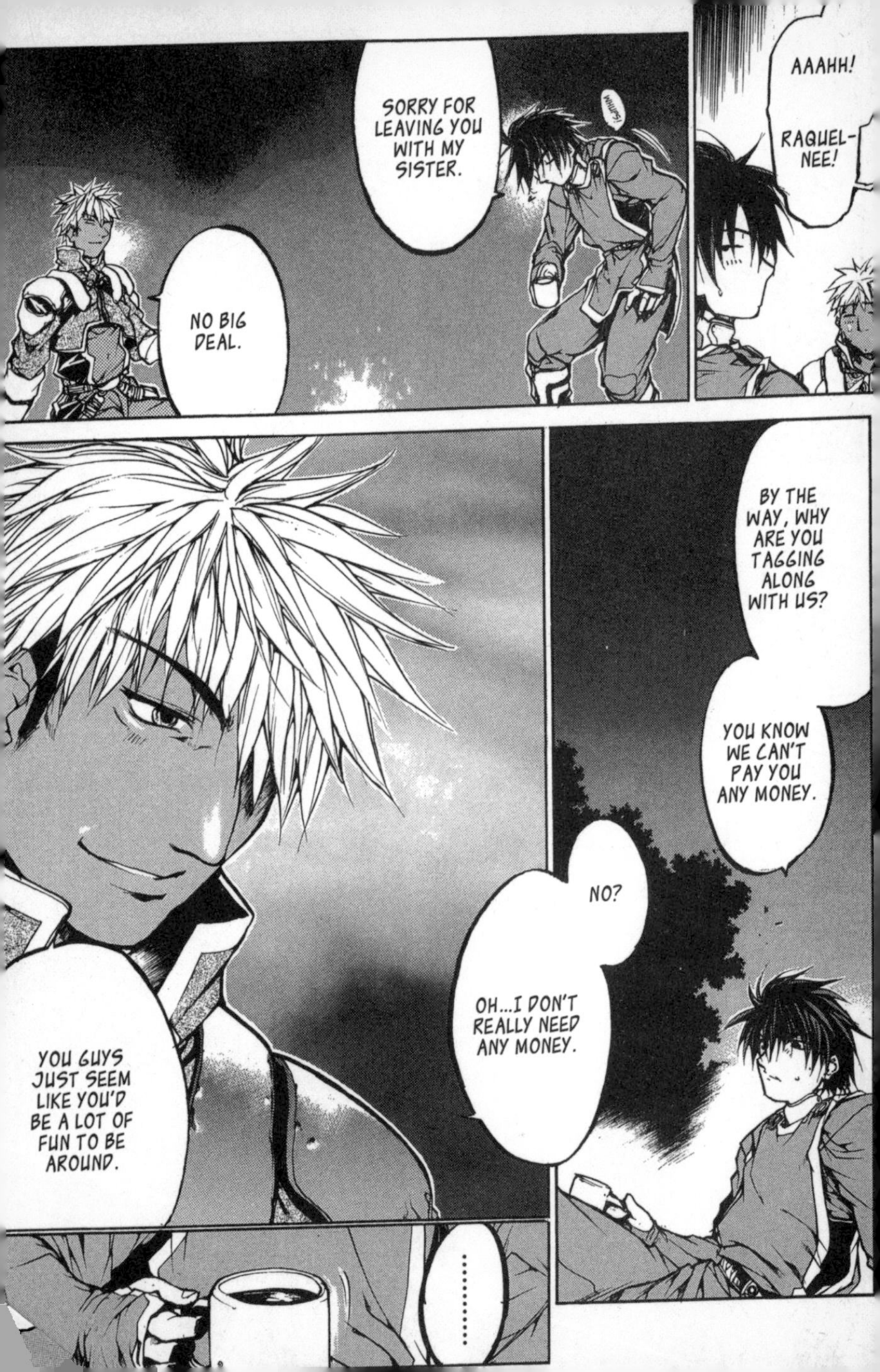
AAAHH!
RAQUEL-NEE!
SORRY FOR LEAVING YOU WITH MY SISTER.
NO BIG DEAL.
BY THE WAY, WHY ARE YOU TAGGING ALONG WITH US?
YOU KNOW WE CAN'T PAY YOU ANY MONEY.
NO?
OH...I DON'T REALLY NEED ANY MONEY.
YOU GUYS JUST SEEM LIKE YOU'D BE A LOT OF FUN TO BE AROUND.
......

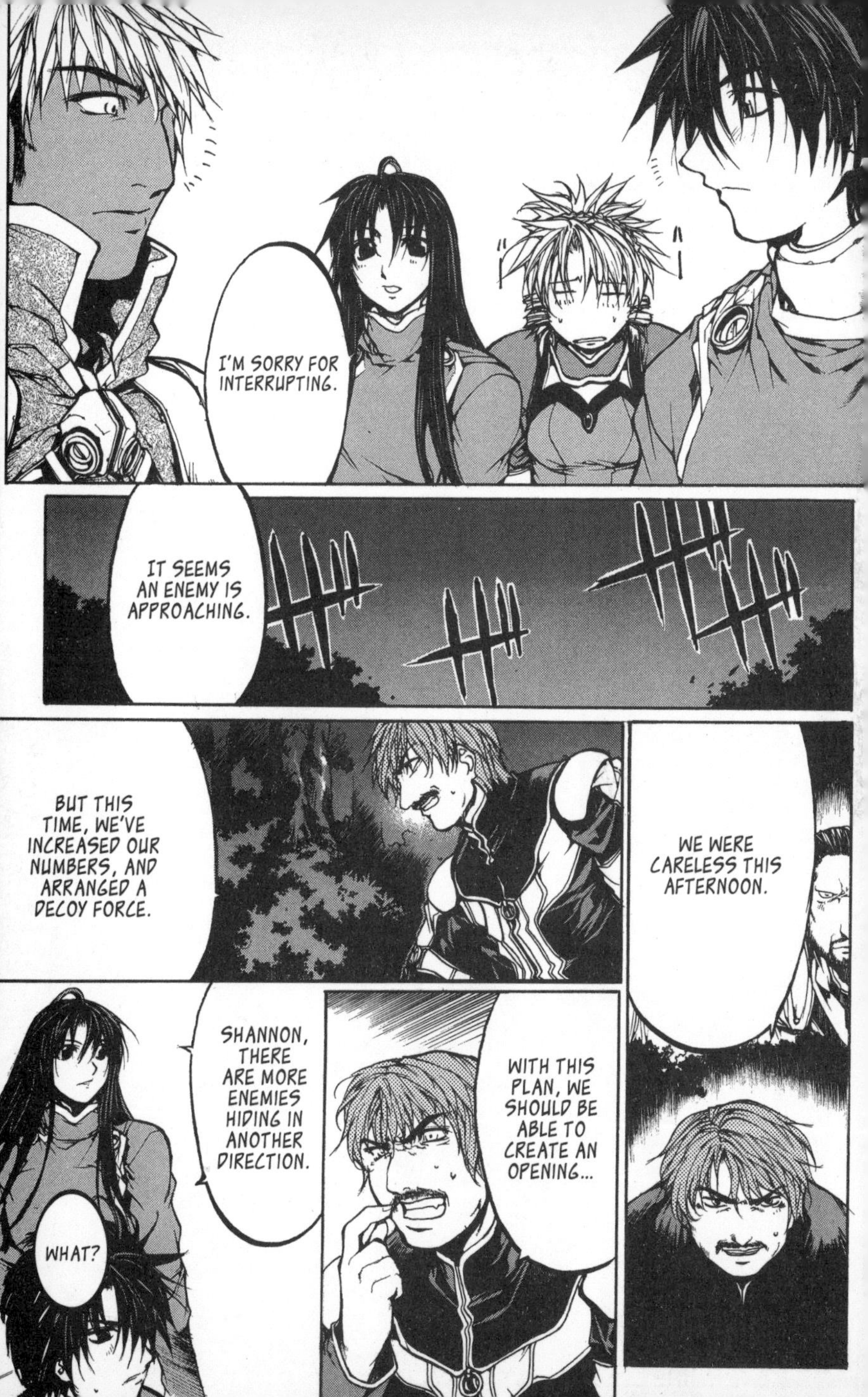

I'M SORRY FOR INTERRUPTING.
IT SEEMS AN ENEMY IS APPROACHING.
WE WERE CARELESS THIS AFTERNOON.
BUT THIS TIME, WE'VE INCREASED OUR NUMBERS, AND ARRANGED A DECOY FORCE.
WITH THIS PLAN, WE SHOULD BE ABLE TO CREATE AN OPENING...
SHANNON, THERE ARE MORE ENEMIES HIDING IN ANOTHER DIRECTION.
WHAT?

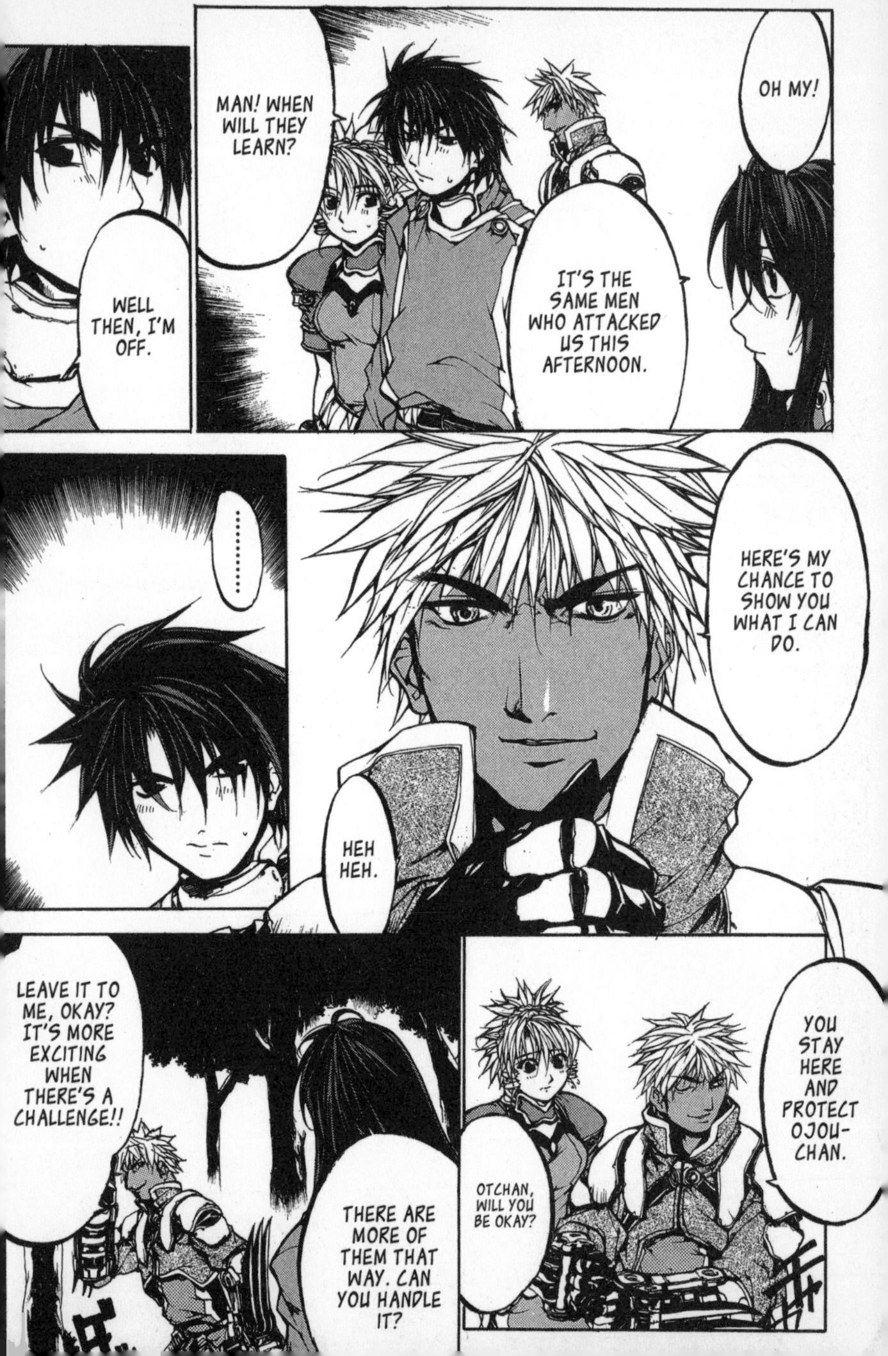
OH MY!
MAN! WHEN WILL THEY LEARN?
IT'S THE SAME MEN WHO ATTACKED US THIS AFTERNOON.
WELL THEN, I'M OFF.
HERE'S MY CHANCE TO SHOW YOU WHAT I CAN DO.
HEH HEH.
....
YOU STAY HERE AND PROTECT OJOU-CHAN.
OTCHAN, WILL YOU BE OKAY?
THERE ARE MORE OF THEM THAT WAY. CAN YOU HANDLE IT?
LEAVE IT TO ME, OKAY? IT'S MORE EXCITING WHEN THERE'S A CHALLENGE!!

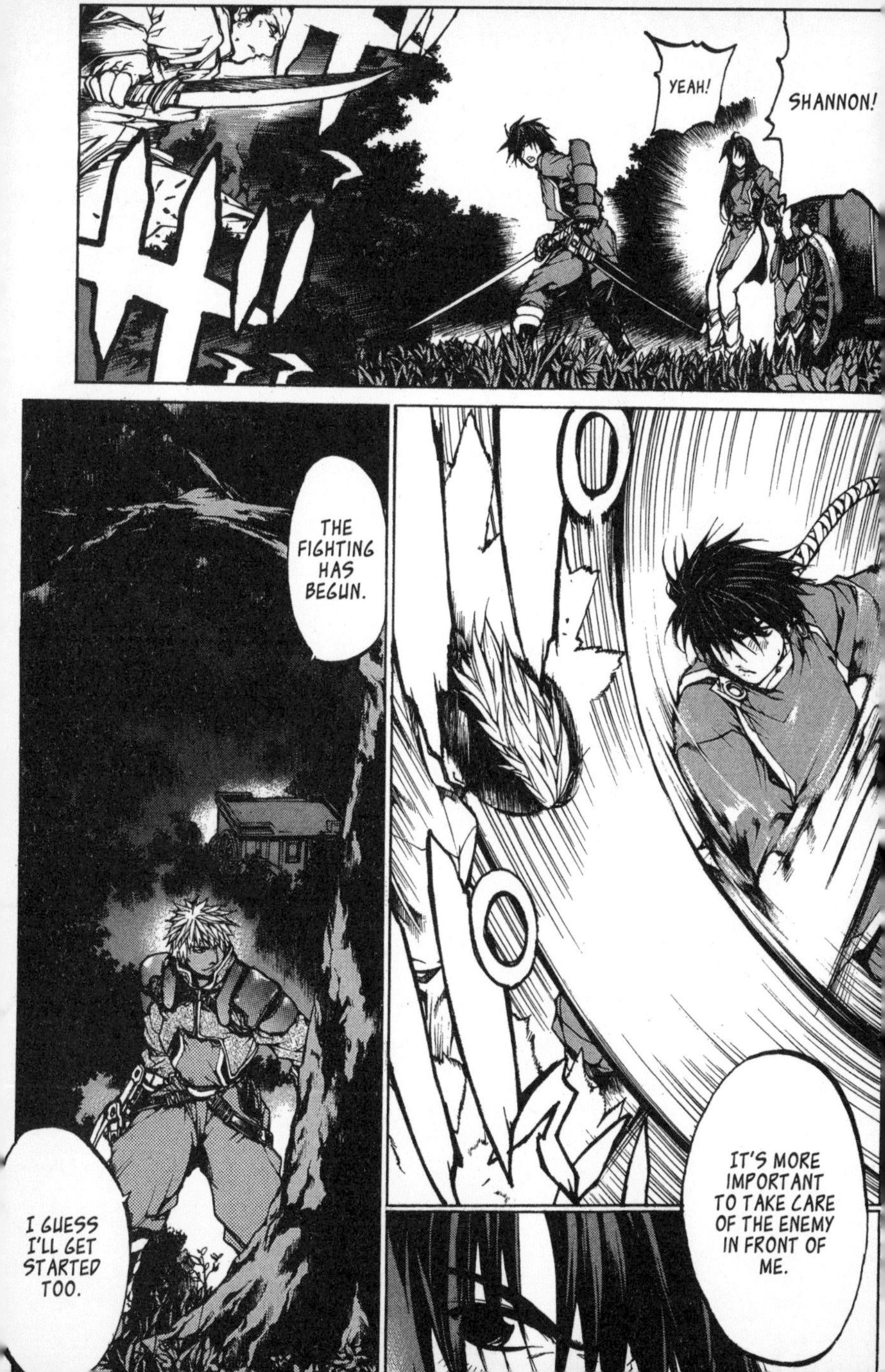
SHANNON!
YEAH!
IT'S MORE IMPORTANT TO TAKE CARE OF THE ENEMY IN FRONT OF ME.
THE FIGHTING HAS BEGUN.
I GUESS I'LL GET STARTED TOO.

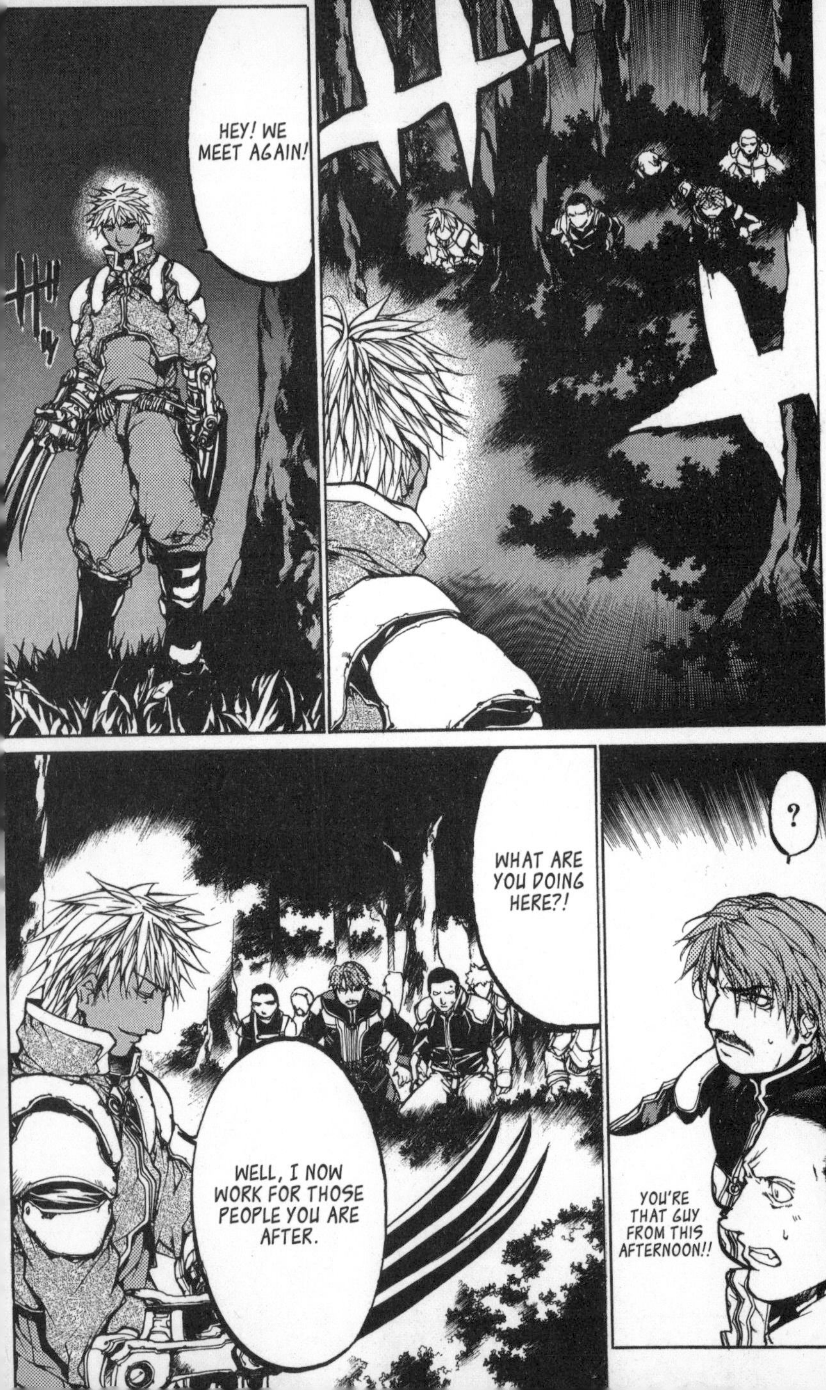
HEY! WE MEET AGAIN!
?
YOU'RE THAT GUY FROM THIS AFTERNOON!!
WHAT ARE YOU DOING HERE?!
WELL, I NOW WORK FOR THOSE PEOPLE YOU ARE AFTER.

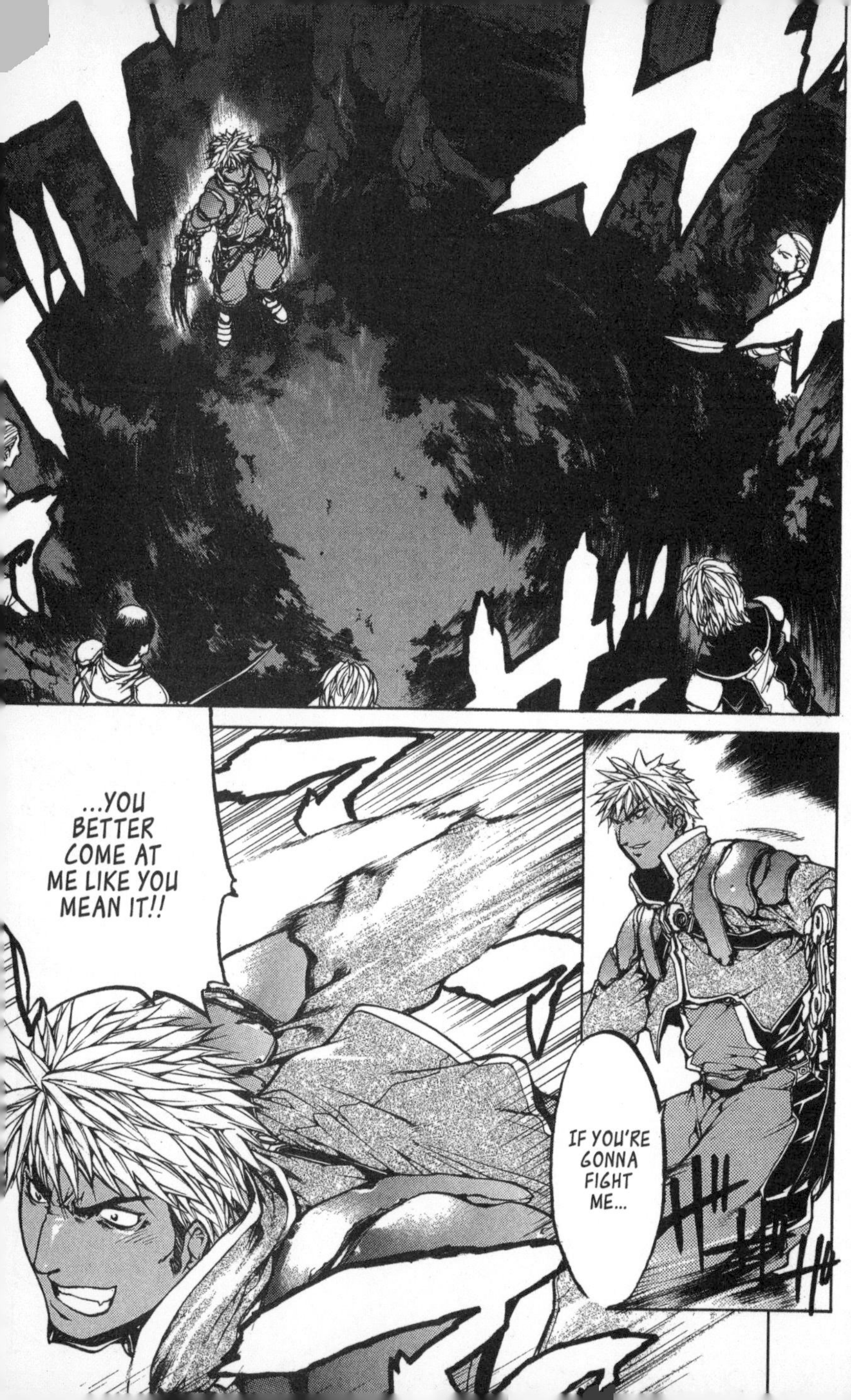
IF YOU'RE GONNA FIGHT ME...
...YOU BETTER COME AT ME LIKE YOU MEAN IT!!

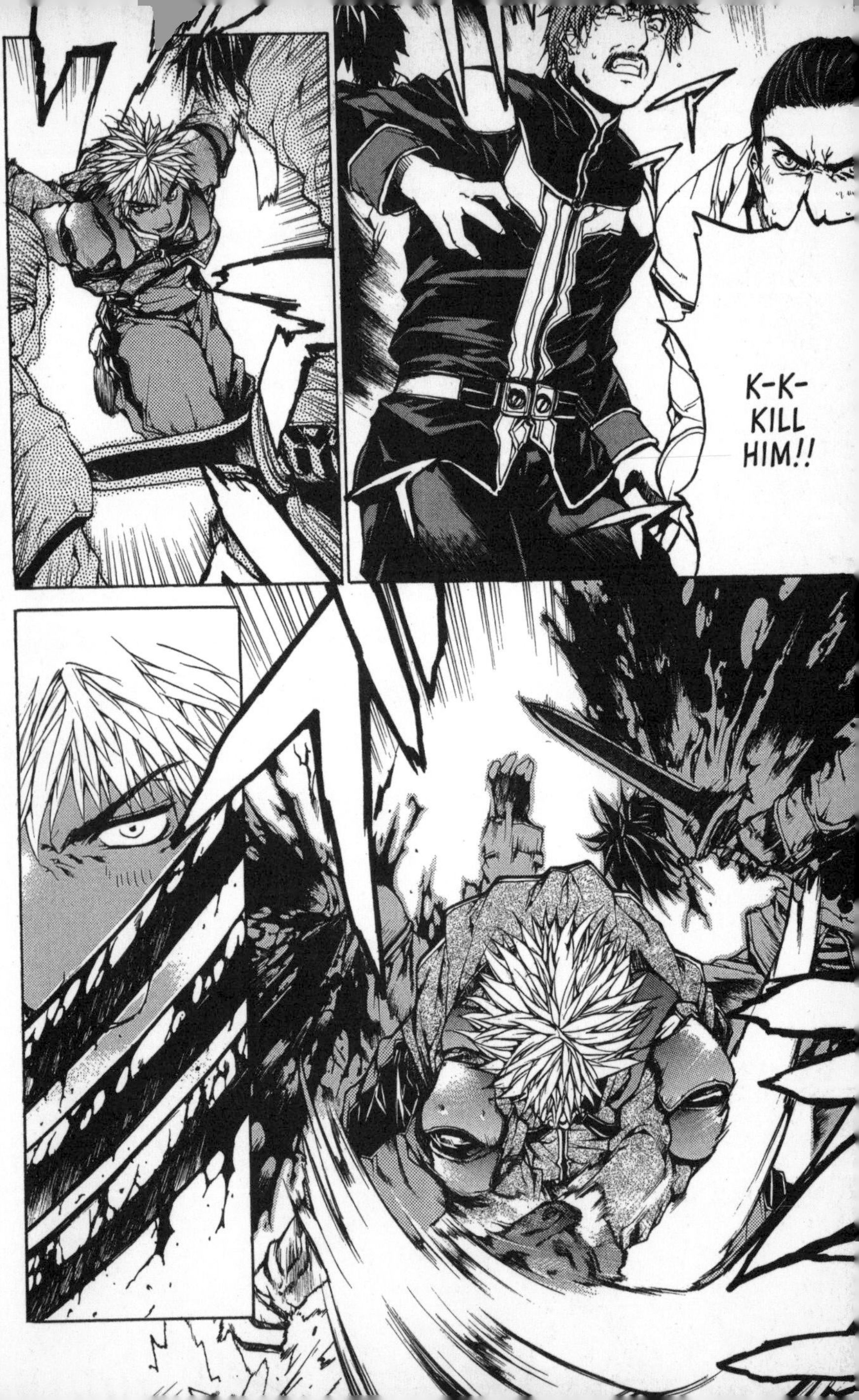
K-K-
KILL
HIM!!

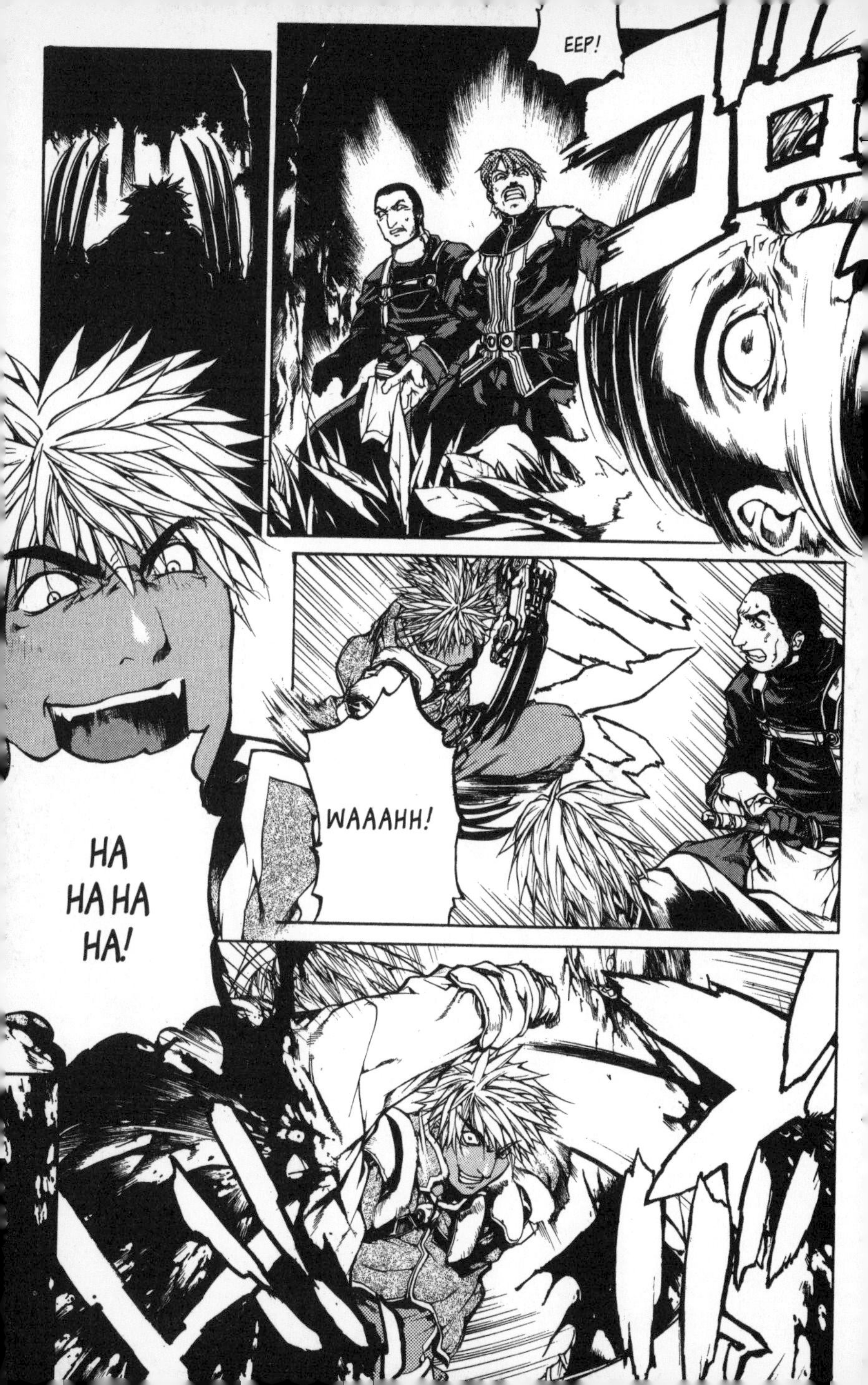
EEP!
WAAAHH!
HA HA HA HA!

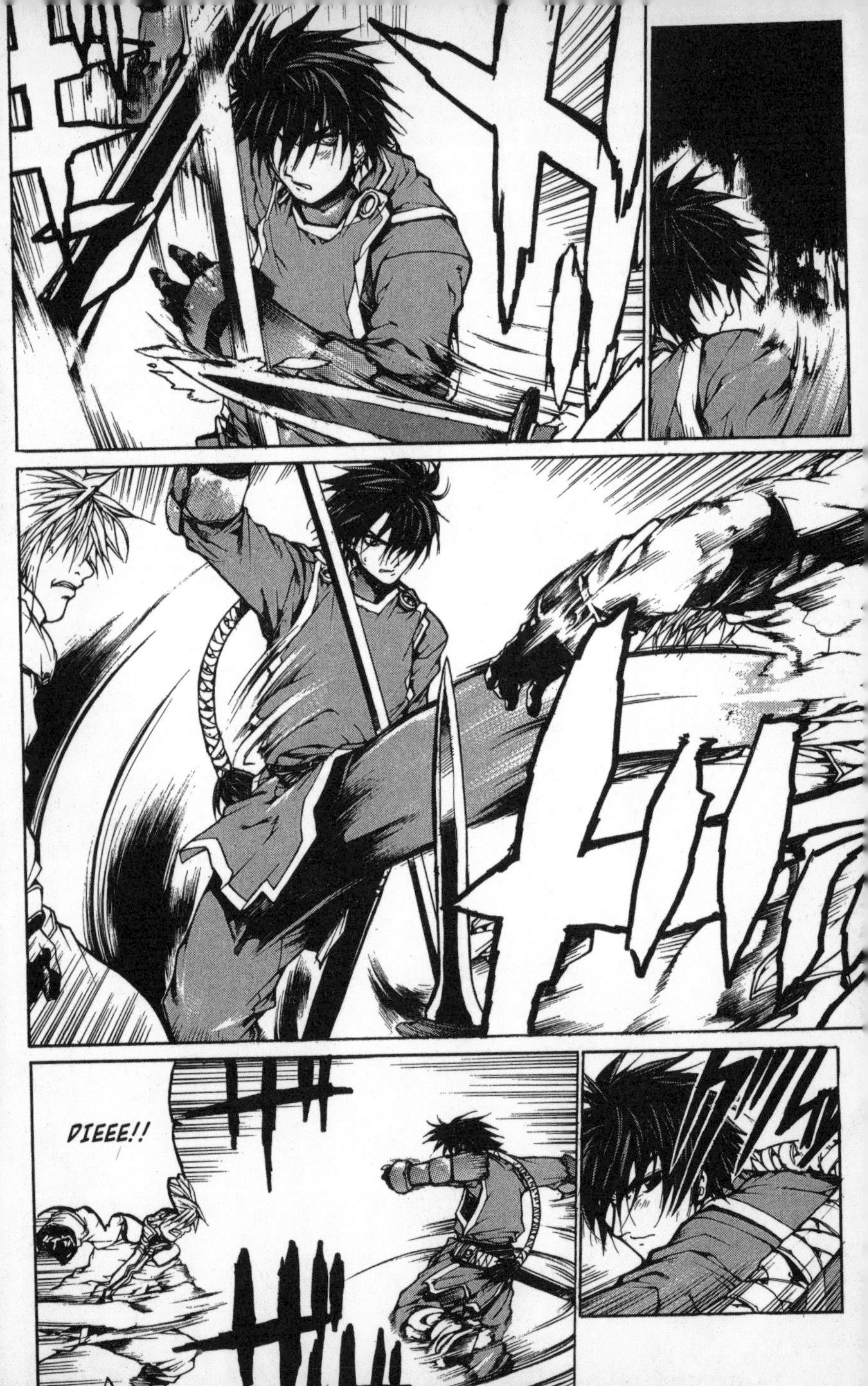
DIEEE!!

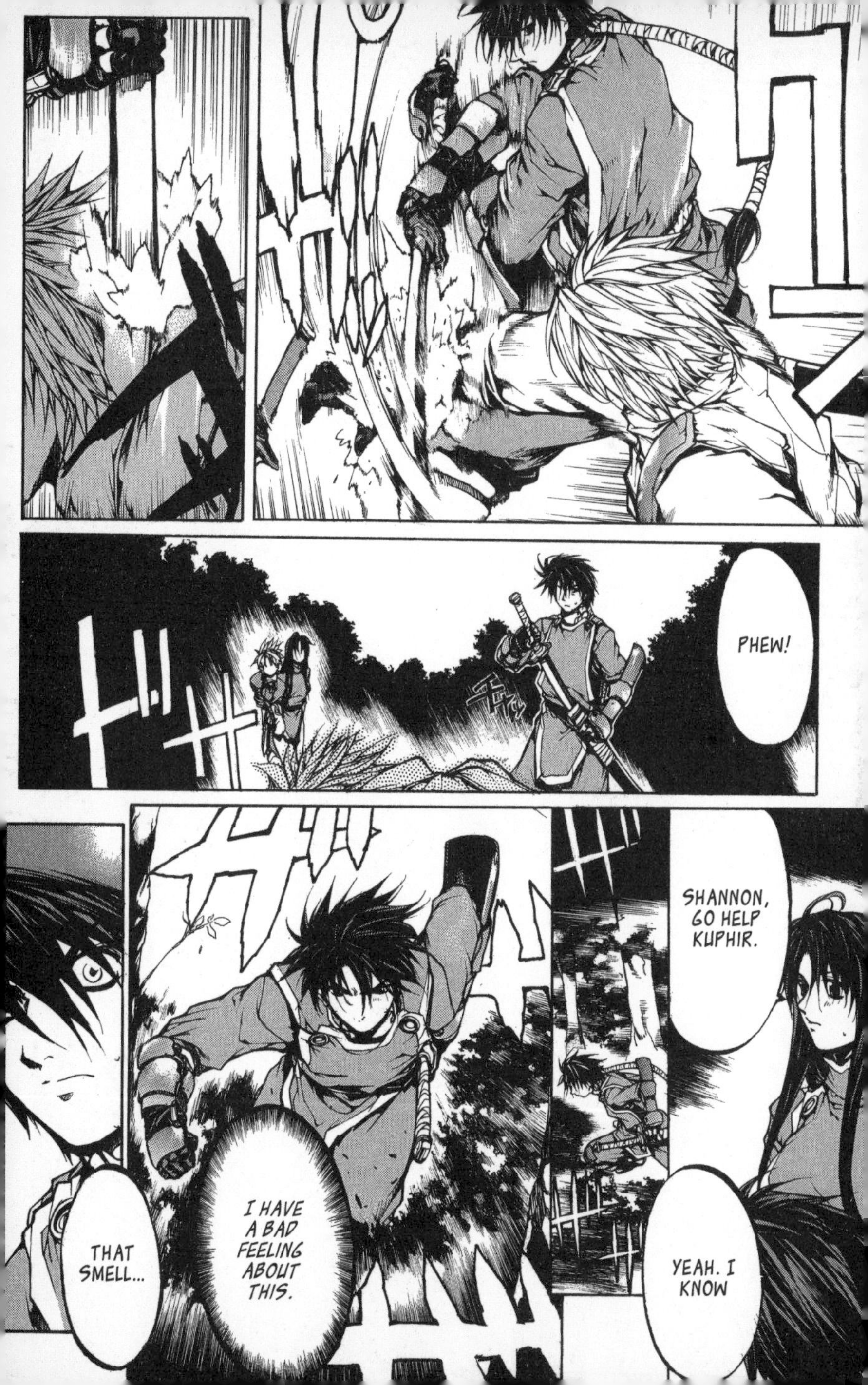
PHEW!
SHANNON, GO HELP KUPHIR.
YEAH. I KNOW
I HAVE A BAD FEELING ABOUT THIS.
THAT SMELL...

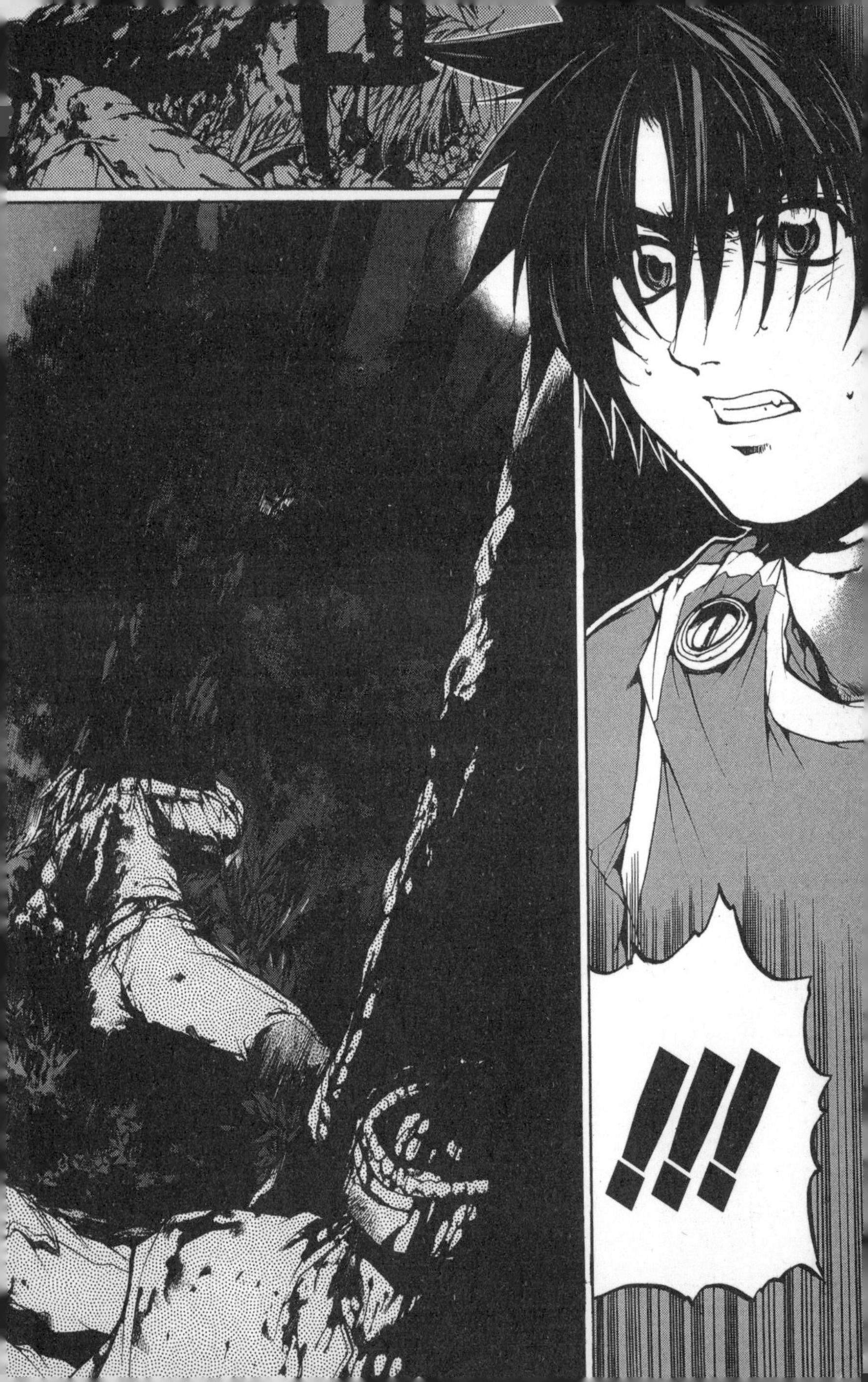
!!!

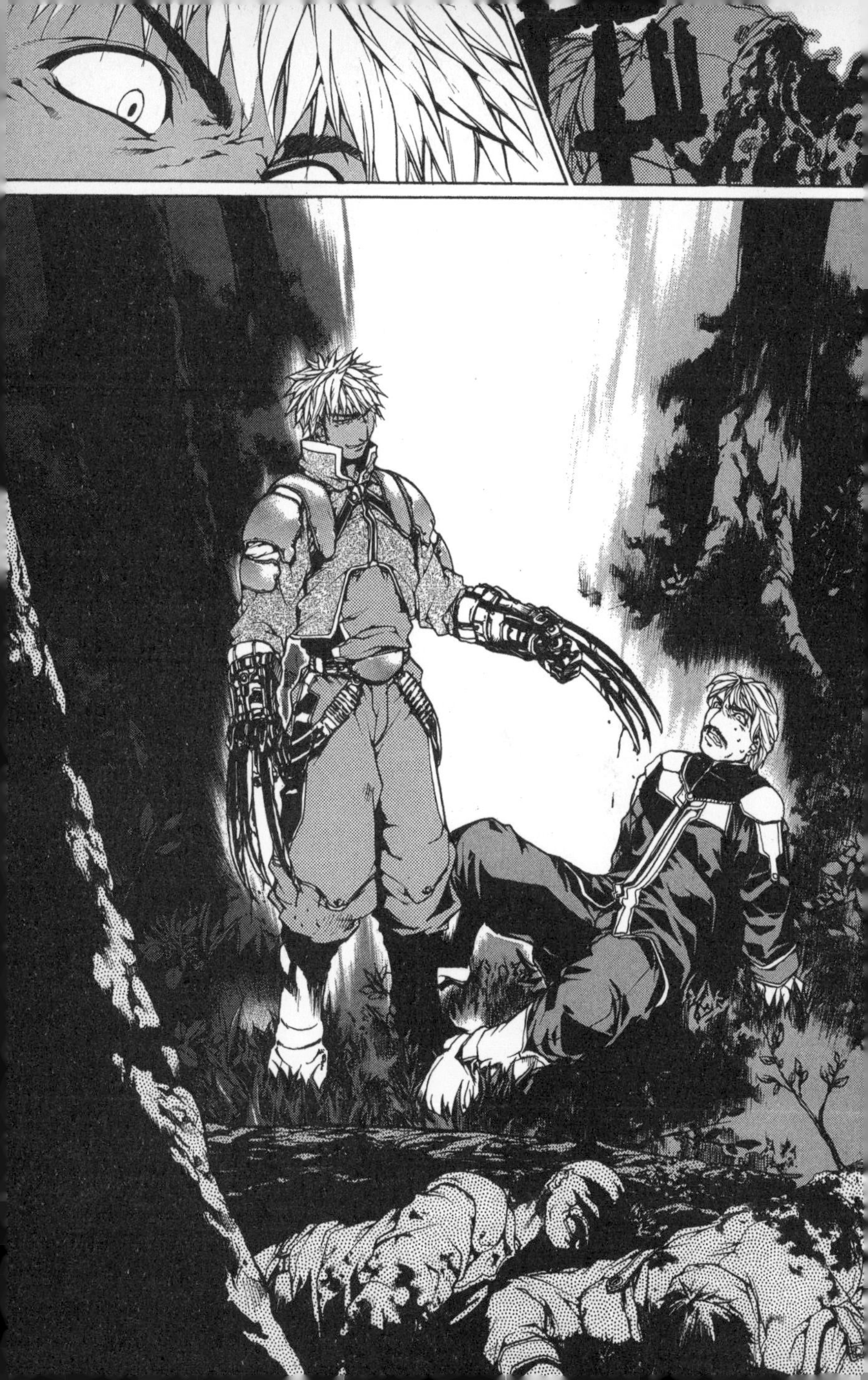

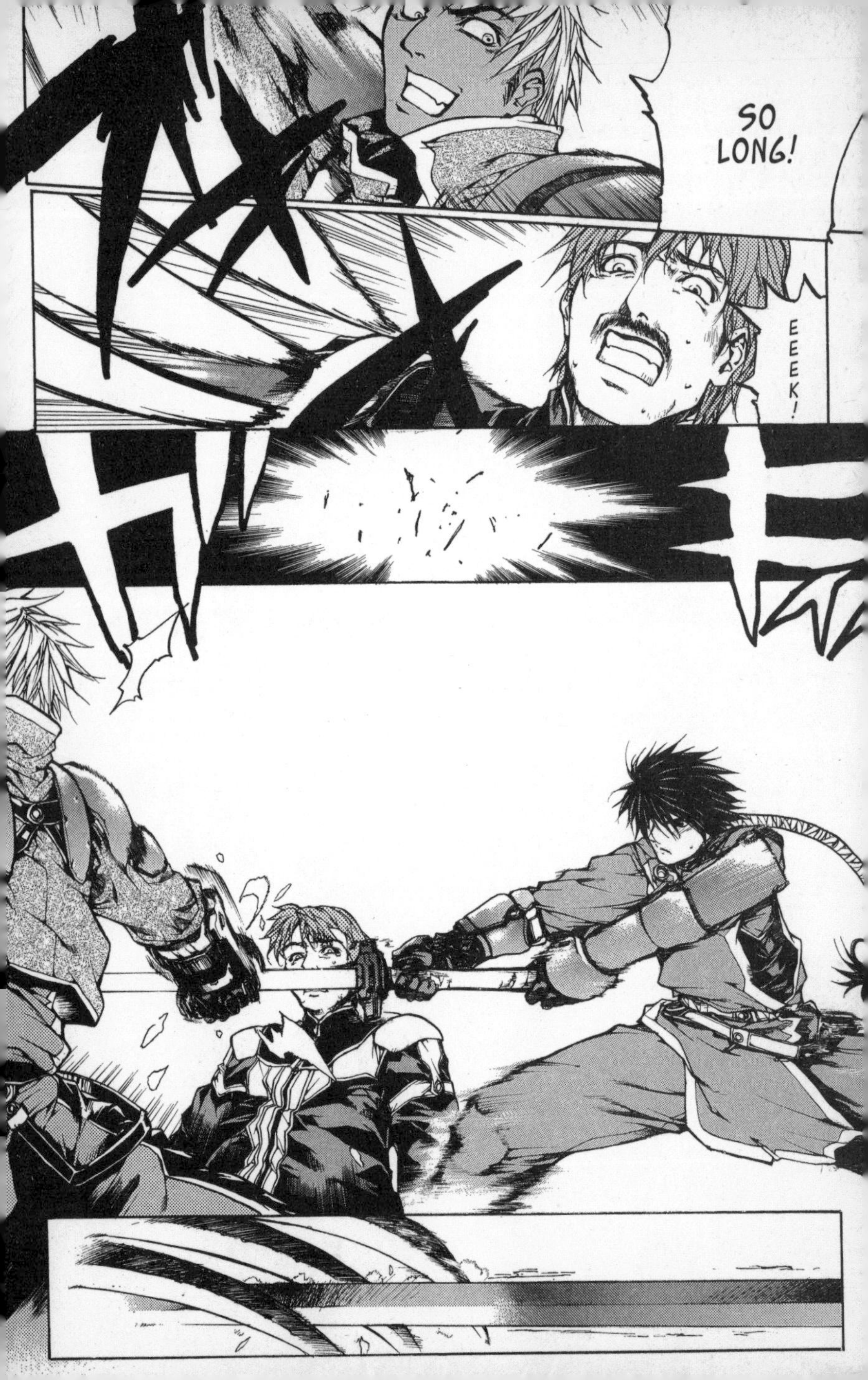
SO LONG!
EEEK!

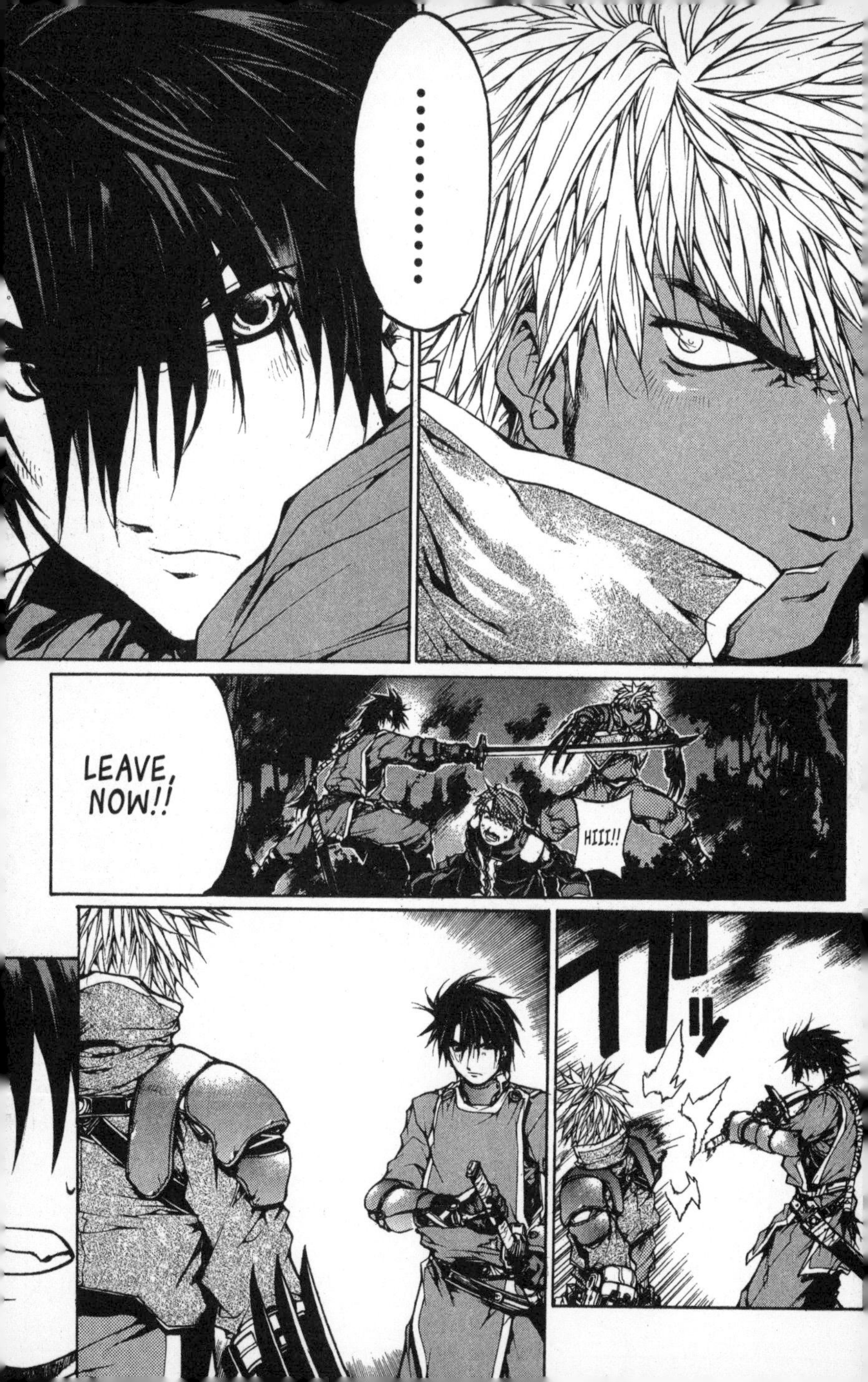
……
HIII!!
LEAVE, NOW!!

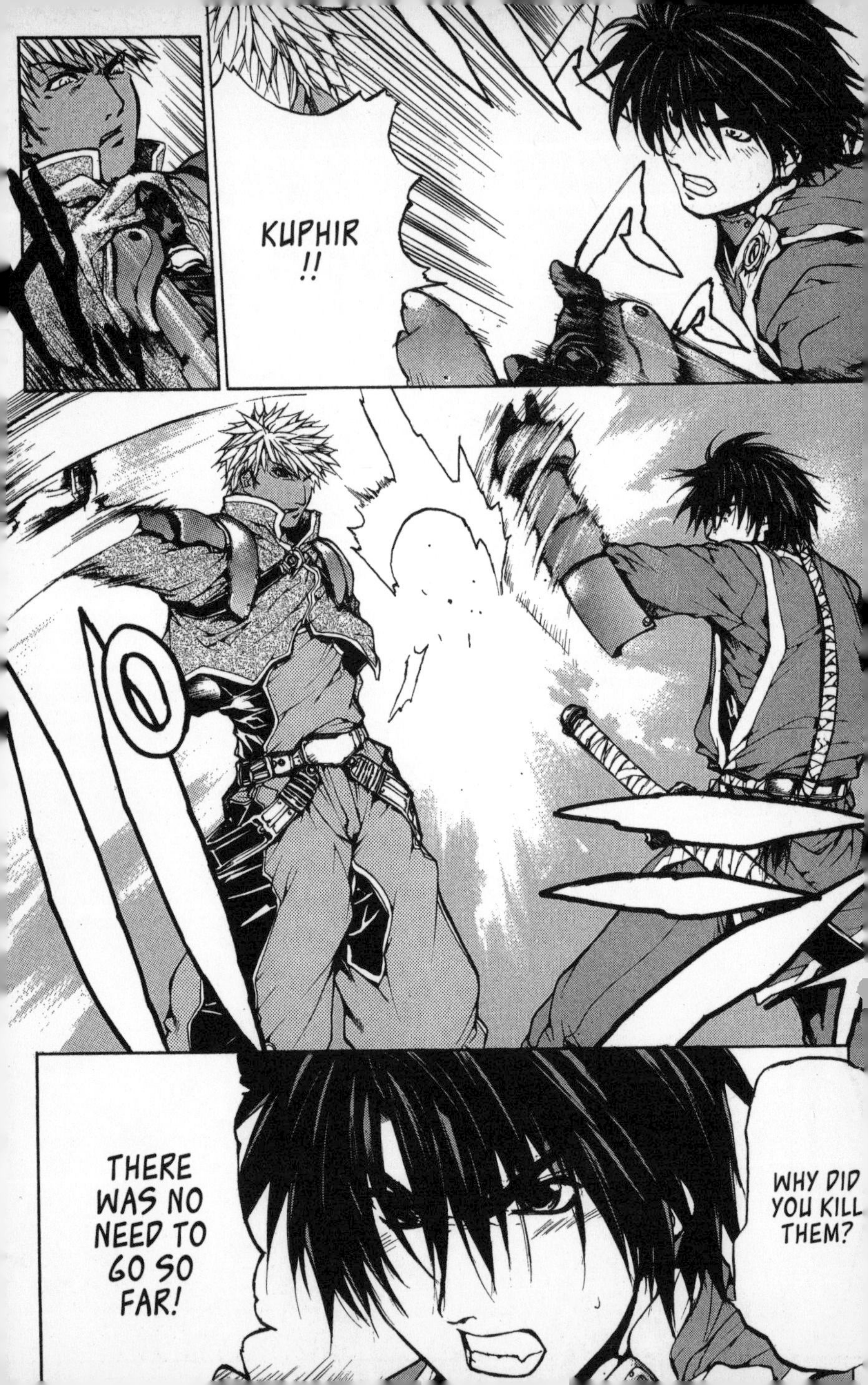
KUPHIR !!
WHY DID YOU KILL THEM?
THERE WAS NO NEED TO GO SO FAR!

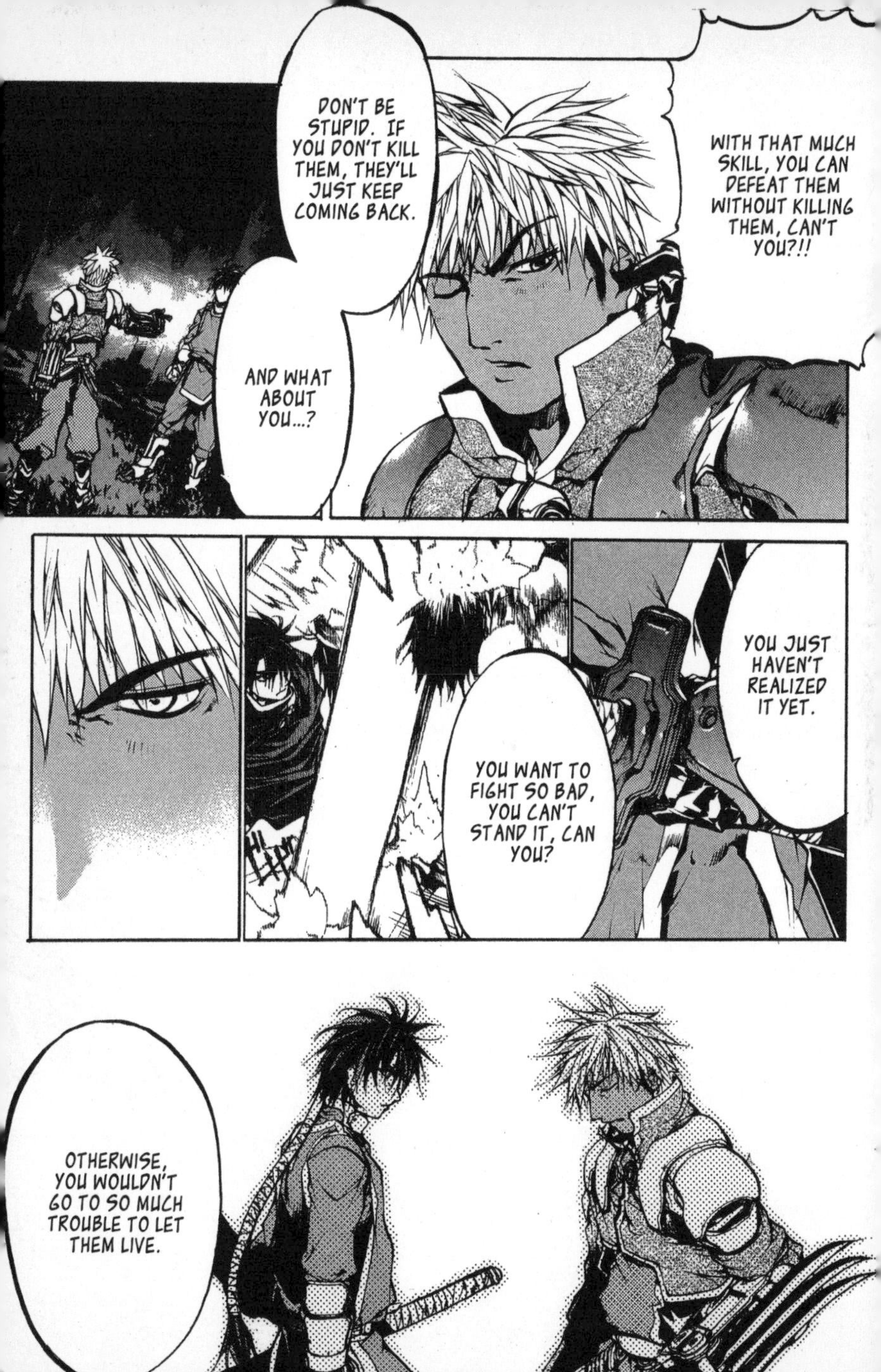
WITH THAT MUCH SKILL, YOU CAN DEFEAT THEM WITHOUT KILLING THEM, CAN'T YOU?!!
DON'T BE STUPID. IF YOU DON'T KILL THEM, THEY'LL JUST KEEP COMING BACK.
AND WHAT ABOUT YOU...?
YOU JUST HAVEN'T REALIZED IT YET.
YOU WANT TO FIGHT SO BAD, YOU CAN'T STAND IT, CAN YOU?
OTHERWISE, YOU WOULDN'T GO TO SO MUCH TROUBLE TO LET THEM LIVE.

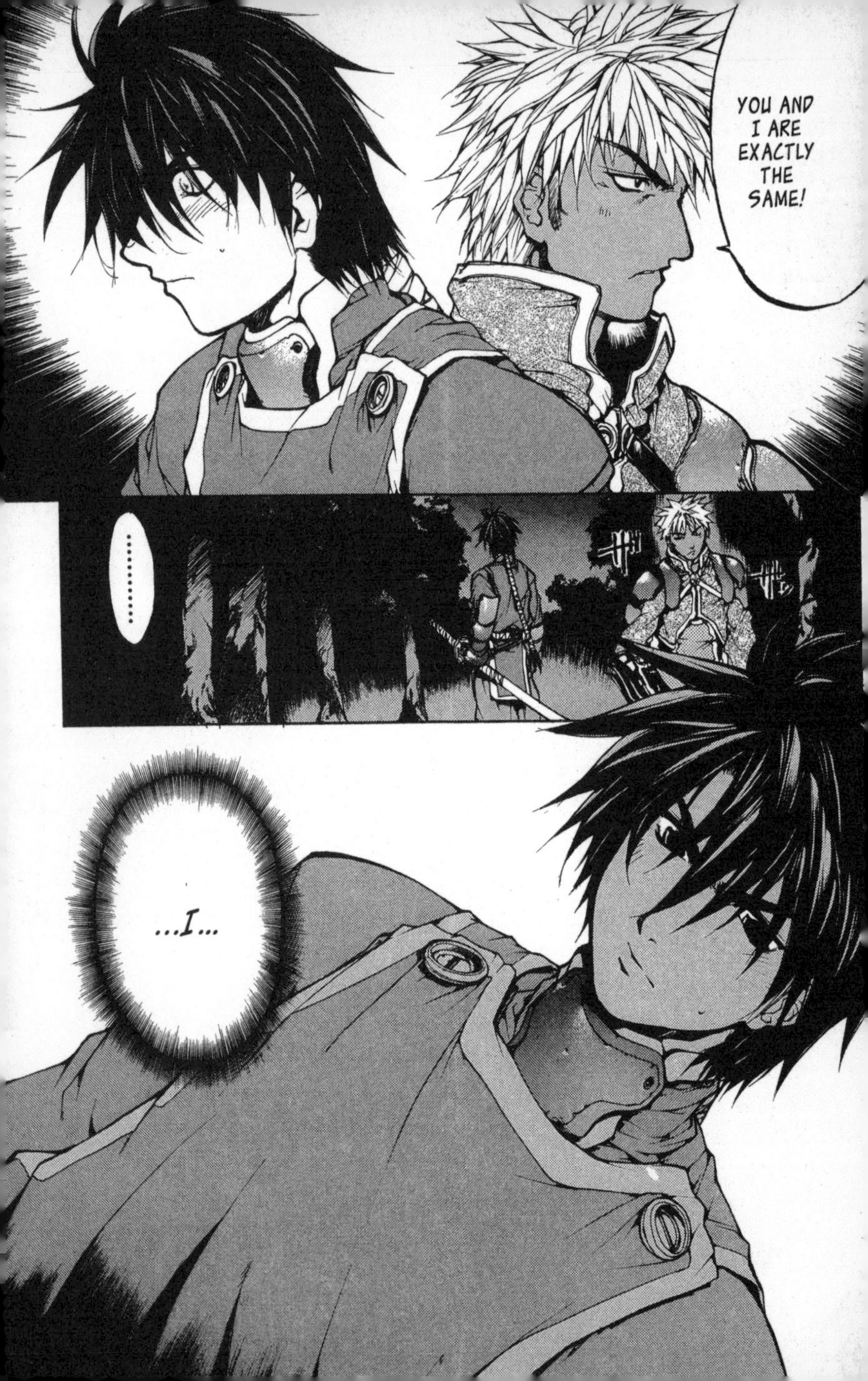
YOU AND I ARE EXACTLY THE SAME!
......
...I...

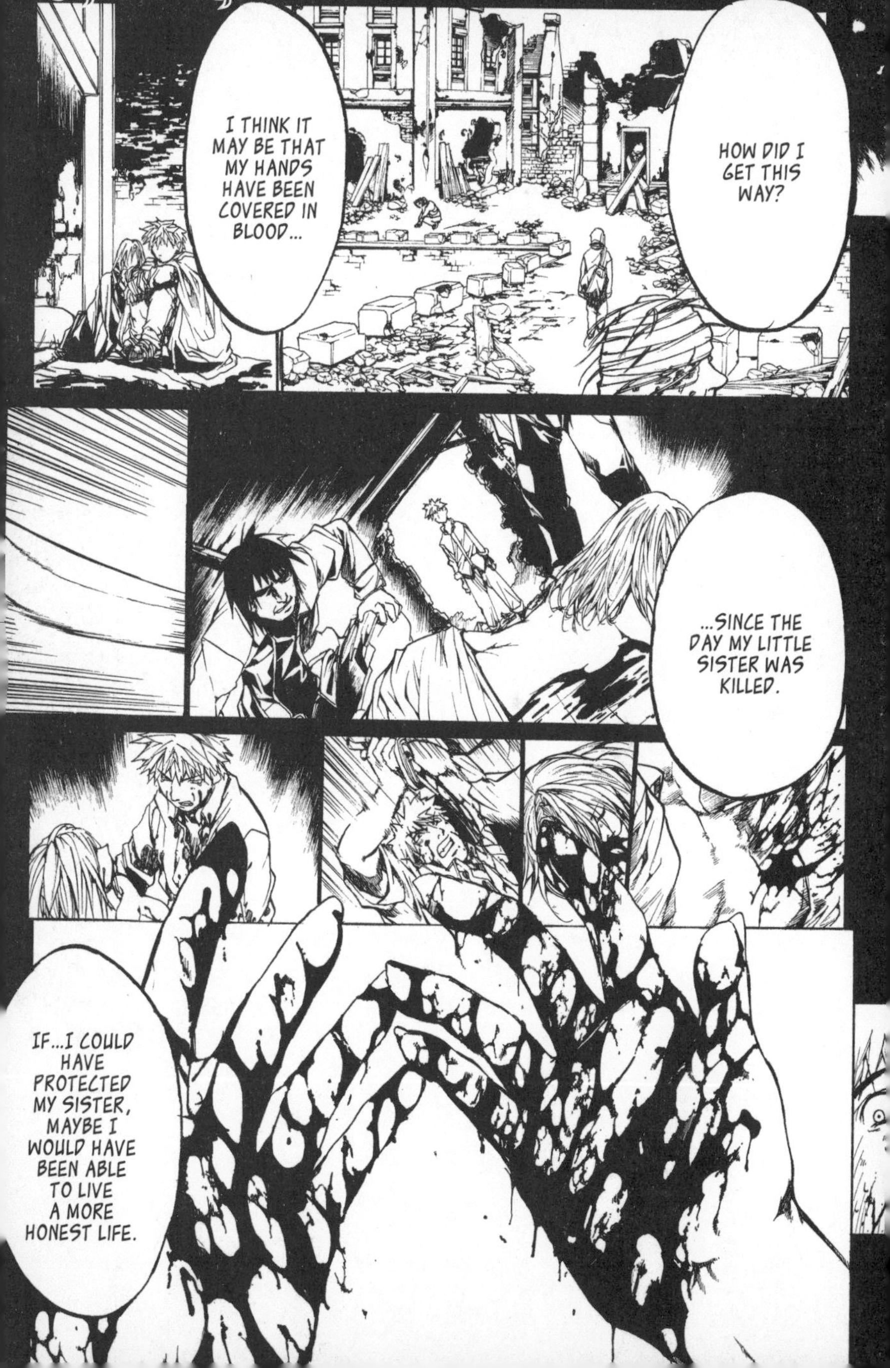
HOW DID I GET THIS WAY?
I THINK IT MAY BE THAT MY HANDS HAVE BEEN COVERED IN BLOOD...
...SINCE THE DAY MY LITTLE SISTER WAS KILLED.
IF...I COULD HAVE PROTECTED MY SISTER, MAYBE I WOULD HAVE BEEN ABLE TO LIVE A MORE HONEST LIFE.

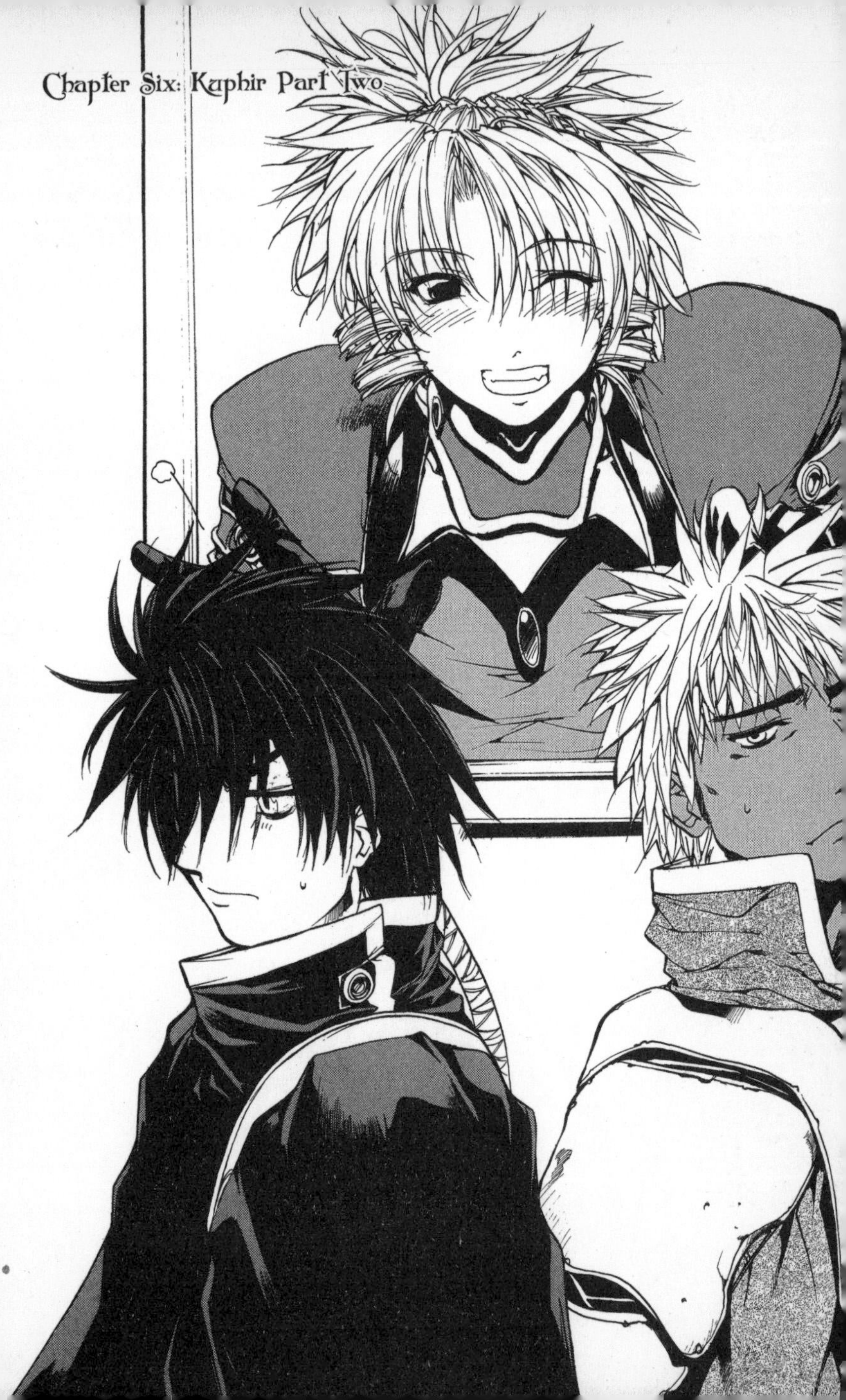
Chapter Six: Kuphir Part Two

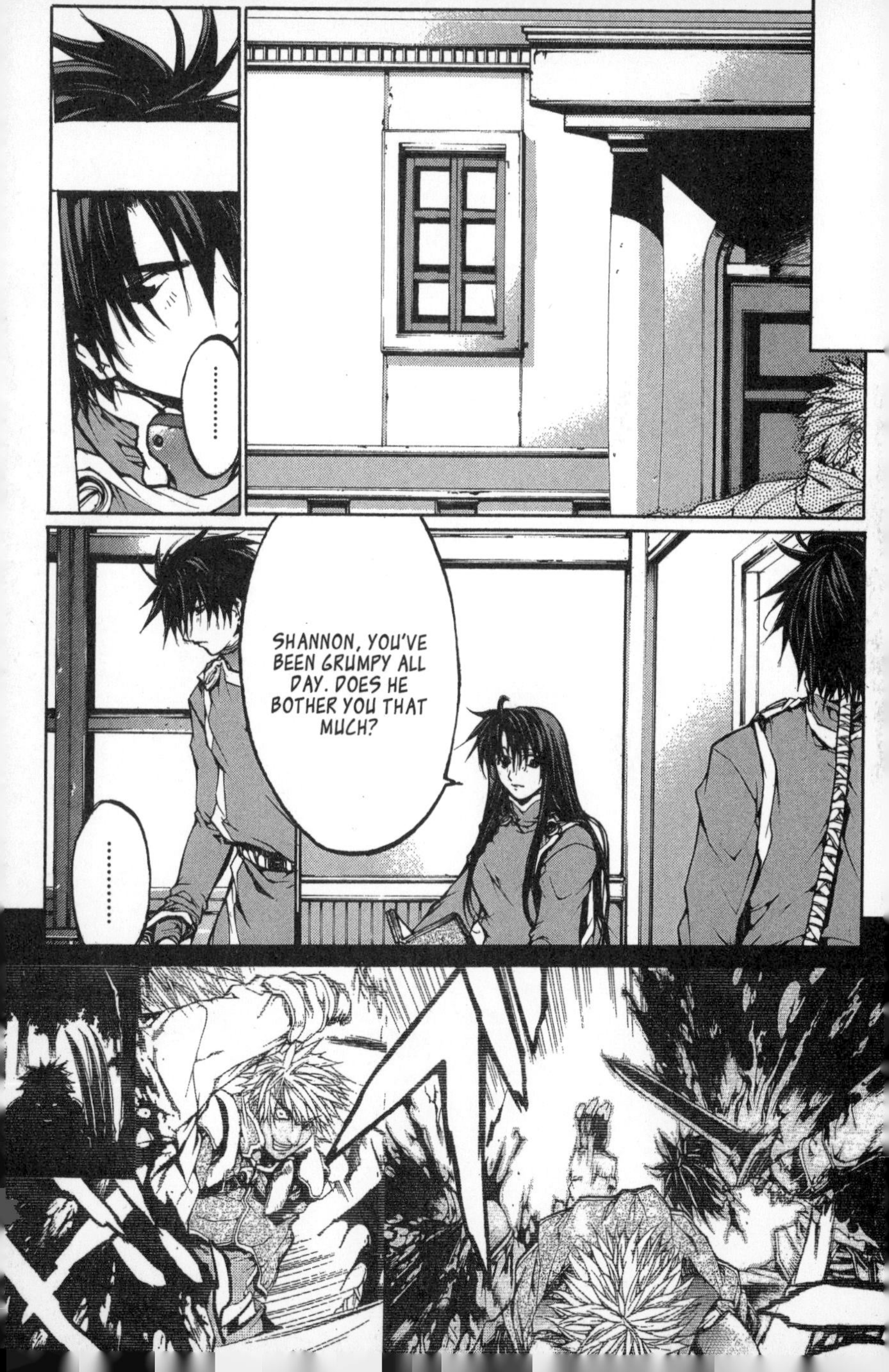
....
SHANNON, YOU'VE BEEN GRUMPY ALL DAY. DOES HE BOTHER YOU THAT MUCH?
....

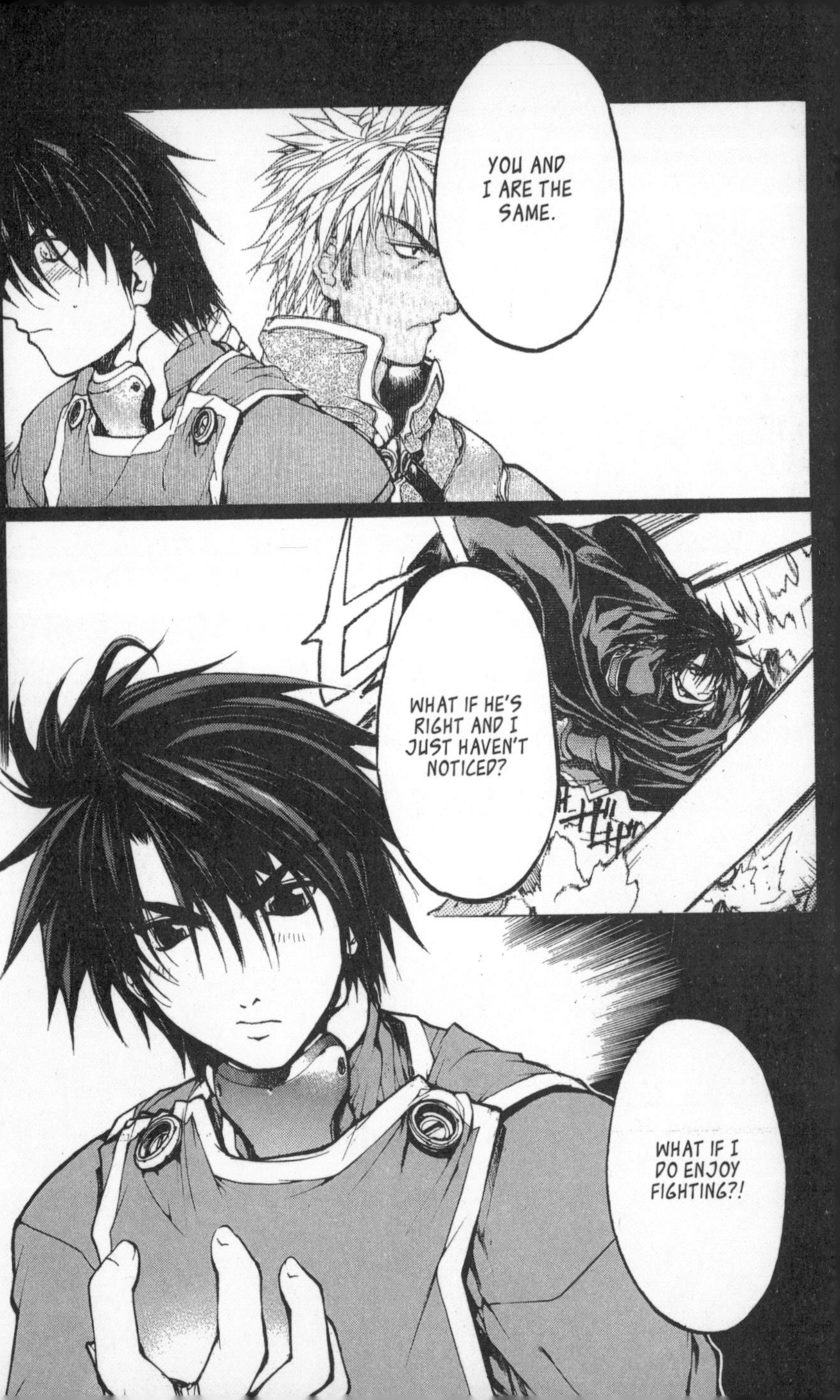
YOU AND I ARE THE SAME.
WHAT IF HE'S RIGHT AND I JUST HAVEN'T NOTICED?
WHAT IF I DO ENJOY FIGHTING?!

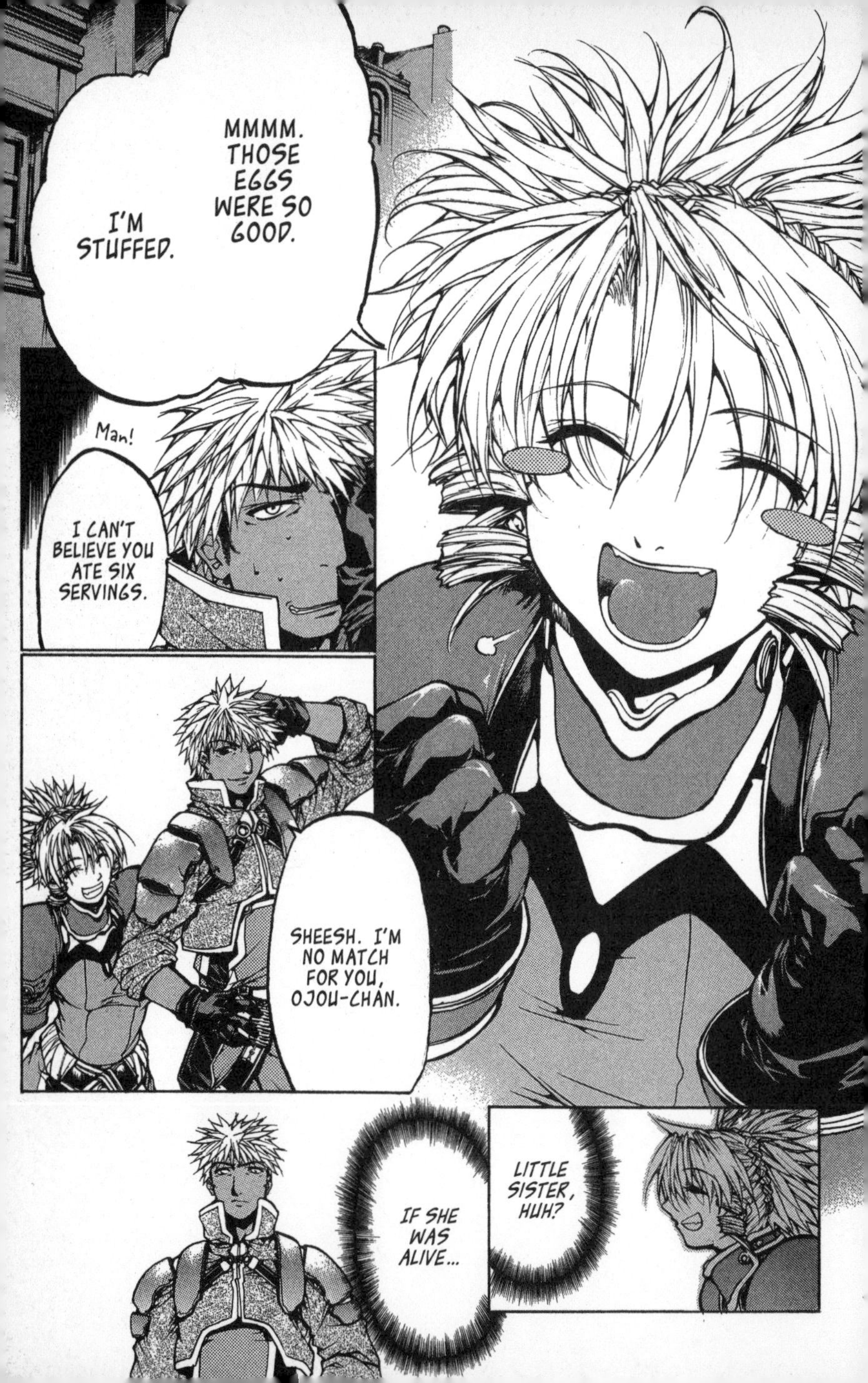
MMMM. THOSE EGGS WERE SO GOOD.
I'M STUFFED.
Man!
I CAN'T BELIEVE YOU ATE SIX SERVINGS.
SHEESH. I'M NO MATCH FOR YOU, OJOU-CHAN.
LITTLE SISTER, HUH?
IF SHE WAS ALIVE...

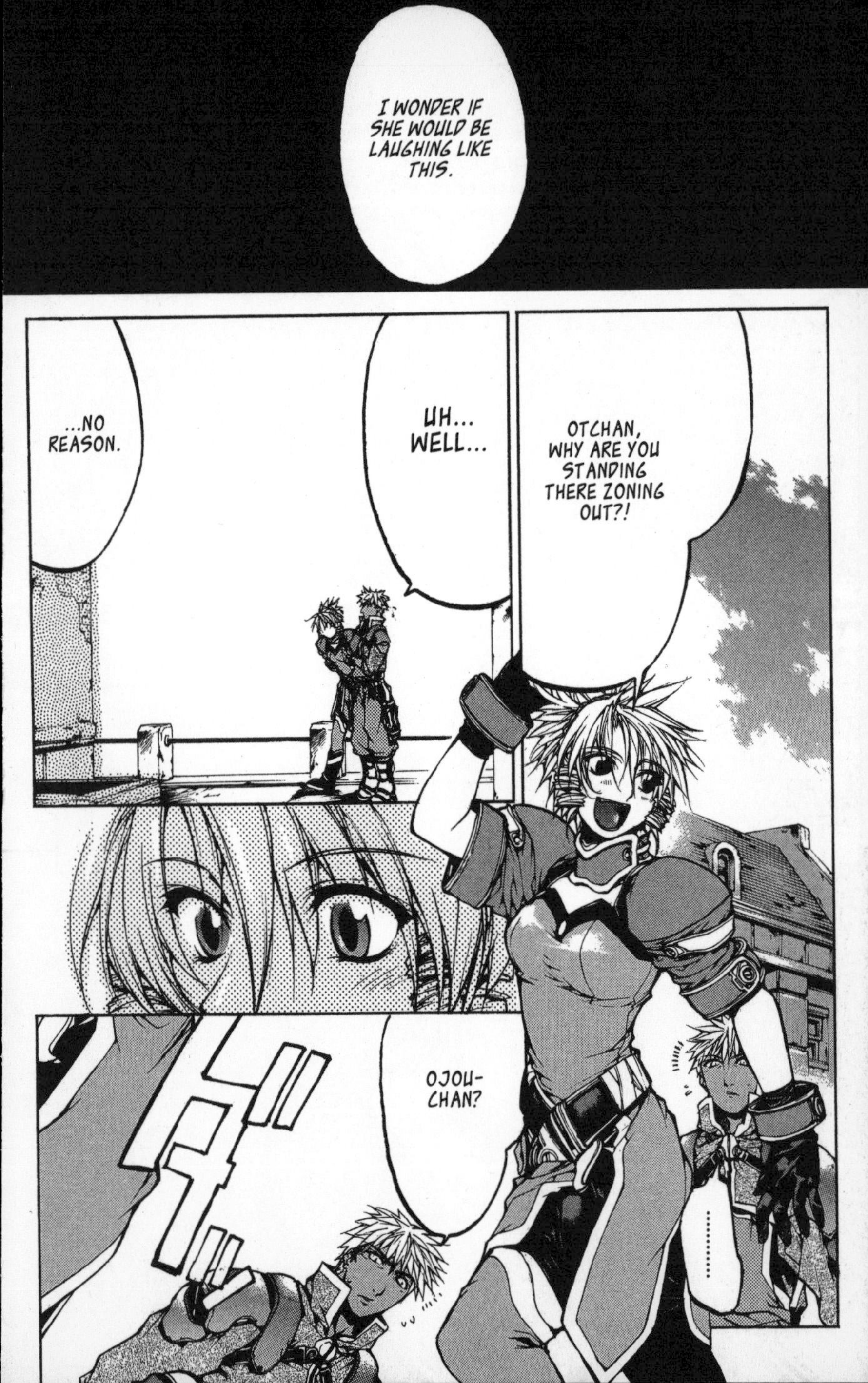
I WONDER IF SHE WOULD BE LAUGHING LIKE THIS.
OTCHAN, WHY ARE YOU STANDING THERE ZONING OUT?!
UH... WELL...
...NO REASON.
OJOU-CHAN?
....

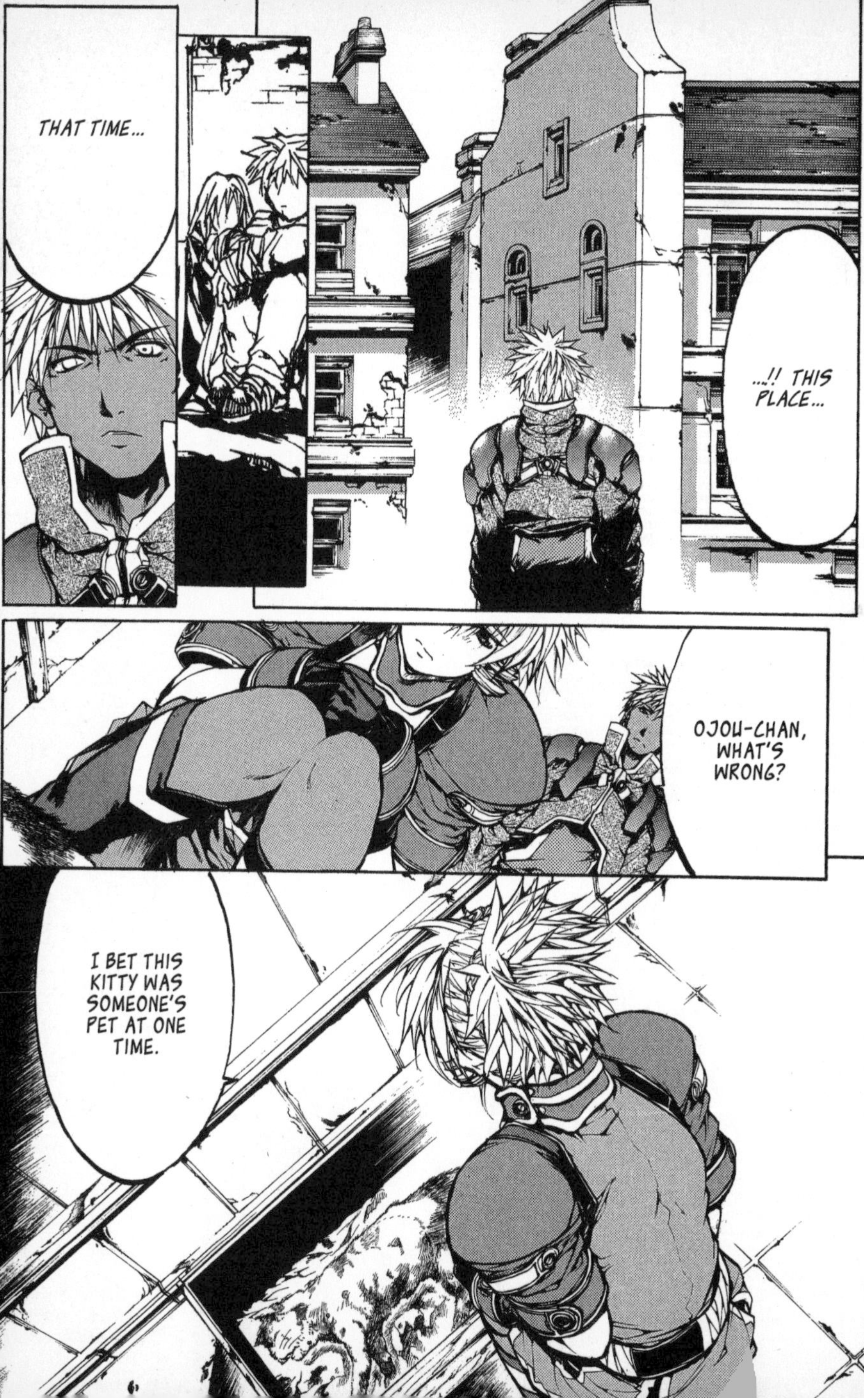

...!! THIS PLACE...
THAT TIME...
OJOU-CHAN, WHAT'S WRONG?
I BET THIS KITTY WAS SOMEONE'S PET AT ONE TIME.

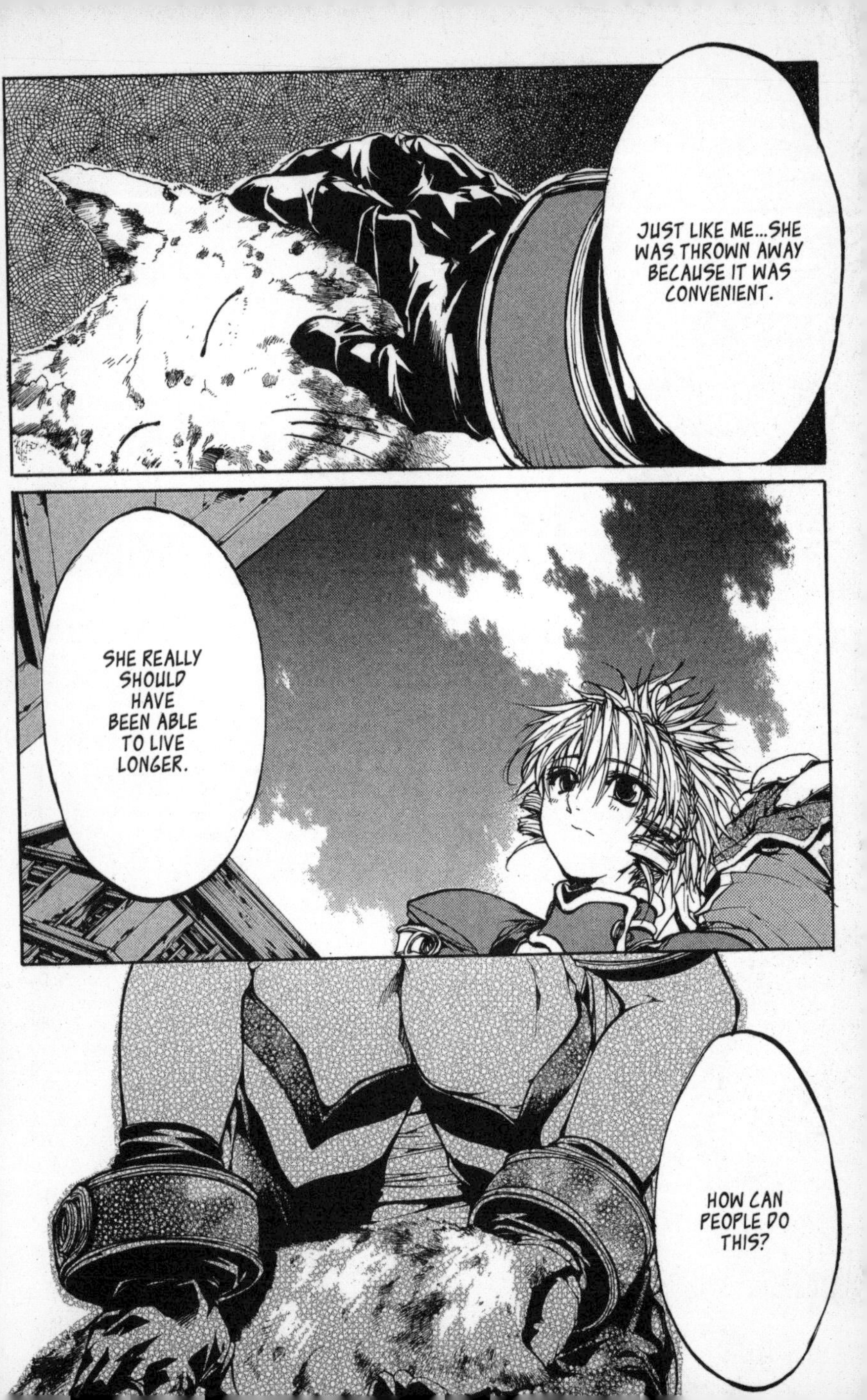
JUST LIKE ME...SHE WAS THROWN AWAY BECAUSE IT WAS CONVENIENT.
SHE REALLY SHOULD HAVE BEEN ABLE TO LIVE LONGER.
HOW CAN PEOPLE DO THIS?

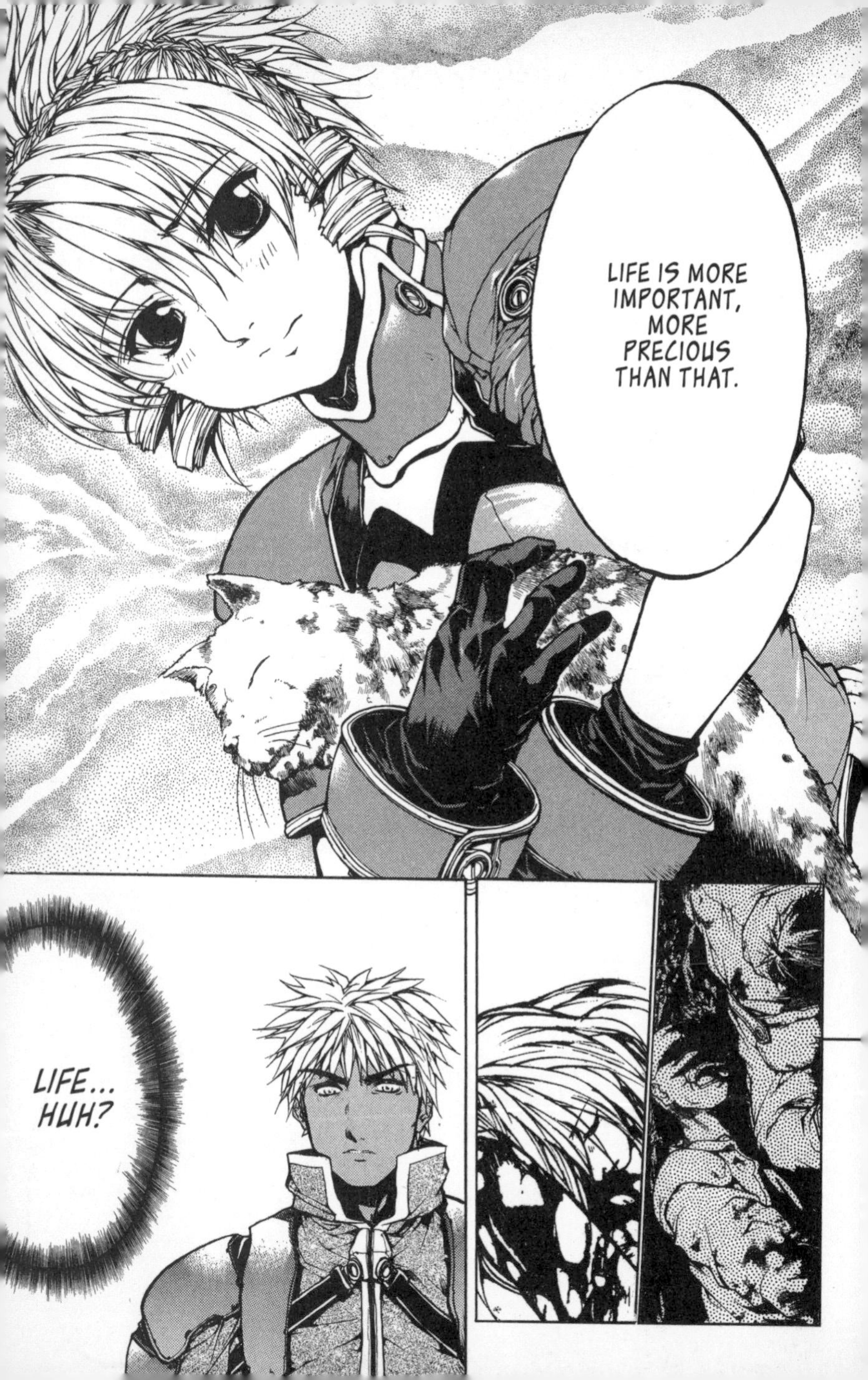
LIFE IS MORE IMPORTANT, MORE PRECIOUS THAN THAT.
LIFE... HUH?

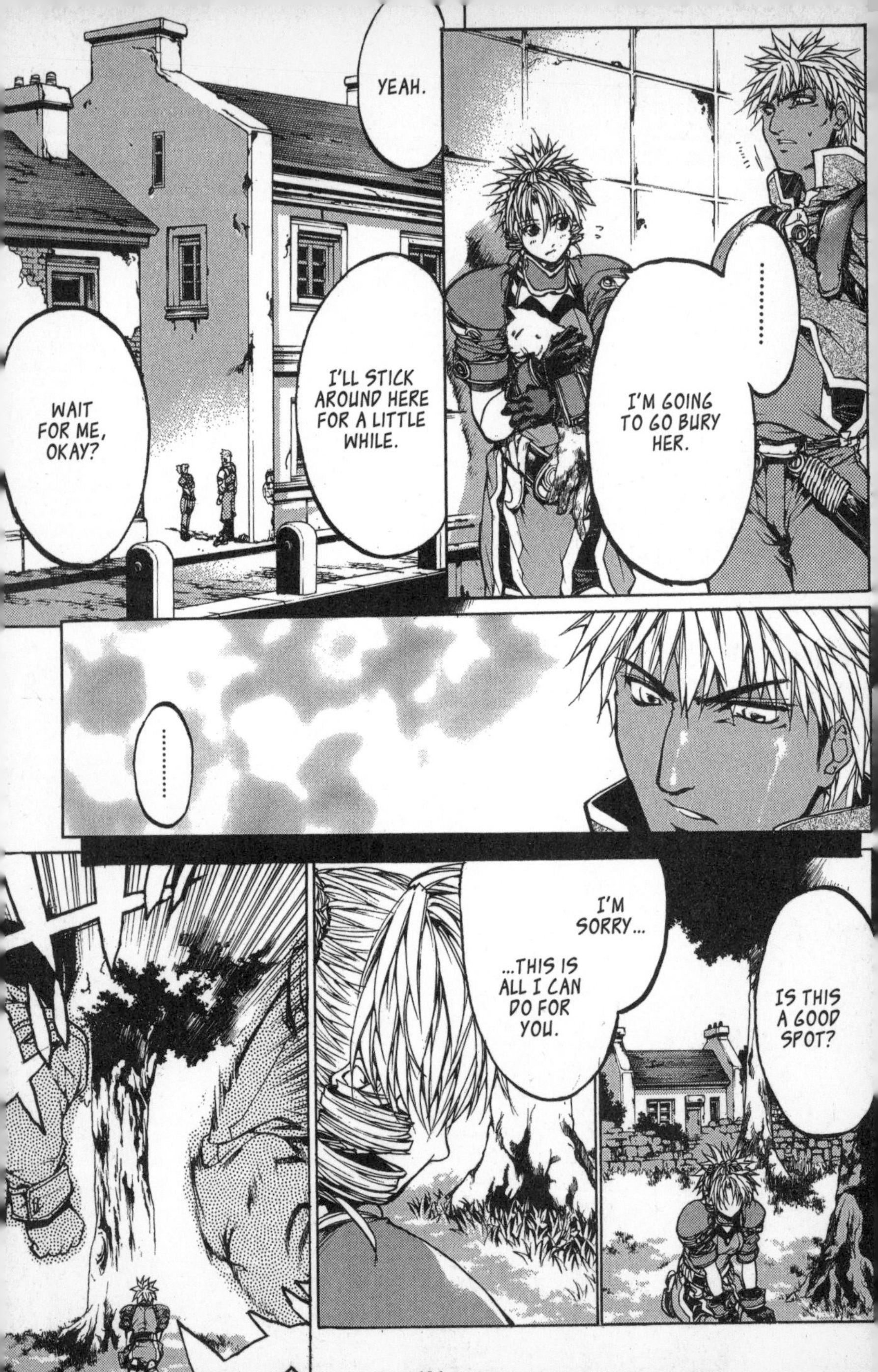

......
I'M GOING TO GO BURY HER.
YEAH.
I'LL STICK AROUND HERE FOR A LITTLE WHILE.
WAIT FOR ME, OKAY?
......
IS THIS A GOOD SPOT?
I'M SORRY...
...THIS IS ALL I CAN DO FOR YOU.

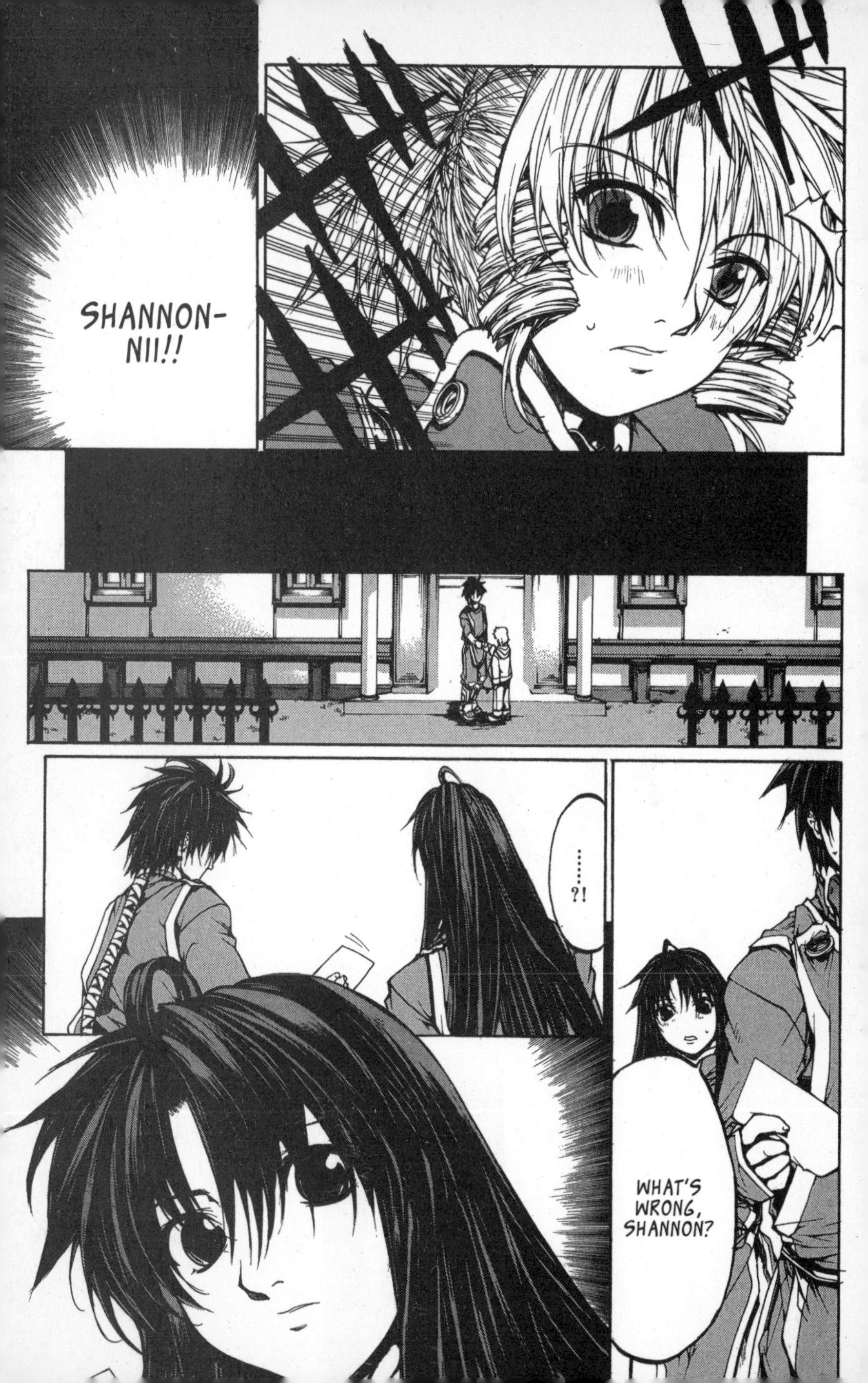
SHANNON-NII!!
WHAT'S WRONG, SHANNON?
......?!

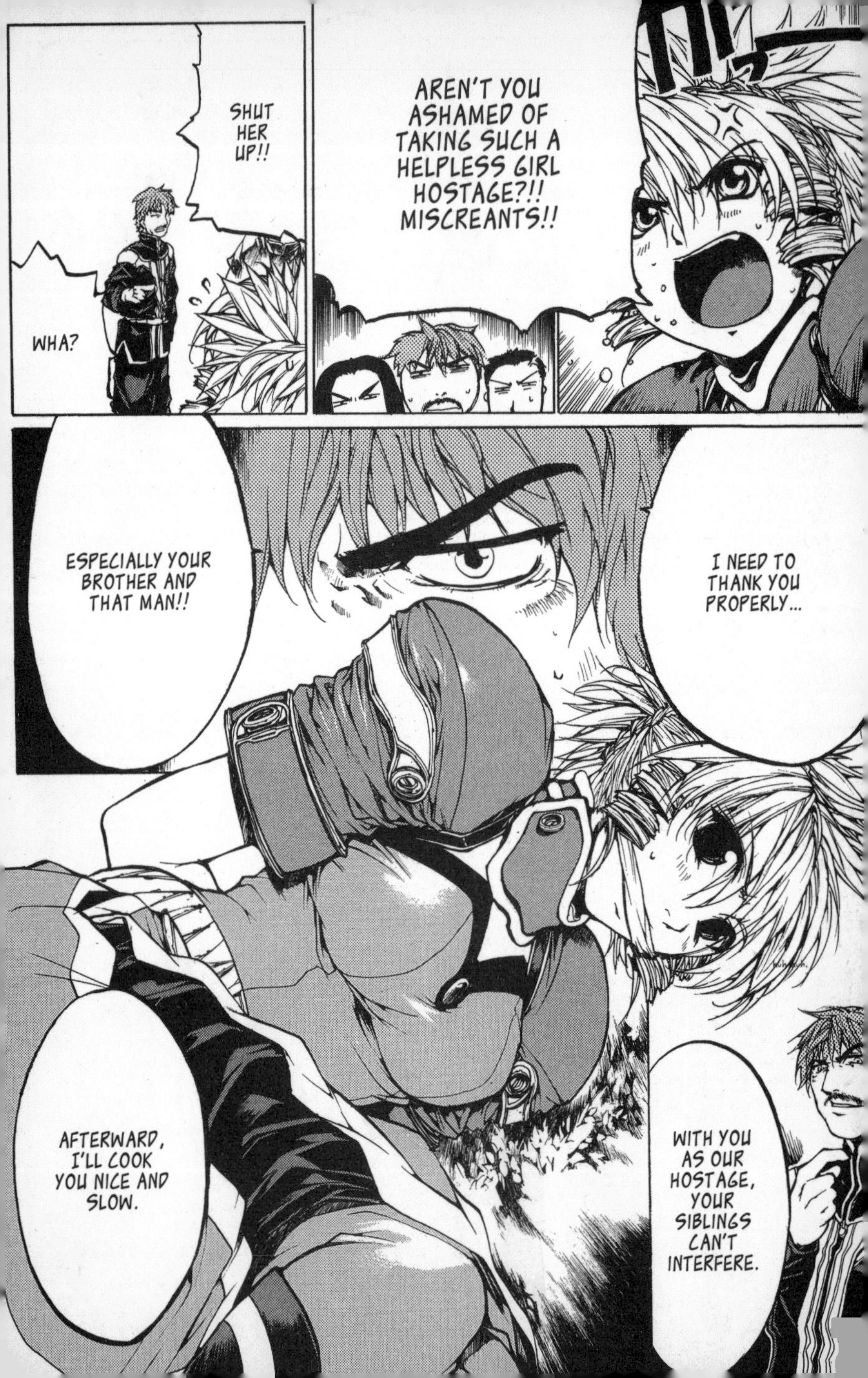
AREN'T YOU ASHAMED OF TAKING SUCH A HELPLESS GIRL HOSTAGE?!! MISCREANTS!!
SHUT HER UP!!
WHA?
I NEED TO THANK YOU PROPERLY...
ESPECIALLY YOUR BROTHER AND THAT MAN!!
WITH YOU AS OUR HOSTAGE, YOUR SIBLINGS CAN'T INTERFERE.
AFTERWARD, I'LL COOK YOU NICE AND SLOW.

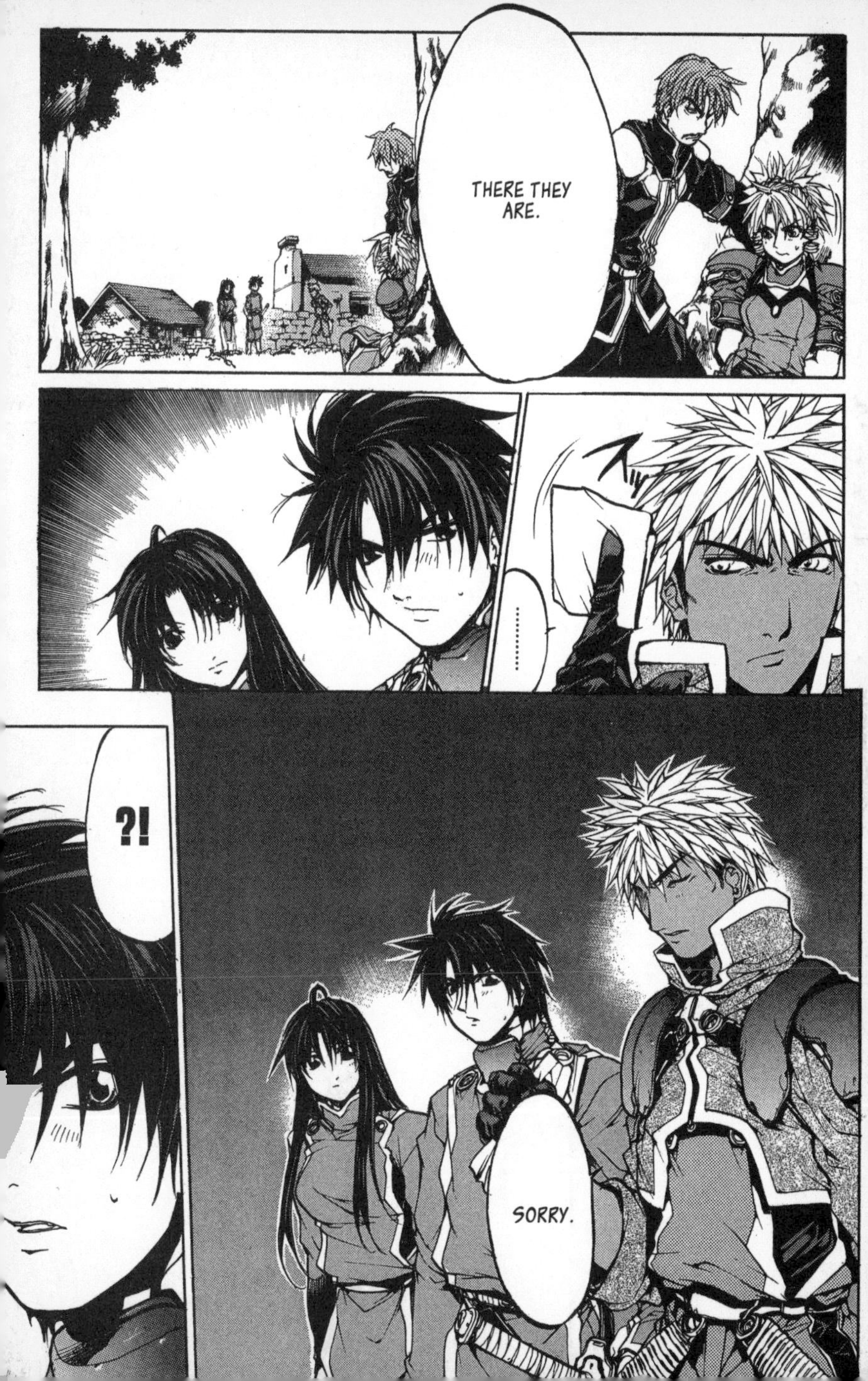
THERE THEY ARE.
......
SORRY.
?!

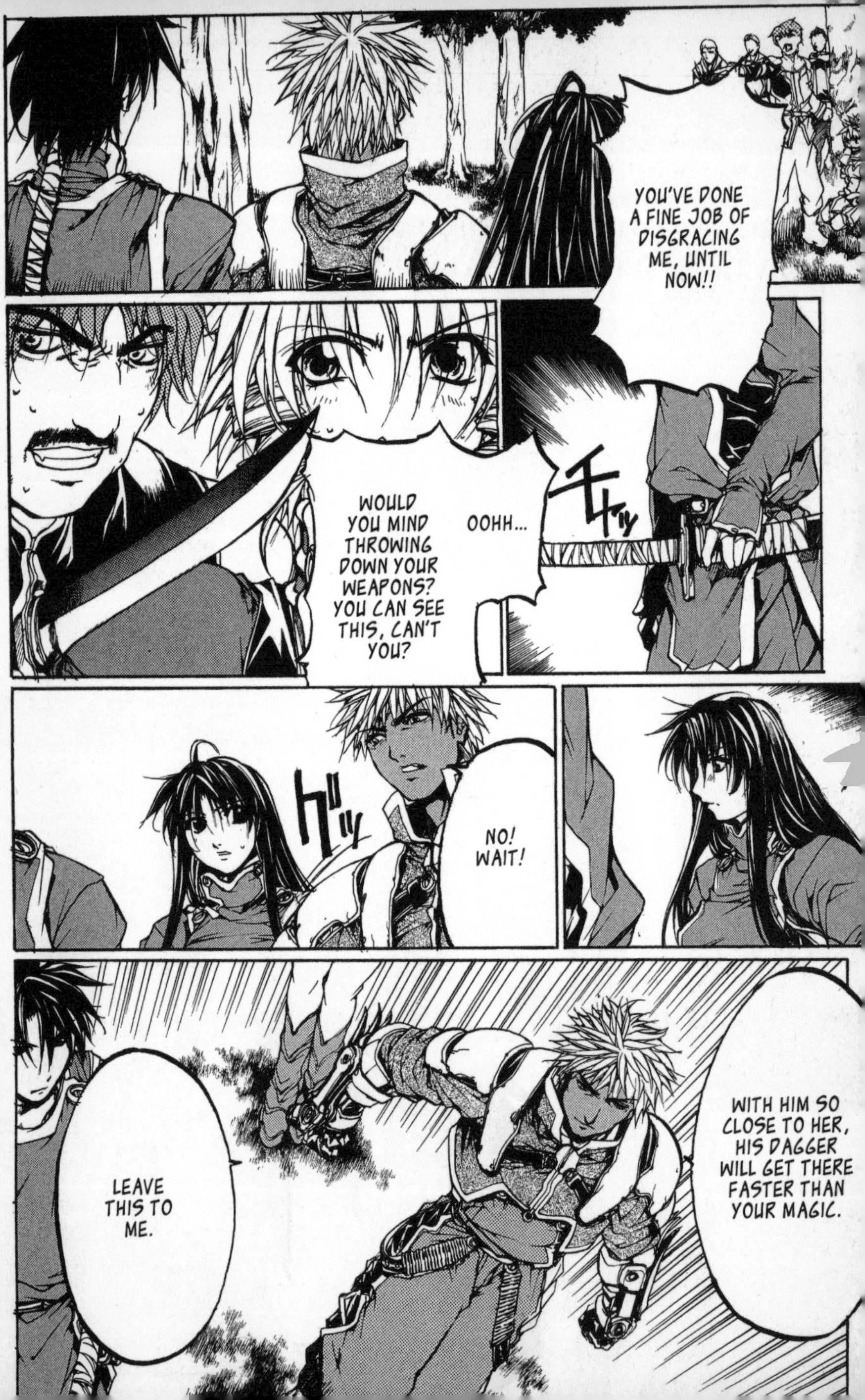
YOU'VE DONE A FINE JOB OF DISGRACING ME, UNTIL NOW!!
OOHH...
WOULD YOU MIND THROWING DOWN YOUR WEAPONS? YOU CAN SEE THIS, CAN'T YOU?
NO! WAIT!
WITH HIM SO CLOSE TO HER, HIS DAGGER WILL GET THERE FASTER THAN YOUR MAGIC.
LEAVE THIS TO ME.

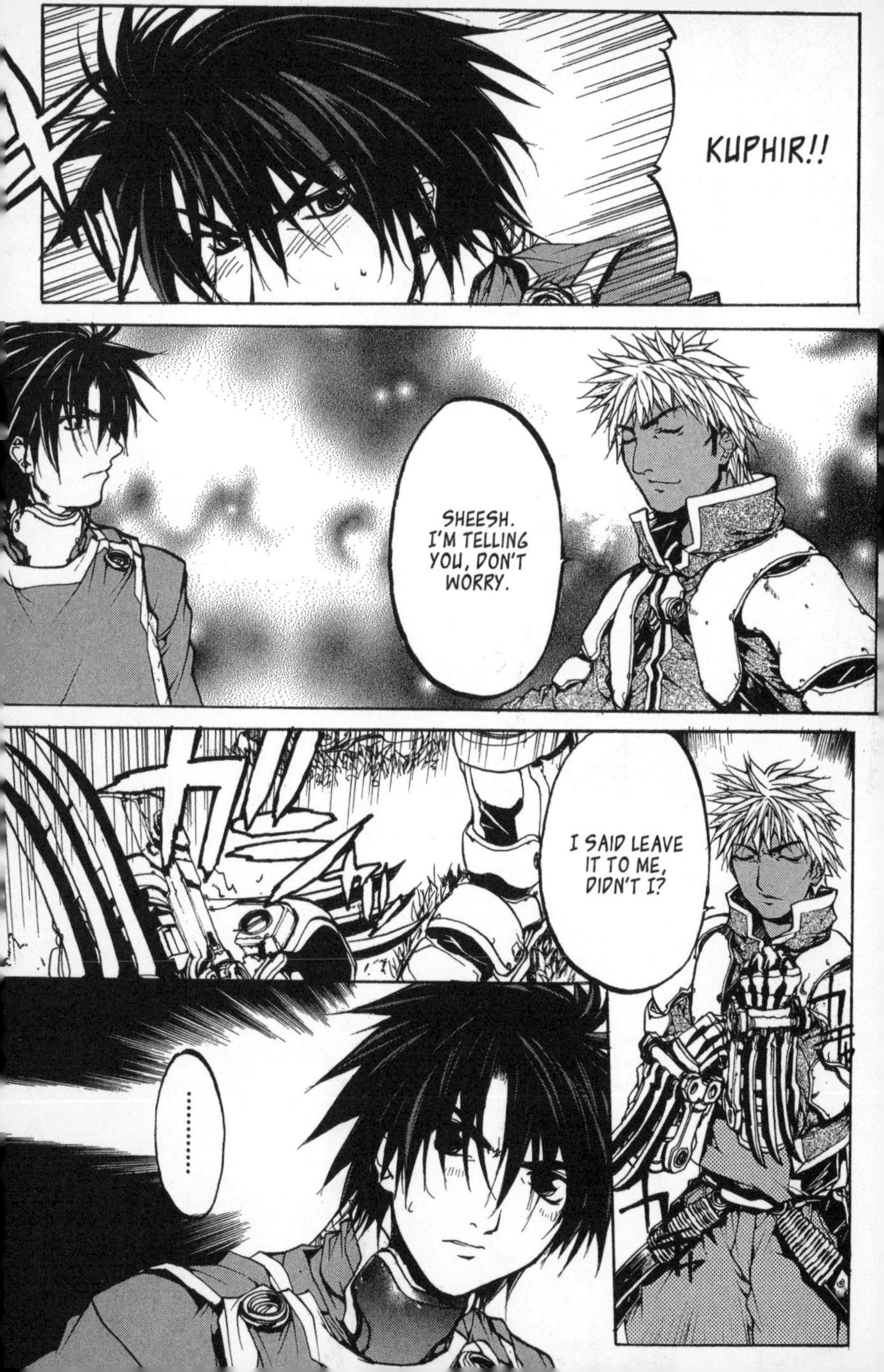
KUPHIR!!
SHEESH. I'M TELLING YOU, DON'T WORRY.
I SAID LEAVE IT TO ME, DIDN'T I?
....

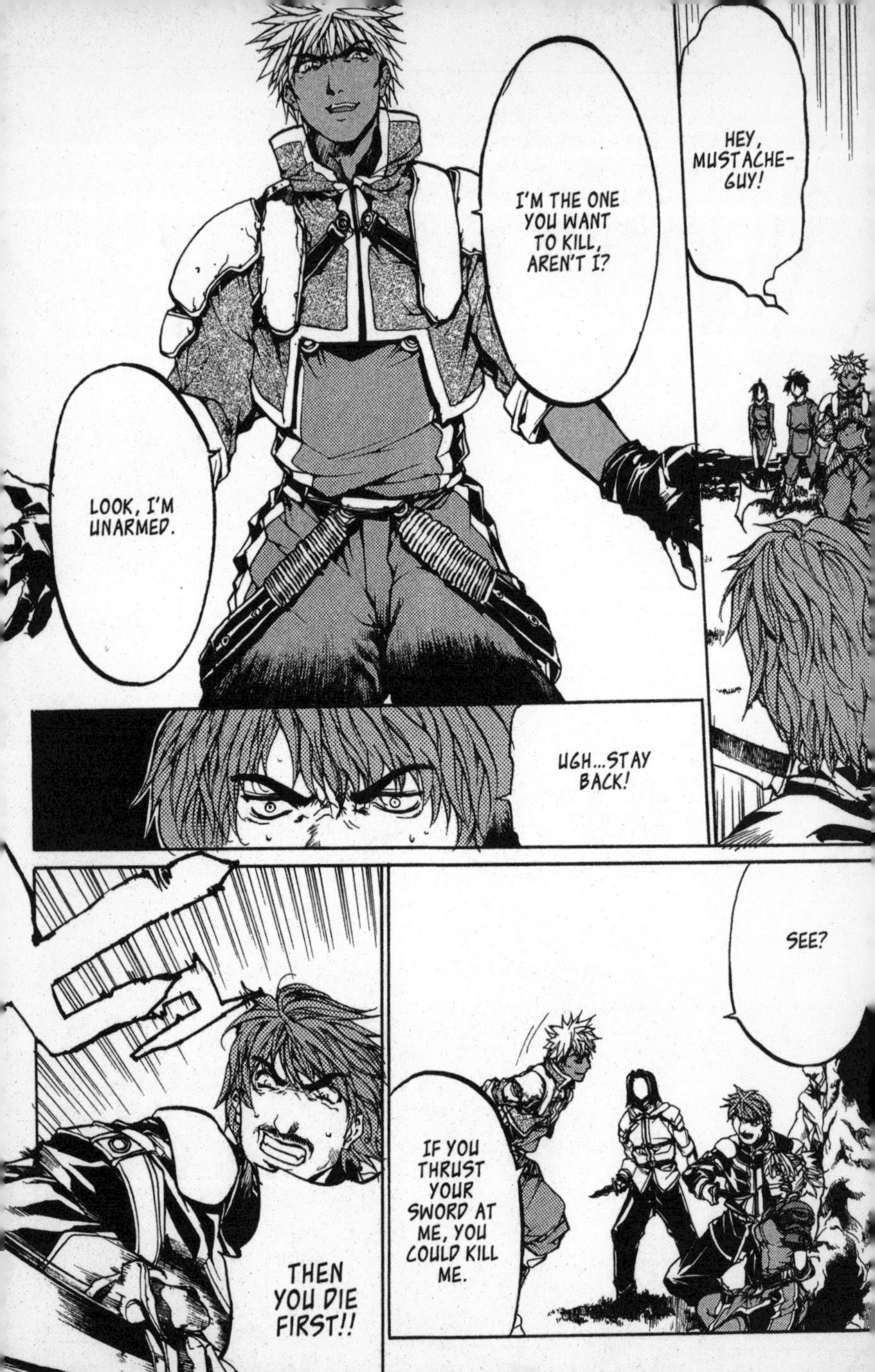
HEY, MUSTACHE-GUY!
I'M THE ONE YOU WANT TO KILL, AREN'T I?
LOOK, I'M UNARMED.
UGH...STAY BACK!
SEE?
IF YOU THRUST YOUR SWORD AT ME, YOU COULD KILL ME.
THEN YOU DIE FIRST!!

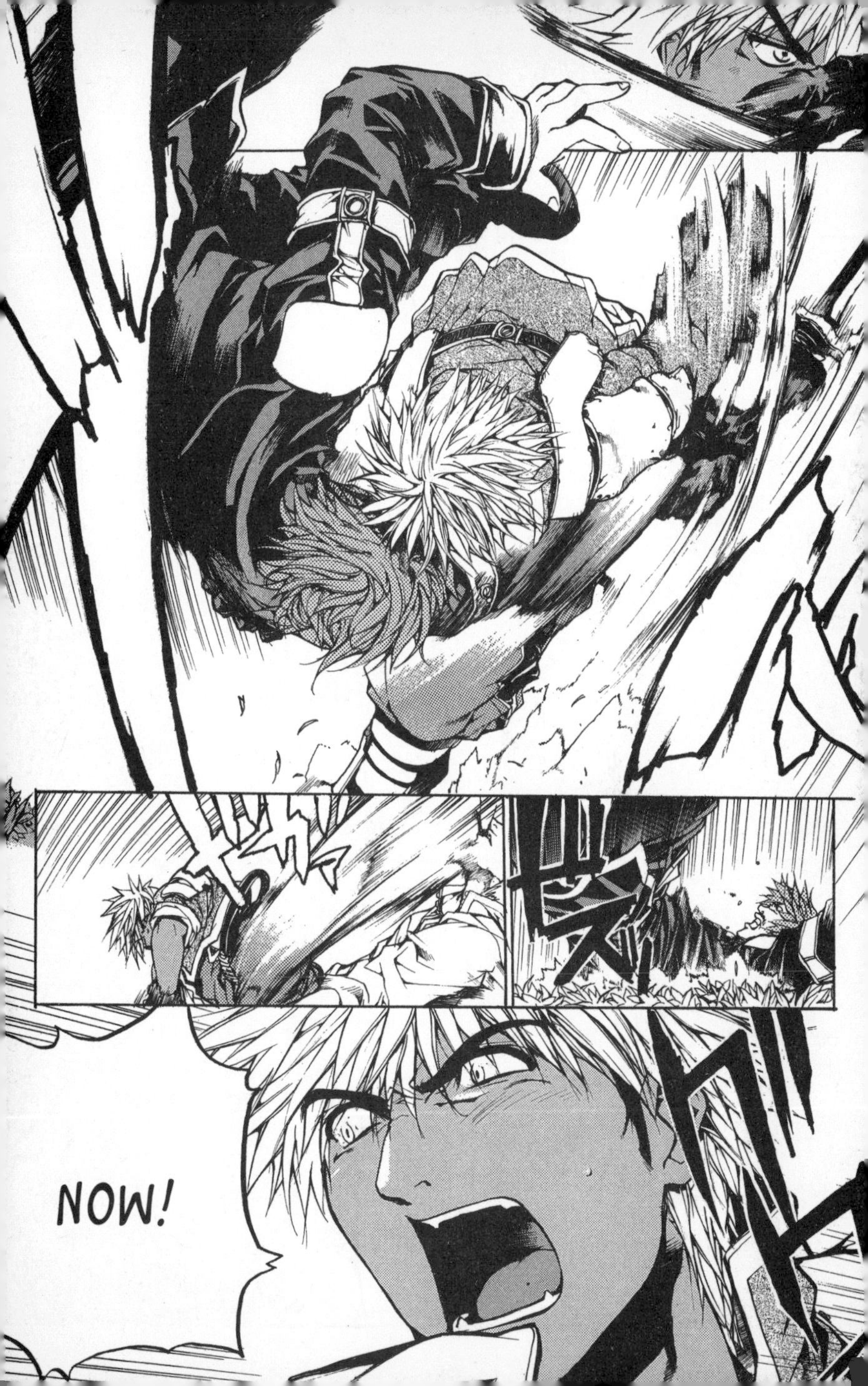
NOW!

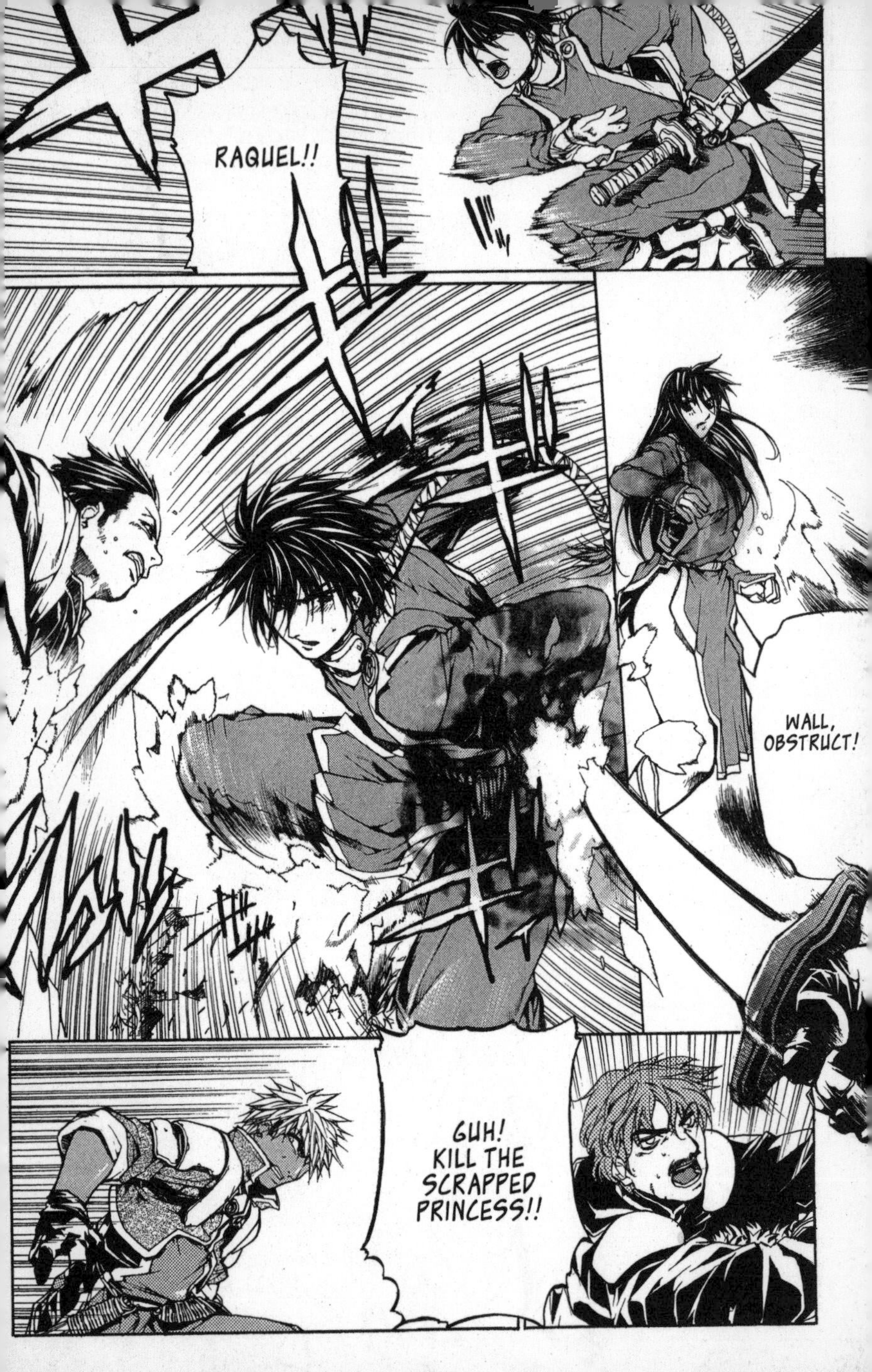
RAQUEL!!
WALL, OBSTRUCT!
GUH! KILL THE SCRAPPED PRINCESS!!

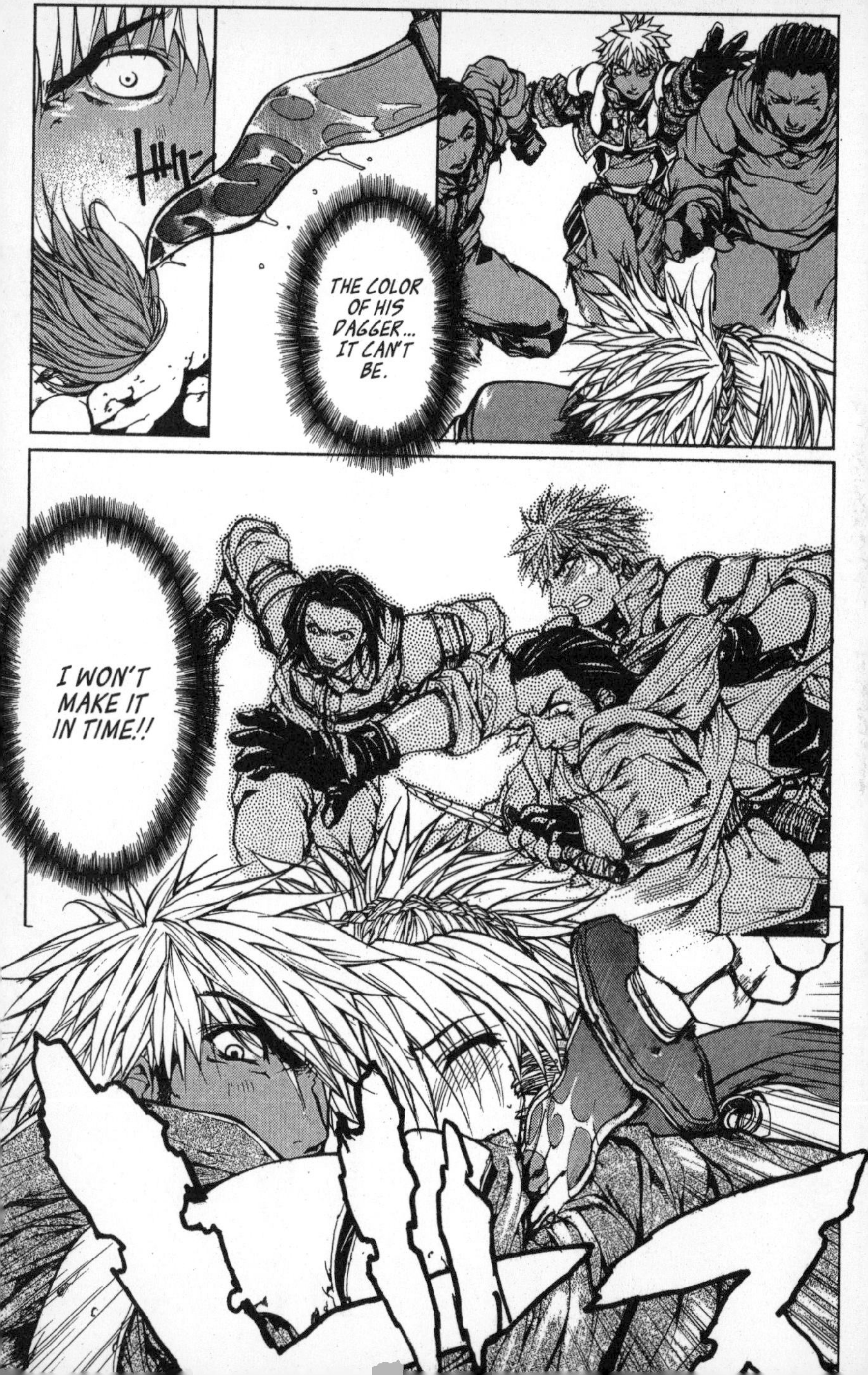
THE COLOR OF HIS DAGGER... IT CAN'T BE.
I WON'T MAKE IT IN TIME!!

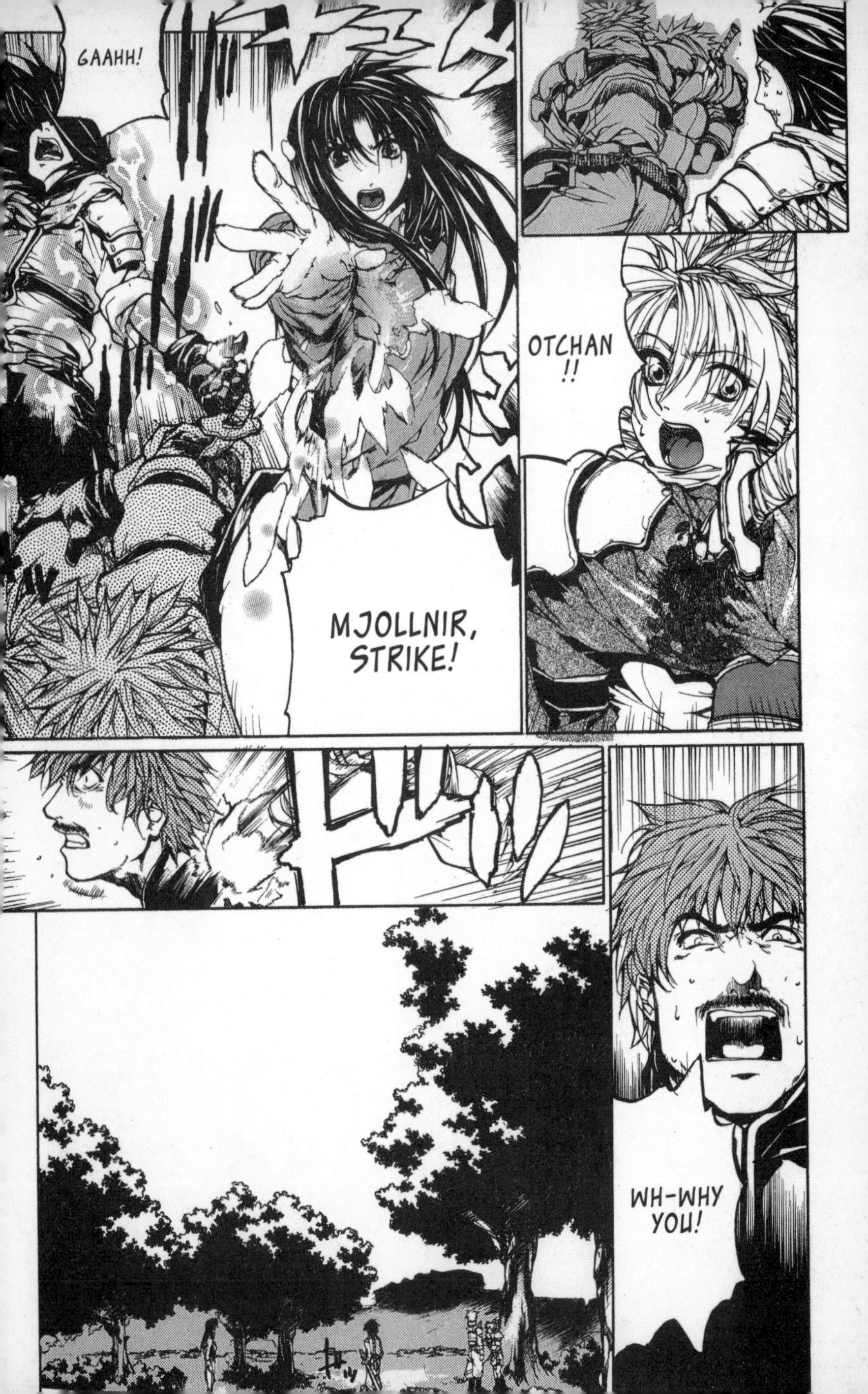
OTCHAN !!
GAAHH!
MJOLLNIR, STRIKE!
WH-WHY YOU!

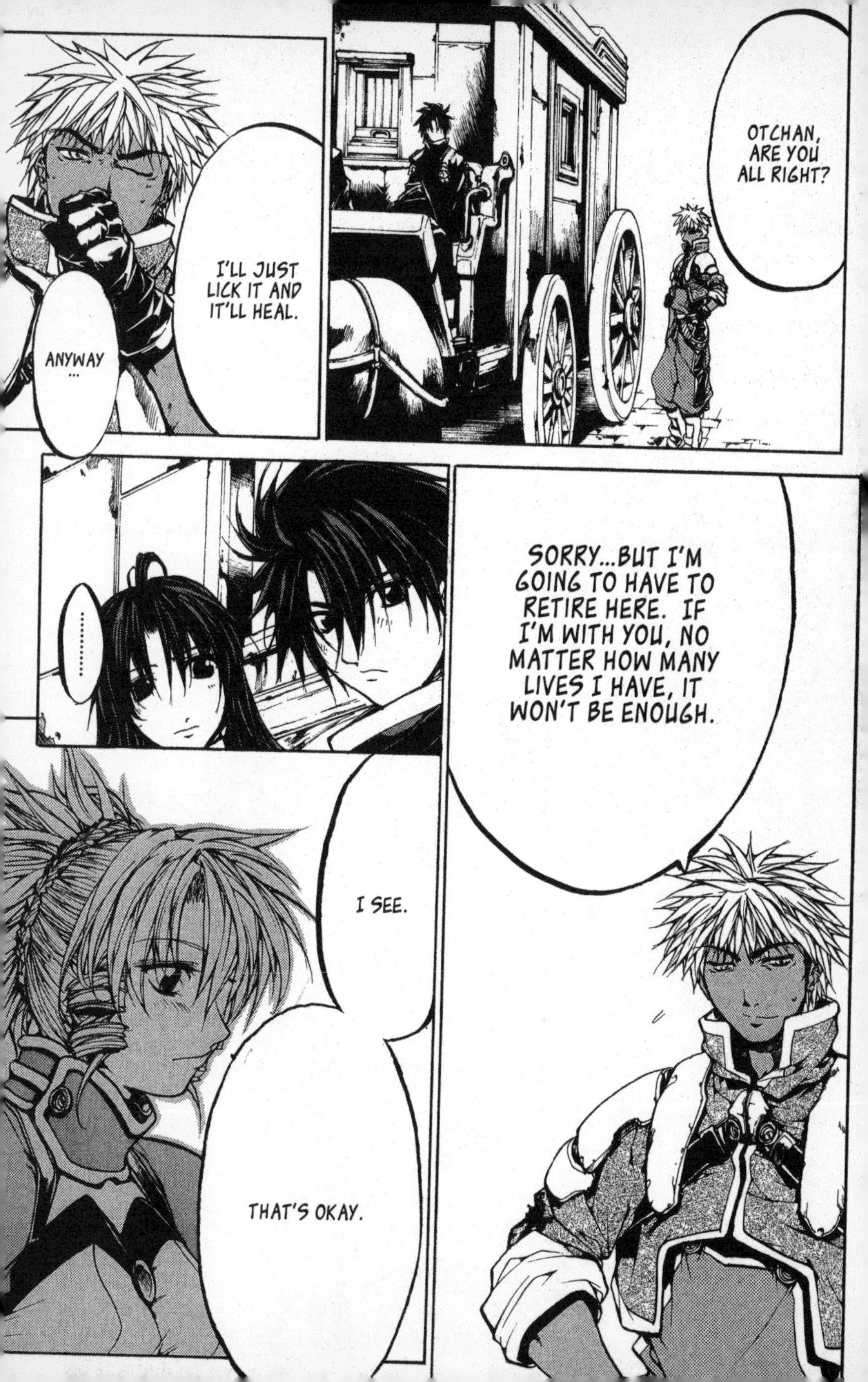
OTCHAN, ARE YOU ALL RIGHT?
I'LL JUST LICK IT AND IT'LL HEAL.
ANYWAY ...
SORRY...BUT I'M GOING TO HAVE TO RETIRE HERE. IF I'M WITH YOU, NO MATTER HOW MANY LIVES I HAVE, IT WON'T BE ENOUGH.
....
I SEE.
THAT'S OKAY.

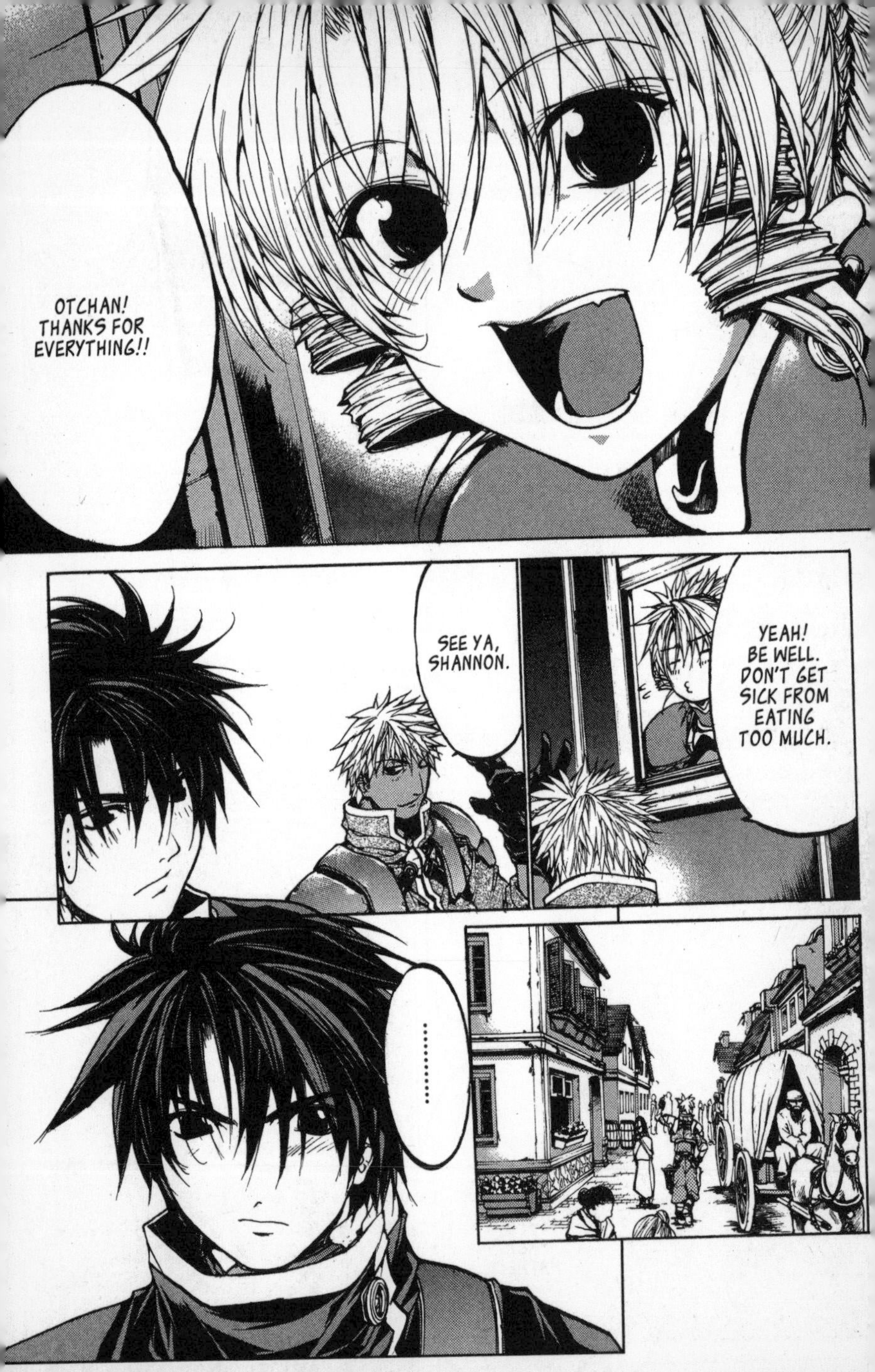
OTCHAN! THANKS FOR EVERYTHING!!
YEAH! BE WELL. DON'T GET SICK FROM EATING TOO MUCH.
SEE YA, SHANNON.
....

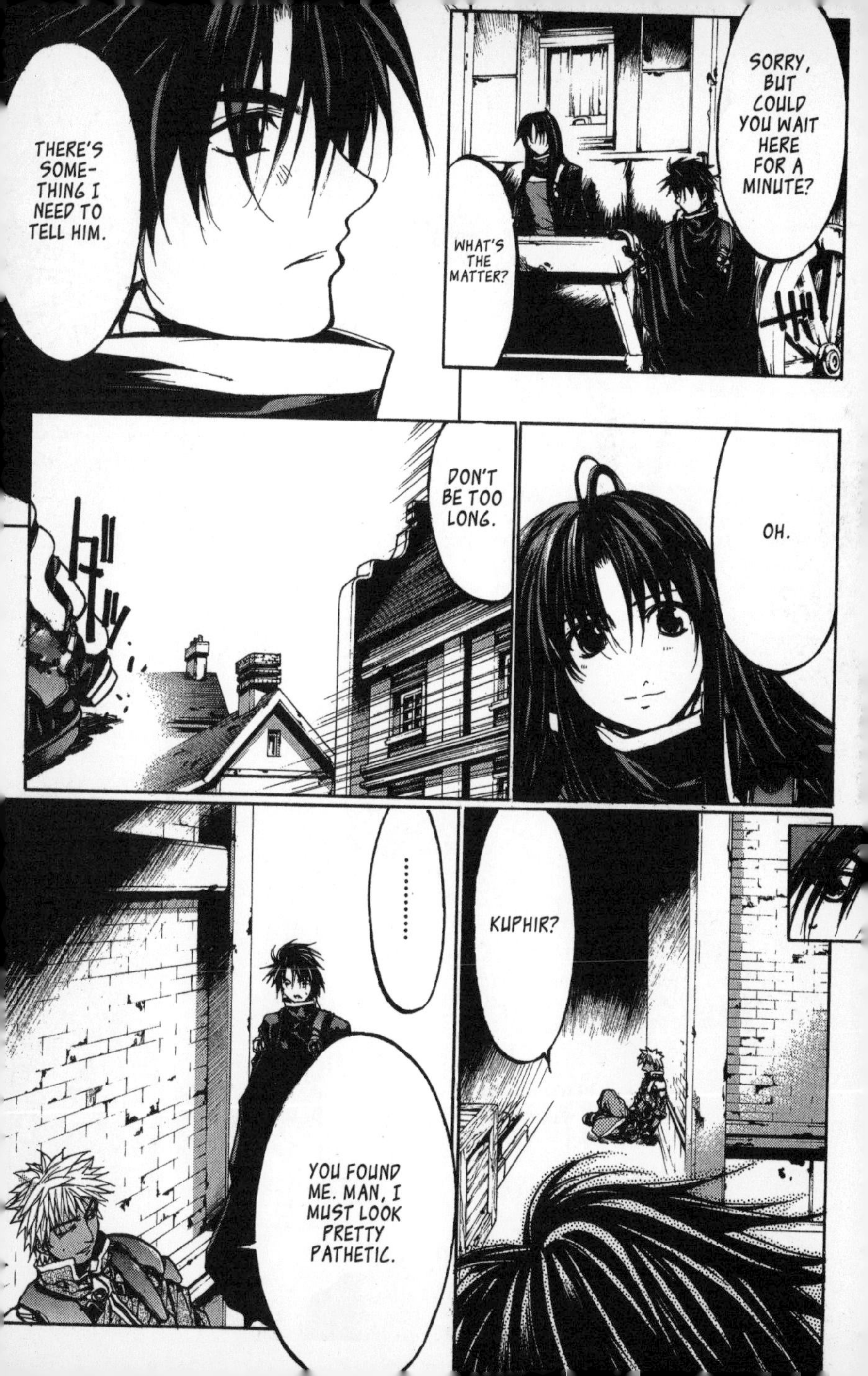
SORRY, BUT COULD YOU WAIT HERE FOR A MINUTE?
WHAT'S THE MATTER?
THERE'S SOME-THING I NEED TO TELL HIM.
OH.
DON'T BE TOO LONG.
KUPHIR?
....
YOU FOUND ME. MAN, I MUST LOOK PRETTY PATHETIC.

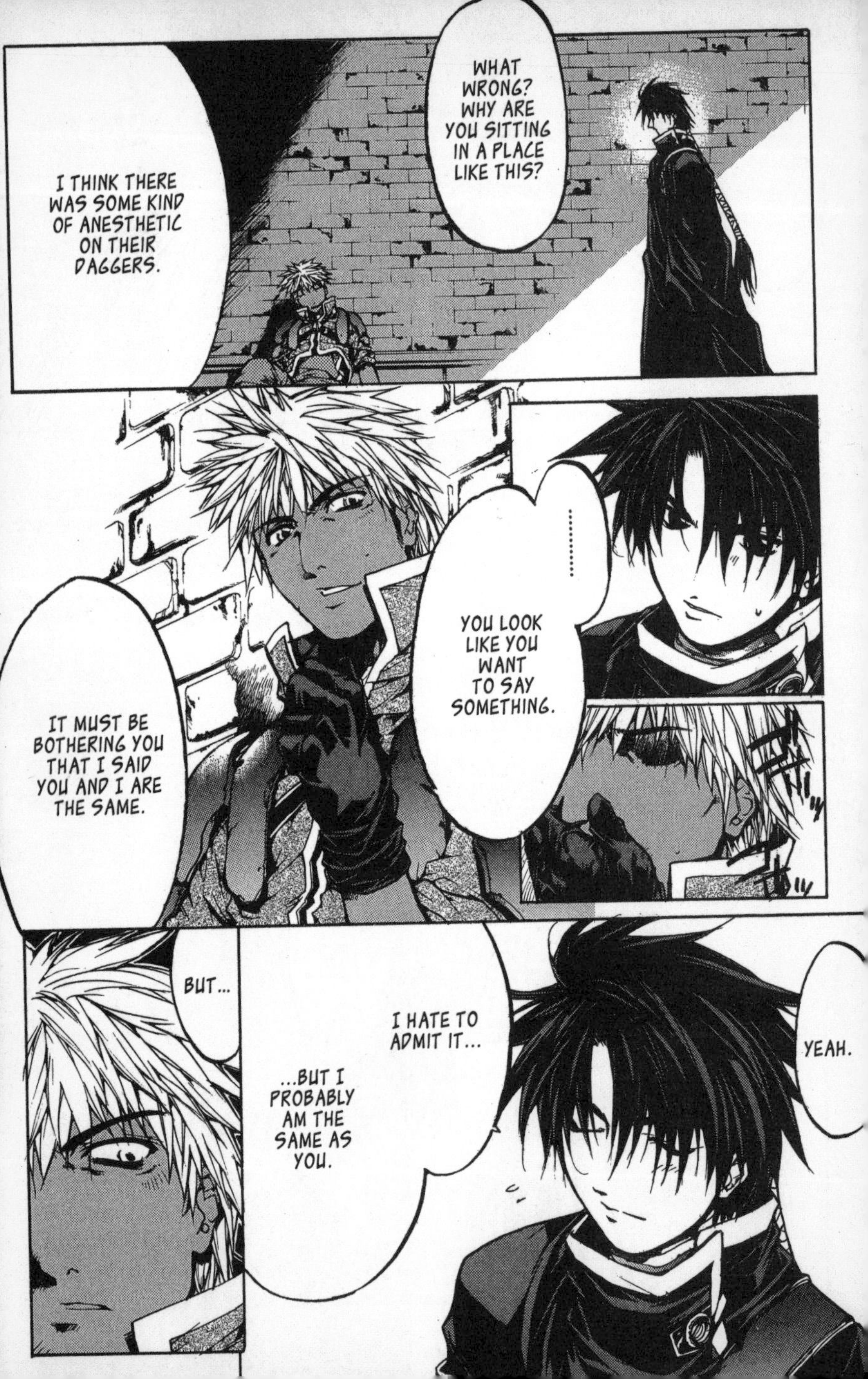
WHAT WRONG? WHY ARE YOU SITTING IN A PLACE LIKE THIS?
I THINK THERE WAS SOME KIND OF ANESTHETIC ON THEIR DAGGERS.
......
YOU LOOK LIKE YOU WANT TO SAY SOMETHING.
IT MUST BE BOTHERING YOU THAT I SAID YOU AND I ARE THE SAME.
YEAH.
I HATE TO ADMIT IT...
...BUT I PROBABLY AM THE SAME AS YOU.
BUT...

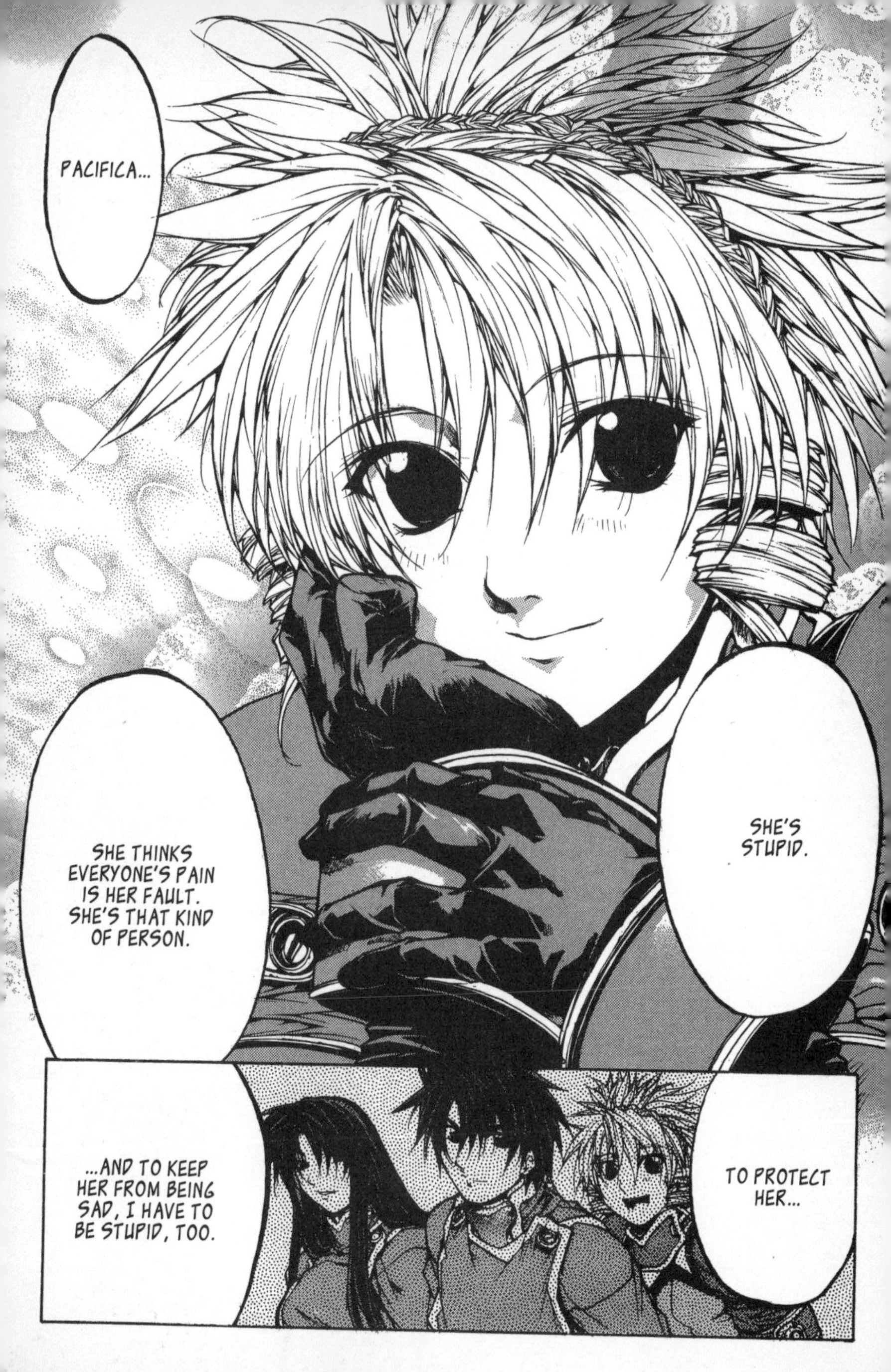
PACIFICA...
SHE'S STUPID.
SHE THINKS EVERYONE'S PAIN IS HER FAULT. SHE'S THAT KIND OF PERSON.
TO PROTECT HER...
...AND TO KEEP HER FROM BEING SAD, I HAVE TO BE STUPID, TOO.

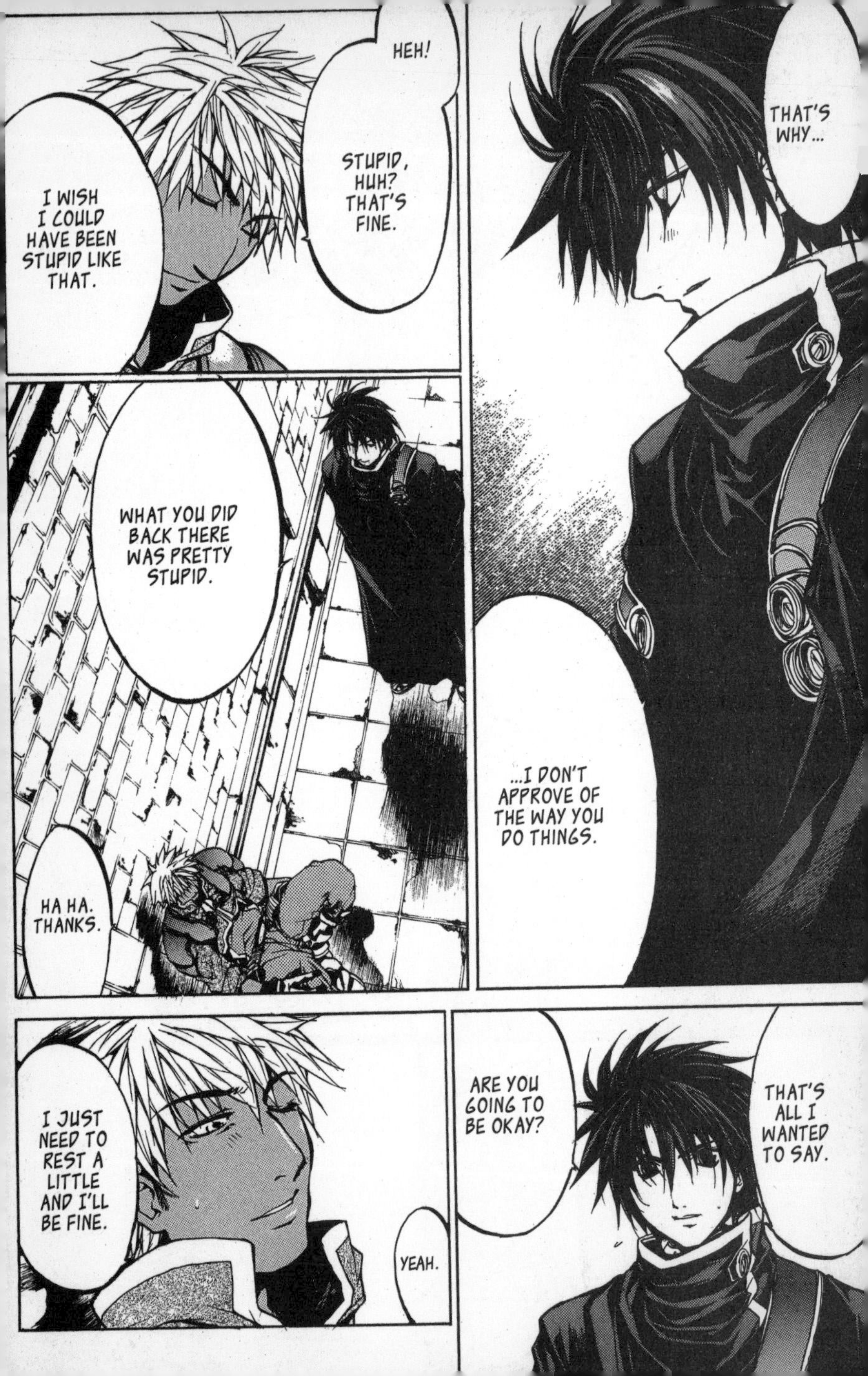
THAT'S WHY...
...I DON'T APPROVE OF THE WAY YOU DO THINGS.
HEH!
STUPID, HUH? THAT'S FINE.
I WISH I COULD HAVE BEEN STUPID LIKE THAT.
WHAT YOU DID BACK THERE WAS PRETTY STUPID.
HA HA. THANKS.
THAT'S ALL I WANTED TO SAY.
ARE YOU GOING TO BE OKAY?
YEAH.
I JUST NEED TO REST A LITTLE AND I'LL BE FINE.

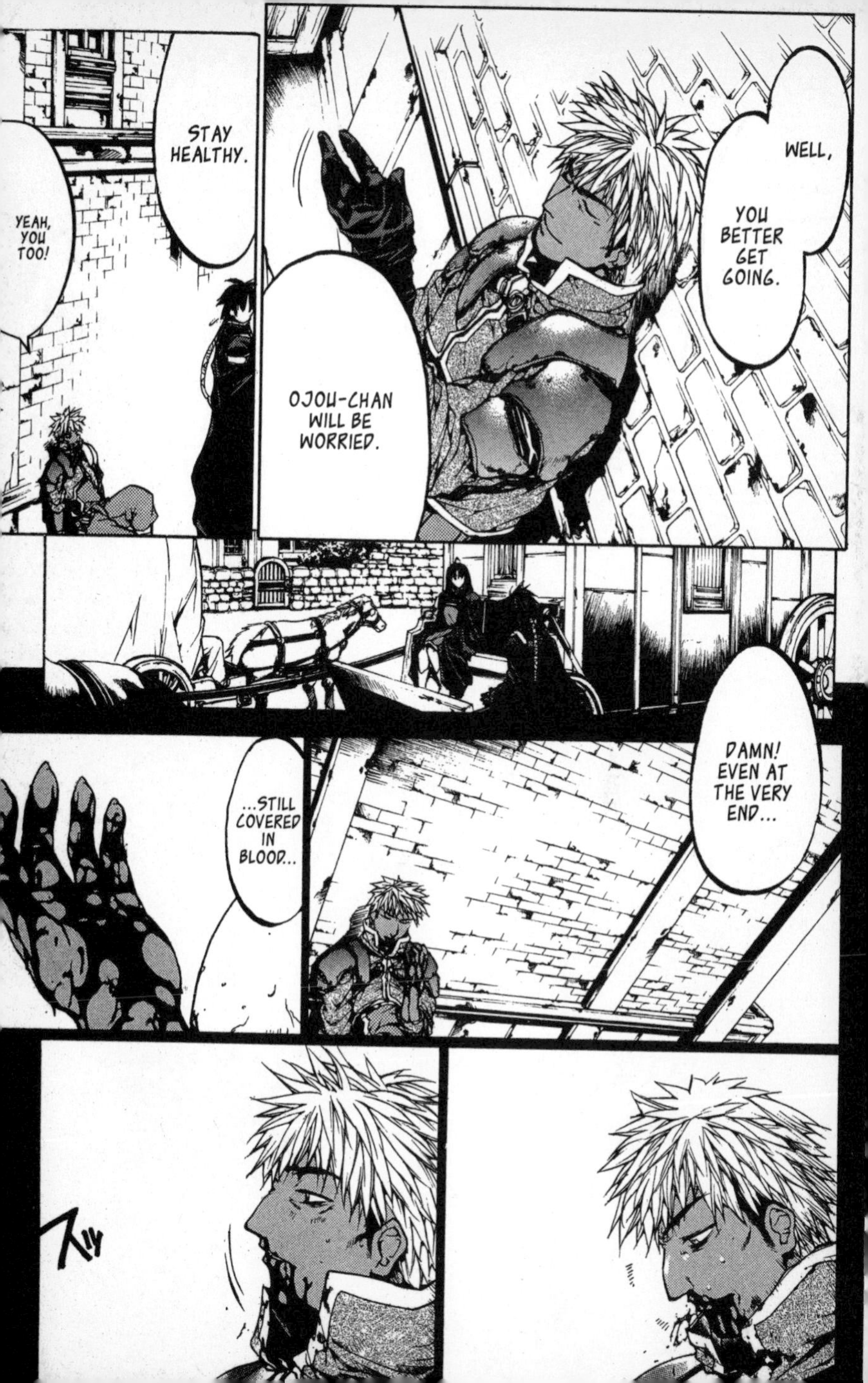
WELL,
YOU BETTER GET GOING.
OJOU-CHAN WILL BE WORRIED.
STAY HEALTHY.
YEAH, YOU TOO!
DAMN! EVEN AT THE VERY END...
...STILL COVERED IN BLOOD...

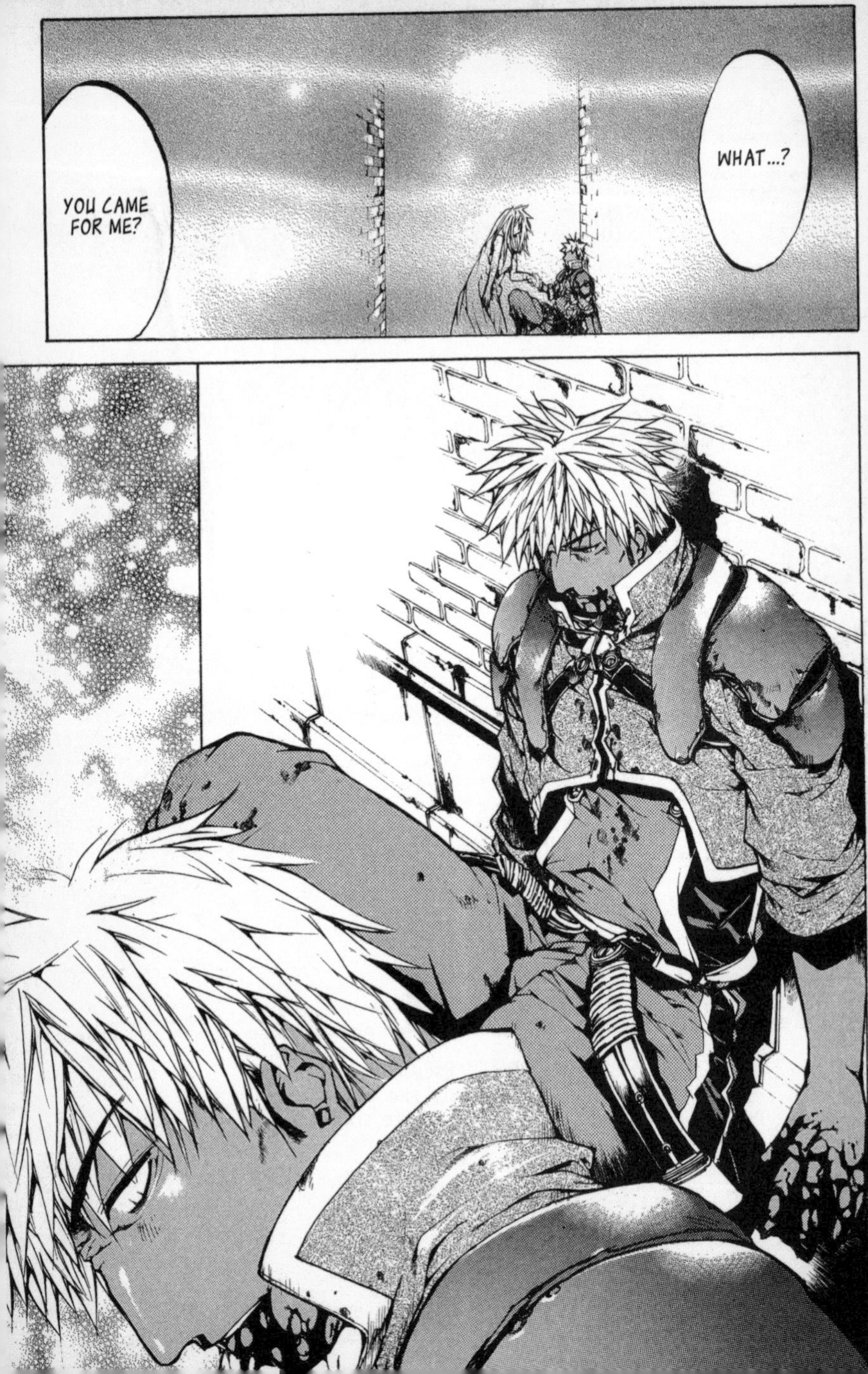
WHAT...?
YOU CAME FOR ME?

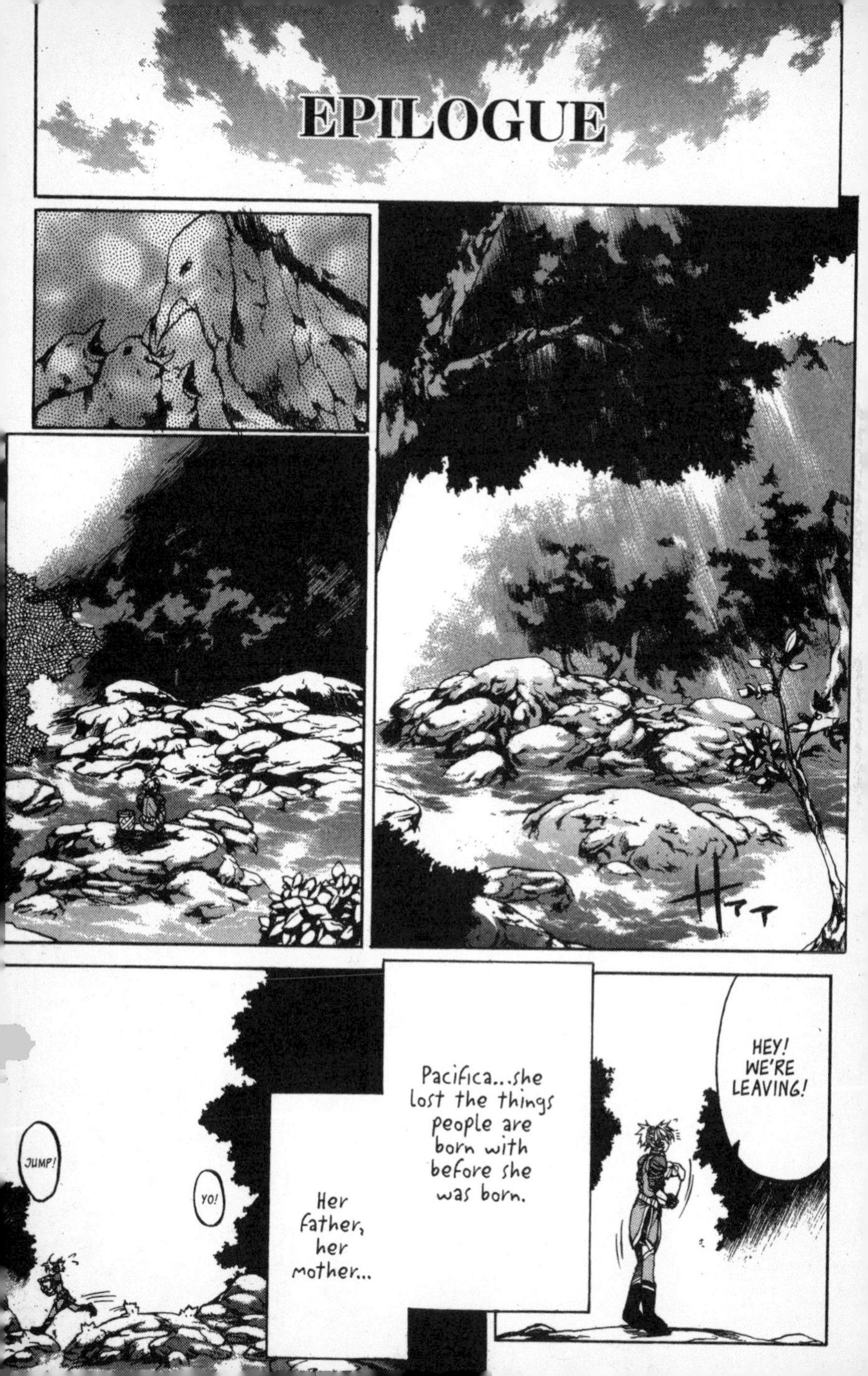
EPILOGUE
HEY! WE'RE LEAVING!
Pacifica...she lost the things people are born with before she was born.
Her father, her mother...
YO!
JUMP!

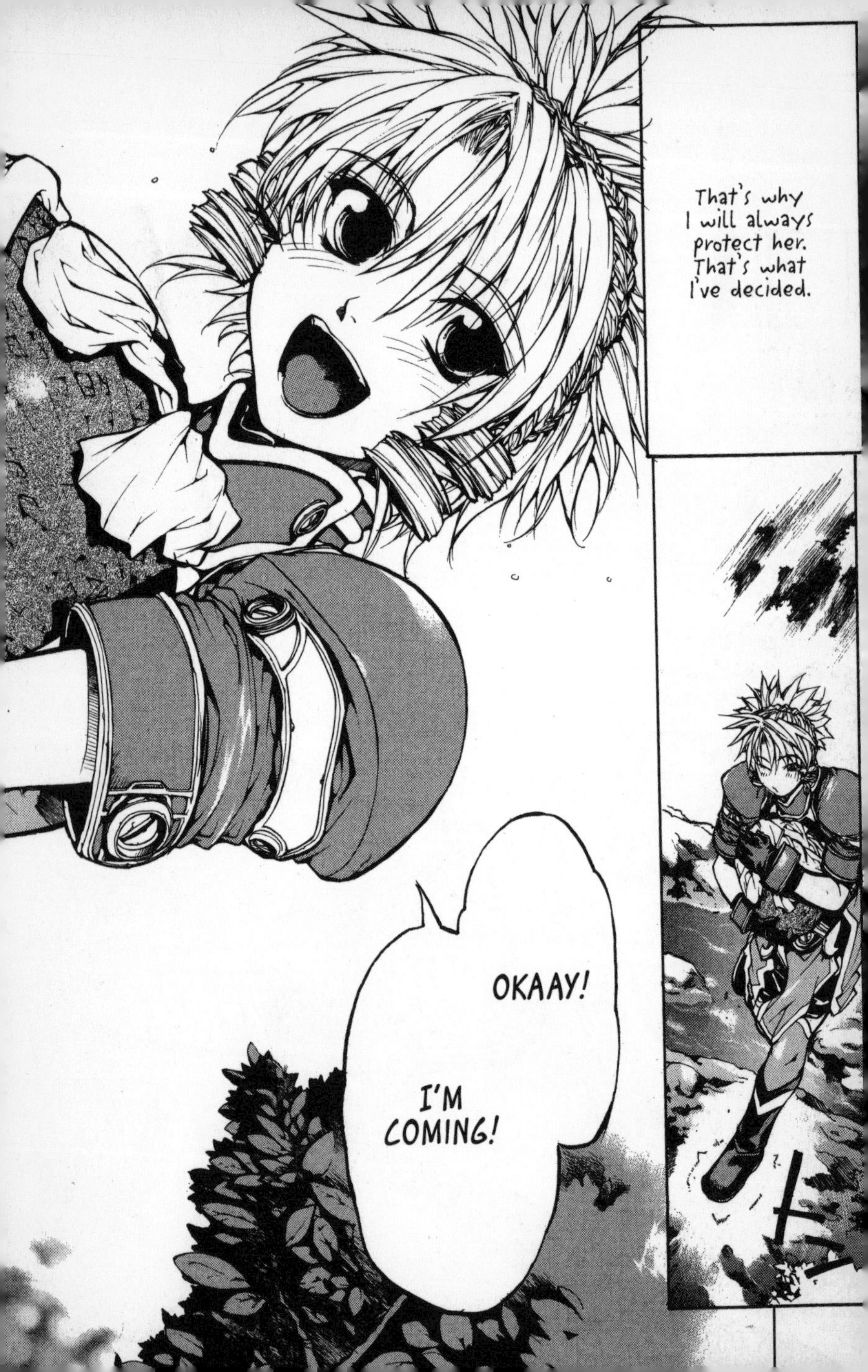
That's why I will always protect her. That's what I've decided.
OKAAY!
I'M COMING!

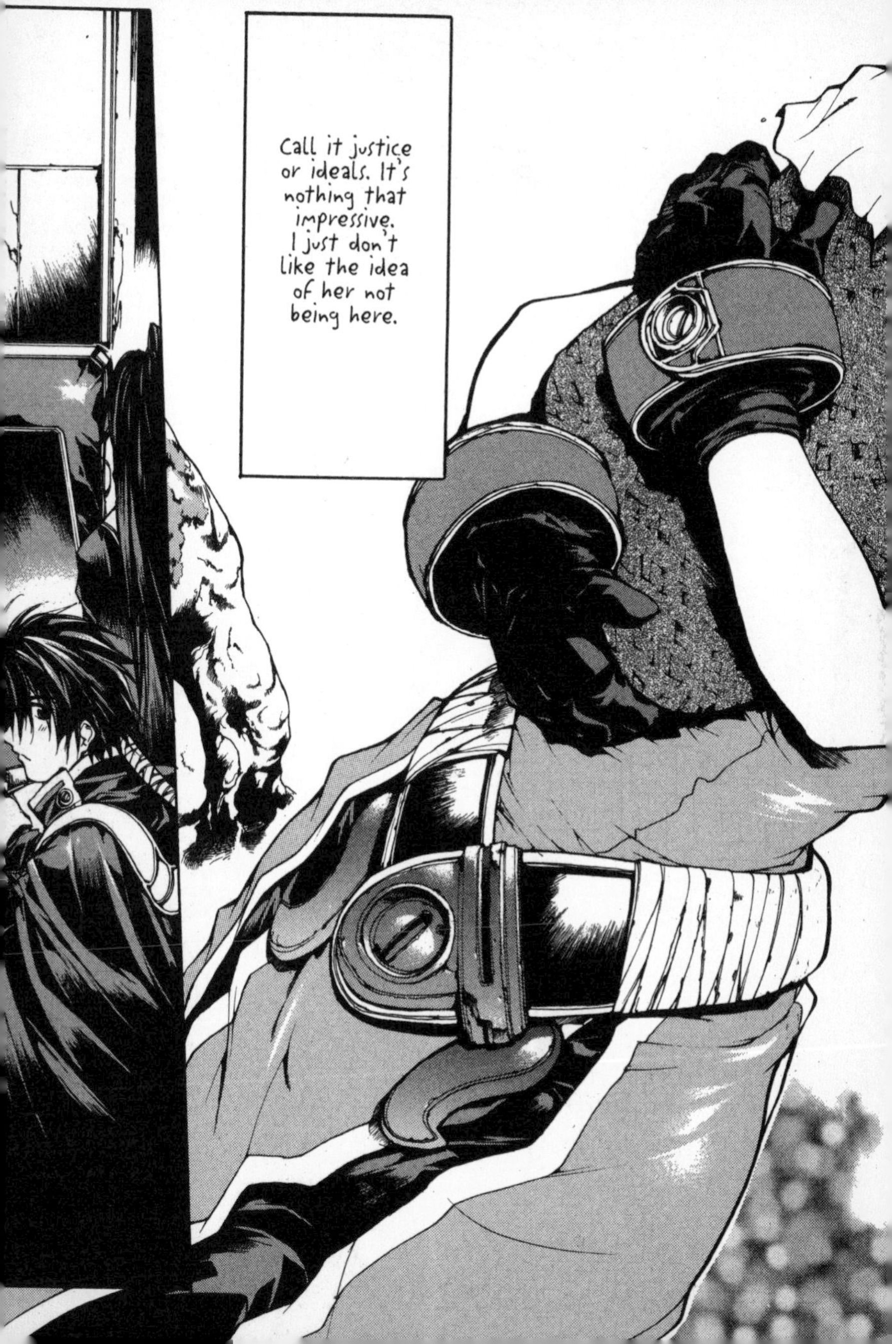
Call it justice or ideals. It's nothing that impressive. I just don't like the idea of her not being here.

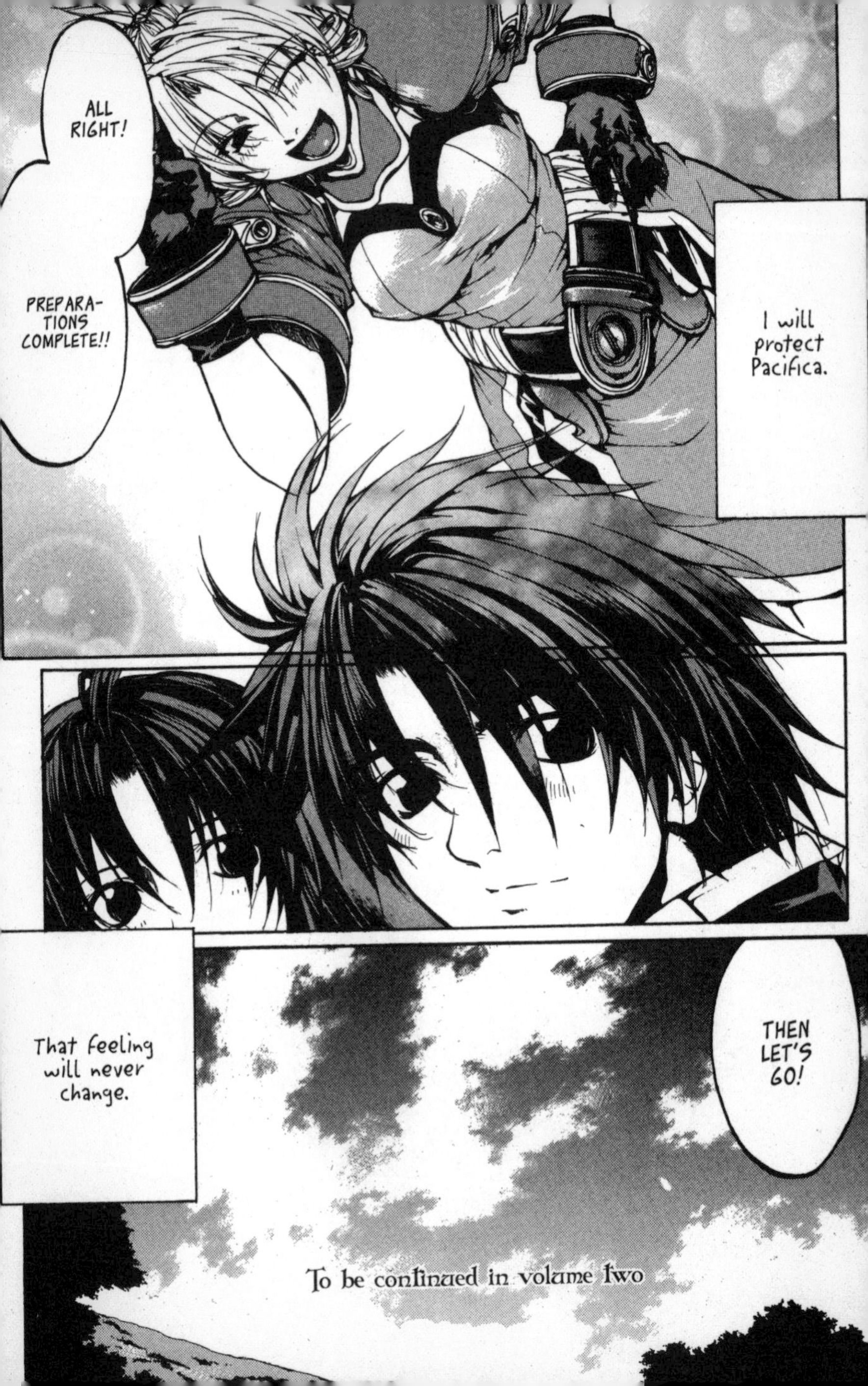
I will protect Pacifica.
ALL RIGHT!
PREPARATIONS COMPLETE!!
THEN LET'S GO!
That feeling will never change.
To be continued in volume two

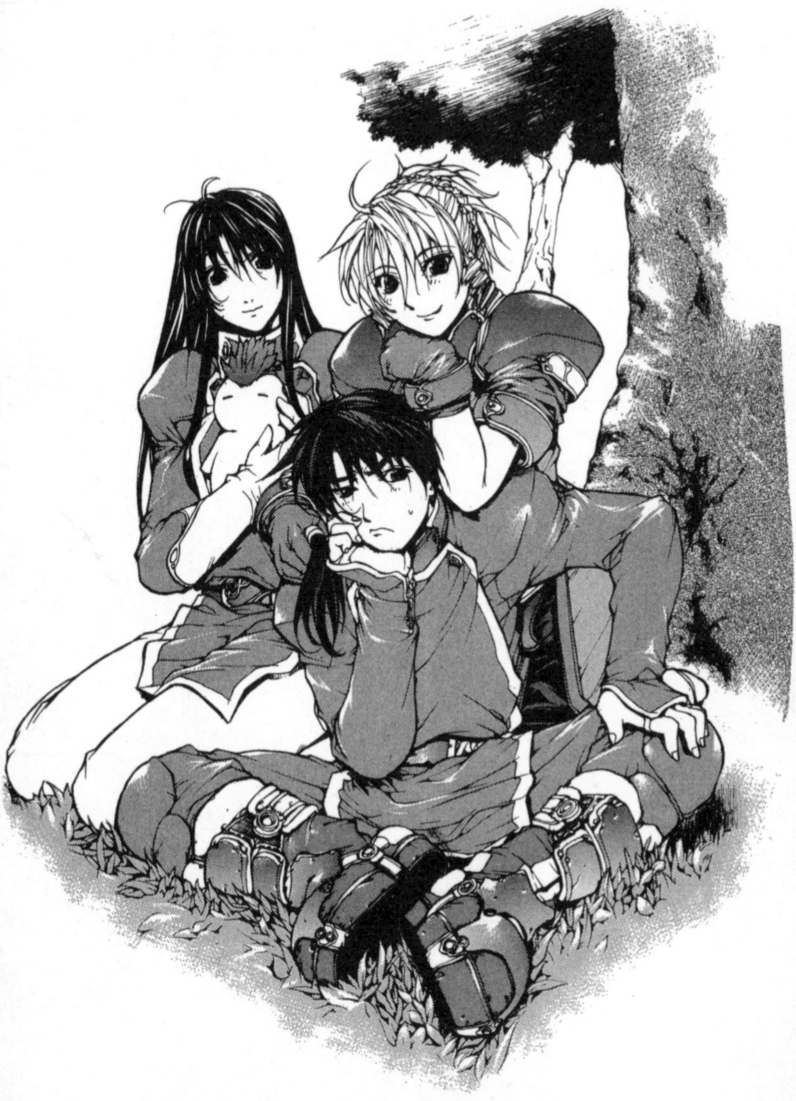

Afterword Manga

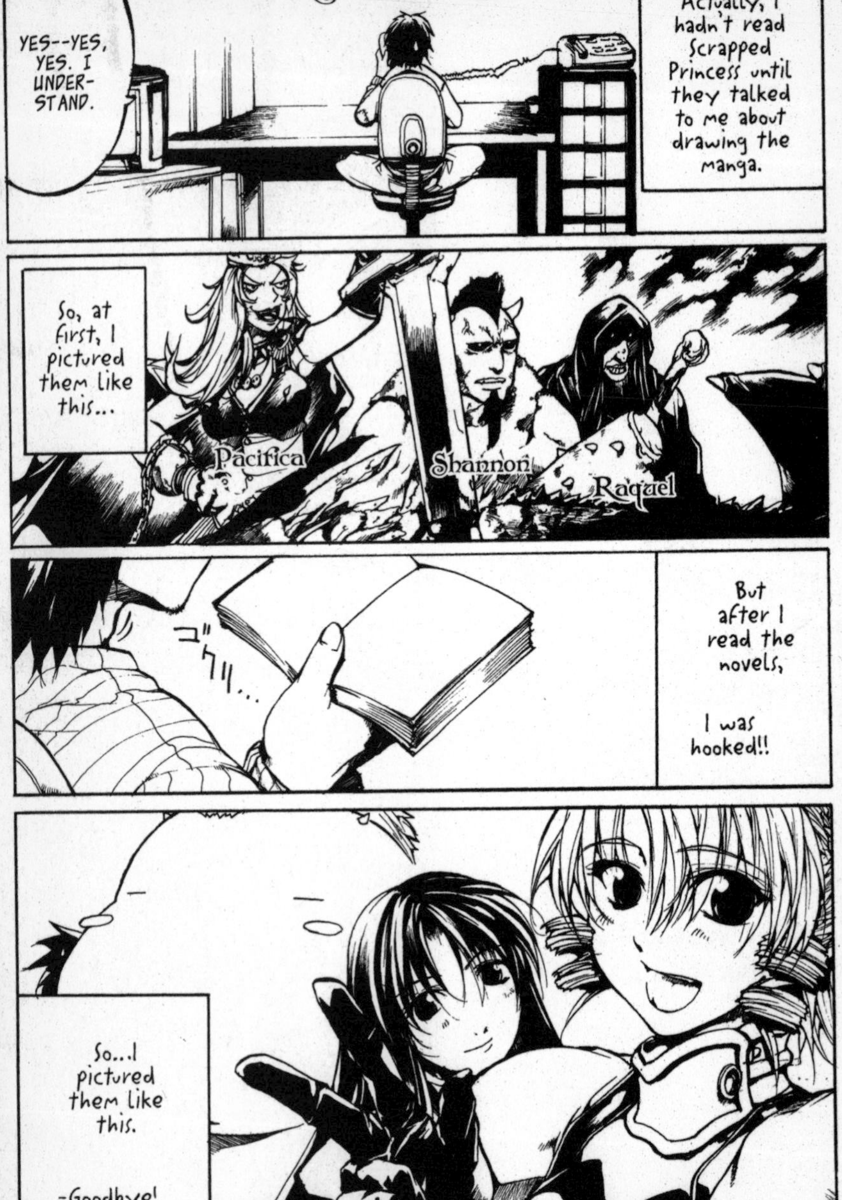
Actually, I hadn't read Scrapped Princess until they talked to me about drawing the manga.
YES--YES, YES. I UNDERSTAND.
So, at first, I pictured them like this...
Raquel
Shannon
Pacifica
But after I read the novels,
I was hooked!!
ゴクリ...
So...I pictured them like this.
-Goodbye!

Please read volume two!

SCRAPPED PRINCESS

榊 一郎 *Ichiro Sakaki*

矢吹 豪 *Go Yabuki*

staff

僕 牧人 *Makito Boku*

多羅澤恭子 *Kyouko Tarasawa*

special thanks

こもりけい *Kei Komori*

柴崎みかる *Mikaru Shibasaki*

外山太一 *Taichi Toyama*

武井雄一郎 *Yuichiro Takei*

中野一平 *Ippei Nakano*

矢口 岳 *Takashi Yaguchi*

なかねかつを *Katsuwo Nakane*

マミー鈴木 *Mammy Suzuki*

田中くん *Tanakakun*

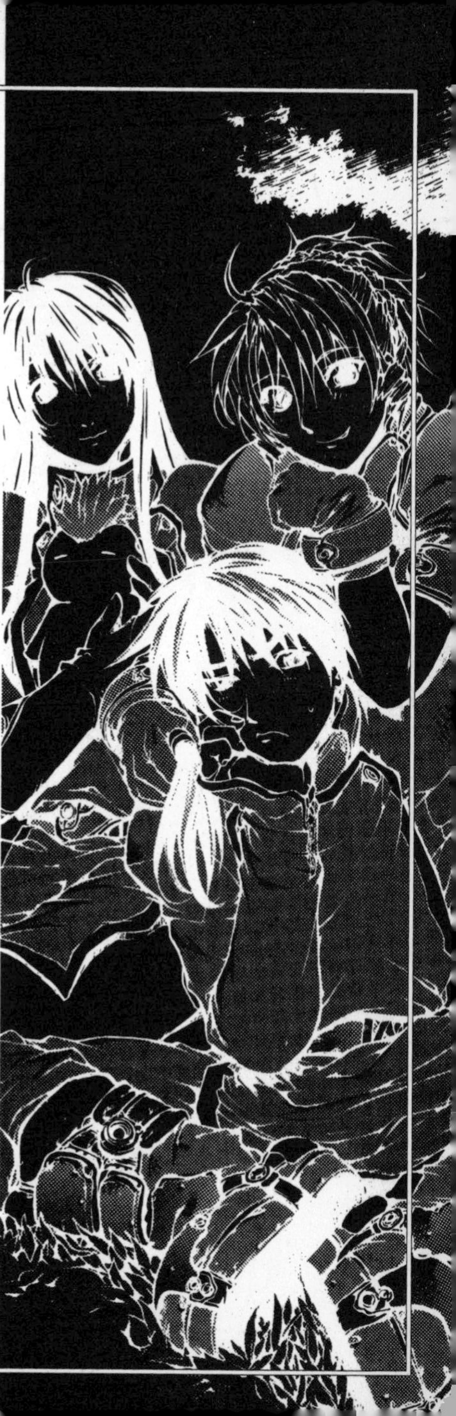

Next Time In

SCRAPPED PRINCESS™

The epic sci-fi fantasy continues as the lives of everyone in the world hang in the balance! While Pacifica, Shannon, and Raquel flee from bounty hunters, Pacifica crosses paths with a frightened girl who has a dark secret and a fatal wish. After the girl disappears, a mysterious pendant might hold the clue to saving her. The three siblings set off to find the girl, but when they finally locate her, she's not quite what she appears to be...

OT
OLDER TEEN
AGE 16+

In the deep South, an ancient voodoo curse unleashes
the War on Flesh—a hellish plague of voracious Ew Chott
hornets that raises an army of the walking dead. This
undead army spreads the plague by ripping the hearts
out of living creatures to make room for a Black Heart
hive, all in preparation for the most awesome incarnation
of evil ever imagined… An unlikely group of five mis-
matched individuals have to put their differences aside to
try to destroy the onslaught of evil before it's too late.

VOODOO MAKES A MAN NASTY!

WAR ON FLESH

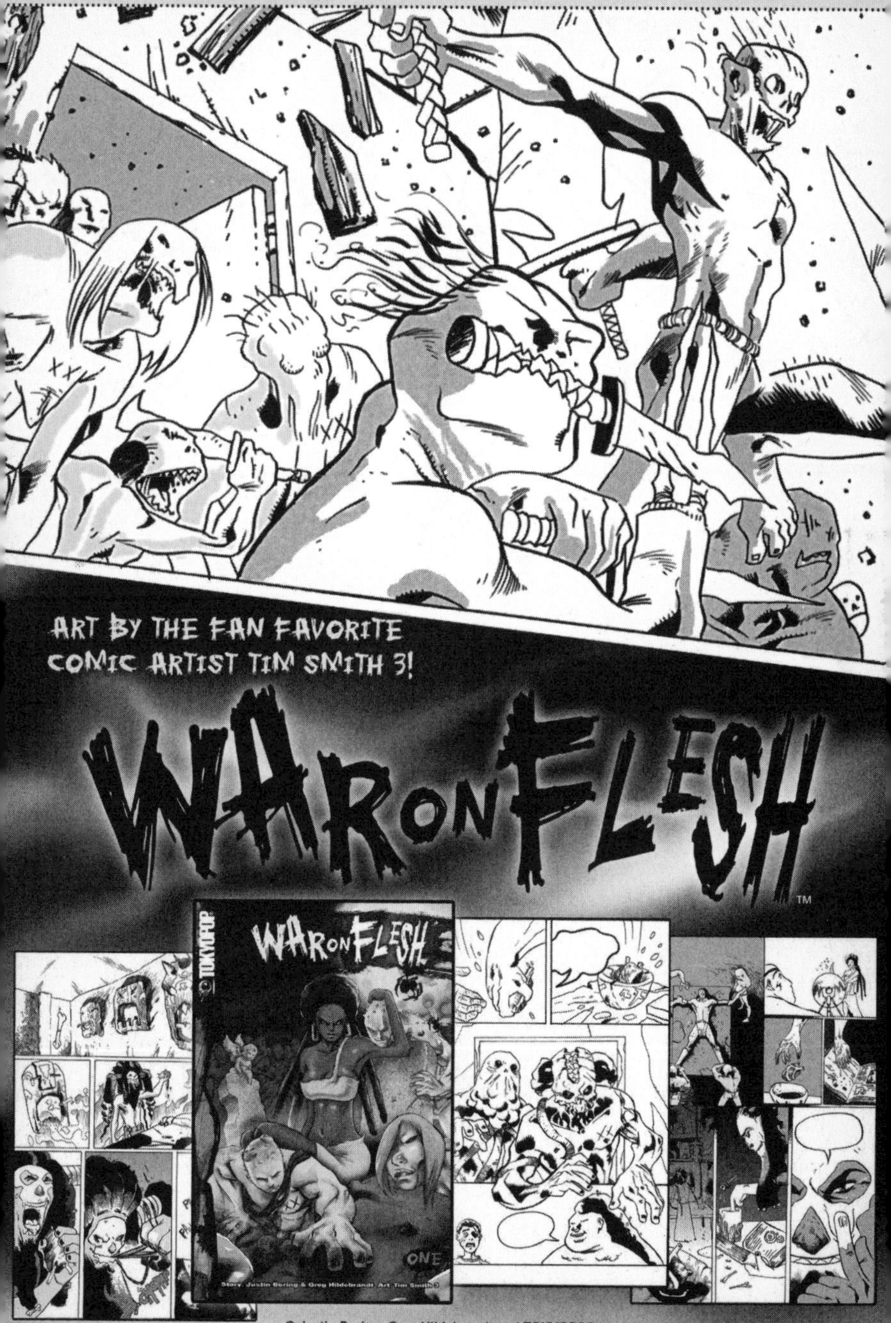
ART BY THE FAN FAVORITE
COMIC ARTIST TIM SMITH 3!
WAR ON FLESH™
TOKYOPOP
WAR ON FLESH
ONE
Story: Justin Boring & Greg Hildebrandt Art: Tim Smith 3

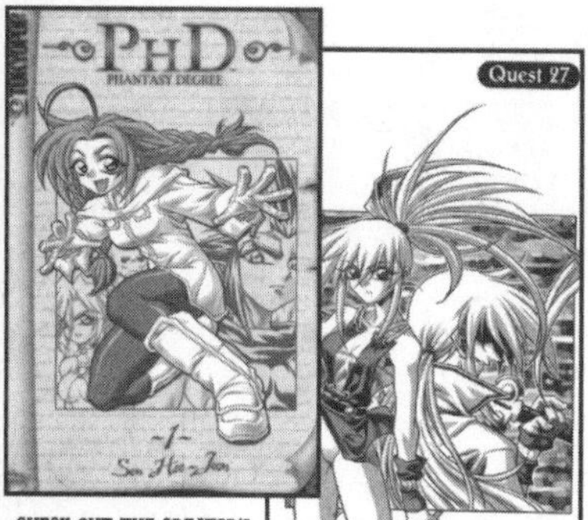
PhD
PHANTASY DEGREE
TOKYOPOP
~1~
Quest 27

CHECK OUT THE CREATOR'S *iD_eNTITY*

BY SON HEE-JOON

PhD: PHANTASY DEGREE

So you think you've got it rough at *your* school? Try attending classes at Demon School Hades! When sassy, young Sang makes her monster matriculation to this arcane academy, all hell breaks loose—literally! But what would you expect when the graduating class consists of a werewolf, a mummy and demons by the score? Son Hee-Joon's underworld adventure is pure escapist fun. Always packed with action and often silly in the best sense, *PhD* never takes itself too seriously or lets the reader stop to catch his breath.

~Bryce P. Coleman, Editor

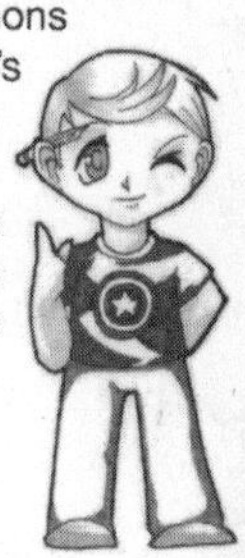

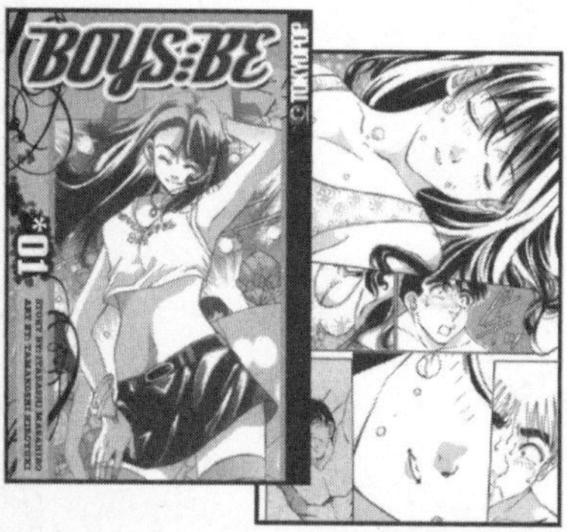
BOYS BE
TOKYOPOP
01

BY MASAHIRO ITABASHI & HIROYUKI TAMAKOSHI

BOYS BE...

Boys Be... is a series of short stories. But although the hero's name changes from tale to tale, he remains Everyboy—that dorky high school guy who'll do anything to score with the girl of his dreams. You know him. Perhaps you *are* him. He is a dirty mind with the soul of a poet, a stumblebum with a heart of sterling. We follow this guy on quest after quest to woo his lady loves. We savor his victory; we reel with his defeat...and the experience is touching, funny and above all human.

Still not convinced? I have two words for you: fan service.

~Carol Fox, Editor

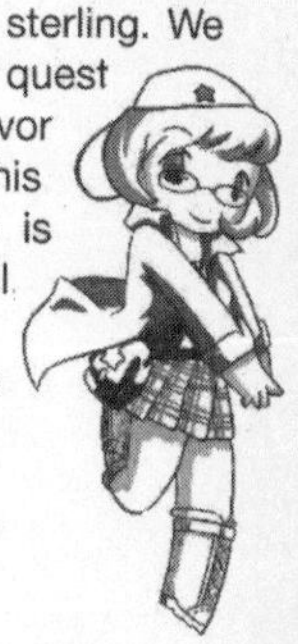

STOP!

This is the back of the book.
You wouldn't want to spoil a great ending!

This book is printed "manga-style," in the authentic Japanese right-to-left format. Since none of the artwork has been flipped or altered, readers get to experience the story just as the creator intended. You've been asking for it, so TOKYOPOP® delivered: authentic, hot-off-the-press, and far more fun!

DIRECTIONS

If this is your first time reading manga-style, here's a quick guide to help you understand how it works.

It's easy... just start in the top right panel and follow the numbers. Have fun, and look for more 100% authentic manga from TOKYOPOP®!